1991

THE COMPLETE HANDBOOK OF

PRO

BASKETBALL

W0010792

1991
THE COMPLETE HANDBOOK OF
PRO
BASKETBALL

EDITED BY

ZANDER HOLLANDER

AN ASSOCIATED FEATURES BOOK

A SIGNET BOOK

ACKNOWLEDGMENTS

We thank all who in one way or another helped make possible this 17th annual edition: contributing editors David Kaplan and Eric Compton, the writers listed on the contents page and Lee Stowbridge, Fred Cantey, Kevin Mulroy, Richard Rossiter, Linda Spain, Henri Cauvin, Alex Sachare, Brian McIntyre, Terry Lyons, Marty Blake, the NBA team publicity directors, Elias Sports Bureau, Dot Gordineer of Libra Graphics and Westchester/Rainsford Book Composition.

Zander Hollander

PHOTO CREDITS: Cover—Focus on Sports, Inside photos—Tom Brownold, Ira Golden, Michael Hirsch, George Kalinsky, Mike Maicher, Mitch Reibel, Mary Schroeder, (Detroit Free Press), NBC-TV, Wide World and the NBA and college team photographers.

SIGNET
Published by the Penguin Group
Penguin Books USA Inc., 375 Hudson Street,
New York, New York 10014, U.S.A.
Penguin Books Ltd, 27 Wrights Lane,
London W8 5TZ, England
Penguin Books Australia Ltd, Ringwood,
Victoria, Australia
Penguin Books Canada Ltd, 2801 John Street,
Markham, Ontario, Canada L3R 1B4
Penguin Books (N.Z.) Ltd, 182–190 Wairau Road,
Auckland 10, New Zealand

Penguin Books Ltd, Registered Offices:
Harmondsworth, Middlesex, England

First Signet Printing, November, 1990
10 9 8 7 6 5 4 3 2 1

CONTENTS

The Enigma of Isiah Thomas..... By Corky Meinecke 8

Marv "Yesss!" Albert Welcomes
   A New Era for NBC and NBA.......... By Hal Bock 18

The Funniest Men in the Game.......By David Moore 26

Next Magic:
   The Suns' Kevin Johnson........By Steve Weston 34

Inside the NBA ...... By Fred Kerber and Frank Brady 40

Atlanta Hawks 44	Dallas Mavericks 199
Boston Celtics 56	Denver Nuggets............211
Charlotte Hornets............69	Golden State Warriors......222
Chicago Bulls................81	Houston Rockets 232
Cleveland Cavaliers...........93	Los Angeles Clippers........243
Detroit Pistons.............105	Los Angeles Lakers.........253
Indiana Pacers.............118	Minnesota Timberwolves.....265
Miami Heat 130	Orlando Magic..............275
Milwaukee Bucks...........141	Phoenix Suns...............286
New Jersey Nets 154	Portland Trail Blazers 297
New York Knicks 166	Sacramento Kings 307
Philadelphia 76ers 178	San Antonio Spurs 317
Washington Bullets 189	Seattle SuperSonics.........328
Utah Jazz 339		

NBA College Draft...................... 350

NBA Statistics........................... 356

NBA Schedule............................ 371

NBC-TV Games........................... 381

TNT Games.............................. 383

Editor's Note: The material herein includes trades and rosters up to final printing deadline.

THE ENIGMA
OF
ISIAH THOMAS

By CORKY MEINECKE

Isiah Thomas looked around the crowded room and tried his best to smile.

It was a hazy Saturday afternoon in the Detroit area, less than 48 hours after the Pistons had clinched their second consecutive NBA title. To Thomas' left sat Tom Wilson, the Pistons' chief executive officer. To Thomas' right stood John Caponigro, his attorney. Surrounding Thomas were several reporters and photographers, some of whom had waited hours to see the Pistons' point guard.

The mood was not light.

Only a few hours earlier, in the same suburban Detroit office, Thomas had met with agents from the FBI and the IRS. Thomas set up the meeting late Friday night, after watching a televised report that linked him to an FBI investigation of an alleged multimillion-dollar sports betting ring. The report was aired only a couple hours after the Pistons had returned from Portland.

"I am not the target of any investigation," Thomas said, scowling. "Nor am I suspected of doing anything wrong. I know that. And more importantly, the FBI knows that."

Less than 48 hours later, at about the same time of the Pistons' glitzy championship celebration at the Palace, local FBI officials held a press conference for the sole purpose of clearing Thomas' name. And in less than a week, the incident was dismissed as one of those unfortunate things that happen to the rich and famous.

As a feature writer, formerly the beat man on the Detroit Pistons, Corky Meinecke of the Detroit Free Press *has been a close follower of the Isiah Thomas odyssey.*

Well, what'll it be? Another title for Isiah's Pistons?

The playoff MVP presents Detroit jersey to the President.

Two weeks after the end of the season, things were pretty much back to normal. Thomas spent a week at his basketball camp, lecturing to and scrimmaging against a host of spellbound youngsters. They hung on his every word, breaking into laughter when he told them, "I'm like Kentucky Fried Chicken. I only do one thing, and I do it right. Basketball."

Thomas went from his camp to the Bahamas for a week-long vacation with coaches and teammates, courtesy of Pistons' owner Bill Davidson. The following week, he stopped by the Pistons' rookie camp to check on the progress of center William Bedford and the team's top draft pick, University of Texas guard Lance Blanks.

At about the same time, Thomas finalized the details of his annual charity basketball game. Last year, he raised nearly $300,000 for the beleaguered Detroit Public Schools sports program. And he had hoped to give just as much money to Comic Relief, a national fund drive for the homeless sponsored by comedians, and to a local organization that aids the homeless, Detroit Health Care.

"I don't have a pet charity," Thomas said. "I go on a need-to-need basis. Helping the homeless is something my wife always preached to me, so I think this will make her happy."

Superstar. Role model. Concerned teammate. Humanitarian. Thoughtful husband.

That's hardly the profile of a high-stakes gambler.

"How could something like that happen?" Thomas said, repeating a question and smiling. "Hey, we've been through this before, haven't we?"

Indeed, Thomas' nine-year NBA career has been equal parts triumph and trouble. He is a splendid point guard—unbelievably quick, amazingly clever and absolutely fearless—but his best position might very well be center of controversy. Magic Johnson is considered a better point guard, but Thomas has no peer at center of controversy.

To be sure, Thomas' critics never lacked for ammo.

If he wasn't being accused of hosting high-stakes dice games in his suburban Detroit home, he was being fingered as the trigger man in the Adrian Dantley-Mark Aguirre trade. Or the ringleader in the alleged freeze-out of Michael Jordan in the 1987 All-Star Game. Or the bug in the ear of then-rookie forward Dennis Rodman, who after the 1987 Eastern Conference finals insisted that Boston's Larry Bird would be considered just another player if he were black.

Thomas' critics delighted in the comments of Dantley's mother, Virginia, who called Thomas "a con artist" and added that "whatever his royal highness wants, he gets." And they were quick to rally to Jordan, who said an apology from Thomas two days after the game was "mostly for show." And they enjoyed watching Thomas squirm during a press conference in which Bird mercifully took him off the hook.

Most of all, Thomas' critics enjoyed watching the emergence of Joe Dumars, Thomas' running mate at guard and Dantley's best friend. Dumars was said to be everything Thomas wasn't—quiet and humble off the court, unselfish and consistent on it. Because of Dumars' MVP award in the 1989 Finals, and because of his friendship with Dantley, it was believed that he and Thomas didn't get along.

"Yeah," Thomas said, shaking his head in disbelief. "People said that to me."

And as the 1990 playoffs began, Thomas was said to be feuding with Pistons' coach Chuck Daly about his role and that of Mark Aguirre, his childhood buddy. There were rumors of a locker-room shouting match between Daly and Thomas, of Thomas demanding that Daly redesign the offense to better suit his skills.

None of the involved would comment, but the Pistons' .500 record in the last 16 regular-season games confirmed that all was not right.

Thomas took most of the heat for the late-season slide. The slump actually took form on March 24, when Dumars broke a bone in his left hand, an injury that kept him out of the lineup for 16 days and seven games. Thomas was expected to pick up the slack, but was physically unable. Two days before Dumars went down, the Pistons' medical staff considered giving Thomas' aching left knee a few days off.

"But with Joe out," Thomas said, "we just couldn't do it."

As is his custom, Thomas kept quiet about the injury, even as his turnovers increased and his shooting percentage decreased. Neither would he allow Daly or Pistons' trainer Mike Abdenour to make excuses for him. "I never use injuries as an excuse," he said. "If you do that, you give yourself an easy way out if you lose. I don't want that. If I get beat, it's because I'm not good enough."

A four-day break between the end of the season and the start of the playoffs proved to be the perfect tonic for Thomas. By the first game of the Pistons' opening-round series against the Indiana Pacers, his knee was back to 100 percent—and so was his game, which he honed late at night inside the gymnasium of his home.

"Over the years," Thomas said, "I noticed that Magic and Bird would always come into the playoffs with some new shot, some extra weapon. I knew I wasn't going to develop a hook shot at my height, so I began working on my three-point shooting."

Thomas had never been much of a three-point shooter. He made just 19-of-98 (.194) in the 1986-87 season, and his career average (.285) was 31 percentage points below that of 6-11 Bill Laimbeer and 22 percentage points below that of Scott Hastings, a 6-11 journeyman power forward.

Thomas had a terrific series against the Pacers—"The best I've seen him play all year," assistant Brendan Malone said—but it didn't start raining threes until Game 2 of the Pistons' second-round series against the New York Knicks, who were coming off a stunning upset of the Boston Celtics in the opening round.

The Knicks knew all about Thomas, about his uncommon ball-handling, driving and passing skills. They knew that he is not to be trifled with, especially during crunch time in any game played in May or June. But they never dreamed he had the ability to reach out and torch someone from outside the three-point arc.

They do now.

"He was just hitting them with ease, and I can't think of a

three-point contest that he's won,'' Knick guard Gerald Wilkins said after the Pistons took a 2-0 series lead with a 104-97 victory. Added guard Maurice Cheeks: "I'd rather he shoot from there than drive, but he shot them pretty easily. He shot them like he knew what he was doing.''

Thomas had a so-so offensive series against the Chicago Bulls in the Eastern Conference finals—18.0 points, 8.7 assists, .440 shooting—but he turned it up a notch defensively, in the deciding seventh game especially.

The Pistons were leading, 28-27, when Jordan collided with John Salley, who tumbled to the court as Jordan took the ball to the basket. Thomas, giving away five inches, rushed over to challenge Jordan. Thomas got so high that he forced Jordan to make a last-second pass. It ended up in the hands of Rodman, who fed Dumars for a breakaway basket that signaled the beginning of a 20-6 run and the end of the Bulls.

"My whole life,'' Thomas said, "I was the leading scorer. The star. 'Stop Isiah, stop Isiah.' That's all the people ever said. But I enjoy doing more than scoring. I like hurting teams with rebounding and passing and defense. Tell you the truth, I always considered myself a better defensive player than an offensive player.''

Trouble was, nobody else did. And until Thomas destroyed Terry Porter, the Portland Trail Blazers' terrific point guard, in the NBA Finals, few considered Thomas a true student of the game. Even Thomas admits that in his early years he did more reacting than thinking, more creating than plotting.

"I'd score 25 points, have 16 assists and I couldn't tell you how we won the game,'' he said. "I like the mental part of the game, and I missed that early in my career. I have to think now and I like that. It's like a chess game every night. I get to read the whole game and get involved in the total package.

"Sometimes, I want to take charge and score a lot of points, but if I do that every night, the team gets accustomed to it. If you let other guys get involved, you're giving them a chance to get confidence. Then, when it's time for the playoffs, we have eight or nine confident people instead of just two who can put the ball in the hole.''

But in the Finals, no Piston put the ball in the hole with the consistency and creativity of Thomas.

In Game 1, he scored 16 of his 33 points in the fourth quarter to lead the Pistons to a come-from-behind, 105-90 victory; in Game 4, a 112-109 Pistons' victory, he scored 22 of his 30 second-half points in the third quarter; in Game 5, he kept the Pistons in the hunt by scoring 20 first-half points. For the series, he averaged 27.6 points, shot .542 and made an incredible 11-of-16 three-point shots.

Thomas saved the best for last, but it wasn't a clutch three-point shot or one of his fearless drives into heavy traffic. It was a subtle and unselfish move, one Thomas supposedly wasn't capable of making. With time running out and the final game tied at 90, Thomas passed up a potential game-winning shot. He fed Vinnie Johnson on the wing, then took a couple steps toward midcourt.

"You don't know what a great play that was," Laimbeer said.

When Thomas moved outside the arc, Porter had no choice but to move with him. Porter certainly couldn't let Thomas try another trey. That left Johnson one-on-one against forward Jerome Kersey. Johnson froze Kersey with a fake, then went over the 6-7 forward and nailed the series-clinching jumper with just :00.7 showing on the clock.

"Isiah saw that Vinnie was the open guy, and that he had the hot hand," Laimbeer said. "Isiah had just come back into the game after hurting his nose. So, he gave Vinnie the ball and Vinnie knew what to do with it. What a great play that was."

Johnson made the shot, but Thomas was the unanimous choice as playoff MVP. It was clearly Thomas' finest moment, considering that six other guards, including Dumars, were selected ahead of Thomas on the three All-NBA teams this season.

"If you ask anybody on our team or anybody who has watched us play, this is Isiah's team," Laimbeer said. "The team has his personality. The determination, the desire and the heart revolve around him. Joe won the MVP last season, and we were the happiest people in the world for him. But I had a sinking feeling in my heart. I felt it should have been Isiah for all the years he put into it."

Thomas put it best when he said, "You can say whatever you want about me, but you can't say I don't know how to win."

The Pistons partied late into the night, then boarded their private jetliner, Roundball I, for the long trip back to Detroit. Thousands greeted the Pistons at the airport, but Thomas didn't want to linger too long because it was the second birthday of his son, Joshua. But when Thomas got home, he found wife Lynn in front of the television, crying.

"They say you've been gambling," she said.

"What?" Thomas said.

The report, by Detroit television station WJBK, said Thomas wasn't the target of the investigation, but that investigators were

Isiah drives past Portland's Jerome Kersey in NBA Finals.

MVP Isiah celebrates Indiana's NCAA championship in 1981.

interested in checks from Thomas that were cashed by Emmet Denha, a close friend and former neighbor. More disturbing was an allegation that Aguirre had approached a former FBI agent, Ned Timmons, during the playoffs and told him that Thomas had a gambling problem.

Thomas explained that he often had Denha cash checks for him at one of Denha's stores. He learned the practice from his mother, who wouldn't cash her checks at westside Chicago banks, "because she would get robbed when she came outside." Thomas did it because he trusted Denha, and because it saved him the hassle of signing autographs and making small talk while standing in line at a bank.

As for Aguirre, "Mark told me he never spoke to any FBI agents," Thomas said.

Nevertheless, their friendship has been strained. Aguirre refused to comment on the report, leading some to believe that Thomas had instituted a gag order. They should be able to patch up their differences, but reconciliation between Thomas and Denha might never take place.

"I love Emmet," Thomas said, "but just because you love a rattlesnake, you don't let him bite you."

Thomas came out of the controversy relatively unscathed. If anything, his popularity in Detroit reached another level. Local newspapers and television stations were flooded with letters of support for Thomas, who at a downtown rally promised to "never let the city of Detroit down."

Later, at the Palace, he told fans to use him as an example. "When you have a problem," he said, "think of me. Say to yourself, 'If Isiah can handle what happened to him, I can handle my problem.'"

But those close to Thomas worry that he'll become less trusting and less open to the public. He admits that he had only two close friends outside of basketball—Denha and Matt Dobek, the Pistons' public relations director. Now, it appears that he's down to just one, and that doesn't seem natural for someone as personable and accessible as Thomas.

"I just didn't deserve this," he said.

Marv "Yesss!" Albert Welcomes a New Era For NBC and NBA

By HAL BOCK

Last spring, when the network television bosses were whipping out their checkbooks in a frenzied, megabucks battle to scoop up sports properties and programming, NBC sportscaster Marv Albert was at a cocktail party for the introduction of the New York Knicks' team video. Albert, the voice of the Knicks for the last two decades, strolled over to an NBA executive and struck up a conversation. It was small talk, really, nothing out of the ordinary at a gathering like this. One thing led to another and eventually the subject of NBA television rights came up.

"I said, 'CBS, right?' " Albert recalled.

It was a logical guess. CBS had been aggressive in the sports marketplace, buying baseball for better than $1 billion and grabbing the NCAA basketball tournament for the same price. The NBA had been a longtime CBS property, virtually the cornerstone of the network's sports package.

The man from the NBA nodded at Albert. CBS, it seemed, was a done deal.

"The next night, Dick Ebersol [president of NBC sports] called," Albert said. "He said, 'Guess what?' "

That kind of open-ended line, especially from your boss, can mean trouble. Not for Albert, though. Ebersol didn't keep him in suspense very long. "You're going to be doing the NBA," he said.

Very quietly, Ebersol and Arthur Watson, his predecessor, had won the NBA rights fight for the next four years with a $600 million bid and, in doing so, the network had dropped Marv Albert

Hal Bock, a feature sports writer at Associated Press, wrote Yesss! Marv Albert on Sportscasting.

A new NBC team: Marv Albert (right) and Mike Fratello.

in the proverbial pot of jam. "It was a major upset and I couldn't believe it," Albert said. "It seemed like a CBS lock right along. Four years of the NBA. That's very exciting."

It's particularly exciting for Albert because for all the NFL games he's done, for all the fights, for all the hockey and baseball, for all of that, he's basically a basketball guy, an ex-Knick ballboy with a special feel for the game.

Albert grew up playing basketball on concrete in the play-grounds of Brooklyn, N.Y., shooting hoops with pals like Moe—"A Charles Barkley type with no outside touch"—and Slats—"A good one-handed shot from the outside. Today, he'd be a three-point specialist."

It was in those pickup games that Albert first began using his trademark call—"Yesss! And it counts!"—borrowed from NBA ref Sid Borgia's emphatic calls. Moe would drive to the hoop, toss one up off his ear and Marv would celebrate the basket with a hearty "Yesss!"

All of this took place on the playground's ancillary courts. "We never made it to Basket No. 1," Albert said. "We played on No. 3. No. 1 was for guys like Billy Cunningham and Connie Hawkins. On No. 1, I was strictly an observer."

Those were Albert's boyhood basketball contemporaries—masters of the sport who could make the ball do everything but talk. The talking part they left up to Marv, and he's thrived with it.

Following a frenetic pace that often kept him on the go seven days a week—an NFL game and college basketball on the weekend, a couple of NBA and NHL games during the week and studio sportscasts in between—Albert became one of the most popular voices in the business. Now he gets the opportunity to do the one thing he's wanted most all along—network play-by-play of the NBA. It is like tossing Br'er Rabbit in the Briar Patch. Let the good times roll.

"For me, it's fulfilling a fantasy," Albert said. "I've always wanted to do the NBA nationally."

Network audiences will be treated to a different listen from Albert and a different look from NBC. "I thought CBS did an excellent job, but I think we'll have a harder edge," he said. "The game is still the game, but there are things we'll be doing that have never been done before. We've got a half-hour pre-game show with [ex-Laker Coach] Pat Riley for every game. That's unprecedented. There's more time allotted. There are more games."

The schedule includes four doubleheaders and is heavy on the league's marquee attractions. Two-time champion Detroit has a minimum of five appearances and the Los Angeles Lakers play half a dozen games for NBC.

It sounds like hoop heaven for Albert, the unreconstructed schoolyard shooter. He'll be paired with ex-Atlanta coach Mike Fratello while Bob Costas works with Steve Jones on NBC's other broadcast team. And like teams on the court, they'll practice to get accustomed to each other's style and establish the proper chemistry between them. There are some preseason games in Barcelona and the Charlotte Invitational, where the NBA's four expansion teams will play each other.

"We'll use those games to get used to the replays, to get comfortable with the producer and the directors," Albert said.

And each other?

"We have rapport," Albert said of himself and Fratello. "We know each other."

That's because Fratello spent time as an assistant coach with the Knicks, who are Albert's NBA anchor. Marv was a ballboy for the team as a youngster and was the play-by-play voice of New York's 1969-70 and 1972-73 champions. To this day, he remembers the chill that went up his spine the moment an injured Willis Reed limped out to warm up for the seventh game of the 1970 championship series against the Lakers. In a lifetime of

As a Warrior, 7-7 Manute Bol matched up with 6-foot Marv.

broadcasting memorable moments, that moment still stands out for Albert.

"We were on the air and I remember the Knicks and Lakers were on the court warming up. Then Reed came out of the runway. I said, 'And here comes Willis.' The Lakers stopped and stood there, just watching him. The crowd went crazy."

Reed scored just two baskets but the emotional lift he gave the Knicks carried them and Albert to the championship. "You never forget times like that," he said. "Those were my broadcasting roots, radio play-by-play. There was very little basketball on TV at the time and that was very fortunate for me. With no cable, the only way to listen to the games was on radio."

And when you did, there was Albert, painting a vivid word picture, careful to give the listener the geography of the court so that he could visualize where the ball was at all times, how the play was developing. Frontcourt, backcourt, left corner, right corner, circle, key, lane—all there like spots on a map, landmarks that Albert used as the ball passes through them.

Don't expect all of that when you tune Albert in on NBC's telecasts, though.

"On television, you have to pull back a little bit, have more of a laid-back style," he said. "You have to be succinct and set up the color guy. It's more analysis rather than call. There's less of the feeling that you're the game, the way you are on radio."

Still, the run-and-gun, non-stop style of the NBA can have a significant impact on the broadcast. "When the level of play rises, you feel it at courtside," Albert said. "The greatness of certain players pulls you along. I always try to maintain controlled enthusiasm."

That can be hard to do when Magic is performing his basketball legerdemain or Bird is throwing that sidearm outlet pass or Isiah is drilling a three-pointer or Air Jordan is soaring toward the hoop. The pace of the game has quickened. The pressing defenses can turn games around in no time and the broadcaster had better be paying attention, just in case that happens.

"I used to be able to relax between baskets," Albert said. "No more, though. You don't want to have your head down when something happens out there."

And if you miss something or butcher a call, you'll hear about it from a variety of sources. Albert has learned that everybody is a critic, including players and coaches. Say something they don't like and they let you know about it.

"Every locker room has a lounge and every lounge has a TV," he said. "With satellites, the games are picked up everywhere.

The teams are watching and if they're not, people tell them what you've said anyway. Sometimes, guys kid around about it. Butch Beard [Albert's ex-broadcast partner and now head coach at Howard University] used to tell players if I said something about them. M.L. Carr used to be upset with me all the time. I'd call him a hatchet man and he took exception. Kevin McHale would come up to me and say, 'How can you say that?'

"One time, when he was still in Milwaukee, Don Nelson made a trade involving Jack Sikma. We had some critical things to say about it. A couple of nights later, we were in Milwaukee. He came over, sat down and told me what he thought about my comments."

It's all in a day's work and it comes under the umbrella of objectivity. Without that, Albert said, a broadcaster can pack up his microphone. Today's sophisticated listeners can see right through a phony call.

"It's antiquated thinking to have an announcer say all good things when a team is dragging," he said. "How can the listener believe him? Your credibility is on the line."

So the Knicks can expect no hometown hoopla from Albert, who calls his games down the middle. Opposing teams get the ultimate Albert call of "Yesss!" if their shots earn it. Earning it, however, is no simple bit of business.

"I use 'Yesss!' for special baskets, shots that bring fans right up out of their seats," Albert said. "A line drive that rattles against the hoop as it goes through. That's a 'Yesss!' So is a spinning reverse layup. I try to reserve 'Yesss!' for really deserving plays. You can tell how good a game is by the number of times I use it. The more 'Yesss!' baskets you hear, the better the game I'm broadcasting."

Over the years, Albert has assembled some favorites, players whose performances stood out, either on the court with a ball in their hands, or off it with a microphone in their faces. Michael Jordan deserves a special mention here because he made both sets of Albert All-Stars.

The starting five for the All-Interview team has Charles Barkley and Kevin McHale—his past criticisms notwithstanding—at the forwards, Mychal Thompson at center and Jordan and Kevin Johnson in the backcourt. They are backed up by John Salley—you'd have to have somebody from Brooklyn on an all-talk team—James Worthy, Mike Gminski, Danny Ainge and Darrell Walker.

Not a bad bunch. And they can play a bit, too.

For his on-the-court team, Albert limited his selections to players he had broadcasted. That simplified the traditional Wilt Cham-

Knick ballboy Marv with Richie Guerin and Ron Sobie (c.).

berlain-Bill Russell center debate because both of them were near the end of their careers when Albert arrived. So he picks Kareem Abdul-Jabbar as his center and surrounds him with Larry Bird, Julius Erving, Magic Johnson and Jordan. Behind that five, Albert's bench has Rick Barry, Dave DeBusschere, Willis Reed and Walt Frazier with Jerry West and Oscar Robertson sharing the second guard spot because they, too, were near the end of their brilliant careers when Albert began broadcasting.

"I respect the guys I watched growing up," Albert said, "people like Bob Cousy, Bob Pettit, Russell. But you wonder if they could have played today. Cousy would have adjusted. He had quickness. But a guy like George Mikan, I don't know. He was slow. In today's game, he might be a backup center."

And just as basketball has changed, so has the style of broadcasting. The audience is more knowledgeable and the announcer must fit that into the equation that makes up his call of the game.

"You don't have to talk after every play," Albert said. "My biggest gripe as a listener is that color men tend to talk too much."

Hear that, Fratello?

"A good rule to follow is, if there's nothing to say, don't say anything. Otherwise, you wind up saying the obvious and people are sitting at home saying, 'C'mon, I know that.' What you want to do is add to the telecast, give the listener fresh, meaningful information that adds to his enjoyment of the broadcast.''

What's meaningful?

"Say a guy can't go to his left and then he does that in a game," Albert said. "It's nice to have that kind of material at your fingertips. Al McGuire, who does college basketball for NBC, makes a list before every game he works of 15 facts people don't know, tendencies of teams or players. I do the same thing. Then you're ready when something happens.''

That's part of pre-game preparation, the kind of homework broadcasters must do before working an event. You visit with coaches, watch practices if you can, talk with people around the teams to get a feel for the way things are going. When you're moving from one club to another every week, that's vital in order to deliver a solid broadcast. You want to know what you're talking about.

What's remarkable about Albert is his ability to cross from one sport to another. He is a broad-based broadcaster, comfortable doing just about any sport.

"I'd go crazy with just one sport," he said. "I love football. Boxing is so bizarre with its cast of characters. But basketball is my favorite sport.''

How thoughtful, then, of the folks at NBC to corral the NBA for him. He'll warm up for the assignment with the usual diet of NFL, boxing and college basketball on TV as well as his regular hockey and basketball on radio, a stay-busy schedule that would wear down most folks. It is, however, less frantic than it once was for Albert. "Sometimes," he said, "I look back and wonder how I did it.''

The absence of baseball from NBC's summer lineup for the first time in many years allowed the network to give Albert a month off. It was an opportunity for him to think about the winter schedule—an NBA broadcast every Sunday beginning Jan. 27 with the traditional matchup of Boston and the Lakers. There are a couple of Saturdays to spice the schedule, the All-Star Game at Charlotte on Feb. 10 and then the playoffs beginning the last week of April.

The deal has NBC excited and Albert exuberant. It is viewed by the network as a rejuvenation after losing baseball. And it is viewed by Albert as the final piece of his personal portfolio—a chance to spread the gospel of ''Yesss!'' from coast to coast, broadcasting the best basketball players in the world. In Brooklyn, these would all be Basket No. 1 guys.

THE FUNNIEST MEN IN THE GAME

Piston John Salley revs up at a New York comedy club.

By DAVID MOORE

It is May and Detroit's John Salley is asked how the Pistons will defend Michael Jordan in the playoffs.

"You distract him," he says.

Makes sense. The Pistons can run a different player at Jordan when he gets the ball. Or they can trap him at different spots on the court.

"No," Salley says, shaking his head. "You just talk about things he doesn't like to talk about."

Like what?

"Like baldness."

Jordan may be one of the best players in the NBA, but Salley is one of the funniest. The Pistons' forward has done stand-up routines in comedy clubs in New York and Detroit. He's not afraid to take on Jordan and his receding hairline one-on-one for the sake of a laugh.

There's something about the grind of a six-month schedule that demands comic relief in the NBA. Sometimes it's the ironic that elicits a chuckle. Sometimes it's the inadvertent. Sometimes it's the outrageous.

Whatever the case, one-liners and humorous anecdotes are churned out like jump shots. And no one spins them out more than Philadelphia's Charles Barkley.

After Detroit tried to pry Jon Koncak away from Atlanta with a $2.5-million offer sheet, Barkley said, "I think it's unfair for a guy to be making $1.5 million more than me, especially one who can't play." Barkley signed a nine-year, $29.5-million contract a few weeks later. He also joined his partner in basketball crime, forward Rick Mahorn, to form one of Philadelphia's finest comedy teams.

Mahorn refers to his teammate as "a fat doughboy." When asked what Mahorn means to the Sixers, Barkley said, "It means people will be able to see I don't have the biggest butt in the league." The two also agreed to donate $3,000 to charity last season each time one of them was ejected. "We were going to donate the money to the homeless," Barkley said, "but they would have had better houses than we have."

David Moore, who previously was the Dallas Mavericks' beat man for the Fort Worth Star-Telegram, *is the national NBA writer for the* Dallas Morning News.

And what does he think of the Big Apple?

"New York is my kind of town," Barkley said, "because I have a gun."

Some of the more amusing moments in the league are provided by players who aren't even trying to be funny.

Last season, Atlanta's Dominique Wilkins noticed a familiar face as he watched the tape of a game between Sacramento and New Jersey before the Hawks played the Nets.

"Hey, Kenny, come over here," Wilkins said to guard Kenny Smith, who was acquired from the Kings before the trading deadline. "Is that you?"

"Yeah, that's me," Smith said. "Number 30."

"I thought that's who it was," Wilkins said.

Smith went back to his locker. Wilkins continued to tie his shoes. He then stopped and turned to the reporter sitting next to him.

"Hey," Wilkins asked, pointing to the screen, "is this game live?"

He was serious. And Nets' forward Chris Morris was serious when he happened upon teammate Rick Carlisle sitting at a piano in a hotel lobby and asked him "to play some Picasso."

When Mike McGee was with the Los Angeles Lakers, there was a day where nothing went right. Coach Pat Riley yelled at him throughout practice for busting his assignments. Finally, Riley whistled practice to a stop and got in McGee's face.

"I keep calling your house and nobody's home," Riley said. McGee looked puzzled.

"Gee, coach," McGee said. "I was home all day and didn't hear the phone ring once."

Others have unwittingly stumbled into this comic realm. After San Antonio hired Larry Brown, forward Walter Berry wondered if their relationship would work. "He's a fundamentally sound coach, and my game does not consist of fundamentals," declared Berry, who was later traded to New Jersey. Not to be outdone, here's what guard David Rivers said about Minnesota coach Bill Musselman after he was released by the Timberwolves last season.

"I didn't fit in," Rivers explained. "He (Musselman) wants to have a guard run the offense, pass the ball and play defense. That's not me at all."

Players don't have a monopoly on humor in the NBA. Frank Layden, the former coach and president of the Utah Jazz, leads the league in average laughs.

The NBA's version of Jackie Gleason, he was being heckled by the fans in Portland in a game during the 1984-85 season. That

76er Charles Barkley does his act on Jess Kersey.

was the year the Trail Blazers drafted Sam Bowie instead of Michael Jordan. Layden looked around the 12,880-seat Memorial Coliseum and said, "Now I see why your team didn't draft Michael Jordan. Not enough seats."

When Layden was named as coach of the West team in the 1984 All-Star Game, he said, "It's a good thing for the Utah Jazz, a good thing for Salt Lake City. In fact, it's a great thing for the human race and the universe."

This is the same Frank Layden who said when things were going bad a few seasons earlier: "We formed a booster club in Utah, but by the end of the season it had turned into a terrorist group."

Layden often turned to himself—all 300 pounds of him—for a laugh. To wit:

"A waist is a terrible thing to mind."

"They'd worship this body in India."

"I only put on weight in certain places—pizzerias, ice cream parlors, bakeries."

"It's hard to feel fit as a fiddle when you're shaped like a cello."

The move upstairs to the front office didn't affect Layden's wit. After watching San Antonio rookie David Robinson, lieutenant, U.S. Navy, tear up the league last season, Layden offered this observation: "Have you noticed ever since David Robinson has come into the NBA, the Navy has gone to hell?"

When the league's owners gave commissioner David Stern a five-year, $27.5-million contract, Layden put it all in perspective.

"The head of our Colombian cartel doesn't make that much money," Layden said.

Stern's contract also proved to be fodder for Pat Williams, the president and GM of the Orlando Magic. "One of David's sons asked his father if he could buy him a chemistry set now," Williams said. "David went out and bought the DuPont Co."

Williams went on to say that "David is about to move into a neighborhood where the Girl Scouts go door-to-door selling croissants. Every spring, kids sign up for Little League Polo. The Salvation Army band has a string section. The bird feeders have salad bars."

Williams can be counted on for frequent three-point pot shots. Before the start of last season, he sent a singing telegram to the Minnesota front office. It was "Who's Afraid of the Timberwolves?"—set to the tune of "Who's Afraid of the Big Bad Wolf?"

When Los Angeles Clippers center Benoit Benjamin reported at 280 pounds last season—about 30 pounds more than he weighed the previous year—Williams said, "Benoit has given new meaning to the term expansion player."

Weight has always been a big source of NBA laughs. Center Mel Turpin, after being traded from Cleveland to Utah before the start of the 1987-88 season, flew to Salt Lake City and held a press conference. Turpin, who wrestled with a weight problem, told writers that he weighed 268 pounds. The next day, at his physical, he checked in at 282 pounds.

"I always did like airplane food," Turpin said.

Of the league's entertaining coaches, Denver's Doug Moe stands out. Unfortunately, much of Moe's humor will never reach print. By the count of one enterprising reporter, Moe spewed out 624 profanities when he picked up his 600th NBA victory in March.

New Jersey's Bill Fitch has also been known to utter a few X-rated words in his day—and had ample opportunity last season. The Nets finished with the league's worst record at 17-65.

"Well, we know no one is going to take us prisoner," Fitch said in one of his calmer moments. "Who would pay the ransom?"

Fitch, along with Sacramento coach Dick Motta and Phoenix coach Cotton Fitzsimmons, are part of the old guard. That means they employ a more classical sense of humor.

Fitzsimmons went an entire decade without picking up a victory at The Forum in Los Angeles. That frustration came to an end last May when the Suns beat the Lakers in the Western Conference semifinals. Asked if he remembered the last time a team he coached won in The Forum, Fitzsimmons said, "Yes, I believe it was right after Lincoln was assassinated."

Motta returned to coaching last season after a 2½-year absence. A few months before he returned, Motta bought the Bluebird Candy Co. in Logan, Utah. "I'm up to my ass in chocolate," Motta told a reporter just before the holiday rush.

What will it take to win in Sacramento?

"We're not going to trot out virgins or anything so dramatic, but there will be some sacrifice," Motta said.

Atlanta coach Bob Weiss, who used to be Motta's assistant in Dallas, apparently inherited some of Motta's humor. Weiss played in the same Chicago Bulls' backcourt as Jerry Sloan in the late '60s.

"In your prime, you would have stopped Michael Jordan cold," Weiss told Sloan. "Of course, in your prime, Jordan would have been 12 years old."

A man with a very long prime was Earl Strom, who was referee for more than three decades before retiring in June.

"Earl, you can't retire," backup center Chuck Nevitt told Strom on his last trip to Houston. "You're famous. Everyone will miss you."

"Great refs are like great painters," Strom said. "They're not famous until after they're dead."

Nevitt didn't miss a beat. "Yeah," he said. "And that's probably when you will call your best game."

Strom was the official for Julius Erving's last game with the Philadelphia 76ers. He tossed Milwaukee coach Don Nelson out in the second quarter of the game. At the half, he was told someone called the switchboard and threatened to blow his head off.

"What else are you gonna do in Milwaukee on a Sunday afternoon?" Strom said. "But I was scared. They shoot popes and presidents. Why wouldn't they shoot a stupid referee?"

Strom didn't take any chances. He ran over to retrieve the ball once the game ended. He handed it to Erving then walked off the court arm-in-arm with the star. As a friend noted: "Strom knew nobody was going to take a shot at him with Dr. J standing there."

Others in the league have the ability to make people laugh on a regular basis. The Lakers' Mychal Thompson, for one, specializes in topical humor. Thompson missed six games with a sore left heel last December. This was at the same time the U.S. was trying to bring Panama president Manuel Noriega to justice.

"My heel has been just like that heel down in Panama—very irritating and it will not go away," Thompson said.

Boston's Kevin McHale, Indiana coach Dick Versace, Sacramento GM Jerry Reynolds, and former Clippers' coach Don Casey, who is now with the Celtics, all have graced the sport with a choice quip from time to time.

That's not to imply the league in the past has been a comic wasteland. Earl Tatum·was a classic. Once, when Tatum was at Marquette, he had to be helped to the bench after an injury. When asked where he had been hurt, Tatum pointed to the spot on the floor where he went down.

The NBA didn't deprive Tatum of that sense of the absurd. Tatum was running line drills with his Laker teammates one day when he suddenly dropped to his hands and knees and began scouring the court. Los Angeles GM Jerry West walked over and asked what he was doing.

"Looking for my contact lens," Tatum said.

"You don't wear contacts," West said.

"Oh," Tatum said. "That's right."

Darryl Dawkins, who hailed from a planet named Lovetron, and World B. Free have been known for their comical contributions. But one of the most underrated was San Antonio's Edgar Jones. Here's what the forward had to say the day he stopped talking to the press:

"I'm not talking anymore," Jones said. "That's it. No more words. It's over. Wanna know the deal? Mum is the word here. My game talks and my conversation walks. That's food for thought for the people.

"All those fancy quotes were from my early days when I was a young buck. I've gotta take all the brashness of them now and give 'em a coat of coolness. Wanna know why? Not that they're not true. I have no limitations. It's just that I'm basically a quiet guy who keeps to himself. I don't like to talk.

"By the way, I'm probably retiring after the season because I can make more money outside of basketball. Wanna know why?"

John Drew, who played for Atlanta and Utah, was asked to fill out an insurance form. He put down Sept. 30 for his birthday.

"What year?" the secretary asked.

Drew looked at her like she didn't know what she was talking about.

"Every year," he said.

The Suns traded All-Star guard Dennis Johnson to the Celtics for All-Stiff center Rick Robey in 1983. It turned out to be a horrible deal for Phoenix. Robey played for three seasons and never averaged more than 5.6 points a game and everyone gave Phoenix GM Jerry Colangelo grief for making the trade.

Everyone. In 1984, a man named Ronald Turney was found guilty of burglary and first-degree murder. "I do have one thing I'd like to get on the record," Turney said as he was hauled off to prison. "Tell Colangelo not to make any more deals with Boston. Red Auerbach really took him in that Robey deal."

And the final word comes from Bulgaria's Georgi Glouchkov, who played for the Suns during the 1985-86 season. After Glouchkov suffered through a particularly bad game, picking up five fouls in 11 minutes, he was asked to assess his performance.

"I am not all that pleased," Glouchkov said in his fractured English. "But I did not do anything for which I should be hung or beaten."

NEXT MAGIC: THE SUNS' KEVIN JOHNSON

By STEVE WESTON

Only a truly devoted, not to mention demented, masochist would wait around, gleefully anticipating the appearance of a glitch in Kevin Johnson's personality.

He is all these Boy Scoutish things: trustworthy, loyal, helpful, friendly, courteous, kind, obedient, cheerful, thrifty, brave, clean and reverent.

And rich. And talented. And genuine.

The rumors of his kindness and generosity are true. Did he write a check for $5,000 to help a security guard at his apartment complex out of a financial jam? Yes.

Did he hand the keys to his RX-7 to a friend in need of a car and tell that friend not to bother returning it? Yes.

Does he buy 10 tickets to every Suns' home game and give them out to people he meets on the street? Yes.

Is he building a home in the Sacramento ghetto of his childhood in an effort to help some of that neighborhood's youngsters to find a meaningful life? Yes.

Does he meticulously go over every piece of fan mail, dutifully answer each, say "thank you," "ma'am" and "sir," sign every autograph with a smile, take youngsters aside for a kind word of encouragement, return messages, not drink, not chase women and party because that would "distract" him from his goals, never duck the tough question, remain devoutly religious, an organizer of locker-room Christianity and a dedicated bookworm? Yes, yes, yes, yes and YES!

This is point guard Kevin Johnson, whose star has risen in the

Steve Weston, a sportswriter for more than three decades, follows KJ and the Suns for the Phoenix Gazette.

Young Kevin Johnson has emerged as one of the NBA's elite.

NBA West with the Phoenix Suns rather than in a major media market in the East, where he would have achieved sainthood long ago.

Saint Kevin. It has a ring to it. As it is, lionization has occurred soon enough. "If you had a son," said JoAnn Fitzsimmons, wife of Suns' coach/player personnel director Cotton Fitzsimmons, and KJ's confidant and condominium decorator, "you would want him to be like Kevin. If you had a daughter, you would want her to marry someone like him."

Personally perfect, professionally perfect.

"It's hard to believe," the 24-year-old Johnson said, "that I am in the position that I am in right now."

The position he is in is that of a budding superstar in a profession where the word superstar is more often used than deserved. KJ, as he is known to the Suns' faithful, deservedly wears that tag.

Referred to by many as The Next Magic, Kevin Johnson must at least be considered at the head of the class of the small, mobile, versatile guards who have become such major factors in the success of the NBA's elite teams. Isiah Thomas, John Stockton, Mark Price, Joe Dumars and Terry Porter are in that class.

Only rarely does Saint Kevin's halo slip askew. And even then, it's not too exciting. He did attract a modicum of attention early last season when both he and Magic Johnson were thrown out of a game between the Suns and Lakers at The Forum. They got into a kind of pushing match and Magic ended up shoving Kevin in the face with an open hand because of something Kevin had called him.

"You big punk," reportedly was KJ's admonishment. Strong stuff there for KJ. He won't talk about it.

And there's a technical foul here and there. After being elbowed and hurt by Portland center Kevin Duckworth in the 1990 playoffs, KJ rather unwisely seized an opportunity to fire the basketball at the seven-foot, 270-pound Trail Blazer.

And once in a while you can catch Johnson snapping back at Fitzsimmons, whose verbosity has irritated older and wiser players (not to mention general managers, other coaches and media types).

"We have some of the same traits," Fitzsimmons said. "We both like to feel in control. This can clash sometimes, but we work it out."

Said Johnson: "I have to mature. I have to handle it." It's become obvious after only a little more than two full seasons as a starter in his pro career that Kevin is on the way to becoming one of the great double-threat guards in the history of the NBA.

In his first full season with the Suns (1988-89), he became only the fifth player—following Oscar Robertson, Magic, Isiah and Nate Archibald—to average more than 20 points (20.4) and 10 assists (12.2) in a single season. He was voted the Most Improved Player.

He came back in 1989-90 and did it again—22.5 points, 11.4 assists. In the process, KJ has led the Suns to 55- and 54-win regular-season records and appearances in the Western Conference championship playoff series both years.

There might not be a guard in the league today with a quicker first step, and he certainly is among the best at driving the basket, or pulling up to take the short-, medium- or long-range jumper, or getting the ball to an open teammate.

He has yet to fully recognize and understand his abilities not

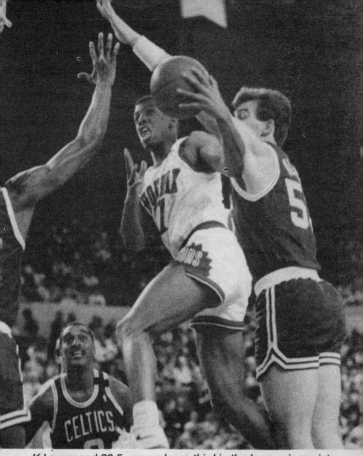

KJ averaged 22.5 ppg and was third in the league in assists.

only at playing the game, but in leading his teammates. But he's just a baby, although perhaps only in chronological terms.

Being born in the ghetto, as he was in Sacramento, offers plenty of quick-growth opportunities. And even more if one parent was white, the other black, and the child sent to live with the mother's parents because the mother was only 16 years old.

His father, Lawrence "Frog" Johnson, drowned when Kevin was three years old. "I'm not really curious about him," Johnson said. "I guess if someone came to me and wanted to talk about him, I would listen. But I don't seek information."

Johnson has managed to turn the negatives of his beginnings

and a ghetto upbringing into nothing but positives. His grandparents became the most important people in his life.

"I had a lot of love and support," Johnson said, "and that was very unusual in our neighborhood. I came in at dark, didn't go to parties and didn't run with guys who got into trouble."

Johnson noted that through his grandparents, George Peat and the late Georgia Peat, and his mother, who remained close as he grew up and still is close to her son, he was able to isolate himself from the pitfalls of the inner city. "I wanted to be the best," he said. "I didn't want to be one of the guys."

His ticket out came through athletics. Oddly, it was initially stamped "baseball."

"While everybody else was playing basketball," he said, "I spent my time throwing the baseball as high as I could and catching it, over and over and over."

Even when he finished his senior year at Sacramento High School with the best scoring average (32.5) in the state of California, baseball was the lure. He had batted .470 as a switch-hitting senior shortstop and kept dabbling at the sport even while on a basketball scholarship at Cal-Berkeley, where he majored in political science.

The Oakland A's had shown interest in Johnson while he was still in high school and, saying it was "something I had to get out of my system," Johnson took the A's up on his 23rd-round draft selection in the 1986 amateur draft. He worked out with the parent club in the summer after his junior year and played two games as a minor-league shortstop with Modesto, Cal.

A's scouting director Dick Bogard said Johnson had the talent to make the majors, but clearly his best shot would be at an NBA career.

Although he finished his college basketball career as Cal's all-time leader in scoring, assists and steals, he had problems with coach Lou Campanelli, who kept a leash on his point guard. Johnson does not perform well on a leash.

The Cleveland Cavaliers made Johnson the seventh player selected in the 1987 draft. But Mark Price, who had struggled in his first year with the Cavs, emerged in 1987-88 and whipped Kevin consistently, starting in training camp. Kevin wound up playing behind Price and before the February 25, 1988 deadline, he was traded to Phoenix with Mark West and Tyrone Corbin for Larry Nance and Mike Sanders.

"I knew what Kevin could do," Fitzsimmons said. "I wouldn't turn over a team to just anybody."

At first, he startled some teammates and angered others with his take-charge approach. But it didn't take long for them—including veteran forward Tom Chambers, who would be acquired through unrestricted free agency in the summer—to realize the potential for improvement in their game rested in KJ's success.

The results have been vividly demonstrated by the Suns' achievements since KJ's arrival and by his individual highlights, including selection for the 1990 All-Star Game and his All-NBA second-team designation two years in a row.

If he were in Los Angeles, New York, Chicago or any other "major media market," KJ would be smiling from billboards, grinning from national television commercials, speaking on league promotional videotapes.

He's big at his local bank, of course, where he deposits checks from a salary that's in the vicinity of $2 million a year for the next six seasons. He's easily recognizable locally, too. And despite the fact a player from the market size of Phoenix normally isn't mobbed by autograph-seekers and well-wishers all across the nation, Johnson is attracting his share, and feeling the loss of privacy.

"The way I try to deal with it," he said, "is that when I'm out in public, that's their space and I'm invading it. They have every right to expect me to give autographs and talk basketball and whatever. When I'm not in the mood, I stay home and do things in the privacy of my home."

His "endorsements" are limited to a local tire company and Dial Soap, which is headquartered here. KJ has a shoe contract with Fila that he says is "worth a considerable amount as far as shoe endorsements go," but hardly comparable to those "six-figure" deals held by people like Magic, Isiah and Michael Jordan.

The Fila deal had a kicker. They had to agree to donate clothing each year to St. Hope Academy. That brings him to his favorite subject, the building under construction in the Oak Park area of South Sacramento, where drug and alcohol abuse are commonplace, as is unemployment.

Johnson is building a youth center, St. Hope Academy, which will provide counselling and job training for kids from nine to 16 years of age. KJ envisions it as a "ticket" out of the ghetto.

Hope is KJ's favorite word and seven is his number and the position he was drafted. His shiny black Porsche has a license plate reading Hope VII.

Watch him on the Suns' team bus and airplane rides. He reads the Bible, the works of Emerson, Thoreau and Martin Luther King.

Watch him relate to people of all races and denominations.

The most-asked question about him: "Is he for real?"

Believe it.

INSIDE THE NBA

By FRED KERBER and FRANK BRADY

PREDICTED ORDER OF FINISH

ATLANTIC	CENTRAL	MIDWEST	PACIFIC
Philadelphia	Detroit	San Antonio	Phoenix
New York	Cleveland	Utah	L.A. Lakers
Boston	Chicago	Dallas	Portland
Washington	Indiana	Houston	L.A. Clippers
New Jersey	Milwaukee	Denver	Seattle
Miami	Atlanta	Minnesota	Sacramento
	Charlotte	Orlando	Golden State

EASTERN CONFERENCE: Chicago
WESTERN CONFERENCE: Phoenix
CHAMPION: Chicago

Among life's basic precepts such as "Don't Wear Tin Hats in Rain Storms," is the simple adage of "Never Go Against a Defending Champ," unless, of course, one views indigestion as a viable alternative life style.

We tried to stay in the mainstream. We couldn't. Pass the antacids. Yes, it's hard to go against the Pistons with their marvelous three-guard rotation of Isiah Thomas and Joe Dumars and Vinnie Johnson; with their suffocating defense led by Dennis Rodman; with coach Chuck Daly returning for one more season. But how much longer can Michael Jordan be denied a spot in the NBA

Fred Kerber covers the Knicks for the New York Daily News *and Frank Brady, formerly the Lakers' beat man on the* Los Angeles Herald-Examiner, *now writes for the* San Diego Tribune. *Brady wrote the Western Conference, Kerber the Eastern Conference and the introduction after consultation with his counterpart.*

Utah's John Stockton adds to assists legend.

Finals? Television doesn't want to wait any longer.

And so 1990-91 is forecast as the season His Airness and the Bulls get past the obstacle that has denied them two seasons running. Last year, the Eastern Finals went to seven games—one more than two seasons ago. This time, Chicago takes the Finals step—and one step beyond to the title.

The Bulls are like the Pistons of a few years back. Always, it seemed Detroit had the stuff to get past the Celtics and failed. The Pistons learned through losing. The Bulls have earned their doctorate in defeat and are ready to advance.

And it says here that they'll advance to see a team that also learned from losing, the Phoenix Suns under coach Cotton Fitzsimmons. Cotton's swabs found ways to lose the Western Finals to the Blazers last season. This time, they should find enough ways to properly celebrate their 15th-year reunion in the Finals.

Nothing will come easy. The Bulls could find themselves no better than third-place finishers in the awesomely fierce Central

The Knicks hope for an encore from Maurice Cheeks.

Division. Detroit, especially with Daly directing his farewell season, should again finish atop that blue-collar heap. And the Cavs, winners of 57 games two seasons ago, will be a legit contender with health and Danny Ferry aboard, two elements missing in 1989-90.

The Atlantic Division should feature a fierce three-team go-for-the-jugular fight as Philadelphia, New York and Boston all scramble for home-court advantage in the playoffs. The Sixers last season dethroned the Knicks, who had dethroned the Celtics the previous season. The Knicks will be one of the most intriguing stories. How much can venerable veteran guard Maurice Cheeks deliver in support of a front line that boasts beasts in Patrick Ewing and Charles Oakley?

In Boston, the question is how much quickness (and happiness after the courts ordered him to stay stateside) will Brian Shaw deliver? But with Charles Barkley and Rick Mahorn thumping and bumping through 82 games, the Sixers remain the Atlantic choice. Can't always go against the champs. There are only so many antacids in the galaxy. The Sixers' bench, though, again should be the Achilles heel that prevents legit title contention. "It's no secret," Barkley said, "we need more players."

The West should prove equally fierce. The Midwest Division could be a veritable bloodbath with the David Robinson-led Spurs at the top. The Jazz have added the outside element of Jeff Malone to complement his Mailman namesake Karl and the splendid John Stockton. In Dallas, the addition of forwards Alex English and Rodney McCray plus do-everything guard Fat Lever should offset the stinging loss of free agent Sam Perkins to the Lakers. Lever, joining Derek Harper and Rolando Blackman, provides a back-court rotation to rival the Pistons.

"I think it stacks up with Detroit," Lever said. "Derek is pretty similar to Isiah, I'm pretty similar to Joe Dumars and Ro has the scoring ability to light it up as quickly as Vinnie."

Phoenix will have to contend with Magic Johnson and the Lakers, who found themselves out of the Finals for the first time since the Taft Administration—or so it seemed. And Portland didn't get to the Finals with mirrors. The Blazers are solid and will again pose a formidable presence.

When it's all done next June, there should be a new champ. The bonafide contenders are as numerous as in any season of recent memory: Detroit, Chicago, Utah, Phoenix, San Antonio, Dallas, Portland, Cleveland, the Lakers. And even though it may be plain dumb to go against the Pistons, we'll take our chances, and our antacids, with the Bulls.

ATLANTA HAWKS

TEAM DIRECTORY: Pres.: Stan Kasten; GM: Pete Babcock; Dir. Pub. Rel.: Arthur Triche; Coach: Bob Weiss; Asst. Coaches: Kevin Loughery, Johnny Davis. Arena: The Omni (16,371). Colors: Red, white and gold.

SCOUTING REPORT

SHOOTING: The Hawks' shooting percentage was nothing to sneer at: .487, eighth-best in the league. The big problem was what they gave up, an embarrassing .496.

Some of the individual offensive numbers were impressive: Dominique Wilkins, for example, had his best shooting season (.484) since his rookie campaign. Ten Hawks came in at .477 or better. Nope, putting the ball in the basket wasn't the problem. Stopping opponents from doing the same was. The presence of Alexander Voltov, the 6-10 Soviet forward and a good outside shot, should diversify a predictable offense.

PLAYMAKING: With the drafting of Rumeal Robinson, the Hawks have four point guards, including Kenny Smith, Doc Rivers and Spud Webb. Rivers, though, figures to spend a lot more time at shooting guard this season so the Hawks will need all the passing help they can get at the point. Webb probably will continue spot duty and Smith has yet to prove he can handle the point consistently. Above all, the Hawks need to re-establish consistency in their running game, which often bogged down through Moses Malone's lumbering style.

DEFENSE: The Hawks should have picked up an early clue last season: their first three non-expansionist opponents on the schedule shot .540, .553 and .529. And that darn near qualified as the highlight of a defensive campaign that was an utter bust. For the season, opponents shot a staggering .496, placing the Hawks 25th in the league—ahead of only Charlotte and Orlando. Forced turnovers were way down, to 15.8 from a third-best 18.1 the previous season. Teams regularly beat them in transition, something unthinkable a few seasons back when "athleticism" was the key Atlanta watchword.

But improvement looms, mainly because it can't get any worse. With the intimidation of his contract a year behind him, Jon Koncak figures to be an interior presence again. Ditto Kevin Willis,

Dominique Wilkins shot less and improved percentage.

who has found some security through the deletion of Antoine Carr. Transition defense, where teams took advantage of the aging Malone, will remain one of new coach Bob Weiss' target areas.

REBOUNDING: While the perennial search in Atlanta has always been for more perimeter shooting, the quest may start turning toward rebounding as the Hawks' downward board spiral continued: they ranked No. 18 in the league in rebounding.

The key to a resurgence could be Willis, who was a fearsome rebounder in the latter stages last season. Rebounding is largely a hustle, desire and positioning stat and those were three elements missing in a disappointing, disenchanted team.

OUTLOOK: Atlanta often disappointed in past playoffs. They didn't last season. They never got the chance, failing to qualify for the first time since 1985. Now it will be a comparatively low-

HAWK ROSTER

No.	Veterans	Pos.	Ht.	Wt.	Age	Yrs. Pro	College
10	John Battle	G	6-2	175	27	5	Rutgers
32	John Koncak	C	7-0	260	27	5	SMU
33	Duane Ferrell	F	6-7	209	25	2	Georgia Tech
53	Cliff Levingston	F	6-8	210	29	8	Wichita State
34	John Long	G	6-5	195	34	12	Detroit
2	Moses Malone	C	6-10	255	35	14	None
22	Roy Marble	G	6-6	190	23	1	Iowa
25	Glenn Rivers	G	6-5	185	29	7	Marquette
31	Kenny Smith	G	6-3	170	25	3	North Carolina
8	Alexander Volkov	F	6-10	218	26	1	Kiev Institute
4	Anthony (Spud) Webb	G	5-7	135	27	5	N.C. State
21	Dominique Wilkins	F	6-8	200	30	8	Georgia
42	Kevin Willis	F	7-0	235	28	5	Michigan State

Rd.	Rookies	Sel. No.	Pos.	Ht.	Wt.	College
1	Rumeal Robinson	10	G	6-2	195	Michigan
2	Trevor Wilson	36	F	6-7	211	UCLA
2	Steve Bardo	41	G	6-5	191	Illinois

key approach from Weiss—in contrast to the intense, cerebral, undeniably professional approach of ousted Mike Fratello—that tries to level out one of the NBA's most puzzling clubs of the past decade.

Like recent years, the 1989-90 Hawks were often super, often rotten. A healthy overhaul was predicted and has started with new faces in GM Pete Babcock and Weiss. The Hawks, though, will enter this season as perhaps more of an enigma than ever before as they try to work with virtually the same problems and strengths in a different system.

HAWK PROFILES

DOMINIQUE WILKINS 30 6-8 200   Forward

Can't keep blaming him . . . Had a quality season in otherwise lost season for Hawks . . . Shot .484, highest since rookie season . . . Incredible athletic skills . . . Still can leap over redwoods . . . True, he shoots at every opportunity, but he launched the fewest shots since his second season . . . Vastly underrated defender . . . May have lost half a step . . . Won Slam Dunk cham-

pionship for second time... An 80 percent career shooter from line... Good offensive rebounder, keeps the ball alive with leaps and taps... Gerald's big brother... One of league's best interviews... Left Georgia after three years, where he earned "Human Highlight Film" sobriquet... Born Jan. 12, 1960, in Sorbonne, France... Real first name is Jacques... Earned $1.8-million salary.

Year	Team	G	FG	FG Pct.	FT	FT Pct.	Reb.	Ast.	TP	Avg.
1982-83	Atlanta	82	601	.493	230	.682	478	129	1434	17.5
1983-84	Atlanta	81	684	.479	382	.770	582	126	1750	21.6
1984-85	Atlanta	81	853	.451	486	.806	557	200	2217	27.4
1985-86	Atlanta	78	888	.468	577	.818	618	206	2366	30.3
1986-87	Atlanta	79	828	.463	607	.818	494	261	2294	29.0
1987-88	Atlanta	78	909	.464	541	.826	502	224	2397	30.7
1988-89	Atlanta	80	814	.464	442	.844	553	211	2099	26.2
1989-90	Atlanta	80	810	.484	459	.807	521	200	2138	26.7
	Totals	639	6387	.469	3724	.804	4305	1557	16695	26.1

JON KONCAK 27 7-0 250   Center

Jon Contract... Was he supposed to say no to ludicrous amount of money?... Career lows in points (198), average (3.7), rebounds (226), blocks (34), field goals (78), shots (127) and free-throw percentage (.532)... Other than that, he was worth every penny of the staggering $12.5-million contract that came courtesy of Piston offer sheet... Totally intimidated by his newfound fortune... Got $2.7 million last year, gets a mere $1.8 million this season... Detroit was interested in him because he's always been tough inside defender and rebounder... Hawks feel he can become adequate scorer... Good shot selection, without anything resembling scorer's mentality. Hit .614 from floor ... A lottery pick (No. 5) by Hawks in 1985 out of Southern Methodist... Born May 17, 1963, in Cedar Rapids, Iowa.

Year	Team	G	FG	FG Pct.	FT	FT Pct.	Reb.	Ast.	TP	Avg.
1985-86	Atlanta	82	263	.507	156	.607	467	55	682	8.3
1986-87	Atlanta	82	169	.480	125	.654	493	31	463	5.6
1987-88	Atlanta	49	98	.483	83	.610	333	19	279	5.7
1988-89	Atlanta	74	141	.524	63	.553	453	56	345	4.7
1989-90	Atlanta	54	78	.614	42	.532	226	23	198	3.7
	Totals	341	749	.510	469	.604	1972	184	1967	5.8

GLENN (DOC) RIVERS 29 6-4 185   Guard

Reporter's dream . . . Ask him a question, turn on the recorder and get five hours of great quotes . . . Likeable, decent human being . . . Not a bad player, either . . . Endured "the most frustrating season of my career" . . . Herniated disc limited him to 48 games . . . But upon return, continued huge improvement in three-point shooting: shot .364 on trifectas . . . All-time Hawks assist leader . . . Shot well enough to have Hawks seriously contemplating make him full-time two-guard . . . Never played point until his third year in league . . . Went to Marquette and Hawks grabbed him on second round in 1983 . . . Superb penetrator . . . Good defensively, averaged 2.41 steals, but he should be better . . . Born Oct. 13, 1961, in Chicago . . . Makes $1 million.

Year	Team	G	FG	FG Pct.	FT	FT Pct.	Reb.	Ast.	TP	Avg.
1983-84	Atlanta	81	250	.462	255	.785	220	314	757	9.3
1984-85	Atlanta	69	334	.476	291	.770	214	410	974	14.1
1985-86	Atlanta	53	220	.474	172	.608	162	443	612	11.5
1986-87	Atlanta	82	342	.451	365	.828	299	823	1053	12.8
1987-88	Atlanta	80	403	.453	319	.758	366	747	1134	14.2
1988-89	Atlanta	76	371	.455	247	.861	286	525	1032	13.6
1989-90	Atlanta	48	218	.454	138	.812	200	264	598	12.5
	Totals	489	2138	.460	1787	.775	1747	3526	6160	12.6

MOSES MALONE 35 6-10 255   Center

The war horse is breaking down . . . Future Hall of Famer showed his age . . . Didn't run floor well at all . . . Slowed Hawks' transition game, often to crawl . . . Can still go get 'em on the boards . . . Clogged middle too much and negated some of Dominique Wilkins' post game . . . Scoring (18.9) was second lowest of NBA career . . . For first time since 1977-78, failed to average combined 20 points and 10 rebounds . . . Fewest defensive rebounds of career (448). Ranked in low 30 percent of defensive boarding efficiency . . . Moved past Wes Unseld, Walt Bellamy and Nate Thurmond into fifth place on all-time rebounding list with 14,483 . . . Four free throws short of Oscar Robertson's all-time record of 7,694 . . . One of four players to make jump from high school to pros . . . Born March 23, 1955, in Sugarland, Tex. . . . Signed three-year, free-agent deal with Hawks in

'88 and made $2.4 million last season . . . Originally a third-round pick of Utah Stars in ABA . . . Led Sixers to 1983 NBA title and made finals with Houston in 1981.

Year	Team	G	FG	FG Pct.	FT	FT Pct.	Reb.	Ast.	TP	Avg.
1974-75	Utah (ABA)	83	591	.571	375	.635	1209	82	1557	18.8
1975-76	St. Louis (ABA) . . .	43	251	.512	112	.612	413	58	614	14.3
1976-77	Buf.-Hou.	82	389	.480	305	.693	1072	89	1083	13.2
1977-78	Houston	59	413	.499	318	.718	886	31	1144	19.4
1978-79	Houston	82	716	.540	599	.739	1444	147	2031	24.8
1979-80	Houston	82	778	.502	563	.719	1190	147	2119	25.8
1980-81	Houston	80	806	.522	609	.757	1180	141	2222	27.8
1981-82	Houston	81	945	.519	630	.762	1188	142	2520	31.1
1982-83	Philadelphia	78	654	.501	600	.761	1194	101	1908	24.5
1983-84	Philadelphia	71	532	.483	545	.750	950	96	1609	22.7
1984-85	Philadelphia	79	602	.469	737	.815	1031	130	1941	24.6
1985-86	Philadelphia	74	571	.458	617	.787	872	90	1759	23.8
1986-87	Washington	73	595	.454	570	.824	824	120	1760	24.1
1987-88	Washington	79	531	.487	543	.788	884	112	1607	20.3
1988-89	Atlanta	81	538	.491	561	.789	956	112	1637	20.2
1989-90	Atlanta	81	517	.480	493	.781	812	130	1528	18.9
	Totals	1208	9429	.499	8177	.757	16105	1728	27039	22.4

KEVIN WILLIS 28 7-0 225   Forward-Center

Superbly gifted athlete who's also terribly insecure . . . But from day Antoine Carr was traded, he played like a new man in starting lineup. Averaged over 15 points, 10 rebounds, shot better than 60 percent . . . Has always felt unappreciated and underpaid—he made $500,000 last year . . . Should be much better defensively, doesn't rotate that well . . . Plus, makes a lot of bad decisions . . . Doesn't have the wingspan to be quality shot-blocker . . . Nice jump hook and he runs court well, even if he doesn't see it . . . Could be a monster this year, if end of last year is any indication . . . Born in Los Angeles on Sept. 6, 1962 . . . Atlanta picked him 11th overall out of Michigan State in 1984.

Year	Team	G	FG	FG Pct.	FT	FT Pct.	Reb.	Ast.	TP	Avg.
1984-85	Atlanta	82	322	.467	119	.657	522	36	765	9.3
1985-86	Atlanta	82	419	.517	172	.654	704	45	1010	12.3
1986-87	Atlanta	81	538	.536	227	.709	849	62	1304	16.1
1987-88	Atlanta	75	356	.518	159	.649	547	28	871	11.6
1988-89	Atlanta					Injured				
1989-90	Atlanta	81	418	.519	168	.683	645	57	1006	12.4
	Totals	401	2053	.514	845	.673	3267	228	4956	12.4

CLIFF LEVINGSTON 29 6-8 210   Forward

Repeat after him: "I should have signed, I should have signed..."...Hawks offered healthy contract last season, but Wichita State product declined, figuring to play for free agency...Bad move...Came in overweight, never got going...Career lows in points and rebounds...Always had problem with playing time with Atlanta forward logjam...
Rep as a good, strong athlete offensive rebounder. Run and jump is his game, thrives in transition. Gets snuffed in half court...A team player...Happy-go-lucky, fun to be around...Born Jan 4. 1961, in St. Louis...Undergrad first-round pick by Pistons in 1982, traded to Hawks with rights for Antoine Carr in 1984 for Dan Roundfield...Made $450,000 last year, could have made more.

Year	Team	G	FG	FG Pct.	FT	FT Pct.	Reb.	Ast.	TP	Avg.
1982-83	Detroit	62	131	.485	84	.571	232	52	346	5.6
1983-84	Detroit	80	229	.525	125	.672	545	109	583	7.3
1984-85	Atlanta	74	291	.527	145	.653	566	104	727	9.8
1985-86	Atlanta	81	294	.534	164	.678	534	72	752	9.3
1986-87	Atlanta	82	251	.506	155	.731	533	40	657	8.0
1987-88	Atlanta	82	314	.557	190	.772	504	71	819	10.0
1988-89	Atlanta	80	300	.528	133	.696	498	75	734	9.2
1989-90	Atlanta	75	216	.509	83	.680	319	80	516	6.9
	Totals	616	2026	.525	1079	.688	3731	603	5134	8.3

ROY MARBLE 23 6-6 190   Guard

Wasted year. Hopefully, not a wasted life ...Hit with drug woes, missed half a season ...Relentless worker, a run-and-jump type... Seemed completely unprepared for rigors and style of pro game...Hawks took him 23rd in 1989 draft after steady four-year career at Iowa ...Cameo role performer who displayed no semblance of a shot—.276 accuracy over 24 games...Born Dec. 13, 1966, in Flint, Mich....Paid $275,000.

Year	Team	G	FG	FG Pct.	FT	FT Pct.	Reb.	Ast.	TP	Avg.
1989-90	Atlanta	24	16	.276	19	.655	24	11	51	2.1

KENNY SMITH 25 6-3 170   Guard

Got to get Sacramento nightmare out of his head ... Hawks hoping he's not as bad as they saw after getting him for Antoine Carr in February ... Rarely penetrated, and still dribbles ball too high and gets stripped ... Poor defender ... Shoots a knuckleball ... At least he's polite ... Still must be considered a project after three years in league ... Some tools, such as quickness and good hands, but Hawks wanted an impact point guard immediately and he wasn't ... Born March 8, 1965, in Queens, N.Y. ... Another in long line of North Carolina pro products who played with Michael Jordan, Brad Daugherty and Sam Perkins ... A hard worker who was Kings' first-round pick (No. 6) in 1987 draft ... Made $600,000.

Year	Team	G	FG	FG Pct.	FT	FT Pct.	Reb.	Ast.	TP	Avg.
1987-88	Sacramento......	61	331	.477	167	.819	138	434	841	13.8
1988-89	Sacramento......	81	547	.462	263	.737	226	621	1403	17.3
1989-90	Sac.-Atl.........	79	378	.466	161	.821	157	445	943	11.9
	Totals	221	1256	.467	591	.781	521	1500	3187	14.4

JOHN BATTLE 27 6-2 175   Guard

If he had a third knee, probably would have had surgery on that, too ... Decent year considering both knees underwent knife ... Another team player ... Tough one-on-one defender ... Nice jumper from 17-18 feet. And he penetrates well ... Career highs in scoring (10.9) and shooting (.506) ... So what's the drawback? His confidence, for one ... If he misses a few, he treats shot opportunities like a dreaded disease ... When he and Doc Rivers started together, Hawks were 20-11. But he's a better weapon off bench ... Decent passer and ball-handler ... Can play point in a pinch ... Born Nov. 9, 1962, in Washington, D.C. ... A fourth-round find out of Rutgers in 1985 ... Made $350,000 last season.

Year	Team	G	FG	FG Pct.	FT	FT Pct.	Reb.	Ast.	TP	Avg.
1985-86	Atlanta	64	101	.455	75	.728	62	74	277	4.3
1986-87	Atlanta	64	144	.457	93	.738	60	124	381	6.0
1987-88	Atlanta	67	278	.454	141	.750	113	158	713	10.6
1988-89	Atlanta	82	287	.457	194	.815	140	197	779	9.5
1989-90	Atlanta	60	275	.506	102	.756	99	154	654	10.9
	Totals	337	1085	.467	605	.766	474	707	2804	8.3

ALEXANDER VOLKOV 26 6-10 218   Forward

He made good comrade Hawk, no?... Showed flashes of brilliance and Hawks are more than pleased with this free agent from Kiev, USSR ... Had a problem with the culture and language—no, he never ordered earmuffs for lunch... Biggest problem was fatigue... The guy never had a break... Played with Russian national team and then came right to NBA... Swing player, but not quick enough for most small forwards, not strong enough for most power forwards... Still, there's a niche somewhere in between... Superb penetrator, excellent passer, good work ethic... Too much clutch and grab on defense and is foul prone—probably as result of playing European zones... Earned $700,000 (American)... Born March 29, 1964, in Omsk, USSR.

Year	Team	G	FG	FG Pct.	FT	FT Pct.	Reb.	Ast.	TP	Avg.
1989-90	Atlanta	72	137	.482	70	.583	119	83	357	5.0

SPUD WEBB 27 5-7 133   Guard

The original NBA Munchkin... Had best statistical year of five-season career... Improved shooting was a must and he came through... Starting for the injured Doc Rivers, he thrived some with his broken-field full-court dashes... Only Hawk to play all 82 games—first time in last six seasons just one Hawk has done so... Temperamental player at times... Doesn't seem to understand what makes him an undersized asset also makes him oversized liability... Born July 13, 1963, in Dallas... Won Slam Dunk title in 1986 in his home town and captured nation's heart... Still gets letters from appreciative short people... Thrilled ACC fans with exploits at N.C. State... Drafted by Pistons on fourth round in 1985, was waived and signed as free agent by Hawks.

Year	Team	G	FG	FG Pct.	FT	FT Pct.	Reb.	Ast.	TP	Avg.
1985-86	Atlanta	79	199	.483	216	.785	123	337	616	7.8
1986-87	Atlanta	33	71	.438	80	.762	60	167	223	6.8
1987-88	Atlanta	82	191	.475	107	.817	146	337	490	6.0
1988-89	Atlanta	81	133	.459	52	.867	123	284	319	3.9
1989-90	Atlanta	82	294	.477	162	.871	201	477	751	9.2
	Totals	357	888	.472	617	.815	653	1602	2399	6.7

JOHN LONG 34 6-5 195   Guard

With properly spotted minutes, still an asset . . . Came in January with a couple of 10-day contracts and was signed for rest of season after he failed to hook on with Dallas . . . Played over half of season, providing 8.4 points per game and some solid play during Doc Rivers' absence . . . Shot abominable .409 two seasons ago when he was cast adrift by Indiana . . . A streak shooter all the way . . . Gave some quality minutes but is at the stage where too much is simply too much . . . Tough physical defender who fights through screens . . . Got minimum wage of $125,000 . . . Born Aug. 28, 1956, in Romulus, Mich. . . . Detroit's second-round pick in 1978 out of U. of Detroit.

Year	Team	G	FG	FG Pct.	FT	FT Pct.	Reb.	Ast.	TP	Avg.
1978-79	Detroit	82	581	.469	157	.826	266	121	1319	16.1
1979-80	Detroit	69	588	.505	160	.825	337	206	1337	19.4
1980-81	Detroit	59	441	.461	160	.870	197	106	1044	17.7
1981-82	Detroit	69	637	.492	238	.865	257	148	1514	21.9
1982-83	Detroit	70	312	.451	111	.760	180	105	737	10.5
1983-84	Detroit	82	545	.472	243	.884	289	205	1334	16.3
1984-85	Detroit	66	431	.487	106	.862	190	130	973	14.7
1985-86	Detroit	62	264	.482	89	.856	98	82	620	10.0
1986-87	Indiana	80	490	.419	219	.890	217	258	1218	15.2
1987-88	Indiana	81	417	.474	166	.907	229	173	1034	12.8
1988-89	Ind.-Det.	68	147	.409	70	.921	77	80	372	5.5
1989-90	Atlanta	48	174	.453	46	.836	83	85	404	8.4
	Totals	836	5027	.469	1765	.861	2420	1699	11906	14.2

THE ROOKIES

RUMEAL ROBINSON 23 6-2 195   Guard

Somewhat curious pick for Hawks at No. 10 on first round. They sought shooting guard, wound up with point guard . . . Michigan's 1989 NCAA title-game hero when he sank two OT free throws at :03 to beat Seton Hall. Says something about his nerves because he was just a .666 career free-throw shooter . . . All-Big Ten, All-American second team as senior when he averaged 19.2 points . . . Attended Rindge & Latin High in Cambridge, Mass., Patrick Ewing's alma mater . . . Born Nov. 13, 1966.

TREVOR WILSON 22 6-7 211   **Forward**

Three-year All-Pac 10 selection out of UCLA was grabbed as the 36th pick in the second round... His 90 double-figure scoring games are second in Bruin history to Kenny Fields. Played more games, 126, than any Bruin ever... "Good, aggressive NBA player," projects Marty Blake, the league's director of scouting services... Has good ball-handling skills and runs the court well ... Free-throw shooting saw peculiar four-year decline: from .726 to .621 to .576 to embarrassing .507... Question with Hawks is: Where will minutes come from?... Born March 16, 1968.

STEPHEN BARDO 22 6-5 191   **Guard**

Hawks made the Big Ten's two-time defensive Player of the Year the 41st pick in the draft... Sixers' assistant GM Bob Weinhauer said Bardo "might be the best defensive guard in the country."... Defend isn't all he does, either. He led Illinois in three-point shooting (.438) and assists (4.7)... Played some forward in college, but could probably double up at either guard spot as pro... Born April 5, 1968, in Carbondale, Ill.

COACH BOB WEISS: Players' coach... Named to succeed  Mike Fratello, whose intensity level set new standards... Weiss, naturally, is much more laid back... Ideal coaching situation is letting players work and perform... Had a 12-year NBA career with six different teams, averaging 7.6 points and 3.7 assists... From 1968-74, played an ironman streak of 538 straight games ... Selected 25th in 1965 draft by Philadelphia after career at Penn State... Born May 7, 1942, in Nazareth, Pa.... Twice was picked in expansion drafts: from Philly by Seattle, from Seattle by Milwaukee... Was fine third guard in Chicago behind Jerry Sloan and Norm Van Lier... Was assistant to Gene Shue for two seasons with Clippers... Assistant in Dallas for six seasons before landing San Antonio head job. In two years, teams struggled to 59-105 record... Assistant in Orlando last season.

GREATEST REBOUNDER

Before there was Atlanta, there was St. Louis (by way of Milwaukee) and before there was Dominique Wilkins there was Bob Pettit.

When Pettit broke into the league in the 1954-55, the Hawks were in their final year in Milwaukee. But while that season marked the end of one era, it signaled the start of another as the 6-9 Pettit began an 11-year career that finished with him owning the third-greatest rebound average in history, 16.2 rpg.

The Louisiana State product was a magnificent shooter and he won two league scoring titles. But Pettit was an equally terrific board man; he still holds the franchise records for most rebounds in a half (21), a game (35, twice) and career (12,851). Nine times, he had over 1,000 rebounds. And in 1957-58, he led the Hawks to their only NBA title.

ALL-TIME HAWK LEADERS

SEASON

Points: Bob Pettit, 2,429, 1961-62
Assists: Glenn Rivers, 823, 1986-87
Rebounds: Bob Pettit, 1,540, 1960-61

GAME

Points: Dominique Wilkins, 57 vs. Chicago, 11/10/86
    Dominique Wilkins, 57 vs. New Jersey 4/10/86
    Lou Hudson, 57 vs. Chicago, 11/10/69
    Bob Pettit, 57 vs. Detroit, 2/18/61
Assists: Glenn Rivers, 21 vs. Philadelphia, 3/4/86
Rebounds: Bob Pettit, 35 vs. Cincinnati, 3/2/58
    Bob Pettit, 35 vs. New York, 1/6/56

CAREER

Points: Bob Pettit, 20,880, 1954-65
Assists: Glenn Rivers, 3,526, 1983-90
Rebounds: Bob Pettit, 12,851, 1954-65

BOSTON CELTICS

TEAM DIRECTORY: Chairman: Don Gaston; Sr. Exec. VP: David Gavitt; Exec. VP/GM: Jan Volk; Dir. Pub. Rel.: Jeff Twiss; Coach: Chris Ford; Asst. Coaches: Don Casey, John Jennings. Arena: Boston Garden (14,890) and Hartford Civic Center (15,134), Colors: Green and white.

SCOUTING REPORT

SHOOTING: Nothing wrong here. At .498 from the floor, the Celtics trailed only Utah, while their .832 from the line not only was the best in the NBA, but established a team record. The Celtics simply are a smart team and smart teams take smart shots. Although Larry Bird displayed stretches of mortality and finished at .473, the lowest figure of any healthy season in his career, he came on strong and should have a big year. Robert Parish (.580) and Kevin McHale (.549) perennially are among the league leaders in FG percentage and there's no reason to expect that to change.

PLAYMAKING: As long as Bird is around, creativity will always flourish along the front line. An era apparently is ending with Dennis Johnson, so the Celtics will look to Brian Shaw and top draft pick Dee Brown to create and spark in the backcourt. The Celtic offense often became predictable, lacking necessary movement in recent seasons, and under new coach Chris Ford, the Celtics likely will feature a game plan calling for alterations in everybody's game.

DEFENSE: The Celtics are masters in halfcourt at both ends. So in the playoffs, the Knicks sought to run, run, run them into the ground, create some fatigue and look for the easy baskets. On any given night, that can work, but the Celtics are infusing fresher legs—albeit gradually—with the likes of Shaw and the rookie Brown. Up front, McHale and Parish are both superb defenders while Bird is a typical three spot defender. The loss of Johnson, for years one of the finest defensive guards in the league with astounding anticipation, will be felt. The Celtics, through fresher legs, will need to find some way to create a semblance of pressure; they were dead last in creating turnovers last season, with just 12.2 a game.

A healthy Larry Bird launches his 12th season.

CELTIC ROSTER

No.	Veterans	Pos.	Ht.	Wt.	Age	Yrs. Pro	College
5	John Bagley	G	6-0	192	30	9	Boston College
33	Larry Bird	F	6-9	220	33	11	Indiana State
34	Kevin Gamble	G-F	6-5	215	24	3	Iowa
53	Joe Kleine	C	7-0	271	28	5	Arkansas
35	Reggie Lewis	G-F	6-7	195	24	3	Northeastern
32	Kevin McHale	F	6-10	225	32	10	Minnesota
00	Robert Parish	C	7-0	230	37	14	Centenary
4	Jim Paxson	G	6-6	210	33	11	Dayton
54	Ed Pinckney	F	6-9	215	27	5	Villanova
—	Brian Shaw	G	6-6	190	24	1	Cal-Santa Barbara
13	Charles Smith	G	6-1	160	22	1	Georgetown
11	Michael Smith	F	6-10	225	25	1	BYU

Rd.	Rookies	Sel. No.	Pos.	Ht.	Wt.	College
1	Dee Brown	19	G	6-1	161	Jacksonville

REBOUNDING: Again, the Celts' front line will go down in history as one of the best ever. Parish, McHale or Bird on any night are individually capable of double-figure rebounds. McHale and Parish are among the best offensive rebounders around—their arms simply don't come down as they board, catch and shoot. Each member of the trio had at least 677 boards. In the backcourt Reggie Lewis is one of the NBA's best rebounding guards.

OUTLOOK: A lot healthier than it was last season, but there are plenty of question marks. The return of Shaw is a major plus, the absence of D.J. is a major minus. Bird will be better with a full season separating him from his surgery. The age-old question in Boston always deals with old age and this season will be no exception.

The Celtics pulled out 52 victories, but could have a tough time repeating that feat as Ford—even though he has been around them for seven seasons—installs a new system. But the bottom line is the playoffs, where the Celtics were embarrassingly ousted by the Knicks. Maybe they can last another round, but that's about it. They don't appear that significantly improved.

CELTIC PROFILES

LARRY BIRD 33 6-9 220   Forward

The Legend lives . . . Got better and stronger as season progressed after missing most of 1988-89 following surgery for bone spurs on heels . . . There was enough of the stuff of legend—10 triple-doubles, 17 double-figure assist games and 71 straight free throws, the second-greatest run in NBA history. Also team free-throw record of 93 percent, which led league . . . Had trouble working with Jimmy Rodgers' team concept. That's ex-coach Jimmy Rodgers, by the way . . . Only non-guard among top 30 assist leaders . . . Had seven games of 40 or more points, but shot career-low .473 . . . Will make $1.5 million this season . . . Born Dec. 7, 1956, in West Baden, Ind. . . . Red Auerbach made him sixth pick as junior eligible in 1978 from Indiana State . . . You knew something was wrong last season when he failed to win three-point shootout for first time . . . So what? Hall of Fame in Springfield, Mass., is still holding a wing for him.

Year	Team	G	FG	FG Pct.	FT	FT Pct.	Reb.	Ast.	TP	Avg.
1979-80	Boston	82	693	.474	301	.836	852	370	1745	21.3
1980-81	Boston	82	719	.478	283	.863	895	451	1741	21.2
1981-82	Boston	77	711	.503	328	.863	837	447	1761	22.9
1982-83	Boston	79	747	.504	351	.840	870	458	1867	23.6
1983-84	Boston	79	758	.492	374	.888	796	520	1908	24.2
1984-85	Boston	80	918	.522	403	.882	842	531	2295	28.7
1985-86	Boston	82	796	.496	441	.896	805	557	2115	25.8
1986-87	Boston	74	786	.525	414	.910	682	566	2076	28.1
1987-88	Boston	76	881	.527	415	.916	703	467	2275	29.9
1988-89	Boston	6	49	.471	18	.947	37	29	116	19.3
1989-90	Boston	75	718	.473	319	.930	712	562	1820	24.3
	Totals	792	7776	.500	3647	.884	8031	4958	19719	24.9

KEVIN McHALE 32 6-10 225   Forward

With all the talk of aging in Boston, shouldn't he be senile by now? . . . But senility doesn't average 20.9 points and 8.3 rebounds a game . . . Discovered the joys of three-point shooting last season and knocked in 23 of 69 attempts . . . Underwent thumb surgery following play-offs . . . Destroyed Knicks for two games, then was stopped cold when Patrick Ewing began covering him . . . The power forward on the greatest front line in history . . . Knows moves in the post that haven't been invented yet and remains one of the league's finest defenders and offensive rebounders . . . Born Dec. 19, 1957, in Hibbing, Minn. . . . First player to finish in top 10 in field-goal and free-throw percentage since 1969-70 . . . Third overall pick in 1980 after starring at Minnesota . . . Guaranteed $1.6 million this season.

Year	Team	G	FG	FG Pct.	FT	FT Pct.	Reb.	Ast.	TP	Avg.
1980-81	Boston	82	355	.533	108	.679	359	55	818	10.
1981-82	Boston	82	465	.531	187	.754	556	91	1117	13.
1982-83	Boston	82	483	.541	193	.717	553	104	1159	14.
1983-84	Boston	82	587	.556	336	.765	610	104	1511	18.
1984-85	Boston	79	605	.570	355	.760	712	141	1565	19.
1985-86	Boston	68	561	.574	326	.776	551	181	1448	21.
1986-87	Boston	77	790	.604	428	.836	763	198	2008	26.
1987-88	Boston	64	550	.604	346	.797	536	171	1446	22.
1988-89	Boston	78	661	.546	436	.818	637	172	1758	22.5
1989-90	Boston	82	648	.549	393	.893	677	172	1712	20.
	Totals	776	5705	.563	3108	.793	5954	1389	14542	18.7

REGGIE LEWIS 24 6-7 195   Guard

Yes, he can play . . . Enters final year of deal that will pay him $450,000 . . . Knick coach Stu Jackson calls him "the most underrated player in the league" . . . Runs floor extremely well, misses an open shot about once a month and has improved his defensive immeasurably . . . Quick enough to handle some small forwards, big enough to post up a lot of guards . . . Best athlete on the team . . . Averaged 17.0 ppg and shot career-best .496 . . . Born Nov. 21, 1965, in Baltimore . . . Out of famed Dunbar High, where he was sixth man on team that included Reggie Williams and Muggsy Bogues . . . Top all-time scorer at Northeastern, which was 102-26 in his four years there . . . Celts' first-round pick (22d overall) in 1987.

Year	Team	G	FG	FG Pct.	FT	FT Pct.	Reb.	Ast.	TP	Avg.
1987-88	Boston	49	90	.466	40	.702	63	26	220	4.5
1988-89	Boston	81	604	.486	284	.787	377	218	1495	18.5
1989-90	Boston	79	540	.496	256	.808	347	225	1340	17.0
	Totals	209	1234	.489	580	.789	787	469	3055	14.6

ROBERT PARISH 37 7-0½ 230   Center

Incredible specimen, this Chief . . . Every season, he's not supposed to do it any more and he does . . . He does it with a great spin move in the post, accurate jumper, picking his spots to run the break—which he still does with the best . . . Took up offseason conditioning program and shot 58 percent from the floor, second-best total of career . . . Gave Patrick Ewing his usual fits in the playoffs . . . Averaged 15.7 points and 10.1 boards in regular season . . . Signed on for two more years worth $5.5 million . . . Born Aug. 30, 1953 A.D., in Shreveport, La. . . . Part of one of greatest swindles in NBA history when Celts landed him from Warriors along with first-rounder (which became Kevin McHale) for two first-rounders . . . Played at Centenary.

Year	Team	G	FG	FG Pct.	FT	FT Pct.	Reb.	Ast.	TP	Avg.
1976-77	Golden State	77	288	.503	121	.708	543	74	697	9.1
1977-78	Golden State	82	430	.472	165	.625	680	95	1025	12.5
1978-79	Golden State	76	554	.499	196	.698	916	115	1304	17.2
1979-80	Golden State	72	510	.507	203	.715	783	122	1223	17.0
1980-81	Boston	82	635	.545	282	.710	777	144	1552	18.9
1981-82	Boston	80	669	.542	252	.710	866	140	1590	19.9
1982-83	Boston	78	619	.550	271	.698	827	141	1509	19.3
1983-84	Boston	80	623	.546	274	.745	857	139	1520	19.0
1984-85	Boston	79	551	.542	292	.743	840	125	1394	17.6
1985-86	Boston	81	530	.549	245	.731	770	145	1305	16.1
1986-87	Boston	80	588	.566	227	.735	851	173	1403	17.5
1987-88	Boston	74	442	.589	177	.734	628	115	1061	14.3
1988-89	Boston	80	596	.570	294	.719	996	175	1486	18.6
1989-90	Boston	79	505	.580	233	.747	796	103	1243	15.7
	Totals	1100	7540	.540	3232	.717	11130	1806	18312	16.6

BRIAN SHAW 24 6-6 190   Guard

Seems like he's in court more than on court . . . Took the Eurobucks and ran last year . . . Was supposed to return to Boston after extricating himself from two-year contract with Il Messagero Roma in Italian league and signed five-year, $6.2-million pact with Celts last January . . . Then changed his mind about returning and matter again wound up before a judge . . . Still, Celtics plan on him running them in the '90s . . . Good solid defender with quick hands, gets back well in transition... All-Rookie second team two seasons ago after Celts made him their first-round pick (No. 24) out of Cal-Santa Barbara... Then prior to second season, he signed two-year deal with Il Messagero Roma in Italian league, where he teamed with Danny Ferry... Not the answer to all of Celtics' problems, but he's part of the solution ... Born March 22, 1966, in Oakland.

Year	Team	G	FG	FG Pct.	FT	FT Pct.	Reb.	Ast.	TP	Avg.
1988-89	Boston	82	297	.433	109	.826	376	472	703	8.6

JIM PAXSON 33 6-6 210 — Guard

Had bizarre season... First, folks in Boston thought it was he who said those discouraging works about Larry Bird (''he's tearing us apart'') to a New York writer... Paxson swears he didn't say it... Second, he was plagued by injuries, including Achilles tendon strain... Averaged 6.4 points, lowest since his rookie season... Strictly a role player whose role will get even smaller if Celtics come up with another outside shooter... But until then, he's still a perimeter threat... Born July 9, 1957, in Kettering, Ohio... Younger brother John plays for Bulls... Came to Celts from Portland for Jerry Sichting in 1988... Played at Dayton until Blazers made him No. 12 pick in 1979 draft... Has contract so complex that Ph. Ds can't figure it out, but basically he'll get $700,000 this season.

Year	Team	G	FG	FG Pct.	FT	FT Pct.	Reb.	Ast.	TP	Avg.
1979-80	Portland	72	189	.411	64	.711	109	144	443	6.2
1980-81	Portland	79	585	.536	182	.734	211	299	1354	17.1
1981-82	Portland	82	662	.526	220	.767	221	231	1552	18.9
1982-83	Portland	81	682	.515	388	.812	174	231	1756	21.7
1983-84	Portland	81	680	.514	345	.841	173	251	1722	21.3
1984-85	Portland	68	508	.514	196	.790	222	264	1218	17.9
1985-86	Portland	75	372	.470	217	.889	148	278	981	13.1
1986-87	Portland	72	337	.460	174	.806	139	237	874	12.1
1987-88	Port.-Bos.	45	137	.460	68	.861	45	76	347	7.7
1988-89	Boston	57	202	.454	84	.816	74	107	492	8.6
1989-90	Boston	72	191	.453	73	.811	77	137	460	6.4
	Totals	784	4545	.498	2011	.807	1593	2300	11199	14.3

JOHN BAGLEY 30 6-0 192   Guard

Former Boston College star, hardly a Boston Celtic star . . . Was insurance for Dennis Johnson last season after Brian Shaw's defection . . . Missed over a month with separated shoulder . . . Doubtful he'll be anything more than bench fodder for Celts . . . Can push the ball and is tough against presses and traps. When Rick Pitino coached Knicks, he said one guard he never wanted to press against was Bagley . . . Still, his inconsistency and lack of height hurt . . . Came over from Nets prior to 1989 season for a pair of second-round picks . . . Born April 23, 1960, in Bridgeport, Conn. . . . Was 12th overall pick of 1982 draft by Cavs and was fourth in NBA in assists in 1986-87 . . . Will earn $550,000 this season.

Year	Team	G	FG	FG Pct.	FT	FT Pct.	Reb.	Ast.	TP	Avg.
1982-83	Cleveland	68	161	.432	64	.762	96	167	386	5.7
1983-84	Cleveland	76	257	.423	157	.793	156	333	673	8.9
1984-85	Cleveland	81	338	488	125	.749	291	697	804	9.9
1985-86	Cleveland	78	366	.423	170	.791	275	735	911	11.7
1986-87	Cleveland	72	312	.426	113	.831	252	379	768	10.7
1987-88	New Jersey	82	393	.439	148	.822	257	479	981	12.0
1988-89	New Jersey	68	200	.416	89	.724	144	391	500	7.4
1989-90	Boston	54	100	.459	29	.744	89	296	230	4.3
	Totals	579	2127	.437	895	.784	1560	3477	5253	9.1

MICHAEL SMITH 25 6-10 225   Forward

"He plays like Larry Bird—we hope." . . . Those were immortal words of Red Auerbach when Celts drafted him out of Brigham Young with 13th pick in 1989 . . . Sorry, Red. He's no Larry Bird . . . Did flash some streaks of talent, though, during a seven-game starting streak when he averaged 14.6 points and shot 50 percent . . . But his defense is suspect at power forward and with one Larry Joe Bird on the parquet, there aren't too many minutes to earn at the three spot . . . Good free-throw shooter . . . BYU's second all-time leading scorer (behind Danny Ainge), he missed two years while serving on mission in

Argentina... Born May 19, 1965, in Rochester, N.Y.... Will get $525,000 this season.

Year	Team	G	FG	FG Pct.	FT	FT Pct.	Reb.	Ast.	TP	Avg.
1989-90	Boston	65	136	.476	53	.828	100	79	327	5.0

CHARLES SMITH 22 6-1 160   Guard

Former Georgetown standout is strictly bench material... A real Hoya harrasser on defense, he can be had in halfcourt game in pros... Offensive skills limited... Needs to hone talents and to do so, needs minutes which weren't in large supply last season (519 in 60 games)... Played on 1988 U.S. Olympic team ... Earned $150,000, but will make at least $250,000 if Celtics keep him... Signed as undrafted free agent ... Born Nov. 29, 1967, in Washington, D.C.

Year	Team	G	FG	FG Pct.	FT	FT Pct.	Reb.	Ast.	TP	Avg.
1989-90	Boston	60	59	.444	53	.697	69	103	171	2.9

KEVIN GAMBLE 24 6-5 215   Guard-Forward

Everyone was just dying to see what he could do when given proper minutes... Now everyone can go on living... He's very erratic... Got lots of time early in season, but his play was hardly reminiscent of last six games of 1988-89, when he torched foes for 22.8 ppg on .655 shooting... Made minimum of $125,000 and ended last season as restricted free agent ... Born Nov. 13, 1965, in Springfield, Ill.... Drafted by Portland on third round in 1987 out of Iowa... Was leading CBA (Quad City) in scoring when Celtics rescued him in December 1988.

Year	Team	G	FG	FG Pct.	FT	FT Pct.	Reb.	Ast.	TP	Avg.
1987-88	Portland	9	0	.000	0	.000	3	1	0	0.0
1988-89	Boston	44	75	.551	35	.636	42	34	187	4.3
1989-90	Boston	71	137	.455	85	.794	112	119	362	5.1
	Totals	124	212	.482	120	.741	157	154	549	4.4

JOE KLEINE 28 7-0 271   Center/Forward

Able to jump over a phone book with a stiff wind behind his back... Actually, a solid backup for Celtic purposes... Averaged 16.9 minutes and could tack on a minute or two as Robert Parish and Kevin McHale don't get any younger... Averaged 5.1 points, shot career-high .480... Can shoot, although he'll never display the .587 form he did at Notre Dame and Arkansas... Prime asset is his bulk... Made Twit of the Year move in playoffs when he pushed away teammate Michael Smith, who tried to help fallen Knick Eddie Lee Wilkins to his feet... Will earn $850,000 this season... Born Jan. 4, 1962, in Colorado Springs, Colo.... No. 6 pick of 1985 draft by Sacramento, which traded him and Ed Pinckney for Danny Ainge and Brad Lohaus in February 1989.

Year	Team	G	FG	FG Pct.	FT	FT Pct.	Reb.	Ast.	TP	Avg.
1985-86	Sacramento......	80	160	.465	94	.723	373	46	414	5.2
1986-87	Sacramento......	79	256	.471	110	.786	483	71	622	7.9
1987-88	Sacramento......	82	324	.472	153	.814	579	93	801	9.8
1988-89	Sac.-Boston	75	175	.405	134	.882	378	67	484	6.5
1989-90	Boston.........	81	176	.480	83	.830	355	46	435	5.4
	Totals	397	1091	.460	574	.808	2168	323	2756	6.9

ED PINCKNEY 27 6-9 215   Forward

The Suns drafted this guy ahead of Karl Malone?... Has been a mega-disappointment since leading Villanova's miracle team to 1985 NCAA title... Bombed in Phoenix. Nondescript in Sacramento. And hasn't quite made folks forget Steve Kuberski in Boston... Celtics tried every which way to give him a starting job but it just hasn't worked out... Nickname in college was E-Z Ed, but nothing's been easy in the pros... Lacks strength to mix it up with big guys and quickness to beat little guys... Celts still feel he can produce in up-tempo game ... Born March 27, 1963, in the Bronx, N.Y.... Phoenix made him No. 10 pick of 1985 draft after college heroics . . . Will make $750,000 this season.

Year	Team	G	FG	FG Pct.	FT	FT Pct.	Reb.	Ast.	TP	Avg.
1985-86	Phoenix	80	255	.558	171	.673	308	90	681	8.5
1986-87	Phoenix	80	290	.584	257	.739	580	116	837	10.5
1987-88	Sacramento	79	179	.522	133	.747	230	66	491	6.2
1988-89	Sac.-Bos.	80	319	.513	280	.800	449	118	918	11.5
1989-90	Boston	77	135	.542	92	.773	225	68	362	4.7
	Totals	396	1178	.543	933	.747	1792	458	3289	8.3

THE ROOKIE

DEE BROWN 21 6-1 161   Guard
Two basic speeds: Fast and "Pull over, Buddy, where's the fire?" . . . Celtics, desperate for speed and youth, made him the 19th overall pick in the draft . . . Question about Brian Shaw availability made drafting of point guard nearly imperative . . . Former Virginia coach Terry Holland said with Brown on floor, his team "can explode at any time" . . . Led Jacksonville in scoring, steals and assists and set school record for three-pointers . . . Perimeter shooting somewhat suspect, however . . . Born Nov. 29, 1968.

COACH CHRIS FORD: Popular choice with players as successor of fired Jimmy Rodgers on June 12, 1990 . . . Served as Celtic assistant since 1983 . . . Promised to restore "fire and passion" of great Boston teams . . . Knows this team as well as anyone and should know what buttons to push . . . Appeared to be No. 2 choice of new honcho Dave Gavitt, but Celts maintained Duke's Mike Krzyzewski was never tended an offer . . . Played 10 years with Pistons and Celtics after career at Villanova . . . Averaged 9.2 points as pro, but was regarded for smart, turnover-free play . . . Only he, K.C. Jones, Bill Russell and Tom Heinsohn have championship rings as player and member of Celtic coaching staff . . . Scored first three-point field goal in NBA history, Oct. 12, 1979 . . . Made 126 treys in three seasons . . . Born Jan. 11, 1949, in Atlantic City, N.J.

Underrated Reggie Lewis shot career-high .496.

GREATEST REBOUNDER

One of the pleasures of sports is debating who's better: Magic or Michael? DiMaggio or Williams? But when it comes to determining the greatest Celtic rebounder ever, there is absolutely no room for debate.

Bill Russell ranks second only to Wilt Chamberlain as the greatest rebounder in the history of the game. His 13 seasons produced a staggering 21,620 boards, an average of 22.5 a game. By comparison, Wilt totaled 23,924 and 22.9 rpg.

Russell, the lifeblood of the Celtic dynasty that captured 11 NBA titles—including eight in a row—failed to grab 1,000 rebounds only in his rookie season when he got 942 in 48 games, a mere 19.6 per. Three times, he had 17 rebounds in a quarter. His 51 rebounds against Syracuse on Feb. 8, 1960, is the second greatest one-game total ever recorded. And in two other games, he had 49, giving him three of the four greatest board games ever.

No, there is absolutely no room for debate on this one.

ALL-TIME CELTIC LEADERS

SEASON

Points: John Havlicek, 2,338, 1970-71
Assists: Bob Cousy, 715, 1959-60
Rebounds: Bill Russell, 1,930, 1963-64

GAME

Points: Larry Bird, 60 vs. Atlanta, 3/12/85
Assists: Bob Cousy, 28 vs. Minneapolis, 2/27/59
Rebounds: Bill Russell, 51 vs. Syracuse, 2/5/60

CAREER

Points: John Havlicek, 26,395, 1962-78
Assists: Bob Cousy, 6,945, 1950-63
Rebounds: Bill Russell, 21,620, 1956-69

CHARLOTTE HORNETS

TEAM DIRECTORY: Owner George Shinn; Exec. VP: Tony Renaud; VP-Basketball: Allan Bristow; Dir. Pub. Rel.: Harold Kaufman; Coach: Gene Littles; Asst. Coach: Mike Pratt. Arena: Charlotte Coliseum (23,901). Colors: Teal, purple and white.

SCOUTING REPORT

SHOOTING: Does the phrase "...the broad side of a barn" mean anything? Well, the Hornets couldn't hit it last season. In fact, they couldn't hit the barn, period.

Their .455 wretchedness settled in above only Minnesota and New Jersey. Rex Chapman was the chief offender, tossing up

Muggsy Bogues was fifth in the NBA in assists per game.

brick after brick and often showing absolutely no concept of the NBA game. He finished at .408, which many suspected might have finished him in Charlotte. He wasn't alone. Kelly Tripucka (.430), J.R. Reid (.440)—and he was in the middle, don't forget—and Robert Reid (.391) also were way off. The Hornets are looking for a Western-style game and hope Johnny Newman (.476), the newly-acquired former Knick, will settle into the up-tempo.

Of course, with such a weak rebounding game, a rotten percentage was only natural. The Hornets hope they've solved their perimeter woes for the future with the drafting of Illinois sharpshooter Kendall Gill.

PLAYMAKING: They're hoping Gill can help out a bit in this area, too. Muggsy Bogues for the second straight season led the NBA in assists-to-turnovers ratio and does a creditable job. But he is not the franchise point guard the Hornets need and seek. Charlotte racked up over 2,000 assists—with 867 of them by Bogues. And it could get better with coach Gene Littles favoring the motion, movement game.

DEFENSE: We were always told that if you can't say something nice, don't say anything at all. And there was nothing nice to be said about a gosh-awful effort that allowed opponents to: shoot .497, average 108.2 points (seventh worst), and finish dead last in blocked shots with 262 (which would place the entire Hornet team fourth in the league individual race behind Olajuwon, Ewing and Robinson). The Hornets need something inside resembling an intimidator. J.R. Reid's butt takes up a lot of space, but they need help going vertically, not just horizontally.

REBOUNDING: The pits. Worst in the East. Now you know the reasoning behind the acquisition of Armon Gilliam. With no real center, the Hornets enter battle night in, night out at a huge board disadvantage. Both Gilliam and J.R. Reid have nice power-forward numbers, but they're not enough. And with the way the Hornets shoot, rebounding is a critical need.

OUTLOOK: Entering their third season of existence, the Hornets appear headed for a year as undistinguished as their first two. The whole franchise—aside from attendance—was an utter mess last season. Perhaps some stability—like finally signing Littles, a player's coach—will help. But not much. To make matters worse, the Hornets are plucked down into the Central Division this season, so the slaughters should come with even more regularity.

HORNET ROSTER

No.	Veterans	Pos.	Ht.	Wt.	Age	Yrs. Pro	College
35	Richard Anderson	C-F	6-10	240	29	6	Cal-Santa Barbara
1	Tyrone Bogues	G	5-3	140	25	3	Wake Forest
3	Rex Chapman	G	6-4	185	23	2	Kentucky
30	Dell Curry	G	6-5	195	26	4	Virginia Tech
33	Kenny Gattison	G	6-8	252	26	4	Old Dominion
45	Armon Gilliam	F	6-9	245	26	3	Nevada-Las Vegas
6	Michael Holton	G	6-4	185	29	6	UCLA
42	Dave Hoppen	C	6-11	235	26	3	Nebraska
31	Randolph Keys	F	6-7	195	24	2	Southern Miss.
4	Johnny Newman	F	6-7	190	26	4	Richmond
34	J.R. Reid	C-F	6-9	256	22	1	North Carolina
41	Doug Roth	C	6-11	255	23	1	Tennessee
32	Brian Rowsom	F	6-10	230	25	3	UNC-Wilmington
7	Kelly Tripucka	F	6-6	225	31	9	Notre Dame

Rd.	Rookies	Sel. No.	Pos.	Ht.	Wt.	College
1	Kendall Gill	5	G	6-5	200	Illinois
2	Steve Scheffler	39	C	6-9	250	Purdue

HORNET PROFILES

MUGGSY BOGUES 25 5-3 140   Guard

Would you believe he actually blocked three shots? . . . Has shown he can play while starting at others' kneecaps. For second straight season, led NBA in assists to turnover ratio with 5.94 . . . Great ball-handler, ideal for team pushing ball . . . Guess what his biggest drawback is? . . . Still, teams don't always try to post him up because it takes them out of offense . . . Has his own apparel line for kids . . . Always a bad shooter, he made huge strides last year by hitting .491 of shots after dreadful .408 first two seasons . . . High-school teammate of Reggie Williams and Reggie Lewis at famed Dunbar in Baltimore . . . Born Jan. 9, 1965, in Baltimore . . . Selected on first round by Washington in 1987 after career at Wake Forest . . . Scooped up by Hornets in expansion draft . . . Earned about $400,000.

Year	Team	G	FG	FG Pct.	FT	FT Pct.	Reb.	Ast.	TP	Avg.
1987-88	Washington	79	166	.390	58	.784	136	404	393	5.0
1988-89	Charlotte	79	178	.426	66	.750	165	620	423	5.4
1989-90	Charlotte	81	326	.491	106	.791	207	867	763	9.4
	Totals	239	670	.444	230	.777	508	1891	1579	6.6

REX CHAPMAN 23 6-4 185   Guard

Kind of like the Scarecrow from ''The Wizard of Oz.'' If he only had a basketball brain... Incredible athletic ability. Unquestioned talent ...Incredibly stupid shot selection...Shot .408 from the floor, which sort of means his shots are bad or he couldn't hit the barn, let alone the broad side...Strong trade rumors surfaced...Has a 42-inch vertical leap. Or in the words of Sir Charles Barkley: ''He's got black legs.''... Often acts like he doesn't understand the rudimentary laws of the game. No clue on entry passes...But remember, he should be a senior just now coming out of Kentucky...First-ever pick by Hornets, No. 8 overall in 1988 draft...Averaged 17.5 points in injury-plagued campaign...Born Oct. 5, 1967, in Bowling Green, Ky. ...Earned $750,000.

Year	Team	G	FG	FG Pct.	FT	FT Pct.	Reb.	Ast.	TP	Avg.
1988-89	Charlotte	75	526	.414	155	.795	187	176	1267	16.9
1989-90	Charlotte	54	377	.408	144	.750	179	132	945	17.5
	Totals	129	903	.411	299	.773	366	308	2212	17.1

DELL CURRY 26 6-5 195   Guard

Minnesota coach Bill Musselman said he's one of five best pure shooters in the game...So how come Utah and Cleveland have given up? ...Defense and attitude are two pretty good reasons...Plays the lanes well, but is horrid in man-to-man defense...Really is a great outside threat...Minutes a problem as Hornets are committed to development of Rex Chapman ...New contract for $1 million has somewhat eased his ego, though...Shot 47 percent, a shade above career mark...Standout baseball pitcher, once clocked at 95 mph. Great wrists help him on long-distance shots...Born June 25, 1964, in Harrisburg, Va....Utah's first-round pick out of Virginia Tech in 1986... Came to Hornets in expansion draft from Cleveland.

Year	Team	G	FG	FG Pct.	FT	FT Pct.	Reb.	Ast.	TP	Avg.
1986-87	Utah	67	139	.426	30	.789	78	58	325	4.9
1987-88	Cleveland	79	340	.458	79	.782	166	149	787	10.0
1988-89	Charlotte	48	256	.491	40	.870	104	50	571	11.9
1989-90	Charlotte	67	461	.466	96	.923	168	159	1070	16.0
	Totals	261	1196	.464	245	.848	516	416	2753	10.3

KELLY TRIPUCKA 31 6-6 225   Forward

Self-proclaimed dinosaur . . . Said he and Adrian Dantley are last of dying—or retiring—breed of undersized small forwards still playing . . . Always an offensive threat . . . Got into a terrible shooting slump where he couldn't hit the water from a rowboat . . . Never, ever has been a good defender. Or even an average one. He did try, though . . . Rapped fans over P.A. system after one game for booing team. Was promptly booed . . . From an illustrious seven-child sports family that dominated Bloomfield, N.J., high-school sports for over a decade . . . Father, Frank, was pro quarterback . . . Born Feb. 16, 1959, in Glen Ridge, N.J. . . . After career at Notre Dame, he was selected 12th overall by Pistons in 1981 draft . . . In final year of contract worth $1.1 million.

Year	Team	G	FG	FG Pct.	FT	FT Pct.	Reb.	Ast.	TP	Avg.
1981-82	Detroit	82	636	.496	495	.797	443	270	1772	21.6
1982-83	Detroit	58	565	.489	392	.845	264	237	1536	26.5
1983-84	Detroit	76	595	.459	426	.815	306	228	1618	21.3
1984-85	Detroit	55	396	.477	255	.885	218	135	1049	19.1
1985-86	Detroit	81	615	.498	380	.856	348	265	1622	20.0
1986-87	Utah	79	291	.469	197	.872	242	243	798	10.1
1987-88	Utah	49	139	.459	59	.868	117	105	368	7.5
1988-89	Charlotte	71	568	.467	440	.866	267	224	1606	22.6
1989-90	Charlotte	79	442	.430	310	.883	322	224	1232	15.6
	Totals	630	4247	.474	2954	.846	2527	1931	11601	18.4

J. R. REID 22 6-9 256   Center-Forward

How to win friends and influence people . . . Tried to prove he was non-creampuff rookie, then cheap-shotted everyone short of Mother Teresa . . . David Robinson said no one ever made him angrier on court . . . A power forward playing center, he averaged 11.1 points and played all 82 games . . . Typically foul-prone . . . Unlimited potential with bulk and muscle . . . Very limited offensive skills, though. Basically owns a jump hook and 10-foot fadeaway . . . Problems grasping system and some basics. Like figuring out a pick and roll . . . Good position and tough to box out because of a rump the size of the Pacific . . . Signed four-year, escalating deal that averages out to $1.1 million . . . Born March 31, 1968, in Virginia Beach, Va. . . . Skipped senior year at North Carolina so Hornets could make him the fifth pick of 1989.

Year	Team	G	FG	FG Pct.	FT	FT Pct.	Reb.	Ast.	TP	Avg.
1989-90	Charlotte	82	358	.440	192	.664	691	101	908	11.1

ARMON GILLIAM 26 6-9 245   Forward

Getting into a practice fight with Tom Chambers had nothing to do with Suns trading him after 16 games for Kurt Rambis ... Yeah, right ... Sensational scorer in low post where vast majority of his 18.8 ppg (with Hornets) came from ... Doesn't defend ... With size and strength, should be a better rebounder. Still, in 60 games was Hornets' second best boarder ... Took ex-coach Dick Harter about a week to develop an ulcer for his lack of defense and inability to run floor ... Born May 28, 1964, in Pittsburgh ... After career at Nevada-Las Vegas, he was drafted as second pick in 1987 by Suns, behind David Robinson ... Earned $1 million.

Year	Team	G	FG	FG Pct.	FT	FT Pct.	Reb.	Ast.	TP	Avg.
1987-88	Phoenix	55	342	.475	131	.679	434	72	815	14.8
1988-89	Phoenix	74	468	.503	240	.743	541	52	1176	15.9
1989-90	Phoe.-Char.	76	484	.515	303	.723	599	99	1271	16.7
	Totals	205	1294	.500	674	.721	1574	223	3262	15.9

DAVE HOPPEN 26 6-11 235   Center

Another who popped in for a little visit ... Played in only 10 games, courtesy of a chronic shoulder problem ... That on top of a blown-out knee that curtailed his college days at Nebraska ... Real soft, but not as bad as Brad Sellers. Still, he wouldn't mix it up with a gnat ... The 6-11 guys always find employment ... No post-up game whatsoever ... Decent little shot up to 15 feet ... Runs floor well ... Was Charlotte starter in early games of first year ... Born March 13, 1964, in Omaha, Neb. ... Was third-round pick (No. 65 overall) of Atlanta in 1986 ... Hornets took him in expansion pool from Warriors ... $225,000 wage earner.

Year	Team	G	FG	FG Pct.	FT	FT Pct.	Reb.	Ast.	TP	Avg.
1987-88	Mil.-G.S.	39	84	.459	54	.871	174	32	222	5.7
1988-89	Charlotte	77	199	.564	101	.727	384	57	500	6.5
1989-90	Charlotte	10	16	.390	8	.800	36	6	40	4.0
	Totals	126	299	.518	163	.773	594	95	762	6.0

JOHNNY NEWMAN 26 6-7 190   Forward

The Knicks didn't match the Hornets' offer sheet and he wound up with a four-year, $5-million contract . . . Lost starting job in late March as Knicks sought shakeup . . . Averaged 8.4 ppg off bench . . . Prototype streak shooter. Some nights couldn't miss blindfolded, others couldn't dunk with a step ladder . . . Never lacks for confidence or moxie, but another who felt unappreciated . . . Not bad defensively, but he's usually muscled by bigger forwards . . . Marvelous playoff series vs. Celtics, averaging 18.0 points. But then met Rodman and Co. in second round and dropped to 5.4 . . . Earned $575,000 last year before restricted free agency . . . Pickup in 1987 after being waived by Cleveland . . . Was Cavs' second-round pick out of Richmond in 1986 . . . Born Nov. 28, 1963, in Danville, Va.

Year	Team	G	FG	FG Pct.	FT	FT Pct.	Reb.	Ast.	TP	Avg.
1986-87	Cleveland	59	113	.411	66	.868	70	27	293	5.0
1987-88	New York	77	270	.435	207	.841	159	62	773	10.0
1988-89	New York	81	455	.475	286	.815	206	162	1293	16.0
1989-90	New York	80	374	.476	239	.799	191	180	1032	12.9
	Totals	297	1212	.459	798	.821	626	431	3391	11.4

RICHARD ANDERSON 29 6-10 240   Center-Forward

Fifth team in six seasons . . . Maybe it has something to do with him doing all things centers aren't supposed to do . . . Fine jumpshooter, exceptionally weak rebounder for 6-10 . . . Has shown court smarts. Also, has shown he doesn't always use them . . . Really a forward who always winds up at center . . . Not a bad three-point shooter . . . Born Nov. 19, 1960, in San Pedro, Cal. . . . Second-round pick of San Diego in 1982 out of Cal-Santa Barbara . . . Came to Charlotte from Portland for Robert Reid in 1989 trade . . . Made $600,000.

Year	Team	G	FG	FG Pct.	FT	FT Pct.	Reb.	Ast.	TP	Avg.
1982-83	San Diego.	78	174	.404	48	.696	272	120	403	5.2
1983-84	Denver.	78	272	.426	116	.773	406	193	663	8.5
1986-87	Houston	51	59	.424	22	.759	79	33	144	2.8
1987-88	Hou.-Port.	74	171	.390	58	.753	303	112	448	6.1
1988-89	Portland	72	145	.417	32	.842	231	98	371	5.2
1989-90	Charlotte	54	88	.417	18	.783	127	55	231	4.3
	Totals	407	909	.412	294	.762	1418	611	2260	5.6

RANDOLPH KEYS 24 6-7 195 Forward

A tweener... Not consistent enough shooter for big guard, gets posted up and bullied at small forward... What to do? Send him to an expansion team, which is what Cavs did for a second-round pick... Inconsistent jumper is biggest flaw... Raw athletic skills, he runs court well... Someone has to do it and this guy can draw a charge as well as anyone in the league... Needs bulk... A project who might make it in right system... Cavs' first-round pick in 1988 after 1,600-point career at Southern Mississippi... Born April 19, 1966, in Collins, Miss.

Year	Team	G	FG	FG Pct.	FT	FT Pct.	Reb.	Ast.	TP	Avg.
1988-89	Cleveland	42	74	.430	20	.690	56	19	169	4.0
1989-90	Clev.-Char.	80	293	.432	101	.721	253	88	701	8.8
	Totals	122	367	.432	121	.716	309	107	870	7.1

MICHAEL HOLTON 29 6-4 185 Guard

His back makes Kiki Vanderweghe's condition seem hale and hearty... Wasted year due to a herniated disc... Played 16 games and moved like Amos McCoy... And he was never fast to begin with... Regarded as a tough defender... Hornets face major decision. They've signed him long-term, for about $500,000 per, but can't afford another season like last... Would be—and has been—a decent backup on other clubs... Gets most out of what he has, which isn't a heckuva lot... Coachable, smart, gutsy, team-concept guy... Born Aug. 4, 1961, in Seattle... UCLA product who came to Hornets in expansion grab bag via Portland... Originally a third-round pick by Golden State.

Year	Team	G	FG	FG Pct.	FT	FT Pct.	Reb.	Ast.	TP	Avg.
1984-85	Phoenix	74	257	.446	96	.814	132	198	624	8.4
1985-86	Phoe.-Chi.	28	77	.440	28	.636	33	55	183	6.5
1986-87	Portland	58	70	.409	44	.800	38	73	191	3.3
1987-88	Portland	82	163	.462	107	.829	149	211	436	5.3
1988-89	Charlotte	67	215	.427	120	.839	105	424	553	8.3
1989-90	Charlotte	16	14	.538	1	.500	2	16	29	1.8
	Totals	325	796	.441	396	.807	459	977	2016	6.2

KENNY GATTISON 26 6-8 252   Forward

Will run through a wall and ask why later... One of the few Hornets who won't shy away from the dirty work... Physically gifted, versatile athlete... Set adrift by Suns, found life in Charlotte and made nice contributions after preseason free-agency pickup... A nice bench complement to any roster... Missed all of 1987-88 with torn interior cruciate ligament of left knee... Born May 23, 1964, in Wilmington, N.C.... Suns made him third round pick in 1986 after he was Sun Belt Conference Player of the Year for Old Dominion... Made $150,000.

Year	Team	G	FG	FG Pct.	FT	FT Pct.	Reb.	Ast.	TP	Avg.
1986-87	Phoenix	77	148	.476	108	.632	270	36	404	5.2
1988-89	Phoenix	2	0	.000	1	.500	1	0	1	0.5
1989-90	Charlotte	63	148	.550	75	.682	197	39	372	5.9
	Totals	142	296	.509	184	.650	468	75	777	5.5

BRIAN ROWSOM 25 6-10 230   Forward

Operates on two speeds: 1) Slow and 2) You Aren't Really A Pro Athlete, Are You?... Feet of stone... Free-agent pickup two seasons ago... Has some skills: decent passer, will work inside, hit boards and do dirty work... And he's even shown flashes of scoring ability... Good desire and willing to work... Bad ball-handler... Was chosen 34th overall by Pacers in 1987 draft out of UNC-Wilmington... Born Oct. 23, 1965, in Newark, N.J.... Minimum wage.

Year	Team	G	FG	FG Pct.	FT	FT Pct.	Reb.	Ast.	TP	Avg.
1987-88	Indiana	4	0	.000	6	1.000	5	1	6	1.5
1988-89	Charlotte	34	80	.494	65	.802	137	24	226	6.6
1989-90	Charlotte	44	78	.436	68	.819	131	22	225	5.1
	Totals	82	158	.455	139	.818	273	47	457	5.6

THE ROOKIES

KENDALL GILL 22 6-4 200   Guard

Superb long-range shooter... Hornets getting sick of Rex Chapman's gunner act... Led Illini to Final Four as a junior... Top scorer as senior with 20.0 ppg... His .500 FG percentage included so-so .348 efficiency from three-point range... Said he can play

Hornets made Illinois' Kendall Gill fifth in draft.

point guard in the pros, which would help alleviate another Hornet headache . . . Led Big Ten in scoring, first Illini to do so since 1943 . . . A 76 percent career free-throw shooter . . . "Well-rounded, classy, intelligent," says T-Wolves' player personnel director Billy McKinney . . . Born May 25, 1968.

STEVE SCHEFFLER 22 6-9 250   Forward

A bruiser . . . Purdue stalwart was 39th pick . . . Good low-post game for college, but pro potential a question . . . Strong, plodding type has overcome tremendous odds, including dyslexia, to become All-Big Ten and an honor student . . . Plays linebacker in the middle; wore football pad-like gear on his thighs . . . A 15-point, 8-rebound guy in college.

COACH GENE LITTLES: Part of Hornet scene from start . . . Took over as interim after Dick Harter was axed . . . Players love him . . . Mr. Nice Guy approach, directly opposite to Harter's war-is-hell mentality . . . Exceptional rapport with players, especially younger ones . . . Running and motion-offense proponent . . . All-time leading scorer at NAIA High Point College . . . NAIA Hall of Fame Member . . . Played professionally in ABA with Carolina and Kentucky . . . Began coaching career as assistant at Appalachian State . . . Served two years as head coach at North Carolina A&T, where he was Mid-Eastern Athletic Conference Coach of the Year in '78 after teams compiled two-year 40-15 record . . . Assistant coach in pros at Utah, Cleveland and Chicago before joining Hornets as player personnel director . . . Born June 29, 1943, in Washington, D.C.

GREATEST REBOUNDER

He spent less than a season-and-a-quarter in Carolina and when his career is over, Kurt Rambis will undoubtedly be associated with either the Lakers or the Suns, not the Hornets. But until J. R.

Reid gets a few more boards into his mitts, Rambis ranks as the best rebounder yet to wear the Hornet uniform.

In Charlotte's expansion season of 1988-89, Rambis was brought in to do the dirty work and show a struggling infant team how winners do it. And he did it, leading the club with 703 rebounds, including 269 off the offensive glass. Rambis added another 120 boards in 16 games in 1989-90 before he was traded to Phoenix for Armon Gilliam.

These are team records that undoubtedly will fall soon. But for now, they belong to the bespectacled one.

ALL-TIME HORNET LEADERS

SEASON

Points: Kelly Tripucka, 1,606, 1988-89
Assists: Tyrone Bogues, 867, 1989-90
Rebounds: Kurt Rambis, 703, 1988-89

GAME

Points: Kelly Tripucka, 40 vs. Philadelphia, 1/16/89
Kelly Tripucka, 40 vs. Indiana, 12/14/89
Kelly Tripucka, 40 vs. San Antonio, 2/25/89
Assists: Tyrone Bogues, 19 vs. Boston, 4/23/89
Rebounds: Kurt Rambis, 22 vs. San Antonio, 2/25/89

CAREER

Points: Kelly Tripucka, 2,838, 1988-90
Assists: Tyrone Bogues, 1,487, 1988-90
Rebounds: Kurt Rambis, 823, 1988-89

CHICAGO BULLS

TEAM DIRECTORY: Chairman: Jerry Reinsdorf; VP-Operations: Jerry Krause; Dir. Media Services: Tim Hallam; Coach: Phil Jackson; Asst. Coaches: John Bach, Tex Winter, Jim Cleamons. Arena: Chicago Stadium (17,339). Colors: Red, white and black.

Michael Jordan aims for fifth straight scoring crown.

SCOUTING REPORT

SHOOTING: Whenever a roster lists "Michael Jordan," any phase of the offensive game figures to be better than average. Much better. Which is what the Bulls were last season. And what they'll probably be this season. True, Jordan has long complained about receiving some complementary help, which this season may have arrived in the form of Dennis Hopson, a guy labeled when drafted three years ago as a "can't miss" who did nothing but with the Nets.

Jordan, with his spectacular array of offense, should keep his shooting again above 50 percent, like his .526 last season. And that helped the Bulls to a .498 team mark, tying them for second behind only Utah. Scottie Pippen arrived in All-Star form and will only get better. As will the other baby Bulls: B.J. Armstrong, Horace Grant, etc. With Jordan drawing so much attention, open shots are only to be expected.

PLAYMAKING: John Paxson is the designated starting point guard, but when the Bulls really need something created, when they need a defense broken down, they follow their credo: "Let Michael Do It." Jordan played the point full-time two seasons back and is apt to take over at any given time. And his very presence on the court spreads defenses and makes the Bulls a good playmaking team.

DEFENSE: Not great, not bad, but better than average. The Bulls can confound with the likes of Jordan and Pippen anticipating and stealing: at 2.77 and 2.57, respectively, they ranked first and third in the league in steals last season. Bill Cartwright won't block any shots—he was last in the league among starting centers who played a full season—but he'll bump and grind and force most centers off the blocks. The Bulls, however, lack that inside intimidator, which helped opponents finish with a .493 shooting percentage, the highest by far of any of the four conference finalists.

REBOUNDING: There's no real rebounding stud since Charles Oakley left three years ago, but the Bulls do an adequate job. Jordan, Pippen, Grant and Cartwright all grabbed better than 460 rebounds, with Grant's 629 a team-high. Yes, he was injured, but Cartwright has got to improve on his meager 6.5 average. And, as the center, he was the team's best boarder in only 12 of his 71 games. Grant, when happy, is an emerging inside force and the team's best offensive boarder.

BULL ROSTER

No.	Veterans	Pos.	Ht.	Wt.	Age	Yrs. Pro	College
10	B.J. Armstrong	G	6-2	175	23	1	Iowa
24	Bill Cartwright	C	7-1	245	33	11	San Francisco
54	Horace Grant	F	6-10	220	25	3	Clemson
14	Craig Hodges	G	6-2	190	30	8	Long Beach State
2	Dennis Hopson	G	6-5	203	25	3	Ohio State
23	Michael Jordan	G	6-6	198	27	6	North Carolina
34	Stacey King	F-C	6-11	230	23	1	Oklahoma
5	John Paxson	G	6-2	185	30	7	Notre Dame
32	Will Perdue	C	7-0	240	25	2	Vanderbilt
33	Scottie Pippen	F	6-7	210	25	3	Central Arkansas
42	Jeff Sanders	F	6-8	225	24	1	Georgia Southern

Rd.	Rookies	Sel. No.	Pos.	Ht.	Wt.	College
2	Toni Kukoc	29	F	6-9	205	Yugoslavia

OUTLOOK: The Bulls are no longer considered a rising team: they've risen, if not all the way. Two years running, they've achieved the conference finals. And two years running, the Pistons sent them home. They still need to shed the one-man team image, something Jordan has long fought against by forcing his mates to step forward. A major key could be Hopson, acquired from the Nets for the No. 22 draft pick last June. If the change of scenery helps and if Hopson can anywhere near approach the level for which was predicted and improve a Bulls' bench that has been generally flaccid, then maybe the Bulls can take that next step this season.

BULL PROFILES

MICHAEL JORDAN 27 6-6 198   Guard

An American institution . . . Where do you begin with this god, er, guard? . . . May have hurt image a tad by giving media the freeze in playoffs. Said he wanted players to shoulder responsibility for explaining why Bulls stunk in first two games with Pistons. . . . Hey, he's Michael Jordan, he can do what he wants . . . Most dynamic weapon on the face of the planet in any sport... Led NBA in scoring for fourth straight season, averaging 33.6 ppg... Also was NBA best in steals (2.77) for second straight year... Played all 82 games. Has missed one game in last four years... Bought weight equipment to bulk up against beatings he generally takes... Moved to head of all-time Bulls' scoring list, supplanting Bob Love... Added three-point shot as effective weapon as he knocked down 92—34 more than the total for his first five seasons... Scored a career-high 69 points, ninth best single-game total ever, on March 28, 1990, vs. Cleveland. Also had career-high 18 rebounds in that game... Scored over 30 points 51 times... Didn't foul out of a game... Excellent defender, plays passing lanes as well as anyone, made All-Defensive team again... Averaged 36.1 in playoffs, and suffered world's most publicized bruised butt in Game 1 of Eastern Finals vs. Pistons when he was sent flying to floor. He can't always defy gravity... Born Feb. 17, 1963, in Brooklyn, but grew up in North Carolina, where he brought Dean Smith his only NCAA title... No. 3 pick in 1984 draft behind Akeem Olajuwon and Sam Bowie... Monster eight-year, $25-million contract paid him $2.45 million last season... Pocket change compared to his endorsement salaries.

Year	Team	G	FG	FG Pct.	FT	FT Pct.	Reb.	Ast.	TP	Avg.
1984-85	Chicago	82	837	.515	630	.845	534	481	2313	28.2
1985-86	Chicago	18	150	.457	105	.840	64	53	408	22.7
1986-87	Chicago	82	1098	.482	833	.857	430	377	3041	37.1
1987-88	Chicago	82	1069	.535	723	.841	449	485	2868	35.0
1988-89	Chicago	81	966	.538	674	.850	652	650	2633	32.5
1989-90	Chicago	82	1034	.526	593	.848	565	519	2753	33.6
	Totals	427	5154	.516	3558	.848	2694	2565	14016	32.8

SCOTTIE PIPPEN 25 6-7 210   Forward

Superstar under construction... Improved in every offensive and defensive category... Became something of a mini-Michael with his all-around game... Finished third in the league in steals at 2.57... Runs court well, excellent on break... Hits boards, often takes it up court himself... Second on team in scoring at 16.5, led team in blocks... Not an exceptional shooter, but made good strides with his shot and hit .489... Again weak from foul line... All-Star Game selection... Numbers up a bit in playoffs but was generally inconsistent... Played all 82 games... Came from nowhere, Central Arkansas to be precise, to become the fifth pick by Seattle in the 1987 draft . . . Rights traded to Bulls for Olden Polynice with draft package . . . Born Sept. 25, 1965, in Hamburg, Ark. . . . Earned $660,000.

Year	Team	G	FG	FG Pct.	FT	FT Pct.	Reb.	Ast.	TP	Avg.
1987-88	Chicago	79	261	.463	99	.576	298	169	625	7.9
1988-89	Chicago	73	413	.476	201	.668	445	256	1048	14.4
1989-90	Chicago	82	562	.489	199	.675	547	444	1351	16.5
	Totals	234	1236	.479	499	.650	1290	869	3024	12.9

DENNIS HOPSON 25 6-5 203   Guard

Big guard Bulls were looking for . . . And a big question mark . . . Can he shed "soft" label? . . . Came to Chicago on eve of 1990 draft from New Jersey for No. 1 pick (Tate George) and second-round picks in 1991 and 1992 . . . Actually drew comparisons to Michael Jordan coming out of college . . . Was "can't-miss" No. 3 pick in 1987 out of Ohio State, where he was Big 10 Player of the Year . . . But he missed plenty in three pro years, shooting .404, .419 and .434 . . . Can't create, needs screens . . . Various injuries also sapped his confidence . . . Ball-handling and defense are suspect . . . Led Nets in scoring at 15.8 ppg . . . Born April 22, 1965, in Toledo, Ohio . . . Earned $800,000.

Year	Team	G	FG	FG Pct.	FT	FT Pct.	Reb.	Ast.	TP	Avg.
1987-88	New Jersey	61	222	.404	131	.740	143	118	587	9.6
1988-89	New Jersey	62	299	.419	186	.849	202	103	788	12.7
1989-90	New Jersey	79	474	.434	271	.792	279	151	1251	15.8
	Totals	202	995	.422	588	.797	624	372	2626	13.0

BILL CARTWRIGHT 33 7-1 245   Center

One of great ironies of trade that brought him from Knicks for Charles Oakley is that after two seasons "Medical Bill" has missed fewer games than Oak Tree . . . Strong start, finish weakened by nagging injuries . . . Played perhaps best defense of his 10 playing seasons in first half by holding opposing centers to 10 ppg . . . But tied Kevin Duckworth for the fewest blocks by any starting center in league (34) . . . Topped 2,000 minutes for second straight season . . . Knee and back troublesome down stretch . . . Slipped badly (8.1 ppg) in playoffs . . . Bulls were

9-2 in the 11 games he sat . . . Low-post scorer, has good short-range turnaround . . . No. 3 pick by Knicks in 1979 out of San Francisco . . . Missed all of 1984-85 season with broken foot . . . Played just two games in 1985-86 . . . Born July 30, 1957, in Lodi, Cal. . . . Was paid $1.3 million last season.

Year	Team	G	FG	FG Pct.	FT	FT Pct.	Reb.	Ast.	TP	Avg.
1979-80	New York	82	665	.547	451	.797	726	165	1781	21.7
1980-81	New York	82	619	.554	408	.788	613	111	1646	20.1
1981-82	New York	72	390	.562	257	.763	421	87	1037	14.4
1982-83	New York	82	455	.566	380	.744	590	136	1290	15.7
1983-84	New York	77	453	.561	404	.805	649	107	1310	17.0
1984-85	New York					Injured				
1985-86	New York	2	3	.429	6	.600	10	5	12	6.0
1986-87	New York	58	335	.531	346	.790	445	96	1016	17.5
1987-88	New York	82	287	.544	340	.798	384	85	914	11.1
1988-89	Chicago	78	365	.475	236	.766	521	90	966	12.4
1989-90	Chicago	71	292	.488	227	.811	465	145	811	11.4
	Totals	686	3864	.539	3055	.784	4824	1027	10783	15.7

HORACE GRANT 25 6-10 220   Forward

Good player with rotten timing . . . Waited until eve of playoffs to express his unhappiness over contract that paid him $320,000 base last season . . . After Michael Jordan, was Bulls' most consistent playoff performer . . . Averaged 12.2 points, team-best 9.9 rebounds . . . Made excellent strides, especially on offense, in third season . . . Scored more on break, displayed good post move . . . Runs court well, snags in halfcourt sets . . . Team's best overall rebounder and best offensive rebounder . . . Twin brother of Washington's Harvey . . . Shot over 50 percent for third straight season . . . Had 18-rebound game vs. Lakers . . . Was Clemson's first-ever ACC Player of Year . . . Passing game continued to improve. Only Otis Thorpe and tweener Detlef Schrempf had more assists at power-forward position . . . Born July 4, 1965, in Augusta, Ga. . . . Was Bulls' second first-round pick behind Scottie Pippen (No. 10 overall) in 1987.

Year	Team	G	FG	FG Pct.	FT	FT Pct.	Reb.	Ast.	TP	Avg.
1987-88	Chicago	81	254	.501	114	.626	447	89	622	7.7
1988-89	Chicago	79	405	.519	140	.704	681	168	950	12.0
1989-90	Chicago	80	446	.523	179	.699	629	227	1071	13.4
	Totals	240	1105	.516	433	.680	1757	484	2643	11.0

JOHN PAXSON 30 6-2 185   Guard

Coming off perhaps best season of his seven-year career . . . Second-highest scoring average at 10.0 ppg, career-best .516 shooting . . . Had best shooting mark of any guard in first half of season . . . Intelligent, court-wise veteran who made few mistakes: 85 turnovers in 82 games . . . Terrific perimeter shooter, but quick point guards can give him fits defensively . . . Had a good playoff until ankle sprain negated him in Piston series. Relies on legs for rhythm and it wasn't there . . . Started every game for first time in his career . . . Type of guy who, on paper, appears to be weak link. Then he beats you in several ways . . . Little brother of Celtics' Jim . . . Born Sept. 29, 1960, in Dayton, Ohio . . . Was 19th pick in 1983 draft by San Antonio out of Notre Dame . . . Pulled in $335,000.

Year	Team	G	FG	FG Pct.	FT	FT Pct.	Reb.	Ast.	TP	Avg.
1983-84	San Antonio	49	61	.445	16	.615	33	149	142	2.9
1984-85	San Antonio	78	196	.509	84	.840	68	215	486	6.2
1985-86	Chicago	75	153	.466	74	.804	94	274	395	5.3
1986-87	Chicago	82	386	.487	106	.809	139	467	930	11.3
1987-88	Chicago	81	287	.493	33	.733	104	303	640	7.9
1988-89	Chicago	78	246	.480	31	.861	94	308	567	7.3
1989-90	Chicago	82	365	.516	56	.824	119	335	819	10.0
	Totals	525	1694	.492	400	.803	651	2051	3979	7.6

WILL PERDUE 25 7-0 240   Center

Maybe he has an NBA future after all . . . After his 1988-89 rookie season, even close friends were handing him leaflets to truck-driver school . . . Showed flashes second time around . . . Not enough to stop Bulls from looking for backup center help, but enough for them to realize he can contribute . . . Very inconsistent playing time and his court performance was equally inconsistent . . . Can rebound and play some defense, but concentration level appears to be a problem . . . A long way to go as major contributor, but maybe some day . . . Monstrous feet . . . SEC Player of the Year in senior season at Vanderbilt . . . Selected 11th in 1988 draft with pick that originally belonged to Knicks as teams swapped slot in Charles Oakley-Bill Cartwright deal. Knicks got

Rod Strickland . . . Born Aug. 29, 1965, in Melbourne, Fla. . . . Received $500,000.

Year	Team	G	FG	FG Pct.	FT	FT Pct.	Reb.	Ast.	TP	Avg.
1988-89	Chicago	30	29	.403	8	.571	45	11	66	2.2
1989-90	Chicago	77	111	.414	72	.692	214	46	294	3.8
	Totals	107	140	.412	80	.678	259	57	360	3.4

CRAIG HODGES 30 6-2 190   Guard

Total waste of a season . . . Unless you want to count overtaking Larry Bird as king of Long Distance Shootout during All-Star Weekend . . . Injured much of first half with Achilles tendon problem, enountered more of same the final month . . . Had back problem, too. Needed traction in March . . . Shot career-low .438 with career-worst 6.5 ppg . . . Still showed three-point touch, knocking in 87 of 181 attempts for .481 accuracy . . . Specialist all the way, rarely goes to the line . . . Was 48th pick by San Diego in 1982 after his stint at Long Beach State . . . Born June 27, 1960, in Park Forest, Ill. . . . A $500,000 wage-earner.

Year	Team	G	FG	FG Pct.	FT	FT Pct.	Reb.	Ast.	TP	Avg.
1982-83	San Diego	76	318	.452	94	.723	122	275	750	9.9
1983-84	San Diego	76	258	.450	66	.750	86	116	592	7.8
1984-85	Milwaukee	82	359	.490	106	.815	186	349	871	10.6
1985-86	Milwaukee	66	284	.500	75	.872	117	229	716	10.8
1986-87	Milwaukee	78	315	.462	131	.891	140	240	846	10.8
1987-88	Mil.-Phoe.	66	242	.463	59	.831	78	153	629	9.5
1988-89	Phoe.-Chi.	59	203	.472	48	.842	89	146	529	9.0
1989-90	Chicago	63	145	.438	30	.909	53	110	407	6.5
	Totals	566	2124	.467	609	.821	871	1618	5340	9.4

STACEY KING 23 6-11 230   Forward-Center

Three speeds in rookie development: slowest, slower, slow . . . Frankly, Bulls hoped for more after making Oklahoma stud No. 6 pick in 1989 draft . . . Developed some nice, good offensive moves, but did little to distinguish himself as a rebounder or defender . . . First half of season almost total washout, but still played all 82 games . . . Gets lots of garbage points from all the doubling done on Michael Jordan . . . Knows enough to go to hole when Mr. Jordan slashes. Picks up dumpoffs or offensive boards . . . Showed up for the playoffs, but didn't really hurt or help . . . Paid $1 million . . . Born Jan. 29, 1967, in Lawton, Okla.

Year	Team	G	FG	FG Pct.	FT	FT Pct.	Reb.	Ast.	TP	Avg.
1989-90	Chicago	82	267	.504	194	.727	384	87	728	8.9

B.J. ARMSTRONG 23 6-2 175   Guard

Will somebody proof this kid? . . . One of the baby bulls and he certainly looks the part . . . Was refused entry to Bulls' training facility, being told by worker there, "You must be 18." . . . Inconsistent all season on court. Hence, never developed confidence . . . Shot well (.485), but his game was almost exclusively perimeter . . . Didn't penetrate the way Bulls had hoped . . . Decent passer, earned assist about every 6½ minutes . . . Needs lot of work, but Bulls were encouraged . . . Iowa product was the 18th overall pick in 1989 draft . . . Born Sept. 9, 1967, in Detroit.

Year	Team	G	FG	FG Pct.	FT	FT Pct.	Reb.	Ast.	TP	Avg.
1989-90	Chicago	81	190	.485	69	.885	102	199	452	5.6

JEFF SANDERS 24 6-8 225   Forward

Who? . . . Oh yeah, that other first-round pick. The guy that never played . . . Bulls like his athleticism and can't wait to see if he can do anything on court. Last season, all they did was wait . . . Broke foot in training and missed first 21 games . . . Returned and missed last eight games with sore knee and foot . . . Played just 182 minutes . . . Was drafted to be a small forward, but Bulls discovered even before he broke his foot that's not his spot . . . Long arms, likes to play inside game . . . Was Chicago's third first-round pick (No. 20 overall) out of Georgia Southern . . . Born Jan. 14, 1966, in Augusta, Ga. . . . Was paid $365,000.

Year	Team	G	FG	FG Pct.	FT	FT Pct.	Reb.	Ast.	TP	Avg.
1989-90	Chicago	31	13	.325	2	.500	39	9	28	0.9

All-around Scottie Pippen soared to his best campaign.

THE ROOKIE

TONI KUKOC 22 6-9 205   **Forward**

Michael Jordan said he didn't want to play with any more rookies this season, so the Bulls took Yugoslavia's Kukoc on second round after trading first-round pick . . . Considered a "can't-miss" type. Problem is getting him here. Yugo Army Tour of Duty and all that. Plus, he wasn't exactly thrilled about thoughts of U.S. of A. . . . "He can create, he's a good passer, has good three-point range and he's tough," said NBA superscout Marty Blake . . . Played for Jugoplastika Split . . . Born Sept. 18, 1968.

COACH PHIL JACKSON: Just what Bulls needed . . . Was calming influence after fiery tenure of Doug Collins, whom he replaced on July 10, 1989. . . . Directed Bulls to eight-game regular-season improvement (55-27) and return trip to Eastern Conference finals in his rookie season . . . Became 12th head coach in Bulls' history . . . Was Collins' assistant for two seasons prior and credited with much of Bulls' defensive improvement . . . Cerebral sort who was considered something of a flake as a player . . . Coached at Albany in CBA for five seasons, posting a .558 (134-106) winning percentage . . . Defensive specialist during 13-year NBA career, 11 with Knicks, including 1972-73 championship season. Sat all of 1969-70 title year with chronic back problem . . . Exiled to New Jersey for final two seasons . . . Politically minded, worked on George McGovern's presidential campaign and is good friend of former teammate and N.J. Senator Bill Bradley . . . Averaged 6.7 points as a career backup . . . Two-time All-American at North Dakota under coach Bill Fitch . . . Knicks made him second-round pick in 1967 . . . Born Sept. 17, 1945, in Deer Lodge, Mont.

GREATEST REBOUNDER

The 1968 draft brought two Hall of Fame centers on the first and second picks, Elvin Hayes and Wes Unseld. At No. 4, the selection was another center. And although Tom Boerwinkle didn't have a career like the first two, he still put up some decent numbers, including the most rebounds ever by a Bull.

The 7-foot Tennessee product averaged 12.2 rebounds in his first four seasons, which included a pair of 1,000-board campaigns. But injuries limited him to just 54 games over the next two years, including just eight in 1972-73. He never achieved lofty numbers again but still finished his 635-game career—all in Chicago—with 5,745 rebounds, an average of 9.0.

And he still has the single-game Bulls' record of 37 rebounds, against Phoenix, on Jan. 8, 1970. That mark has withstood challenges by the likes of Charles Oakley, Clifford Ray and Chet Walker.

ALL-TIME BULL LEADERS

SEASON

Points: Michael Jordan, 3,041, 1986-87
Assists: Guy Rodgers, 908, 1966-67
Rebounds: Tom Boerwinkle, 1,133, 1970-71

GAME

Points: Michael Jordan, 69 vs. Cleveland, 3/28/90
Assists: Ennis Whatley, 22 vs. New York, 1/14/84
         Ennis Whatley, 22 vs. Atlanta, 3/3/84
Rebounds: Tom Boerwinkle, 37 vs. Phoenix, 1/8/70

CAREER

Points: Michael Jordan, 14,016, 1984-90
Assists: Norm Van Lier, 3,676, 1971-78
Rebounds: Tom Boerwinkle, 5,745, 1968-78

CLEVELAND CAVALIERS

TEAM DIRECTORY: Chairmen: George Gund III, Gordon Gund; GM: Wayne Embry; Dir. Pub. Rel.: Bob Price; Coach: Lenny Wilkens; Asst. Coaches: Brian Winters, Dick Helm. Arena: The Coliseum (20,273). Colors: Blue, white and orange.

Three-point whiz Mark Price hit treys in 34 straight games.

SCOUTING REPORT

SHOOTING: The tepid .461 shooting mark of 1989-90 is legitimately deceiving. With injuries wiping out much of the front line early (the Cavs lost 154 manpower games to injury, compared to 19 the previous season), Cleveland resorted to a surface-to-air-missile attack, led by the bombing of Mark Price and Steve Kerr, and wound up with the second-greatest total of three-point field goal attempts ever with 851. Their .407 accuracy on three-pointers was an all-time high.

More representative of the Cavs' shooting abilities was the .495 they posted in the final 23 games of the season. This is a smart team that takes smart shots (you'd expect something else from a team coached by Lenny Wilkens?). The Cavs, when healthy, led the NBA in field-goal percentage two seasons ago.

PLAYMAKING: Again, an area where a Lenny Wilkens team should—and does—excel. Of course, Wilkens doesn't do the ball-handling and passing. He leaves that to Price, one of the game's best point guards even if he rarely is mentioned in the same sentence with Magic and Isiah.

Price's speed and quickness are vastly underrated by the general public, if not by the players. He is a superb penetrator and creator who passed for a career-high 666 assists (9.1 average, seventh-best in the NBA). Play his passes, and he'll step back and burn you deep. Craig Ehlo also is a smart decision maker, more effective from the bench. And Brad Daugherty is regarded by most as the best passing center in the game, although a bit turnover-laden. Considering all the injuries, their 10th-place showing in assists (25.7 average) wasn't bad at all. And now they're adding Danny Ferry, an outstanding passer, to the mix.

DEFENSE: The Cavs again were among the league's stingiest teams, surrendering 102.2 points per, fourth-best in the league. And over the last 23 games, when the gang was all there, the Cavs outscored teams, 107.3 to 101.0. Teams shot .479 against the Cavs, a touch high, but no doubt due to the drop in the Cavs' defensive rebounding.

REBOUNDING: The Cavs were 10th from the bottom in defensive rebounding—an area that had been a strong point when health was not a factor. And they improved to just middle-of-the-

CAVALIER ROSTER

No.	Veterans	Pos.	Ht.	Wt.	Age	Yrs. Pro	College
20	Winston Bennett	F	6-7	210	25	1	Kentucky
52	Chucky Brown	F	6-8	214	22	1	N.C. State
33	Derrick Chievous	G-F	6-7	204	22	2	Missouri
43	Brad Daugherty	C	7-0	263	24	4	North Carolina
3	Craig Ehlo	G-F	6-7	205	28	7	Washington State
5	Steve Kerr	G	6-3	180	24	2	Arizona
44	Paul Mokeski	F-C	7-0	270	33	11	Kansas
23	John Morton	G	6-3	183	23	1	Seton Hall
22	Larry Nance	F	6-10	235	31	9	Clemson
25	Mark Price	G	6-0	178	26	4	Georgia Tech
30	Tree Rollins	C	7-1	240	34	13	Clemson
18	John Williams	F	6-11	238	27	4	Tulane

Rd.	Rookies	Sel. No.	Pos.	Ht.	Wt.	College
1	*Danny Ferry	2	F	6-10	230	Duke
2	Milos Babic	50	C	7-0	240	Tennessee Tech

*1989 draft

pack (12th) in offensive rebounding. John Williams, whom the Cavs kept by matching Miami's staggering $26.5-million, seven-year free-agent sheet, easily rates as the team's best all-around rebounder. Daugherty will hold his own when healthy, but the Cavs must have Larry Nance healthy and effective to compete on the boards.

OUTLOOK: The addition of Ferry raises the intelligence and passing level of an already intelligent and fine passing team. Now, if only something can be done about keeping the Cavs healthy . . . To get Ferry, of course, the Cavs traded an All-Star in Ron Harper, thus breaking apart one core member of the once-projected Eastern "Team of the 90s" nucleus. But they feel Ferry is well worth it.

The ingredients are there to place the Cavs in the NBA's upper crust strata: the perimeter game of Price, Ehlo and Kerr, the inside work of Williams and Nance (whose biggest battle appears to be with time); the complete all-around center play of Daugherty. The Cavs are and will be for real, a legit challenger to Detroit's Eastern title.

If they stay out of the hospital, of course.

CAVALIER PROFILES

MARK PRICE 26 6-0 178   Guard

Tarnished choir-boy image when he said ''bull'' in a game and earned his first-ever ejection, let alone technical . . . Next he'll be drinking coffee . . . That was only tarnish on his game that has him as the NBA's all-time three-point accuracy leader (.423 career) . . . Cavs' team MVP . . . Tied his club record with six trifectas in game vs. San Antonio. Also had his first-ever triple double in that game: 25 points, 12 assists, career-high 11 rebounds . . . Hit at least one three-pointer in 34 straight games, second-longest streak ever . . . Exceptional speed, quickness and court sense . . . Led team in scoring at 19.6 and in assists with 9.1 . . . Born Feb. 16, 1964, in Bartlesville, Okla. . . . Real first name William. Goes by middle name . . . Entering third year of five-year, $6-million deal . . . Devout Christian, donates one-tenth of salary to church. And yeah, he was a choir boy . . . Played at Georgia Tech, where scouts questioned his size for pro game . . . Selected by Dallas with 25th pick in 1986 draft, then sent to Cavs for second-rounder and cash. A steal.

Year	Team	G	FG	FG Pct.	FT	FT Pct.	Reb.	Ast.	TP	Avg.
1986-87	Cleveland	67	173	.408	95	.833	117	202	464	6.9
1987-88	Cleveland	80	493	.506	221	.877	180	480	1279	16.0
1988-89	Cleveland	75	529	.526	263	.901	226	631	1414	18.9
1989-90	Cleveland	73	489	.459	300	.888	251	666	1430	19.6
	Totals	295	1684	.485	879	.883	774	1979	4587	15.5

CRAIG EHLO 29 6-7 205   Guard-Forward

Poor man's Michael Cooper . . . Vastly underrated defender by general public. Acknowledged by players and coaches . . . Another long-range gunner as Cavs supplanted Knicks as real ''Bomb Squad'' . . . Shot .419 from long range, seventh-best in NBA . . . Averaged double-figure points (13.6) for first time in seven NBA career seasons . . . Moved into starting lineup after Ron Harper trade, but Cavs feel he is ideally suited to come off bench . . . Has made monumental advancements . . . Another who goes by middle name. First name is Joel . . . Strong offensive rebounder, third on team behind Brad Daugherty and Larry Nance and led Cavs in steals . . . Third-round pick by Houston in 1983 out of Washington State . . . Signed by Cavs as free agent in 1987 . . . Born Aug. 11, 1961, in Lubbock, Tex. . . . Paid $700,000.

Year	Team	G	FG	FG Pct.	FT	FT Pct.	Reb.	Ast.	TP	Avg.
1983-84	Houston	7	11	.407	1	1.000	9	6	23	3.3
1984-85	Houston	45	34	.493	19	.633	25	26	87	1.9
1985-86	Houston	36	36	.429	23	.793	46	29	98	2.7
1986-87	Cleveland	44	99	.414	70	.707	161	92	273	6.2
1987-88	Cleveland	79	226	.466	89	.674	274	206	563	7.1
1988-89	Cleveland	82	249	.475	71	.607	295	266	608	7.4
1989-90	Cleveland	81	436	.464	126	.681	439	371	1102	13.6
	Totals	374	1091	.461	399	.673	1249	996	2754	7.4

LARRY NANCE 31 6-10 235   Forward

Injuries and age are catching up . . . Off-season ankle surgery knocked him out of first 17 games . . . Still a superb shot-blocker with hands the size of Montana . . . Was 11th in league in rejects, second among forwards at 1.97 per game . . . But his 16.3 scoring average was worst since rookie season of 1981-82 . . . Underrated and unappreciated most of his career, he came to Cavs from Phoenix in monster deal for Kevin Johnson on Feb. 25, 1988 . . . Smart, good passer, especially against doubleteaming . . . Complete pro who's unfortunately on down side of career . . . Career .552 shooting mark puts him in top 10 among active players . . . Winner of first-ever Slam Dunk title. Too many associated him with flash over his abundant substance, though . . . Born Feb. 12, 1959, in Anderson, S.C. . . . Earned $1.2 million.

Year	Team	G	FG	FG Pct.	FT	FT Pct.	Reb.	Ast.	TP	Avg.
1981-82	Phoenix	80	227	.521	75	.641	256	82	529	6.6
1982-83	Phoenix	82	588	.550	193	.672	710	197	1370	16.7
1983-84	Phoenix	82	601	.576	249	.707	678	214	1451	17.7
1984-85	Phoenix	61	515	.587	180	.709	536	159	1211	19.9
1985-86	Phoenix	73	582	.581	310	.698	618	240	1474	20.2
1986-87	Phoenix	69	585	.551	381	.773	599	233	1552	22.5
1987-88	Phoe.-Clev.	67	487	.529	304	.779	607	207	1280	19.1
1988-89	Cleveland	73	496	.539	267	.799	581	159	1259	17.2
1989-90	Cleveland	62	412	.511	186	.778	516	161	1011	16.3
	Totals	649	4493	.552	2145	.737	5101	1652	11137	17.2

JOHN WILLIAMS 28 6-11 238　　　　　Forward

"Hot Rod" was hot again . . . Both in play and demand . . . As a restricted free agent, received a $26.5-million, seven-year offer sheet from Miami, but the Cavs matched it . . . Had previously rejected $10.5-million, five-year offer to see what free agency would bring . . . Led all Eastern Conference forwards in blocks . . . Only Cav to play all 82 games—has played in 241 straight . . . Great leaping ability and magnificent fourth-quarter player . . . Played a lot of center with Brad Daugherty out . . . Nickname is from imitating car noises and scooting across floor as a child . . . Born Aug. 9, 1962, in Sorrento, La. . . . Cavs gambled—and won—drafting him as 45th pick in 1985 while Tulane point-shaving mess caused others to shy away.

Year	Team	G	FG	FG Pct.	FT	FT Pct.	Reb.	Ast.	TP	Avg.
1986-87	Cleveland	80	435	.485	298	.745	629	154	1168	14.6
1987-88	Cleveland	77	316	.477	211	.756	506	103	843	10.9
1988-89	Cleveland	82	356	.509	235	.748	477	108	948	11.6
1989-90	Cleveland	82	528	.493	325	.739	663	168	1381	16.8
	Totals	321	1635	.491	1069	.746	2275	533	4340	13.5

STEVE KERR 25 6-3 180　　　　　Guard

Not hard to root for this guy . . . He's overcome a lot . . . His father was killed in Beirut and was target of insensitive college twits who taunted him as a Middle Easterner . . . Also has a knee that has already been ravaged and surgically repaired . . . Outstanding perimeter shooter, led NBA in three-point shooting with .507. First time a Cav has led the league in anything . . . Even had a pair of rare four-point plays . . . Among league leaders in assists to turnover ratio with 3.35 . . . The bad news is that he's weak defensively and a poor penetrator . . . Born Sept. 27, 1965, in Beirut . . . Suns made him 50th pick in 1988 after he helped Arizona into Final Four . . . Cavs got him for 1993 second-rounder . . . Made $250,000.

Year	Team	G	FG	FG Pct.	FT	FT Pct.	Reb.	Ast.	TP	Avg.
1988-89	Phoenix	26	20	.435	6	.667	17	24	54	2.1
1989-90	Cleveland	78	192	.444	63	.863	98	248	520	6.7
	Totals	104	212	.444	69	.841	115	272	574	5.5

BRAD DAUGHERTY 25 7-0 263   Center

Before David Robinson, he was always mentioned as one of NBA's top three young centers (Patrick Ewing and Akeem Olajuwon the others) . . . Not last year, though . . . Got swelling between his toes and missed half a season after surgery . . . A complete player . . . Not a great shot-blocker, but he's best passing center in NBA . . . Features jump hook in a deep offensive repertoire . . . As nice a guy as you'll find in NBA . . . Did get ticked, though, during season when Cavs were hoisting virtually nothing but three-pointers. Spoke his mind, got more involved in offense and Cavs flourished . . . Born Oct. 19, 1965, in Black Mountain, N.C. . . . A North Carolina Tar Heel, of course . . . First pick in 1986 draft . . . Earned $1.5 million.

Year	Team	G	FG	FG Pct.	FT	FT Pct.	Reb.	Ast.	TP	Avg.
1986-87	Cleveland	80	487	.538	279	.696	647	304	1253	15.7
1987-88	Cleveland	79	551	.510	378	.716	665	333	1480	18.7
1988-89	Cleveland	78	544	.538	386	.737	718	285	1475	18.9
1989-90	Cleveland	41	244	.479	202	.704	373	130	690	16.8
	Totals	278	1826	.521	1245	.716	2403	1052	4898	17.6

DERRICK CHIEVOUS 23 6-7 204   Guard-Forward

Calling Dr. Howard, Dr. Fine, Dr. Howard . . . Everywhere he has been, the word that comes to forefront is: "headcase" . . . At Missouri, where he became Tigers' all-time scorer . . . At Houston, where Rockets drafted him with 16th pick of 1988 . . . And now in Cleveland, where Cavs swapped three second-rounders to get him . . . Once claimed he can score on anyone, any place, any time . . . Feels he can take it to hole against anybody, including the Ewings and Robinsons . . . Has a good work ethic, though . . . Needs consistency on outside shot . . . So-so defender one-on-one, often lost in team concept . . . Born July 3, 1967, in Jamaica, N.Y. . . . Earned $325,000.

Year	Team	G	FG	FG Pct.	FT	FT Pct.	Reb.	Ast.	TP	Avg.
1988-89	Houston	81	277	.437	191	.783	256	77	750	9.3
1989-90	Hou.-Clev.	55	105	.477	80	.721	90	31	293	5.3
	Totals	136	382	.447	271	.763	346	108	1043	7.7

WINSTON BENNETT 25 6-7 210   Forward

Not a bad player . . . But he's not the answer at small forward, where he was forced to start due to injuries for final quarter of season . . . No range beyond 10 feet . . . That's why teams sloughed off and dared him to shoot . . . Average rebounder . . . An adventure from the foul line, where he hit just .667 . . . The 64th pick in 1988 draft after career at Kentucky . . Played in Europe, then with Pensacola of CBA . . . Born Feb. 9 1965, in Louisville, Ky. . . . Earned $150,000.

Year	Team	G	FG	FG Pct.	FT	FT Pct.	Reb.	Ast.	TP	Avg
1989-90	Cleveland	55	137	.479	64	.667	188	54	338	6.

CHUCKY BROWN 22 6-8 214   Forward

Born to run . . . Was one of three rookies on Cavs' roster . . . Thrived in running game, but bogged down in half-court offense . . . Started 33 straight games as Cavs played Dial-A-Small-Forward for much of the year . . . Had a 30-point game vs. Orlando . . . Typical rookie learning season . . . But he did well considering he was 43d player selected in 1989 draft . . Good rebounder who led ACC in boards as a senior at North Carolina State . . . Born Feb. 29, 1968, in New York City . . . Earned $180,000.

Year	Team	G	FG	FG Pct.	FT	FT Pct.	Reb.	Ast.	TP	Avg
1989-90	Cleveland	75	210	.470	125	.762	231	50	545	7.3

PAUL MOKESKI 33 7-0 270   Center

Once upon a time, he had mobility . . . Now the knee is blown out . . . Journeyman big man who spent 6½ years of his 11-year career in Milwaukee . . . Good outside touch . . . Prime directive has always been to bang . . . Has never averaged more than 7.1 points—and that was his second season . . . Nothing flashy or special. always does what he's told . . . When Milwaukee Symphony asked him to be guest conductor a few years ago, he did that, too . . . Houston made him 42d pick in 1979 draft out of Kansas . . . Cavs signed him as a free agent in 1989 and paid him $500,000 last season.

Year	Team	G	FG	FG Pct.	FT	FT Pct.	Reb.	Ast.	TP	Avg.
1979-80	Houston	12	11	.333	7	.778	29	2	29	2.4
1980-81	Detroit	80	224	.489	120	.600	418	135	568	7.1
1981-82	Det.-Clev.	67	84	.435	48	.762	208	35	216	3.2
1982-83	Clev.-Mil.	73	119	.458	50	.735	260	49	288	3.9
1983-84	Milwaukee	68	102	.479	50	.694	166	44	255	3.8
1984-85	Milwaukee	79	205	.478	81	.698	410	99	491	6.2
1985-86	Milwaukee	45	59	.424	25	.735	139	30	143	3.2
1986-87	Milwaukee	62	52	.403	46	.719	138	22	150	2.4
1987-88	Milwaukee	60	100	.476	51	.708	221	22	251	4.2
1988-89	Milwaukee	74	59	.360	40	.784	187	36	165	2.2
1989-90	Cleveland	38	63	.420	25	.694	99	17	151	4.0
	Totals	658	1078	.453	543	.692	2275	491	2707	4.1

JOHN MORTON 23 6-3 183   Guard

If you're going to report injured, report injured after the contract is signed . . . That's how Seton Hall product began Cav career last season after becoming their first-round pick . . . Pulled hamstring from start never allowed him to get in flow . . . Stock rose from 35-point game vs. Michigan in 1989 NCAA Final . . . Limited-time player who, when he was good, was very good, when he was bad, was barely CBA quality . . . Lousy assist-turnover ratio: 67 assists, 51 turnovers . . . Gets in middle and penetrates, then often seems clueless what to do . . . Born May 18, 1967, in Bronx, N.Y. . . . Earned $325,000—pulled hamstring and all.

Year	Team	G	FG	FG Pct.	FT	FT Pct.	Reb.	Ast.	TP	Avg.
1989-90	Cleveland	37	48	.298	43	.694	32	67	146	3.9

TREE ROLLINS 35 7-1 240   Center

Aging sultan of swat . . . The NBA's third all-time leading shot-blocker with 2,374 rejects . . . Now perfect 10-12 minute backup material . . . Always a solid defensive presence who couldn't pass ball through an open door—11 players had more assists last season than Tree has amassed in 11 seasons (613) . . . Began as starter last season with Brad Daugherty down, but Cavs couldn't afford his lack of offense . . . No. 14 pick by Atlanta in

1977 out of Clemson... Born June 15, 1955, in Winter Haven, Fla.... Polite, decent sort who was signed by Cavs as free agent in 1988... Made $750,000 last season, due for big cut.

Year	Team	G	FG	FG Pct.	FT	FT Pct.	Reb.	Ast.	TP	Avg.
1977-78	Atlanta	80	253	.487	104	.703	552	79	610	7.6
1978-79	Atlanta	81	297	.535	89	.631	588	49	683	8.4
1979-80	Atlanta	82	287	.558	157	.714	774	76	731	8.9
1980-81	Atlanta	40	116	.552	46	.807	286	35	278	7.0
1981-82	Atlanta	79	202	.584	79	.612	611	59	483	6.1
1982-83	Atlanta	80	261	.510	98	.726	743	75	620	7.8
1983-84	Atlanta	77	274	.518	118	.621	593	62	666	8.6
1984-85	Atlanta	70	186	.549	67	.720	442	52	439	6.3
1985-86	Atlanta	74	173	.499	69	.767	458	41	415	5.6
1866-87	Atlanta	78	171	.546	63	.724	488	22	405	5.4
1987-88	Atlanta	76	133	.512	70	.875	459	20	336	4.4
1988-89	Cleveland	60	62	.449	12	.632	139	19	136	2.3
1989-90	Cleveland	48	57	.456	11	.688	153	24	125	2.6
	Totals	925	2472	.525	983	.700	6286	613	5927	6.4

THE ROOKIES

DANNY FERRY 24 6-10 230　　　　　　　　Forward

Cavs hope he's smooth sailing... He rocked the boat when Clippers chose him as second player in 1989 draft by signing with Il Messaggero Roma in Italian league... Danny Boy enjoyed mucho popularity in Italy, where he was a 22-ppg scorer... Cavs sent two firstrounders, Ron Harper and a second-rounder to Clips for rights to Duke product who won Naismith Award in senior year... First ACC player ever with 2,000 career points, 1,000 rebounds and 500 assists... Son of former pro and ex-Bullets GM Bob Ferry... Cavs' basketball IQ level goes up about 700 points... Court sense, phenomenal passer ... Made it to Final Four in three of his four seasons... Born Oct. 17, 1966, in Hyattsville, Md.... Signed four-year, $10 million deal.

MILOS BABIC 21 7-0 240　　　　　　　　Center

Is Cavalier via Yugoslavia and transaction in which Phoenix traded draft rights (No. 50) to him for draft rights to center Stefano Rusconi (No. 52)... Supposed to have a good shooting touch and surprising footwork for someone his size . . . Born Nov. 23, 1968, in Kraljevo, Yugoslavia . . . Played three years at Tennessee Tech, where he shot 12.4 pgg and averaged 7.3 rebounds as a senior.

COACH LENNY WILKENS: Sought by a slew of teams, but Cavs refused permission to talk . . . Good move. He's one of most respected coaches in game . . . Patient, low-key approach . . . Coaching record of 725-647 after 17 NBA seasons, including title with Seattle in 1978-79 . . . Solid work ethic, good sideline thinker . . . Took over Cavs in 1986-87 and has produced 172-156 (.524) record . . . But his Cleveland teams have not gotten out of first round in playoffs in three trips . . . Producing a plus-.500 record last season, though, was a real accomplishment since team was decimated by injuries . . . Had 15-year Hall of Fame playing career in NBA (St. Louis, Seattle, Cleveland) after two All-American seasons at Providence College . . . Was 32-year-old player-coach with Seattle . . . Born Oct. 28, 1937, in Brooklyn, N.Y.

GREATEST REBOUNDER

In the history of the Cavaliers, there never has been an individual 1,000-rebound season. Nor a season with 900 for that matter. So all-time numbers for the Cavs are relatively modest. And while current center Brad Daugherty appears a lock to one day assume the top position, the leading rebounder in the 20-year history of the Cavs remains Jim Chones.

A 10-year pro performer who began his career in the ABA, Chones spent five iron-man seasons with the Cavs when they started to make some noise in the NBA, including their 1975-76 Central Division championship season. Three times, the 6-11 Marquette product led the Cavs in rebounding and his 3,790 boards still rank as a team high.

Chones also rates as the second-best shot-blocker in Cav history, having relinquished the No. 1 spot this past season to John Williams. His 400-game stint in Cleveland produced an average of 9.5 rebounds a game.

ALL-TIME CAVALIER LEADERS

SEASON

Points: Mike Mitchell, 2,012, 1980-81
Assists: John Bagley, 735, 1985-86
Rebounds: Jim Brewer, 891, 1975-76

GAME

Points: Walt Wesley, 50 vs. Cincinnati, 2/19/71
Assists: Geoff Huston, 27 vs. Golden State, 1/27/82
Rebounds: Rick Roberson, 25 vs. Houston, 3/4/72

GAME

Points: Austin Carr, 10,265, 1971-80
Assists: John Bagley, 2,311, 1982-87
Rebounds: Jim Chones, 3,790, 1974-79

DETROIT PISTONS

TEAM DIRECTORY: Pres.: Bill Davidson; GM: Jack McCloskey; Dir. Pub. Rel.: Matt Dobek; Coach: Chuck Daly; Asst. Coaches: Brendan Malone, Brendan Suhr. Arena: The Palace, Auburn Hills (21,454). Colors: Red, white and blue.

Dennis Rodman revels as Defensive Player of the Year.

SCOUTING REPORT

SHOOTING: The Piston shot a middle-of-the-pack .478 last season, good for 15th in the league. But the Piston approach to shooting is simple: find the hot hand and ride it until it turns cold.

And why mess with success? One night, it's Isiah Thomas. The next, Joe Dumars. Then Vinnie Johnson. James Edwards. Bill Laimbeer. No Piston averaged 20 points. No Piston was Player of the Week. So what? They were the Team of the Year behind offensive democracy that on any given night takes a strict monarchy approach.

The Pistons run about 60 percent of their halfcourt offense off pick-and-rolls and there's no end in sight. Their three-guard rotation—which picked up an apparently sufficient guy-in-waiting in Texas draft pick Lance Blanks—will continue until stopped. Or until someone goes stone cold.

PLAYMAKING: With backcourt starters in Dumars and Thomas, playmaking isn't much of a problem. The key to the Pistons' offense is the sacrifice of individual glory for the team good. It's a simple fact of life. You play in Detroit, you drive an American-made car and you share the wealth. With a starting duo that's interchangeable at point and off-guard, the Pistons have one of the most lethal backcourts in memory.

DEFENSE: The lifeblood of the Pistons' world. Just when it appears they can't get any better, they do just that. They have the finest one-on-one defender in the game in Dennis Rodman. "He's unique," praises coach Chuck Daly. "All he wants to do is defend and rebound. For a coach, he's like walking down the street and finding gold."

The Pistons held teams to a league-low 98.3 ppg, keeping foes under 100 points an incredible 44 times—more than half their games. Yes, they clutch and grab and hold and do things that their reputation now allows them to get away with unscathed. They just do it better than anybody else.

REBOUNDING: They get it from everywhere as the Pistons rebound by committee. A shot goes up and five guys go to the boards. They were the third-best overall rebounding team in the league with the likes of Rodman and John Salley crashing the offensive boards; with Laimbeer using his court smarts and savvy positioning to overcome a vertical leap measured in millimeters working the defensive boards. They went up against the NBA's

PISTON ROSTER

No.	Veterans	Pos.	Ht.	Wt.	Age	Yrs. Pro	College
23	Mark Aguirre	F	6-6	232	30	9	DePaul
00	William Bedford	C	7-1	252	26	3	Memphis State
4	Joe Dumars	G	6-3	195	27	5	McNeese State
53	James Edwards	C	7-1	263	34	13	Washington
35	Scott Hastings	C-F	6-11	245	30	8	Arkansas
12	Gerald Henderson	G	6-2	175	34	11	Va. Commonwealth
15	Vinnie Johnson	G	6-2	200	34	11	Baylor
40	Bill Laimbeer	C-F	6-11	245	33	10	Notre Dame
10	Dennis Rodman	F	6-8	210	29	4	SE Oklahoma
22	John Salley	F-C	6-11	231	26	4	Georgia Tech
11	Isiah Thomas	G	6-1	185	29	9	Indiana

Rd.	Rookie	Sel. No.	Pos.	Ht.	Wt.	College
1	Lance Blanks	26	G	6-4	195	Texas

top rebounding outfit, Portland, in the NBA Finals and yielded nary an inch, pushing the Blazers to the perimeter and handling the boards with cool efficiency.

OUTLOOK: If you've got to have an outlook, it might as well be the one of the two-time defending champs who show little signs of letting up. Need scoring in the low post? Dial Edwards or Mark Aguirre. Need penetration? Call Thomas. Need a clutch shot? Call Dumars. Need a bunch of points quick? Call for Johnson. Defense? Get Rodman on the line. Need another championship ring? Dial 1-800-PISTONS.

PISTON PROFILES

ISIAH THOMAS 29 6-1 185   **Guard**

In the playoffs, the emphasis on Isiah Lord came on the second name. As in, Lord, did he play . . . MVP honors as he led Pistons to repeat NBA championship . . . Probably won award in Game 1 of Finals when he had staggering 16-point fourth quarter, 10 points in 2:27, to rally Pistons . . . And that wasn't even his best play-off quarter ever. Had stunning 25-point third quarter vs. Lakers in Game 6 of 1988 Finals . . . And in 1984, scored 16 points in 94 seconds vs. Knicks . . . One of most dominant little men who ever played game . . . Virtually every point guard in league is at disadvantage against his offensive showcase . . . Outstanding penetration, which may be single most important element to Piston offense . . . Coach Chuck Daly claimed Zeke "gets bored" with regular season . . . Fought off boredom for team-best 18.4 ppg and 9.4 assists . . . Shot below par, though (.438), second-worst of career . . . All-time team leader in steals and assists . . . Pistons are 6-16 when he hasn't played in his nine-year career . . . Led Indiana to NCAA title in 1981 as soph, then left and Detroit chose him second overall in draft . . . Born April 30, 1961, in Chicago . . . Earned $2.2 million.

Year	Team	G	FG	FG Pct.	FT	FT Pct.	Reb.	Ast.	TP	Avg.
1981-82	Detroit	72	453	.424	302	.704	209	565	1225	17.0
1982-83	Detroit	81	725	.472	368	.710	328	634	1854	22.9
1983-84	Detroit	82	669	.462	388	.733	327	914	1748	21.3
1984-85	Detroit	81	646	.458	399	.809	361	1123	1720	21.2
1985-86	Detroit	77	609	.488	365	.790	277	830	1609	20.9
1986-87	Detroit	81	626	.463	400	.768	319	813	1671	20.6
1987-88	Detroit	81	621	.463	305	.774	278	678	1577	19.5
1988-89	Detroit	80	569	.464	287	.818	273	663	1458	18.2
1989-90	Detroit	81	579	.438	292	.775	308	765	1492	18.4
	Totals	716	5497	.460	3106	.762	2680	6985	14354	20.0

JOE DUMARS 27 6-3 195   Guard

If you're going to have a guard-oriented offense, Isiah Thomas and this guy aren't shabby . . . Endured a bittersweet NBA Finals. While helping Pistons to repeat crown, learned after Game 3 that his father had died . . . Decided against going home and remained with club until decisive victory came in Game 5 . . . One of the great clutch shooters in the game . . . Same thing holds for defense . . . Broke his "Just Joe" label in 1989 Finals when all-around play earned him playoff MVP . . . Was an All-Star for, surprisingly, the first time . . . Enjoyed his finest regular season, despite broken left hand suffered last March that brought his numbers down . . . Still scored 17.8 ppg . . . Second straight All-Defense team honor . . . Shot career-best .900 from line . . . Simply a complete player . . . Unheralded first-round pick (No. 18) from McNeese State in 1985 . . . Born May 23, 1963, in Natchitoches, La., same town which was site of filming of "Steel Magnolias"... Contract bumped to $1.33 million... Prefers renting VCR tapes over going to movies for privacy.

Year	Team	G	FG	FG Pct.	FT	FT Pct.	Reb.	Ast.	TP	Avg.
1985-86	Detroit	82	287	.481	190	.798	119	390	769	9.4
1986-87	Detroit	79	369	.493	184	.748	167	352	931	11.8
1987-88	Detroit	82	453	.472	251	.815	200	387	1161	14.2
1988-89	Detroit	69	456	.505	260	.850	172	390	1186	17.2
1989-90	Detroit	75	508	.480	297	.900	212	368	1335	17.8
	Totals	387	2073	.486	1182	.828	870	1887	5382	13.9

JAMES EDWARDS 34 7-1 263   Center

Buddha... Coming to Detroit has almost been a religious experience: strictly reincarnated... Spent years in Phoenix as a soft, stand-around jump shooter. Came to Detroit in 1988 for the immortal Ron Moore and a 1991 second-rounder and has become a fearsome low-post scorer... Gave Patrick Ewing fits in second round of playoffs, averaging 19.4 ppg... Was up and down after that, prone to foul trouble... First option in Piston offense... Started regular season on bench, moved into starting lineup after 12 games. Pistons were 52-18 with him starting... Played all 82 games, averaged 14.5 ppg—16.0 as starter, 5.7 as sub... One of many who played understudy to Kareem Abdul-Jabbar, he was third-round Laker pick in 1977 out of Washington... Also played in Indiana and Cleveland... Born Nov. 22, 1955, in Seattle... Collected $950,000.

Year	Team	G	FG	FG Pct.	FT	FT Pct.	Reb.	Ast.	TP	Avg.
1977-78	L.A.-Ind.	83	495	.453	272	.646	615	85	1252	15.2
1978-79	Indiana	82	534	.501	298	.676	693	92	1366	16.7
1979-80	Indiana	82	528	.512	231	.681	578	127	1287	15.7
1980-81	Indiana	81	511	.509	244	.703	571	212	1266	15.6
1981-82	Cleveland	77	528	.511	232	.684	581	123	1288	16.7
1982-83	Clev.-Phoe.	31	128	.487	69	.639	155	40	325	10.5
1983-84	Phoenix	72	438	.536	183	.720	348	184	1059	14.7
1984-85	Phoenix	70	384	.501	276	.746	387	153	1044	14.9
1985-86	Phoenix	52	318	.542	212	.702	301	74	848	16.3
1986-87	Phoenix	14	57	.518	54	.771	60	19	168	12.0
1987-88	Phoe.-Det.	69	302	.470	210	.654	412	78	814	11.8
1988-89	Detroit	76	211	.500	133	.686	231	49	555	7.3
1989-90	Detroit	82	462	.498	265	.749	345	63	1189	14.5
	Totals	871	4896	.501	2679	.694	5277	1299	12471	14.3

BILL LAIMBEER 33 6-11 245   Center-Forward

May go down with Stalin and Hitler as one of three most-despised individuals in 20th century ... But those two guys didn't earn two championship rings ... A heckuva player who is absolutely hated by rival players ... His perimeter game worked at fever pitch: knocked in 57 three-pointers in regular season ... Continued in playoffs. Witness his six-trifectra barrage in Game 2 of Finals ... Would probably complain about a sunny day ... Always a tough rebounder, averaged a notch below double figures for second straight year ... Couldn't jump over an LP album, but makes up for it with intelligent play, superb position and well-placed (often well-concealed) elbows ... Second straight year he earned a suspension: fought with Charles Barkley ... Terrific free-throw shooter ... Excellent golfer ... Comes from rich family; even his dad makes more than his $880,000 ... Despite Bad Boy image and opponents' loathing, he's a charitable guy whose contributions get little fanfare ... Cleveland's third-round pick in 1979 out of Notre Dame ... Came from Cavs in 1981-82 season with Kenny Carr for Phil Hubbard, Paul Mokeski and draft picks ... Born May 19, 1957, in Boston (where he's hated most) and grew up in California suburbs.

Year	Team	G	FG	FG Pct.	FT	FT Pct.	Reb.	Ast.	TP	Avg.
1980-81	Cleveland	81	337	.503	117	.765	693	216	791	9.8
1981-82	Clev.-Det.	80	265	.494	184	.793	617	100	718	9.0
1982-83	Detroit	82	436	.497	245	.790	993	263	1119	13.6
1983-84	Detroit	82	553	.530	316	.866	1003	149	1422	17.3
1984-85	Detroit	82	595	.506	244	.797	1013	154	1438	17.5
1985-86	Detroit	82	545	.492	266	.834	1075	146	1360	16.6
1986-87	Detroit	82	506	.501	245	.894	955	151	1263	15.4
1987-88	Detroit	82	455	.493	187	.874	832	199	1110	13.5
1988-89	Detroit	81	449	.499	178	.840	776	177	1106	13.7
1989-90	Detroit	81	380	.484	164	.854	780	171	981	12.1
	Totals	815	4521	.501	2146	.833	8737	1726	11308	13.9

DENNIS RODMAN 29 6-8 210   Forward

No one, absolutely no one, plays defense like this guy ... Is afraid of nobody ... Shut down Patrick Ewing in fourth quarter of regular-season game ... And he asked for that assignment ... Voted Defensive Player of the Year ... Hampered in NBA Finals by sprained ankle after snuffing Chuck Person, Kiki Vandeweghe, Johnny Newman and Scottie Pippen in first three rounds ... Maniacal offensive rebounder ... Keeps ball alive by jumping and tapping and jumping and tapping and . . . Only Moses Malone and Charles Barkley had more than his 336 offensive boards . . . Exuberent court persona . . . Jump shot good up to about, oh, eight inches . . . Chuck Daly said he is "unique— like finding gold, all he wants to do is defend." . . . Named to All-Star team by coaches . . . Warm background story. Overcame troubled times and was raised by white farm family . . . Nicknamed "Worm" . . . Born May 13, 1961, in Dallas . . . Second-round steal out of Southeastern Oklahoma State in 1986 . . . Paid $850,000.

Year	Team	G	FG	FG Pct.	FT	FT Pct.	Reb.	Ast.	TP	Avg.
1986-87	Detroit	77	213	.545	74	.587	332	56	500	6.5
1987-88	Detroit	82	398	.561	152	.535	715	110	953	11.6
1988-89	Detroit	82	316	.595	97	.626	772	99	735	9.0
1989-90	Detroit	82	288	.581	142	.654	792	72	719	8.8
	Totals	323	1215	.571	465	.595	2611	337	2907	9.0

MARK AGUIRRE 30 6-6 232   Forward

Notice there haven't been any public funks since he came to Motown? . . . Troubles of Dallas seems a million miles away . . . Still has his moments, though. Like thinking Pistons were down four instead of three when he hoisted trifecta in Game 2 of Eastern Conference finals against Bulls . . . Finished season coming off bench for first time in his career . . . All sides claim it was his idea . . . Still, a dangerous, multi-faceted scorer . . . Superb post-up player, has quality strength that makes him immovable object on blocks . . . And legit three-point threat. Knocked in 31 threes this season . . . Career 49-percent shooter . . . Came to Pistons in midseason trade for Adrian Dantley in 1988-89 . . . While he was reunited with buddy Isiah Thomas, Mavs players darn near openly wept with joy . . . First pick in 1981 draft by Mavs, out of DePaul . . . Born Dec. 10, 1959, in Chicago . . . Got $765,000.

Year	Team	G	FG	FG Pct.	FT	FT Pct.	Reb.	Ast.	TP	Avg.
1981-82	Dallas	51	381	.465	168	.680	249	164	955	18.7
1982-83	Dallas	81	767	.483	429	.728	508	332	1979	24.4
1983-84	Dallas	79	925	.524	465	.749	469	358	2330	29.5
1984-85	Dallas	80	794	.506	440	.759	477	249	2055	25.7
1985-86	Dallas	74	668	.503	318	.705	445	339	1670	22.6
1986-87	Dallas	80	787	.495	429	.770	427	254	2056	25.7
1987-88	Dallas	77	746	.475	388	.770	434	278	1932	25.1
1988-89	Dal.-Det.	80	586	.461	288	.733	386	278	1511	18.9
1989-90	Detroit	78	438	.488	192	.756	305	145	1099	14.1
	Totals	680	6092	.491	3117	.743	3700	2397	15587	22.9

VINNIE JOHNSON 34 6-2 200   Guard

Heated up at the right time . . . The Microwave never made a bigger shot than the one he bagged in Game 5 of NBA Finals . . . Took Jerome Kersey off the dribble for neat 18-footer with all of :00.7 left to provide winning margin in clincher against Portland . . . Scored 14 points in that game, all in last quarter . . . Rallied Pistons by scoring seven of their last nine points in final 2:02 . . . Brick, smokehouse build . . . Has been coming off screens and nailing sweet jumpers for about a zillion years with Detroit. Actually, since November 1981, when he came from Sonics in trade for Greg Kelser . . . Is it too late for Seattle to call a do-over? . . . One of three reasons why Pistons have game's most devastating three-guard rotation . . . Perhaps the ultimate streak shooter . . . Wonderful individual . . . Born in Brooklyn, N.Y., on Sept. 1, 1956 . . . Seattle made him seventh pick in 1979 draft out of Baylor . . . Earned $710,000.

Year	Team	G	FG	FG Pct.	FT	FT Pct.	Reb.	Ast.	TP	Avg.
1979-80	Seattle	38	45	.391	31	.795	55	54	121	3.2
1980-81	Seattle	81	419	.534	214	.793	366	341	1053	13.0
1981-82	Sea.-Det.	74	217	.489	107	.754	159	171	544	7.4
1982-83	Detroit	82	520	.513	245	.778	353	301	1296	15.8
1983-84	Detroit	82	426	.473	207	.753	237	271	1063	13.0
1984-85	Detroit	82	428	.454	190	.769	252	325	1051	12.8
1985-86	Detroit	79	465	.467	165	.771	226	269	1097	13.9
1986-87	Detroit	78	533	.462	158	.786	257	300	1228	15.7
1987-88	Detroit	82	425	.443	147	.677	231	267	1002	12.2
1988-89	Detroit	82	462	.464	193	.734	255	242	1130	13.8
1989-90	Detroit	82	334	.431	131	.668	256	255	804	9.8
	Totals	842	4274	.471	1788	.752	2647	2796	10389	12.3

JOHN SALLEY 26 6-11 231   Forward-Center

If there's a joke to be found, he'll find it . . . One of league's quickest wits . . . Smart-guy answer for everything but usually it's genuinely funny . . . Foes find nothing to laugh at in his game, which is solid at both ends, but could even be better . . . Does it all in spurts . . . Against Knicks in second round, had a block, rebound, outlet pass and dunk in same 10-second sequence . . . Self-promoter . . . Entering option year of contract, which he let world know approximately every 37 seconds last season . . . Provides quality size off bench . . . Runs floor, re-bounds, blocks shots. Shot .512 but mostly on layups and dunks . . . Has added 10-12 footer, but anything else is vastly inconsistent . . . Began season as starter; averaged 8.0 points and 6.2 boards, before being moved back to bench . . . Career-high 153 blocks . . . Out of Georgia Tech, was 11th overall pick by Pistons in 1986 . . . Earned $500,000, wants more, will get it . . . Born May 16, 1964, in Brooklyn, N.Y.

Year	Team	G	FG	FG Pct.	FT	FT Pct.	Reb.	Ast.	TP	Avg.
1986-87	Detroit	82	163	.562	105	.614	296	54	431	5.3
1987-88	Detroit	82	258	.566	185	.709	402	113	701	8.5
1988-89	Detroit	67	166	.498	135	.692	335	75	467	7.0
1989-90	Detroit	82	209	.512	174	.713	439	67	593	7.2
	Totals	313	796	.535	599	.688	1472	309	2192	7.0

GERALD HENDERSON 34 6-2 175 　　　　Guard

Veteran insurance . . . Signed as free agent on Dec. 6, 1989, after he was waived by Bucks . . . Picked up third NBA championship ring. Got two with Celtics in 1981 and 1984 . . . Still very much a legit three-point threat, nailing 17 of 38 attempts . . . Most memorable moment remains steal on James Worthy in Game 2 of 1984 Finals as a Celtic . . . Veteran of 11 NBA seasons was strictly a role-playing specialist . . . Hey, any port in a storm and this port ain't too shabby . . . Was Spurs' third-round pick in 1978 out of Virginia Commonwealth . . . After stint in Boston, did time in Seattle, New York, Philadelphia and Milwaukee . . . Born Jan. 16, 1956, in Richmond, Va. . . . Pro-rated $600,000 salary.

Year	Team	G	FG	FG Pct.	FT	FT Pct.	Reb.	Ast.	TP	Avg.
1979-80	Boston	76	191	.500	89	.690	83	147	473	6.2
1980-81	Boston	82	261	.451	113	.720	132	213	636	7.8
1981-82	Boston	82	353	.501	125	.727	152	252	833	10.2
1982-83	Boston	82	286	.463	96	.722	124	195	671	8.2
1983-84	Boston	78	376	.524	136	.768	147	300	908	11.6
1984-85	Seattle	79	427	.479	199	.780	190	559	1062	13.4
1985-86	Seattle	82	434	.482	185	.830	187	487	1071	13.1
1986-87	Sea.-N.Y.	74	298	.442	190	.826	175	471	805	10.9
1987-88	N.Y.-Phil.	75	194	.428	138	.812	107	231	595	7.9
1988-89	Philadelphia	65	144	.414	104	.819	68	140	425	6.5
1989-90	Mil.-Det.	57	53	.486	12	.800	43	74	135	2.4
	Totals	832	3017	.473	1387	.776	1408	3069	7614	9.2

Joe Dumars: Second straight All-Defensive Team.

WILLIAM BEDFORD 26 7-1 252   Center

They keep him around in case he ever develops
. . . Has the skills . . . Lacks the work ethic and
attitude . . . One problem after another since
leaving Memphis State in 1987 . . . Had surgery
for torn knee ligaments . . . Then had everything cave in as drug abuse surfaced . . . Spent
most of 1988-89 season in rehab . . . Stayed
clean last season, which was his most important
move . . . Hasn't shown he can play in NBA in bits and pieces of
three seasons . . . If self-policing team like Pistons can't get it out
of him, no one can . . . Born Dec. 14, 1963, in Memphis, Tenn.
. . . When Phoenix made him sixth player chosen in 1986 draft
from Memphis State, he was supposed to be aggressive, best
"pure" center in nation . . . Pistons surrendered a No. 1 for him
in 1987 . . . Earned $760,000 (for 246 minutes) last season and

will make $1 million this go-around, which probably thrills all the auto workers.

Year	Team	G	FG	FG Pct.	FT	FT Pct.	Reb.	Ast.	TP	Avg.
1986-87	Phoenix	50	142	.397	50	.581	246	57	334	6.7
1987-88	Detroit	38	44	.436	13	.565	65	4	101	2.7
1989-90	Detroit	42	54	.432	9	.409	58	4	118	2.8
	Totals	130	240	.411	72	.550	369	65	553	4.3

SCOTT HASTINGS 30 6-11 245   Center-Forward

Was supposed to be Jon Koncak . . . That didn't work out so he became the big body for bench . . . And at a lot lower price: $450,000 . . . Fabulous wit, practical joker . . . Didn't really distinguish himself in Detroit except for newspaper column he wrote during playoffs . . . Had plenty of time to write, only played 166 minutes . . . After being grabbed in expansion draft two years ago by Miami, he told a friend, ''I'm worried. I think I'm the best guy here.'' . . . Strictly bench fodder in Detroit. Will bang, rebound a little, put shaving cream in shoes . . . Born June 3, 1960, in Independence, Kan. . . . Was Knicks' second-round pick in 1982 out of Arkansas.

Year	Team	G	FG	FG Pct.	FT	FT Pct.	Reb.	Ast.	TP	Avg.
1982-83	N.Y.-Atl.	31	13	.342	11	.550	41	3	37	1.2
1983-84	Atlanta	68	111	.468	82	.788	270	46	305	4.5
1984-85	Atlanta	64	89	.473	63	.778	159	46	241	3.8
1985-86	Atlanta	62	65	.409	60	.857	124	26	193	3.1
1986-87	Atlanta	40	23	.338	23	.793	70	13	71	1.8
1987-88	Atlanta	55	40	.488	25	.926	97	16	110	2.0
1988-89	Miami	75	143	.436	91	.850	231	59	386	5.1
1989-90	Detroit	40	10	.303	19	.864	32	8	42	1.1
	Totals	435	494	.436	374	.813	1024	217	1385	3.2

THE ROOKIE

LANCE BLANKS 24 6-4 195   Guard

Played in Travis Mays' shadow at Texas but still managed to average 20.3 ppg . . . Transferred to Texas after two years at Virginia . . . Confident type who does a little bit of everything. Averaged 4.3 rebounds and 3.0 assists. Led team in steals

... "Outstanding athletic ability, he could play point guard in the pros," said Texas coach Tom Penders... Pistons' three-guard rotation members are getting up in years, so this guy made perfect sense at No. 26 on the first round... Born Sept. 9, 1966.

COACH CHUCK DALY: Questions abounded all season:  would he stay or hit the NBC trail, trading in the league's most dapper threads for a TV blazer?... Well, he's back... Hit the "Daly Double" with his repeat title... Yeah, he's got the copyright on that phrase... Super, super guy. Will talk basketball forever, will sit and joke forever... Should be given a medal of honor for the way he has juggled a bunch of egos that could have gone homicidal any moment and transformed them into two-time champs... Obviously, a strong proponent of defense... Says he learned valuable lesson from John Madden about defending the crown. Defend it in playoffs, not regular season... Winningest coach in Piston history. Has compiled 363-225 record in seven Detroit seasons... Second most famous celebrity associated with Punxsutawney, Pa. Groundhog Phil is first, ahead of this former Punxsutawney High coach ... First pro head job in Cleveland in 1981-82, then was canned five weeks into season... Spent four years as assistant to Billy Cunningham in Philly... Assisted at Duke, coached Boston College for two years and Pennsylvania for six years, winning four Ivy League titles... Has produced no less than 46 victories each season with Pistons... Born July 20, 1930, in St. Mary's Pa., and graduated from Bloomsburg (Pa.) State in 1955.

GREATEST REBOUNDER

There are feats. And there are feet. And Bob Lanier was up there in both categories.

The pride of St. Bonaventure stomped his size 22s around

Motown for 9½ seasons, producing more points (15,488) and rebounds (8,063) than any Piston ever. While current Pistons Isiah Thomas and Bill Laimbeer are closing in on his point and rebound marks, Lanier—whose feet and Hall of Fame career gained him light-beer commercial immortality—still remains at the head of the Detroit class.

He averaged 11.8 boards in Detroit. And the 6-11, 260-pound giant still holds the single-game Pistons' mark of 33 rebounds, against Seattle on Dec. 22, 1972.

ALL-TIME PISTON LEADERS

SEASON

Points: Dave Bing, 2,213, 1970-71
Assists: Isiah Thomas, 1,123, 1984-85
Rebounds: Bob Lanier, 1,205, 1972-73

GAME

Points: Kelly Tripucka, 56 vs. Chicago, 1/29/83
Assists: Kevin Porter, 25 vs. Phoenix, 4/1/79
       Kevin Porter, 25 vs. Boston, 3/9/79
       Isiah Thomas, 25 vs. Dallas, 2/13/85
Rebounds: Bob Lanier, 33 vs. Seattle, 12/22/72

CAREER

Points: Bob Lanier, 15,488, 1970-80
Assists: Isiah Thomas, 6,985, 1981-90
Rebounds: Bob Lanier, 8,063, 1970-80

INDIANA PACERS

TEAM DIRECTORY: Owners: Herb Simon, Melvin Simon; Pres.: Donnie Walsh; VP/Basketball: George Irvine; Media Rel. Dir.: Dale Ratermann; Coach: Dick Versace; Asst. Coaches: Bob Hill, Bob Ociepka. Arena: Market Square Arena (16,912). Colors: Blue and yellow.

SCOUTING REPORT

SHOOTING: When the Pacers hired Dick Versace, they did so with hopes of getting improved defense. But where they have made the biggest strides is on the offensive end.

Indiana shot .497, the fourth-best mark in the league, as each member of its eventual starting five—Detlef Schrempf, Reggie Miller, Chuck Person, Vern Fleming and Rik Smits—did no worse than .487. And from three-point range, where Indy has one of the league's most potent threats in Miller, the Pacers hit for .382.

PLAYMAKING: The search goes on. And on. And on. The Pacers have looked everywhere for someone better than Fleming to run the offense, but always they come back to the Georgia product, who always compiles steady, though unspectacular, numbers. His turnovers are low—because he's not big on taking risks or creating. Smits' passing in the post has a long way to go, but give him time. And the addition of Schrempf up front has given the Pacers a sound, smart ball-handling forward. The 1989 drafting of off-guard George McCloud as a point guard was an unqualified disaster.

DEFENSE: It stunk when Versace took over. And pretty much still does, although there exist signs of hope. With Smits, for example, the Pacers have developed the intimidation element in the middle—the Dutchman was ninth in shot-blocking. But other areas are horribly lacking: the Pacers forced the third-fewest turn-overs in the league and surrendered the sixth-most points. They still foul too much and are not a good defensive rebounding team. Person sacrificed his offensive game for leadership, which was at times erratic—but not nearly as much as his defense.

REBOUNDING: Weak. Versace longs for a physical power forward, much like LaSalle Thompson, who many times sits under the coach's nose. With erratic minutes, Thompson gave erratic

Reggie Miller shot to the top in Pacer scoring.

performances. Another problem that eventually manifested itself on the boards was the starters playing too many minutes early in the season. Yes, the Pacers vaulted to a good start. But then the legs got weary and they got pounded on the boards.

They wound up the season as the 24th-best—or fourth-worst—rebounding outfit in the league. Smits' continued growth will make them better, but the Pacers are desperate for bench help. And without a first-round pick, they hope it can come from one of the late second-rounders, 6-10 Antonio Davis of UTEP or 6-9 Kenny Williams, a Barton County (Kan.) JUCO product.

PACER ROSTER

No.	Veterans	Pos.	Ht.	Wt.	Age	Yrs. Pro	College
54	Greg Dreiling	C	7-1	250	26	4	Kansas
10	Vern Fleming	G	6-5	180	29	6	Georgia
12	Rickey Green	G	6-0	170	36	12	Michigan
20	George McCloud	G	6-8	215	23	1	Florida State
31	Reggie Miller	G	6-7	185	25	3	UCLA
42	Calvin Natt	F	6-6	220	33	11	NE Louisianna
23	Dyron Nix	F	6-7	210	23	1	Tennessee
45	Chuck Person	F	6-8	220	26	4	Auburn
33	Mike Sanders	F	6-6	210	30	8	UCLA
11	Detlef Schrempf	F	6-10	215	27	5	Washington
24	Rik Smits	C	7-4	250	24	2	Marist
41	LaSalle Thompson	F	6-10	245	29	8	Texas
14	Randy Wittman	G	6-6	210	31	7	Indiana

Rd.	Rookies	Sel. No.	Pos.	Ht.	Wt.	College
2	*Antonio Davis	45	F	6-9	225	UTEP
2	Ken Williams	46	F	6-9	220	Elizabeth City State

*Signed to play in Greece

OUTLOOK: With Miller emerging as one of the best offensive weapons in the East, opponents simply tried to beat the hell out of him with sheer physical play. But Miller withstood the onslaught—much as the Pacers withstood a lot of shortcomings to land back in the playoffs after a two-year absence. There's plenty of room for growth here—and lots of room for improvement.

The Pacers' biggest problem may be their placement in the Central Division, where—like they did with Atlanta last season—they simply have to survive longer than one of the non-expansionists to achieve the playoffs. Versace has reversed a skid. And he must find the necessary depth to continue the forward trend.

PACER PROFILES

RIK SMITS 24 7-4 250　　　　　　　　　　　Center

A monster arises in the Midwest... Dunking Dutchman made giant strides in second season since Pacers made him No. 2 overall pick in 1988... Still a ways to go, but when you start at 7-4 there's a pretty good foundation... Intimidating shot-blocker (ninth in NBA at 2.06) who shot for .533 accuracy... Needs work in weight room to augment good low-post touch ... Must learn when to lay off on defense... Fouled out 11 times, tying teammate LaSalle Thompson and Miami's Grant Long for NBA-high... Tepid playoff showing, averaged 12.3 points and 5.3 boards vs. Pistons... Real nice, unassuming guy out of small Marist College... Born Aug. 23, 1966, in Eindhoven, Holland ... Earned $1.35 million.

Year	Team	G	FG	FG Pct.	FT	FT Pct.	Reb.	Ast.	TP	Avg.
1988-89	Indiana	82	386	.517	184	.722	500	70	956	11.7
1989-90	Indiana	82	515	.533	241	.811	512	142	1271	15.5
	Totals	164	901	.526	425	.770	1012	212	2227	13.6

REGGIE MILLER 25 6-7 185   Guard

Cheryl's little brother has done the family proud ... Attained star status with team-leading 24.6 ppg average—a vast improvement over previous season... Became first Pacer since 1977 to show up at All-Star Game as player, not spectator... Charles Barkley says he has the sweetest shot in the NBA... Takes a physical beating as opponents often use basic thuggery to take him out of game. Still, he played all 82 games... Has scored in double figures in last 94 games, team record... Superb three-point shooter. His 150 of 362 trifectas (.414) was ninth-best in NBA... Complete offensive player who has added quality penetration moves to repertoire... Not a strong one-on-one defender, but plays passing lanes well and led team in steals... No. 11 pick in 1987 draft out of UCLA... Born Aug. 24, 1965, in Riverside, Cal.... Earned $504,000.

Year	Team	G	FG	FG Pct.	FT	FT Pct.	Reb.	Ast.	TP	Avg.
1987-88	Indiana	82	306	.488	149	.801	190	132	822	10.0
1988-89	Indiana	74	398	.479	287	.844	292	227	1181	16.0
1989-90	Indiana	82	661	.514	544	.868	295	311	2016	24.6
	Totals	238	1365	.497	980	.850	777	670	4019	16.9

VERN FLEMING 29 6-5 180   Guard

He's like tape on your heel. Every year, the Pacers try to find someone better but he always sticks around... Not particularly creative point guard, but then he doesn't make many mistakes either... Played all 82 games with an assist to turnover ratio of nearly 3-to-1... Has limited range from outside, but he did connect for .508 accuracy, slightly above career mark... Indiana's all-time assist leader . . . His 610 last season were most by a Pacer in 13 years . . . Strangely, he shot 86 percent from foul line in first half of season, then 66 percent in second half . . . Born Feb. 4, 1961, in Long Island City, N.Y. . . . No. 18 pick by Pacers out of Georgia in 1984 . . . Earned $557,500.

Year	Team	G	FG	FG Pct.	FT	FT Pct.	Reb.	Ast.	TP	Avg
1984-85	Indiana	80	433	.470	260	.767	323	247	1126	14.1
1985-86	Indiana	80	436	.506	263	.745	386	505	1136	14.2
1986-87	Indiana	82	370	.509	238	.788	334	473	980	12.0
1987-88	Indiana	80	442	.523	227	.802	364	568	1111	13.9
1988-89	Indiana	76	419	.515	243	.799	310	494	1084	14.3
1989-90	Indiana	82	467	.508	230	.782	322	610	1176	14.3
	Totals	480	2567	.504	1461	.779	2039	2897	6613	13.8

GEORGE McCLOUD 23 6-8 215   Guard

Everyone on planet felt he was not a point guard . . . Everyone except Pacers, who chose him seventh overall in 1989 . . . Last year was total waste . . . Played fewest minutes (413) of the top 17 picks . . . Never had a real shot . . . Pacers now looking at him as a possible third guard or three-position player . . . Third all-time leading scorer at Florida State, where he averaged 22.8 points as a senior . . . Born May 27, 1967, in Daytona Beach, Fla. . . . Paid $787,000.

Year	Team	G	FG	FG Pct.	FT	FT Pct.	Reb.	Ast.	TP	Avg
1989-90	Indiana	44	45	.313	15	.789	42	45	118	2.7

CHUCK PERSON 26 6-8 220   Forward

Inconsistent Person . . . Tried to sacrifice scoring for leadership and it brought often erratic results . . . First time in his four seasons that he didn't lead club in scoring . . . But he shot respectable .487 from field and had dramatic reduction in turnovers (170, down from 308) . . . Went south in playoffs vs. Pistons, shooting .378 and averaging 13.3 ppg . . . Nicknamed "The Rifleman." Full name is Chuck Connors Person . . . Mom was a big fan of the old TV show starring the old Celtic and former baseball player . . . Great trash talker, rotten defender . . . Awful perimeter defense . . . Can shoot the three-pointer, though . . . Underrated rebounder, particularly on defensive glass . . . No. 4 pick in 1986 draft out of Auburn . . . Born June 27, 1964, in Brantley, Ala. . . . Earned about $2 million last season.

Year	Team	G	FG	FG Pct.	FT	FT Pct.	Reb.	Ast.	TP	Avg.
1986-87	Indiana.	82	635	.468	222	.747	677	295	1541	18.8
1987-88	Indiana.	79	575	.459	132	.670	536	309	1341	17.0
1988-89	Indiana.	80	711	.489	243	.792	516	289	1728	21.6
1989-90	Indiana.	77	605	.487	211	.781	445	230	1515	19.7
	Totals	318	2526	.476	808	.754	2174	1123	6125	19.3

DETLEF SCHREMPF 27 6-10 215   Forward

Late bloomer . . . Becoming a star since his days in Dallas are over . . . Complete offensive game . . . Nice shot with range and accuracy, good driving moves, strong post-up game, sound passer and draws fouls . . . Exceptionally versatile. Can play both forward spots and is good enough ball-handler to swing to big guard . . . Gym-rat type who loves to play . . . Troubled by quicker small forwards defensively . . . Led Pacers with 7.9 rebound average, including 9.0 after All-Star break . . . Born Jan. 21, 1963, in Leverkusen, West Germany . . . Drafted No. 8 in 1985 by Mavericks, who sent him and second-rounder to Pacers for Herb Williams last year. Great deal for Indy . . . Made $900,000.

Year	Team	G	FG	FG Pct.	FT	FT Pct.	Reb.	Ast.	TP	Avg.
1985-86	Dallas	64	142	.451	110	.724	198	88	397	6.2
1986-87	Dallas	81	265	.472	193	.742	303	161	756	9.3
1987-88	Dallas	82	246	.456	201	.756	279	159	698	8.5
1988-89	Dal.-Indiana	69	274	.474	273	.780	395	179	828	12.0
1989-90	Indiana.	78	424	.516	402	.820	620	247	1267	16.2
	Totals	374	1351	.480	1179	.777	1795	834	3946	10.6

LaSALLE THOMPSON 29 6-10 245   Forward

Confused, and rightfully so . . . Here was the rebounding, defensive power forward coach Dick Versace wanted. But this guy's role was never really defined . . . Great hands, good timing, smart positional player . . . One of better defensive rebounders, second on team to Detlef Schrempf in defensive boards, trailing by only 16 and in over 400 fewer minutes . . . Played much of career at center but power forward is his spot . . . Won't beat your mother-in-law in a foot race . . . Came to Pacers with Randy Wittman for Wayman Tisdale in February 1989 . . . Disappeared in three-game playoff with Detroit, getting only 15 boards and 18 points . . . Born June 23, 1961, in Cincinnati . . . No. 5 pick of 1982 draft as U. of Texas undergraduate . . . Earned $1.225 million.

Year	Team	G	FG	FG Pct.	FT	FT Pct.	Reb.	Ast.	TP	Avg.
1982-83	Kansas City	71	147	.512	89	.650	375	33	383	5.4
1983-84	Kansas City	80	333	.523	160	.717	709	86	826	10.3
1984-85	Kansas City	82	369	.531	227	.721	854	130	965	11.8
1985-86	Sacramento	80	411	.518	202	.732	770	168	1024	12.8
1986-87	Sacramento	82	362	.481	188	.737	687	122	912	11.1
1987-88	Sacramento	69	215	.471	118	.720	427	68	550	8.0
1988-89	Sac.-Indiana	76	416	.489	227	.808	718	81	1059	13.9
1989-90	Indiana	82	223	.473	107	.799	630	106	554	6.8
	Totals	622	2476	.501	1318	.738	5170	794	6273	10.1

DYRON NIX 23 6-7 210   Forward

Brian who? Oh sorry, Dyron. . . . Hey, he's the guy who never played . . . Among league leaders in DNP (did not play) . . . Cameoed in 20 games, earning a valuable 109 minutes of experience . . . Drafted by Charlotte out of Tennessee on the second round in 1989 . . . Then shipped to Indiana for Stuart Gray as Pacers began dismantling galaxy's greatest collection of seven-foot Caucasians . . . Good athletic type . . . Unfortunately, he's a good athletic type with no shot . . . Needs time to develop but 109 minutes a season might not do it . . . Born Feb. 11, 1967, in Meridian, Miss. . . . Paid $200,000 last season.

Year	Team	G	FG	FG Pct.	FT	FT Pct.	Reb.	Ast.	TP	Avg.
1989-90	Indiana	20	14	.359	11	.688	26	5	39	2.0

GREG DREILING 26 7-1 250   Center

Well, he's 7-1 . . . Harasses opposing centers well . . . Did we mention he's 7-1? . . . Longest playing time last season was 16-minute job in November . . . Never left bench in playoffs . . . Garbage-time player, averaged 1.3 points . . . Slow and prone to foul trouble . . . Has never had a chance to show what he can do. And with Rik Smits in front of him, doubtful his status will change in foreseeable future . . . Played with Danny

Manning at Kansas... Born Nov. 7, 1963, in Wichita, Kan. ... Pacers' second-round pick in 1986... Delightful guy... Earned $220,000.

Year	Team	G	FG	FG Pct.	FT	FT Pct.	Reb.	Ast.	TP	Avg.
1986-87	Indiana.	24	16	.432	10	.833	43	7	42	1.8
1987-88	Indiana.	20	8	.471	18	.692	17	5	34	1.7
1988-89	Indiana.	53	43	.558	43	.672	92	18	129	2.4
1989-90	Indiana.	49	20	.377	25	.735	87	8	65	1.3
	Totals	146	87	.473	96	.706	239	38	270	1.8

MIKE SANDERS 30 6-6 210   Forward

Not a scorer, never thinks of himself as a scorer, doesn't try to be a scorer or pretend to be a scorer... Good team guy, of course... Best one-on-one defensive player on team... Cut off one of his arms and legs and he'll try to bite you to death... Played all 82 games—including 13 starts in which Pacers were 8-5... Not offensively bankrupt, though... Moves well without the ball, knows how to get good shot position... Tireless, selfless worker that every team needs... Born May 7, 1960, in Vidalia, La.... UCLA product picked by Kansas City on fourth round in 1982... Earned $710,000.

Year	Team	G	FG	FG Pct.	FT	FT Pct.	Reb.	Ast.	TP	Avg.
1982-83	San Antonio	26	76	.484	31	.721	94	19	183	7.0
1983-84	Phoenix	50	97	.478	29	.690	103	44	223	4.5
1984-85	Phoenix	21	85	.486	45	.763	89	29	215	10.2
1985-86	Phoenix	82	347	.513	208	.809	273	150	905	11.0
1986-87	Phoenix	82	357	.494	143	.781	271	126	859	10.5
1987-88	Phoe.-Clev.	59	153	.505	59	.776	109	56	365	6.2
1988-89	Cleveland	82	332	.453	97	.719	307	133	764	9.3
1989-90	Indiana.	82	225	.470	55	.733	230	89	510	6.2
	Totals	484	1672	.485	667	.767	1476	646	4024	8.3

RANDY WITTMAN 31 6-6 210   Guard

In and out... Played well at times. Then he never played... It seemed that when he scored in double figures, he couldn't find a way back into rotation... Privately, some of Pacer brass were irked at way he was handled by coach Dick Versace... Played 61 games, the fewest in a non-injury season of his career... Came with LaSalle Thompson in the Wayman Tisdale deal . . . Has never fouled out of a game . . . Classic off-the-screen shooter . . . Rap has always been he can't create his own shots . . . Born Oct. 28, 1959, in Indianapolis . . . Picked No. 22 in 1983 by Washington out of Indiana, where he was member of Hoosiers' '81 NCAA championship team . . . Paid $450,000.

Year	Team	G	FG	FG Pct.	FT	FT Pct.	Reb.	Ast.	TP	Avg.
1983-84	Atlanta	78	160	.503	28	.609	71	71	350	4.5
1984-85	Atlanta	41	187	.531	30	.732	73	125	406	9.9
1985-86	Atlanta	81	467	.530	104	.770	170	306	1043	12.9
1986-87	Atlanta	71	398	.503	100	.787	124	211	900	12.7
1987-88	Atlanta	82	376	.478	71	.798	170	302	823	10.0
1988-89	Sac.-Indiana	64	130	.455	28	.683	80	111	291	4.5
1989-90	Indiana	61	62	.508	5	.833	30	39	130	2.1
	Totals	478	1780	.503	366	.755	718	1165	3943	8.2

RICKEY GREEN 36 6-0 170   Guard

The NBA beats Social Security . . . Still quick enough to do it in spots . . . Played 11th season with sixth club, though eight of those years were in Utah . . . Michigan product was No. 16 pick by Golden State back in 1977 . . . Injury-plagued much of season, he still saw parts of 69 games . . . Averaged 3.5 points, 2.6 assists in 13.4 minutes . . . Led NBA in steals in 1984 and can still play the tough 'D' . . . Born Aug. 18, 1954, in Chicago . . . On last legs, he was happy to pick up $325,000 as a free agent prior to training camp.

Year	Team	G	FG	FG Pct.	FT	FT Pct.	Reb.	Ast.	TP	Avg.
1977-78	Golden State	76	143	.381	54	.600	116	149	340	4.5
1978-79	Detroit	27	67	.379	45	.672	40	63	179	6.6
1980-81	Utah	47	176	.481	70	.722	116	235	422	9.0
1981-82	Utah	81	500	.493	202	.765	243	630	1202	14.8
1982-83	Utah	78	464	.493	185	.797	223	697	1115	14.3
1983-84	Utah	81	439	.486	192	.821	230	748	1072	13.2
1984-85	Utah	77	381	.477	232	.869	189	597	1000	13.0
1985-86	Utah	80	357	.471	213	.852	135	411	932	11.7
1986-87	Utah	81	301	.467	172	.827	163	541	781	9.6
1987-88	Utah	81	157	.424	75	.904	80	300	393	4.9
1988-89	Char.-Mil.	63	129	.489	30	.909	69	187	291	4.6
1989-90	Indiana	69	100	.433	43	.843	54	182	244	3.5
	Totals	841	3214	.470	1513	.807	1658	4740	7971	9.5

CALVIN NATT 33 6-6 220   Forward

Natt the type to quit... Strong upper body. Unfortunately, it's placed atop ravaged knees ... Injured most of season, appeared in 14 games... In his prime, a terrific rebounder with strong inside game... Underwent right knee surgery for about the 7,000th time in career that has spanned 11 seasons... Was the No. 8 pick in 1979 out of Northeastern Louisiana by New Jersey... Traded to Portland and then became part of the big trade for Kiki Vandeweghe with Denver... Pacers signed him as free agent before camp, hoping something of All-Star form was left... Born Jan. 8, 1957, in Monroe, La.... Earned $450,000... He and brother Kenny (1980-81) form only brother pair to ever play for Pacers.

Year	Team	G	FG	FG Pct.	FT	FT Pct.	Reb.	Ast.	TP	Avg.
1979-80	N.J.-Port.	78	622	.479	306	.730	691	169	1553	19.9
1980-81	Portland	74	395	.497	200	.707	431	159	994	13.4
1981-82	Portland	75	515	.576	294	.750	613	150	1326	17.7
1982-83	Portland	80	644	.543	339	.792	599	171	1630	20.4
1983-84	Portland	79	500	.583	275	.797	476	179	1277	16.2
1984-85	Denver	78	685	.546	447	.793	610	238	1817	23.3
1985-86	Denver	69	469	.504	278	.801	436	164	1218	17.7
1986-87	Denver	1	4	.400	2	1.000	5	2	10	10.0
1987-88	Denver	27	102	.490	54	.740	96	47	258	9.6
1988-89	Den.-S.A.	24	47	.405	57	.722	78	18	151	6.3
1989-90	Indiana	14	20	.645	17	.773	35	9	57	4.1
	Totals	599	4003	.528	2269	.768	4070	1306	10291	17.2

THE ROOKIE

KEN WILLIAMS 21 6-9 225   Forward

With Antonio Davis gone to play in Greece, Ken becomes Pacers' sole rookie... Highly regarded for his inside play and shooting skills, he's had little college experience—one year at Barton County Community College in Kansas, where he averaged 20.5 ppg in 1988-89 and shot 62.7 percent from the field... Transferred to Elizabeth City State, but wasn't eligible because of transfer rule ... Became an early entry and was 46th pick in draft... Born June 9, 1969, in Elizabeth City, N.C.

COACH DICK VERSACE: Has been winner on every level ... When he took Pacers' job, spoke in terms of what he'd do defensively, borrowing from Pistons' system, where he was assistant to Chuck Daly ... Actually, Pacers' biggest gains have been on offensive end, where they averaged 109.3 points ... Claimed this season that those in media around him "had the vision that would fit in a thimble" while his vision would be the "Atlantic Ocean." ... So much for modesty ... Very bright, learned individual—except in his open feuds with the media ... Would last half a day in New York ... Overused starters early in season as Pacers got off to good start ... Still, no denying that Indiana made great strides in his first season ... Wisconsin grad with literature degree ... Came up through high-school ranks, but really made name for himself at Bradley, earning USBWA Coach of Year honors in 1985-86 ... Replaced Jack Ramsay after stint with Daly ... Mother wrote work from which TV show "The Flying Nun" was adapted ... Born April 16, 1940, in Fort Bragg, N.C.

GREATEST REBOUNDER

He played at a time when the Pacers were in the ABA. Mel Daniels was a dominating 6-9, 220-pounder out of the University of New Mexico. A two-time ABA MVP, Mel played for six seasons with the Pacers, hauling in 7,622 rebounds in 479 games—just a shade under 16 a game. He was clearly the ABA Pacers' greatest rebounder.

For Indiana's era in the NBA, Herb Williams, now in Dallas, remains at the top of the team's rebound column. In his eight Pacer seasons, Williams collected 4,494 boards.

ALL-TIME PACER LEADERS

SEASON

Points: George McGinnis, 2,353, 1974-75 (ABA)
       Billy Knight, 2,075, 1976-77
Assists: Don Buse, 689, 1975-76 (ABA)
       Don Buse, 685, 1976-77
Rebounds: Mel Daniels, 1,475, 1970-71 (ABA)
       Clark Kellogg, 860, 1982-83

GAME

Points: George McGinnis, 58 vs. Dallas, 11/28/72 (ABA)
       Billy Knight, 52 vs. San Antonio, 11/11/80
Assists: Don Buse, 20 vs. Denver, 3/26/76 (ABA)
       Don Buse, 17 vs. Boston, 1/26/77
       Vern Fleming, 17 vs. Chicago, 2/17/86
       Scott Skiles, 17 vs. New Jersey, 12/28/88
Rebounds: George McGinnis, 37 vs. Carolina, 1/12/74 (ABA)
       Herb Williams, 25 vs. Denver, 1/23/89

CAREER

Points: Billy Knight, 10,780, 1974-83 (ABA)
       Herb Williams, 8,637, 1981-89
Assists: Vern Fleming, 2,897, 1984-90
       Don Buse, 2,747, 1972-77, 1980-82 (ABA)
Rebounds: Mel Daniels, 7,622, 1968-74 (ABA)
       Herb Williams, 4,494, 1981-89

MIAMI HEAT

TEAM DIRECTORY: Partners: Ted Arison, Zev Bufman, Billy Cunningham, Lewis Schaffel (Managing Partner); Dir. Player Personnel: Stu Inman; Dir. Pub. Rel.: Mark Pray; Coach: Ron Rothstein; Asst. Coaches: Dave Wohl, Tony Fiorentino. Arena: Miami Arena (15,008). Colors: Orange, red, yellow, black and white.

SCOUTING REPORT

SHOOTING: Pretty poor. In all aspects. Only two teams posted a worse field-goal percentage than the Heat's .461. Miami's perimeter game—especially from disappointing two-guard Kevin Edwards (.412)—abandoned them for most of the season. And—with two Syracuse guys on the roster you'd expect this—they were the worst free-throw shooting team in creation, knocking down a pathetic .687. Three starters—Rony Seikaly, Sherman Douglas, Billy Thompson—all were below 70 percent. From the field, the Heat hopes University of Minnesota sharpshooter Willie Burton can supply respectability from the outside.

PLAYMAKING: The Heat made great strides here through the second-round steal of Douglas, who displayed marvelous penetration skills and set a franchise standard with 619 assists. But after that, the passing falls off markedly, one of the reasons why the Heat dealt veteran Rory Sparrow on draft day for the hopefully creative rookie Bimbo Coles. Seikaly simply must improve his passing: his 78 assists in 74 games was easily the worst passing production by a center in the East.

DEFENSE: Again, poor by overall standards, but not that goshawful for a second-year team. The Heat made nice strides in some areas: like steals, where they were 11th in the league. Seikaly and Thompson blocked some shots, but the Heat lacked anything resembling muscle on the bench. It will get better as the Heat undergoes another season under the guidance of Ron Rothstein, widely recognized as a fine defensive mentor.

REBOUNDING: Good in spots, awful in others—like the two-guard and small-forward positions. Seikaly finished as the second-best rebounding center in the East, behind Patrick Ewing. Thompson, the object of season-long trade rumors, does it with

Rony Seikaly burst out as NBA's Most Improved Player.

HEAT ROSTER

No.	Veterans	Pos.	Ht.	Wt.	Age	Yrs. Pro	College
44	Terry Davis	C-F	6-9	225	23	1	Virginia Union
11	Sherman Douglas	G	6-0	180	23	1	Syracuse
21	Kevin Edwards	G	6-3	195	25	2	DePaul
3	Scott Haffner	G	6-3	185	24	1	Evansville
43	Grant Long	F	6-8	235	24	2	Eastern Michigan
41	Glen Rice	G-F	6-7	218	23	1	Michigan
50	Jim Rowinski	F-C	6-8	255	29	3	Purdue
4	Rony Seikaly	C	6-11	252	25	2	Syracuse
20	Jon Sundvold	G	6-2	170	29	7	Missouri
55	Billy Thompson	F	6-7	220	26	4	Louisville

Rd.	Rookies	Sel. No.	Pos.	Ht.	Wt.	College
1	Willie Burton	9	F-G	6-6	203	Minnesota
1	*Alec Kessler	13	F-C	6-11	235	Georgia
2	**Vernell (Bimbo) Coles	40	G	6-1	172	Virginia Tech

*Drafted by Houston, traded to Heat
**Drafted by Sacramento, traded to Heat

leaping and athleticism. The Heat gets little rebounding from the backcourt but the biggest need is the bruiser type, which they had hoped Tellis Frank would be. He disappointed, so now Miami has fingers crossed that rookie Alec Kessler will soon fill that role. Consider that the Heat placed 15th in overall rebounding. And that's not bad at all for a second-year team. They improved on the offensive boards—which they really had to because they were such a poor shooting outfit.

OUTLOOK: Not at all bad for a team entering its third year of existence. And it could have been a lot better had the $26.5-million, seven-year gamble for restricted free agent John Williams gone through. Seikaly has shown huge strides in two years at center. Douglas is a quality point guard with penetrating skills. Glen Rice should improve, especially in going to the basket. Rookies Kessler and Burton will probably play like rookies but will gain the experience.

The Heat needs Edwards to return to some kind of reliable form so Burton can grow at an unforced pace. Sure, they lack a lot but the Heat is not as far away from being a playoff team as would normally be expected. Improvement is the goal and that should be met.

HEAT PROFILES

RONY SEIKALY 25 6-11 252   Center

He can play . . . Found his niche in second season and was named the NBA's "Most Improved Player" . . . Cut down on a lot of the fakes and spins and began taking the ball to the basket with power and authority . . . Developed strong post-up moves, a hook shot and turnaround jumper . . . Led Heat in scoring with 16.6 average, fifth among NBA centers . . . Established team records with 40 points vs. Chicago, 22 rebounds vs. Orlando and eight blocks vs. New Jersey . . . Still needs a radar gun from the line, where he was a dismal .594—which was an improvement over his rookie season . . . Still learning and will only get better . . . Born in Beirut on May 10, 1965 . . . Heat made him ninth pick in 1988 draft out of Syracuse, where he led Orange to NCAA title game in 1987 . . . Worked for $750,000 last season.

Year	Team	G	FG	FG Pct.	FT	FT Pct.	Reb.	Ast.	TP	Avg.
1988-89	Miami	78	333	.448	181	.511	549	55	848	10.9
1989-90	Miami	74	486	.502	256	.594	766	78	1228	16.6
	Totals	152	819	.478	437	.557	1315	133	2076	13.7

SHERMAN DOUGLAS 23 6-0 180   Guard

Classic case of disproving importance of those college All-Star meat markets . . . Because he skipped postseason tourneys after career in Syracuse, slipped to second round (28th pick overall). Ah, but he thrived in rookie season . . . And would have had legit shot at Rookie of the Year if David Robinson had never been born . . . Scored over 1,000 points and passed for over 500 assists, averaging 14.3 ppg and 7.6 assists . . . Super penetrator and already a team leader . . . Needs to improve defensively, has a tendency to sag too much . . . Was 16th in league in steals (1.79) . . . Made $265,000 but contract was expected to be redone and land him near $1-million mark . . . All-time NCAA career assists leader with 960 when he left Syracuse, where he set school record in scoring and assists . . . In typical Orangemen fashion, was a foul-shooting abomination at .687 ... Born Sept. 15, 1967, in Washington, D.C.

Year	Team	G	FG	FG Pct.	FT	FT Pct.	Reb.	Ast.	TP	Avg.
1989-90	Miami	81	463	.494	224	.687	206	619	1155	14.3

GLEN RICE 23 6-7 218　　　　　　　Guard-Forward

Yeah, the guy's a good perimeter threat ... But just 124 free-throw attempts all season? ... Led team in field-goal attempts and took more shots than any rookie except David Robinson ... Switched to big guard for final 11 games after playing most of season at small forward, where he showed inability to get to the line ... Needs to improve ball-handling and defense, but biggest knock was inability—or unwillingness—to take ball to the hole ... Should get more rebounds because of great leaping ability ... All-time scoring leader in Big 10 (before it became Big 11) and averaged 30.7 ppg as senior to lead Michigan to NCAA title two years ago ... Born May 28, 1967, in Flint, Mich. ... Paid $1.5 million.

Year	Team	G	FG	FG Pct.	FT	FT Pct.	Reb.	Ast.	TP	Avg.
1989-90	Miami	77	470	.439	91	.734	352	138	1048	13.6

KEVIN EDWARDS 25 6-3 195　　　　　　　　Guard

Give him a flashlight and a road map and maybe he'll find his shot ... Made the sophomore jinx an art form ... Shot .412 as a "shooting" guard ... And he's still turnover-prone ... Was named to All-Rookie second team after Heat made him No. 20 pick out of DePaul in 1989 ... Not bad on defensive end ... But he dropped offensively after his rookie season—average from 13.8 to 12.0, assists from 4.4 to 3.2 ... College backcourt mate and roommate of Rod Strickland ... Finished DePaul career with best field-goal percentage ever (60 percent) by a guard ... Earned $250,000 last season ... Born Oct. 30, 1965, in Cleveland Heights, Ohio.

Year	Team	G	FG	FG Pct.	FT	FT Pct.	Reb.	Ast.	TP	Avg.
1988-89	Miami	79	470	.425	144	.746	262	349	1094	13.8
1989-90	Miami	78	395	.412	139	.760	282	252	938	12.0
	Totals	157	865	.419	283	.753	544	601	2032	12.9

BILLY THOMPSON 26 6-7 220   Forward

Led team in trade rumors . . . Strong second half may have upped his value, too . . . Started final 14 games and averaged 15.6 points, 10.1 rebounds . . . Outside shot showed dramatic improvement . . . Plays both forward spots. Gets muscled by bigger guys but compensates with terrific leaping ability and long arms . . . Had an 18-rebound game vs. Dallas . . . Made $365,000 . . . Owns two NBA rings, courtesy of Lakers who lost him in expansion draft to Heat in 1988 . . . Starred at Louisville . . . Atlanta took him with 19th pick in 1986 draft and swapped him to Lakers for Mike McGee . . . Two-time high-school All-American in Camden, N.J., where he was born Dec. 1, 1963.

Year	Team	G	FG	FG Pct.	FT	FT Pct.	Reb.	Ast.	TP	Avg.
1986-87	L.A. Lakers......	59	142	.544	48	.649	171	60	332	5.6
1987-88	L.A. Lakers......	9	3	.231	8	.800	9	1	14	1.6
1988-89	Miami	79	349	.487	156	.696	572	176	854	10.8
1989-90	Miami	79	375	.516	115	.622	551	166	867	11.0
	Totals	226	869	.506	327	.663	1303	403	2067	9.1

GRANT LONG 24 6-8 235   Forward

From major surprise to big disappointment in one season . . . An eye-opener as a rookie in 1988-89 after Heat got him on second round with 33d pick . . . Was named Heat's MVP that year . . . But Eastern Michigan product struggled in sophomore year against strong types up front and ball-handling made him suspect against small forwards . . . Still, he showed enough to keep Heat hopes up . . . Has played in all but one of team's games in two years . . . But his struggles saw playing time cut nearly 600 minutes . . . Came into league with absolutely no face-up game . . . Strong work ethic but severe foul problems. Fouled out 11 times last season, tying for NBA-high . . . Born March 12, 1966, in Wayne, Mich. . . . Earned $350,000.

Year	Team	G	FG	FG Pct.	FT	FT Pct.	Reb.	Ast.	TP	Avg.
1988-89	Miami	82	336	.486	304	.749	546	149	976	11.9
1989-90	Miami	81	257	.483	172	.714	402	96	686	8.5
	Totals	163	593	.484	476	.736	948	245	1662	10.2

JON SUNDVOLD 29 6-2 170   Guard

Fact of NBA life: As youth movement progresses, veterans get squeezed out . . . Not exactly out of Book of Revelations but it describes seven-year vet's status . . . Minutes dropped drastically as he failed to reach 1,000 (867) for first time in career . . . May have to accept role as a three-point specialist to hang on . . . Led NBA in three-point shooting in 1989 (52 percent) . . . And he hit 44-of-100 treys last year, also not too shabby . . . Came to Heat in 1988 expansion draft . . . Originally a first-round pick (No. 19) by Seattle out of Missouri . . . Made $385,000 . . . Born July 2, 1961, in Sioux Falls, S.D.

Year	Team	G	FG	FG Pct.	FT	FT Pct.	Reb.	Ast.	TP	Avg.
1983-84	Seattle	73	217	.445	64	.889	91	239	507	6.9
1984-85	Seattle	73	170	.425	48	.814	70	206	400	5.5
1985-86	San Antonio	70	220	.462	39	.813	80	261	500	7.1
1986-87	San Antonio	76	365	.486	70	.833	98	315	850	11.2
1987-88	San Antonio	52	176	.464	43	.896	48	183	421	8.1
1988-89	Miami	68	307	.455	47	.825	87	137	709	10.4
1989-90	Miami	63	148	.408	44	.846	71	102	384	6.1
	Totals	475	1603	.454	355	.845	545	1443	3771	7.9

SCOTT HAFFNER 24 6-3 185   Guard

Has it up top, if not down bottom . . . Academic All-American at Evansville was injury-plagued in rookie season—and missed final 11 games with right ankle sprain . . . Final appearance of season was starting role vs. Orlando and he produced 10 points and five assists . . . Strictly a shooter, which was why he was still available for Miami with 45th pick in 1989 draft . . . Defense definitely needs work . . . Overachieving type who's ever so marginal . . . Born Feb. 2, 1966, in Peoria, Ill. . . . Paid $150,000.

Year	Team	G	FG	FG Pct.	FT	FT Pct.	Reb.	Ast.	TP	Avg.
1989-90	Miami	43	88	.406	17	.680	51	80	196	4.6

TERRY DAVIS 23 6-9 225　　　　　　**Center-Forward**

 A nice find as an undrafted free agent... Stringbean type moved ahead of veteran Pat Cummings—forcing his release—as a backup center as season progressed... Has a decent perimeter game and nice soft touch... Numbers aren't staggering (4.7 ppg and 3.6 boards), but in five starts in late March, he averaged 11.0 points and 8.8 rebounds while shooting .605... Came from Virginia Union, same small school that produced Charles Oakley... Was the Central Intercollegiate Athletic Association Player of the Year in 1988 and 1989... Born June 17, 1967, in Danville, Va.... Made $125,000 minimum.

Year	Team	G	FG	FG Pct.	FT	FT Pct.	Reb.	Ast.	TP	Avg.
1989-90	Miami	63	122	.466	54	.621	229	25	298	4.7

THE ROOKIES

WILLIE BURTON 22 6-6 203　　　　　　**Forward-Guard**
The guy the Heat really wanted, they traded down from No. 3 and plucked the U. of Minnesota product at No. 9 on the first round... A forward in college, he figures to play a lot of off-guard for the Heat... Stock soared when he was voted MVP of the Orlando All-Star Classic... Born May 26, 1968, in Detroit ... Second all-time leading scorer at Minnesota (behind Mychal Thompson) with 1,800 points, 616 of them as a senior when he averaged 19.3 ppg... Ninth on school's rebounding list, averaged 5.6 boards as senior... Shot .511 from field for four-year career.

ALEC KESSLER 23 6-11 235　　　　　　**Forward-Center**
Was the 12th pick on the draft, by Houston, but came to Heat on draft-day deal that sent Dave Jamerson (No. 15) and second-rounder to Rockets... National Scholar Athlete of the Year two years running... Averaged 21.0 points as senior at Georgia, which was nothing compared to 3.91 grade-point average... Degree in microbiology... Doctor's sheepskin to follow... All-time scoring leader at Georgia with 1,788 points. Passed Vern Fleming in his final game when he scored 33 vs. Texas... Nice, soft mid-range touch. Good low-post game... As a junior, was first Bull-

dog to lead SEC in rebounding (9.7) in 16 years . . . Averaged 10.4 boards as a senior, making him only the second SEC player in 10 years to post a 20-point, 10-rebound season. Kenny Walker was the other . . . Born Jan. 13, 1967, in Roswell, Ga.

BIMBO COLES 22 6-1 172   Guard

Drafted on second round by Sacramento and then shipped to Heat for veteran Rory Sparrow on draft night . . . Virginia Tech product was leading scorer in Metro Conference history with 2,484 points, which translated into four-year average of 21.6 . . . Averaged 25.3 as senior . . . And that's despite awful .404 shooting, which probably cost him first-round status . . . Set or tied 31 Metro Conference records . . . Real first name is Vernell . . . Born April 22, 1968.

COACH RON ROTHSTEIN: Intense, defensive-minded guy

who was one of masterminds of Pistons' defensive scheme . . . Was even rumored to replace Chuck Daly, if his old boss decided to retire . . . His Heat made only modest three-victory improvement to 18 wins . . . But made great strides overall with youth movement, especially development of Rony Seikaly and Sherman Douglas . . . Has managed to get Heat more competitive and team appears in better shape for future than Charlotte, their expansionist cousin . . . The losing early wore thin on his nerves but he appears to have accepted reality of situation . . . Graduate of Rhode Island . . . Broke into NBA as an Atlanta scout under Hubie Brown . . . Assisted Mike Fratello in Atlanta before move to Detroit as aide to Daly . . . Born Dec. 27, 1942, in Bronxville, N.Y.

GREATEST REBOUNDER

When the team is only two seasons old, the search for the team's best ever rebounder isn't too hard. Just find the guy whose two-year expansion numbers almost match the best single-season

Sherman Douglas made the NBA All-Rookie Team.

for most other teams. But give Rony Seikaly a few more years with his current progress and his numbers might stand with most career team leaders.

The player on whom the future of the Heat franchise is pegged, Seikaly averaged 10.4 boards in his second season. That mark made him the NBA's sixth-best board man last season and placed him behind only Patrick Ewing among Eastern Conference centers.

The 6-11 Seikaly, born in Beirut and a star at Syracuse, tops the Heat's embryonic rebound totals with 1,315 in two seasons.

ALL-TIME HEAT LEADERS

SEASON

Points: Rony Seikaly, 1,228, 1989-90
Assists: Sherman Douglas, 619, 1989-90
Rebounds: Rony Seikaly, 766, 1989-90

GAME

Points: Rony Seikaly, 40 vs. Chicago, 2/13/90
Assists: Dwayne Washington, 23 vs. Philadelphia, 2/22/89
Rebounds: Rony Seikaly, 22 vs. Orlando, 11/28/89

CAREER

Points: Kevin Edwards, 2,032, 1988-90
Assists: Rory Sparrow, 717, 1988-90
Rebounds: Rony Seikaly, 1,315, 1988-90

MILWAUKEE BUCKS

TEAM DIRECTORY: Pres.: Herb Kohl; VP-Bus. Oper.: John Steinmiller; Dir. Player Personnel: Lee Rose; Dir. Pub. Rel.: Bill King II; Coach: Del Harris; Asst. Coaches: Frank Hamblen, Mack Calvin. Arena: Bradley Center (18,633). Colors: Green, lime and white.

SCOUTING REPORT

SHOOTING: The Bucks shot a disappointing .473. But with the injury plague that wracked the team, every category suffered. In a season of transition, where the Bucks underwent a drastic make-over, their biggest failing was finding an adequate low-post scorer to replace the traded Terry Cummings.

Ex-Spur Alvin Robertson galloped into Buck record book.

Milwaukee hopes new acquisitions Frank Brickowski from San Antonio and Danny Schayes from Denver (at the cost of first-round pick Terry Mills) can fill some of that void.

In center Jack Sikma, the Bucks have the luxury of a big man with inside capabilities who can burn from the perimeter. Sikma knocked down 68 three-pointers, easily a high among league centers.

PLAYMAKING: Ever since Don Nelson introduced the point-forward scheme in his Milwaukee days, the Bucks have always been a good playmaking team. They have a fine overall creative backcourt in Alvin Robertson and Jay Humphries (who combined for 11.3 assists per). They made Paul Pressey expendable in a trade for the needed bulk of Brickowski. The Bucks are a sound fundamental team with a thinking man's approach to offense. And to do so, passing is essential.

DEFENSE: At times, downright scintillating—like the club-record nine consecutive games early on when the Bucks held each opponent under 100 points. But the injury-induced shuttle system eventually wore down continuity in all aspects and the Bucks finished as a middle-of-the-pack defensive team. Except in steals, of course, where the addition of Robertson enabled the Bucks to lead the league in that category with 826, over 10 a game.

REBOUNDING: The Bucks were one of the worst boarding teams on the planet last season—only Indiana among non-Eastern expansion teams, was worse. Injuries played such a large part that Robertson, a guard, emerged as the team's top rebounder. Praise for Robertson, scorn for the rest of the Bucks. There are some nice board men here, like Greg Anderson and hard-working Fred Roberts, who makes the most of limited skills. But the Bucks are going to continue to miss the injured Larry Krystkowiak, who is not expected to return this season after undergoing additional knee surgery.

OUTLOOK: No matter what logic or the names on paper say, the Bucks just always seem to find a way to the playoffs. And this season should be no exception. If they made it last season for the 11th straight year despite a team record—and NBA-high—235 manpower games missed through injury and illness, this should be a piece of cake. Unless they miss 236 manpower games through injury and illness.

That could be the Bucks' biggest concern. Sikma had back

BUCK ROSTER

No.	Veterans	Pos.	Ht.	Wt.	Age	Yrs. Pro	College
34	Greg Anderson	F	6-10	230	26	3	Houston
—	Frank Brickowski	C-F	6-10	240	31	6	Penn State
35	Tony Brown	F-G	6-6	195	30	5	Arkansas
20	Jeff Grayer	G	6-5	200	24	2	Iowa State
50	Tito Horford	C	7-1	245	24	2	Miami
24	Jay Humphries	G	6-3	185	28	6	Colorado
8	Frank Kornet	F	6-9	225	23	1	Vanderbilt
42	*Larry Krystkowiak	F	6-10	240	26	4	Montana
44	Brad Lohaus	C	7-0	235	26	3	Iowa
22	Ricky Pierce	G-F	6-4	210	31	8	Rice
31	Fred Roberts	F	6-10	220	30	7	BYU
21	Alvin Robertson	G	6-4	190	28	6	Arkansas
43	Jack Sikma	C	7-0	250	34	13	Illinois Wesleyan
—	Danny Schayes	C	6-11	260	31	8	Syracuse

*Injured

Rd.	Rookies	Sel. No.	Pos.	Ht.	Wt.	College
2	Steve Henson	44	G	6-1	175	Kansas City
2	**Pat Durham	35	F	6-7	210	Colorado State

**Drafted by Dallas in 1989

problems that limited him. Anderson didn't justify the trading of Cummings after his assortment of ills. And Krystkowiak can't make this his comeback year.

As usual, the Bucks are rock-solid and deep at guard and will find a way to cause headaches with small lineups and sophisticated sets. They figure to be there when the postseason starts. For how long is another matter.

BUCK PROFILES

JACK SIKMA 34 7-0 250   Center

Mr. Inside turned Mr. Outside . . . As a result, he had dismal shooting season, worst of his 13-year career . . . Completely bombed in play-offs, missing 17 of 23 shots as Bulls bounced Bucks in four . . . His 68-of-199 (.342) three-point shooting often gives opposing centers fits . . . Had seven treys in first 11 seasons, 150 in last two . . . Acknowledged team leader . . .

Still a good low-post scorer, average defender . . . Only starting Eastern Conference center playing 50 games with fewer blocks than his 48 was Bill Cartwright . . . Reached several milestones, including 10,000 rebounds, to join Robert Parish and Moses Malone as only active players at that level . . . Good passing center, averaged 3.2 assists . . . Outstanding free-throw shooter, shot .885, best among all NBA centers . . . Born Nov. 14, 1955, in Kankakee, Ill. . . . After starring at Illinois Wesleyan, went to Seattle as No. 8 pick in 1977 . . . Led Sonics to NBA crown in 1978-79 . . . Came to Milwaukee for Alton Lister with exchange of draft picks in 1986 . . . Got $1.6 million last season.

Year	Team	G	FG	FG Pct.	FT	FT Pct.	Reb.	Ast.	TP	Avg.
1977-78	Seattle	82	342	.455	192	.777	678	134	876	10.7
1978-79	Seattle	82	476	.460	329	.814	1013	261	1281	15.6
1979-80	Seattle	82	470	.475	235	.805	908	279	1175	14.3
1980-81	Seattle	82	595	.454	340	.823	852	248	1530	18.7
1981-82	Seattle	82	581	.479	447	.855	1038	277	1611	19.6
1982-83	Seattle	75	484	.464	400	.837	858	233	1368	18.2
1983-84	Seattle	82	576	.499	411	.856	911	327	1563	19.1
1984-85	Seattle	68	461	.489	335	.852	723	285	1259	18.5
1985-86	Seattle	80	508	.462	355	.864	748	301	1371	17.1
1986-87	Milwaukee	82	390	.463	265	.847	822	203	1045	12.7
1987-88	Milwaukee	82	514	.486	321	.922	709	279	1352	16.5
1988-89	Milwaukee	80	360	.431	266	.905	623	289	1068	13.4
1989-90	Milwaukee	71	344	.416	230	.885	492	229	986	13.9
	Totals	1030	6101	.466	4126	.850	10375	3345	16485	16.0

ALVIN ROBERTSON 28 6-4 190   Guard

Typically Arkansas tough . . . Tenacious defender . . . Swept out of San Antonio in Larry Brown's purge, came to Bucks in the deal for Terry Cummings . . . First Milwaukee guard ever to register 1,000 points, 500 rebounds, 400 assists and 200 steals in same season . . . Usually among NBA best in steals. Last season no exception. Fourth in league in steals at 2.56 . . . Had best rebounding season ever by a Bucks' guard with 559 boards, 230 off offensive glass . . . In fact, had more offensive rebounds than any NBA guard last season . . . Best athletic skills on team . . . Scoring comes on drives and off defense . . . High intensity level . . . Led Buck playoff scoring at 23.5 . . . Rap has always been on his decision-making . . . Middle name Cyrrale . . .

Cyrrale? . . . Born July 22, 1962, in Barton, Ohio . . . San Antonio made him No. 7 pick in 1984 out of Arkansas . . . Paid $820,000.

Year	Team	G	FG	FG Pct.	FT	FT Pct.	Reb.	Ast.	TP	Avg.
1984-85	San Antonio	79	299	.498	124	.734	265	275	726	9.2
1985-86	San Antonio	82	562	.514	260	.795	516	448	1392	17.0
1986-87	San Antonio	81	589	.466	244	.753	424	421	1435	17.7
1987-88	San Antonio	82	655	.465	273	.748	498	557	1610	19.6
1988-89	San Antonio	65	465	.483	183	.723	384	393	1122	17.3
1989-90	Milwaukee	81	476	.503	197	.741	559	445	1153	14.2
	Totals	470	3046	.486	1281	.752	2646	2539	7438	15.8

Backcourt ace Jay Humphries had best shooting season.

JAY HUMPHRIES 28 6-3 185   Guard

Inch for inch and pound for pound, may have been Bucks' MVP... Held team together through incredible rash of injuries... All-around point guard who can score with mid-range jumper, with drives, on break where he's exceptional finisher... Quality defender, especially when pressuring ball... Won't blind you with speed, but feet aren't bound together, either... Adept with either hand, one of league's best right or left players... Averaged only 1.9 turnovers... Career high in scoring at 15.3... Can also play the two-guard... Came to Bucks for Craig Hodges in 1988... No. 13 pick by Suns out of Colorado in 1984... Born Oct. 17, 1962, in Los Angeles... Paid $530,000.

Year	Team	G	FG	FG Pct.	FT	FT Pct.	Reb.	Ast.	TP	Avg.
1984-85	Phoenix	80	279	.446	141	.829	164	350	703	8.8
1985-86	Phoenix	82	352	.479	197	.767	260	526	905	11.0
1986-87	Phoenix	82	359	.477	200	.769	260	632	923	11.3
1987-88	Phoe.-Mil	68	284	.528	112	.732	174	395	683	10.0
1988-89	Milwaukee	73	345	.483	129	.816	189	405	844	11.6
1989-90	Milwaukee	81	496	.494	224	.786	269	472	1237	15.3
	Totals	466	2115	.484	1003	.782	1316	2780	5295	11.4

RICKY PIERCE 31 6-4 210   Guard

Best sixth man in league... Can shoot the lights out. Then on. Then out again... Joined Kevin McHale as only two-time Sixth Man Award winners... Had 30 or more points 16 times, with run of four straight such games... Was third in league in points per minutes played (.80), trailing only Michael Jordan and Karl Malone... Team-high 23.0 scoring was best mark of career... Simply had a heckuva offensive year... Lousy medical season, though. Suffered through ankle sprain, groin pulls, strep throat, swollen hand, sprained wrist... Avoided chicken pox... Improved defensively, but doesn't have the quickness to match the swifter two-guards... Earned $800,000... Born Aug. 19, 1959, in Dallas... Was Detroit's first-round choice in 1982 out of Rice... Wound up with Clippers, who made preposterous deal by sending him, Craig Hodges and Terry Cummings to Milwaukee for Harvey Catchings, Junior Bridgeman and Marques Johnson . . . Wife Joyce was former lead singer of Fifth Dimension.

Year	Team	G	FG	FG Pct.	FT	FT Pct.	Reb.	Ast.	TP	Avg.
1982-83	Detroit	39	33	.375	18	.563	35	14	85	2.2
1983-84	San Diego	69	268	.470	149	.861	135	60	685	9.9
1984-85	Milwaukee	44	165	.537	102	.823	117	94	433	9.8
1985-86	Milwaukee	81	429	.538	266	.858	231	177	1127	13.9
1986-87	Milwaukee	79	575	.534	387	.880	266	144	1540	19.5
1987-88	Milwaukee	37	248	.510	107	.877	83	73	606	16.4
1988-89	Milwaukee	75	527	.518	255	.859	197	156	1317	17.6
1989-90	Milwaukee	59	503	.510	307	.839	167	133	1359	23.0
	Totals	483	2748	.515	1591	.854	1231	851	7152	14.8

DAN SCHAYES 31 6-11 260   Center

From April on, the "experts" couldn't finish a sentence about trades without including this veteran's name. And the rumors became reality in the summer when the Nuggets shipped him to the Bucks for Terry Mills, the 16th pick in the draft . . . Three of the four double-figure seasons during his nine-year career have come since 1987-88 . . . Born May 10, 1959, in Syracuse, N.Y. . . . Son of Hall-of-Famer Dolph Schayes . . . A late-bloomer at Syracuse, where he was a chem major and Academic All-American . . . Set Big East record with 23 rebounds vs. Georgetown . . . Utah made him the 13th pick in 1981 . . . Spent only one full season with Jazz, where he was not greatly loved by paying audiences in Salt Palace . . . Nice touch on jumper . . . No soft touch on defense when he wants to be tough . . . Only played in 53 games last year, starting 22, but still fouled out seven times . . . Always one of top free-throwers among centers, had career-best .852 last year.

Year	Team	G	FG	FG Pct.	FT	FT Pct.	Reb.	Ast.	TP	Avg.
1981-82	Utah	82	252	.481	140	.757	427	146	644	7.9
1982-83	Utah-Den	82	342	.457	228	.773	635	205	912	11.1
1983-84	Denver	82	183	.493	215	.790	433	91	581	7.1
1984-85	Denver	56	60	.465	79	.814	144	38	199	3.6
1985-86	Denver	80	221	.502	216	.777	439	79	658	8.2
1986-87	Denver	76	210	.519	229	.779	380	85	649	8.5
1987-88	Denver	81	361	.540	407	.836	662	106	1129	13.9
1988-89	Denver	76	317	.522	332	.826	500	105	969	12.8
1989-90	Denver	53	163	.494	225	.852	342	61	551	10.4
	Totals	668	2109	.499	2071	.805	3962	916	6292	9.4

FRANK BRICKOWSKI 31 6-10 240   Center-Forward

Journeyman who in a quiet way helped San Antonio through some tough times awaiting arrival of David Robinson . . . At least Spurs didn't go winless in his starting tenure . . . And now he's a Buck, traded during the summer for Paul Pressey . . . Born Aug. 14, 1959, in Bayville, N.Y. . . . Played at Penn State and was taken 57th by New York in third round of 1981 draft . . . Waited three years after college for first NBA spot . . . Released by Knicks and then played successive seasons in Italy, France and Israel . . . Came back to U.S., and Seattle used him for parts of two seasons . . . Signed as veteran free agent by Lakers, who then used him as part of a deal to get Mychal Thompson from San Antonio . . . Got only 12 starts and averaged 6.6 points last year after having averaged 16 and 13.7 waiting for David . . . Offcourt pal of Charlie Sheen, the actor.

Year	Team	G	FG	FG Pct.	FT	FT Pct.	Reb.	Ast.	TP	Avg.
1984-85	Seattle	78	150	.492	85	.669	260	100	385	4.9
1985-86	Seattle	40	30	.517	18	.667	54	21	78	2.0
1986-87	LAL-S.A.	44	63	.508	50	.714	116	17	176	4.0
1987-88	San Antonio	70	425	.528	268	.768	483	266	1119	16.0
1988-89	San Antonio	64	337	.515	201	.715	406	131	875	13.7
1989-90	San Antonio	78	211	.545	95	.674	327	105	517	6.6
	Totals	374	1216	.521	717	.721	1646	640	3150	8.4

FRED ROBERTS 30 6-10 220   Forward

How many guys can say they were traded for players, a coach, draft picks and an exhibition game? This guy can . . . Fifth team in seven seasons . . . Once was traded to Nets from Spurs for compensation for signing coach Stan Albeck . . . Also traded by Jazz to Celts for draft picks and home-team rights in an exhibition game . . . Has found a home in Milwaukee . . . Lunchpail, blue-collar type. Defends, rebounds, stands on head if asked . . . Role player had career year . . . Dives for loose balls, boxes out, runs floor and beats opponents through hustle . . . Played all 82 games for first time in career . . . Born Aug. 14, 1960, in Provo,

Utah . . . Originally drafted by Bucks on second round of '82 out of Brigham Young . . . $353,000 salary last year.

Year	Team	G	FG	FG Pct.	FT	FT Pct.	Reb.	Ast.	TP	Avg.
1983-84	San Antonio	79	214	.536	144	.837	304	98	573	7.3
1984-85	S.A.-Utah	74	208	.498	150	.824	186	87	567	7.7
1985-86	Utah	58	74	.443	67	.770	80	27	216	3.7
1986-87	Boston	73	139	.515	124	.810	190	62	402	5.5
1987-88	Boston	74	161	.488	128	.776	162	81	450	6.1
1988-89	Milwaukee	71	155	.486	104	.806	209	66	417	5.9
1989-90	Milwaukee	82	330	.495	195	.783	311	147	857	10.5
	Totals	511	1281	.499	912	.802	1442	568	3482	6.8

JEFF GRAYER 24 6-5 200   Forward-Guard

This wasn't the plan . . . Missed almost entire rookie season with knee injury . . . Then he struggled last year to find a niche in Milwaukee system . . . Defensive liability . . . Yes, he can do the offensive "little things"—like moving without ball, seeing floor, feeding the post. But he's in trouble on defense against any forward . . . Needs minutes at guard to blossom, but in Brew City guard minutes are hard to come by . . . Big upside potential if proper role can be found . . . Born Dec. 17, 1965, in Flint, Mich. . . . All-time leading scorer at Iowa State . . . Bucks made him 13th pick in 1988 and paid him $500,000 last season.

Year	Team	G	FG	FG Pct.	FT	FT Pct.	Reb.	Ast.	TP	Avg.
1988-89	Milwaukee	11	32	.438	17	.850	35	22	81	7.4
1989-90	Milwaukee	71	224	.460	99	.651	217	107	548	7.7
	Totals	82	256	.457	116	.674	252	129	629	7.7

BRAD LOHAUS 26 7-0 235   Center

Felt he was run out of Boston, Sacramento and Minnesota for lack of inside game . . . Probably right . . . But in Milwaukee, they don't want him inside . . . Bucks content to let him play outside, where he doesn't have to get bruised . . . So he floats on perimeter, shoots three-pointers . . . Came to Bucks in January for Randy Breuer and did rather well, actually . . . Averaged 10.0 ppg with Bucks and had back-to-back rebound games of 16 and 14, respectively . . . Typical U. of Iowa player with little concept of pro game after Celts made him second-round pick in 1987 . . . Hit 16 of 33 trifectas for Bucks after missing 35 of 40 previously in career . . . Born Sept. 29, 1964, in New Ulm, Minn., same small town that produced Terry Steinbach of Oakland A's . . . Earned $520,000.

Year	Team	G	FG	FG Pct.	FT	FT Pct.	Reb.	Ast.	TP	Avg.
1987-88	Boston	70	122	.496	50	.806	138	49	297	4.2
1988-89	Bos.-Sac.	77	210	.432	81	.786	256	66	502	6.5
1989-90	Minn.-Mil.	80	305	.460	75	.728	398	168	732	9.2
	Totals	227	637	.457	206	.769	792	283	1531	6.7

FRANK KORNET 23 6-9 225   Forward

Rookie bench fodder . . . Good practice player who showed flashes of being able to run court . . . Provides occasional trifecta bomb . . . Strong, active body . . . Played just 438 minutes after becoming only the third non-first rounder to make Milwaukee's opening-day roster in 1980s . . . Was second-round pick (30th overall) out of Vanderbilt . . . Bucks hoping for same steady improvement he showed throughout college career . . . Three-year deal brought him $175,000 last season . . . Born Jan. 27, 1967, in Lexington, Ky.

Year	Team	G	FG	FG Pct.	FT	FT Pct.	Reb.	Ast.	TP	Avg.
1989-90	Milwaukee	57	42	.368	24	.615	71	21	113	2.0

GREG ANDERSON 26 6-10 230   Forward

The answer to Terry Cummings left a lot of questions . . . Inconsistent season overshadowed by injuries . . . Missed first month with knee surgery, later popped hamstring and quadriceps . . . Averages of 8.8 ppg and 6.2 rpg well below marks of 12.7 and 7.3 for first two seasons . . . A quality shot-blocker and rebounder . . . Used to work out regularly against Akeem Olajuwon in Houston community center while in college, and it helped him become a ferocious offensive rebounder . . . Came from San Antonio with Alvin Robertson and second-rounder for Cummings . . . Known as The Cadillac, from cruising around the University of Houston on his bicycle . . . Still learning the game and has a wealth of athletic skills . . . Plays some backup center . . . Born June 22, 1964, in Houston . . . Sleeper pick by San Antonio on first round in 1987 . . . Earned $247,000.

Year	Team	G	FG	FG Pct.	FT	FT Pct.	Reb.	Ast.	TP	Avg.
1987-88	San Antonio	82	379	.501	198	.604	513	79	957	11.7
1988-89	San Antonio	82	460	.503	207	.514	676	61	1127	13.7
1989-90	Milwaukee	60	219	.507	91	.535	373	24	529	8.8
	Totals	224	1058	.503	496	.550	1562	164	2613	11.7

TITO HORFORD 24 7-1 245   Center

Bucks have forgotten Godot, they're still waiting for Tito . . . And waiting . . . Second year of three-year plan gave no reason to believe it's going to happen in our lifetime . . . Great athletic body, but court smarts are not exactly in abundance . . . Remember, potential is a word meaning a guy hasn't done it . . . Only in seventh season of playing ball, however . . . Ultimate project . . . Was Milwaukee's second-round pick (39th overall) as undergrad in 1988 . . . Played two so-so years at U. of Miami after committing to LSU and not playing there . . . Got $130,000.

Year	Team	G	FG	FG Pct.	FT	FT Pct.	Reb.	Ast.	TP	Avg.
1988-89	Milwaukee	25	15	.326	12	.632	22	3	42	1.7
1989-90	Milwaukee	35	18	.290	15	.625	59	2	51	1.5
	Totals	60	33	.306	27	.628	81	5	93	1.6

TONY BROWN 30 6-6 195   Forward-Guard

He's going. No, staying. Going. Staying . . . Was on the bubble all season and seemed destined for waiver wire as one Buck after another came off injured list . . . But then one Buck after another went back on injury list, saving his job . . . Fifth NBA team with two CBA stints since being fourth-round pick of Nets in 1982 . . . Played collegiately at Arkansas . . . Good role player, known for defensive intensity . . . Frank Layden once said,

"That Tony whatzisname is a pretty good player." . . . Inconsistent outside jumper has always haunted him . . . Ideal 11th or 12th man . . . Never complains . . . Born July 29, 1960, in Chicago . . . Earned $150,000 last season.

Year	Team	G	FG	FG Pct.	FT	FT Pct.	Reb.	Ast.	TP	Avg.
1984-85	Indiana.	82	214	.460	116	.678	288	159	544	6.6
1985-86	Chicago	10	18	.439	9	.692	16	14	45	4.5
1986-87	New Jersey.	77	358	.442	152	.738	219	259	873	11.3
1988-89	Hou.-Mil.	43	50	.424	24	.774	44	26	128	3.0
1989-90	Milwaukee	61	88	.427	38	.679	72	41	219	3.6
	Totals	273	728	.444	339	.711	639	499	1809	6.6

THE ROOKIE

STEVE HENSON 22 6-1 180   Guard
Real gym rat . . . Four-year starter at Kansas State, became the No. 44 overall pick in the draft . . . Fabulous free-throw shooter, shot .900 for four years, including national-best .925 as a soph . . . First player ever to lead Wildcats two years running in scoring and assists . . . Averaged 17.4 ppg as a senior and shot 46 percent from three-point range . . . May have trouble with his size landing a spot with guard-heavy Bucks . . . Born Feb. 2, 1968, in Junction City, Kan.

COACH DEL HARRIS: Yes, he resembles Man From Glad.

And yes, he has been known as Dull Harris. But yes, he is a terrific coach . . . Only third Bucks' head coach since franchise inception in 1968 . . . Begins fourth year in Milwaukee . . . Faced unenviable task of replacing highly popular Don Nelson and has survived slings and arrows . . . Guided Bucks through a staggering rash of injuries to 44-victory season . . . Bucks established team record and led NBA with 235 manpower games lost to injury . . . NBA coaching record is 276-296 . . . Coached four years in Houston and brought Rockets to NBA Finals in 1981 . . . Big preparation guy. Low-key exterior hides intense, competitive fire . . . Born June 18, 1937, in Orleans, Ind. . . . Played at Milligan (Tenn.) College and studied religion . . . A former minister . . . Coached for nine years at Earlham College in Richmond, Ind.

GREATEST REBOUNDER

He'll no doubt always be thought of as a Laker, but in his first six NBA seasons, Kareem Abdul-Jabbar performed with brilliance Milwaukee will never forget.

The man who began the Bucks on their perennial drive toward consistency—not to mention their first NBA title—grabbed more rebounds (7,161) and scored more points (14,211) than any Buck ever. His 467 games in Milwaukee, back when he had hair, produced a rebounding average of 15.3.

Abdul-Jabbar, whose hyphenated name is synonymous with NBA records, remains the greatest single-season Buck boarder, thanks to the 1,346 he grabbed in 1971-72.

ALL-TIME BUCK LEADERS

SEASON

Points: Kareem Abdul-Jabbar, 2,822, 1971-72
Assists: Oscar Robertson, 668, 1970-71
Rebounds: Kareem Abdul-Jabbar, 1,346, 1971-72

GAME

Points: Kareem Abdul-Jabbar, 55 vs. Boston, 12/10/71
Assists: Guy Rodgers, 22 vs. Detroit, 10/31/68
Rebounds: Swen Nater, 33 vs. Atlanta, 12/19/76

CAREER

Points: Kareem Abdul-Jabbar, 14,211, 1969-75
Assists: Paul Pressey, 3,272, 1982-90
Rebounds: Kareem Abdul-Jabbar, 7,161, 1969-75

NEW JERSEY NETS

TEAM DIRECTORY: Chairman: Alan Aufzien; Pres.: Bernie Mann; Exec. VP-Chief Operating Officer: Bob Casciola; Sr. VP-Basketball Oper.: Willis Reed; Dir. Pub. Rel.: John Mertz; Coach: Bill Fitch; Asst. Coach: Rick Carlisle. Arena: Brendan Byrne Meadowlands Arena (20,039). Colors: Red, white and blue.

Nets pray Syracuse's Derrick Coleman justifies No. 1 pick.

SCOUTING REPORT

SHOOTING: AARGH!!! Absolutely, positively the worst anywhere. The Nets shot an incredibly inept .426, the worst mark in the NBA history of the franchise, the worst mark by any team since the 1975-76 Bulls put up blind-man .414 numbers.

The Nets achieved this staggering low point in a variety of ways: through shot selection that should have warranted execution, rather than benching; through stupidity, and through a basic lack of talent. Of the 19 players who appeared in games last season, only two were above 50 percent: Roy Hinson (who played all of 25 games) and Stanley Brundy (who played 16 games and was bounced for drugs).

Newcomer Reggie Theus was only .439 in Orlando, but he'll definitely help. He certainly won't shy away from any shots and he's a proven scorer.

Offender Dennis Hopson, a .434 bust, was traded to Chicago. What remains are alleged professionals so the Nets should get better, but only if they improve their awful decision-making.

PLAYMAKING: The Nets came up with a good one in Mookie Blaylock, who assumed the starter's role, then broke a finger and wound up playing only 50 games. But being a playmaker on a team with such shooting deficiencies as the Nets is like being a great swimmer in the desert. They should get better—they have to—and the addition of Tate George, the 6-5 rookie from Connecticut, will help. He is fundamentally sound and can play either guard spot.

DEFENSE: Double AARGH!!! Opponents shot .485 and outscored the Nets by nearly eight points a game. There actually are some bright points here, though. Like Sam Bowie, who in his first full season in eons, showed nice shot-blocking capabilities. And Lester Conner, a competent reserve point who simply had to start. He came up with 2.10 steals per to rank him in the top 10.

Chris Morris also showed a good penchant for playing the passing lanes, as his 130 steals attest. But overall, the Nets suffered too many defensive breakdowns, too often failed to rotate or bring help. Perhaps in the second year of coach Bill Fitch's reign, things will improve.

REBOUNDING: Hate to be redundant, but AARGH!!! again. Not only didn't the Nets shoot, but they didn't rebound their misses

NET ROSTER

No.	Veterans	Pos.	Ht.	Wt.	Age	Yrs. Pro	College
10	Mookie Blaylock	G	6-1	185	23	1	Oklahoma
31	Sam Bowie	C	7-1	240	29	6	Kentucky
21	Stanley Brundy	F	6-7	215	22	1	DePaul
15	Lester Conner	G	6-4	185	30	7	Oregon State
22	Chris Dudley	C-F	6-11	242	25	3	Yale
24	Derrick Gervin	F	6-8	215	27	1	Texas-San Antonio
44	Jack Haley	F-C	6-10	240	26	2	UCLA
23	Roy Hinson	F-C	6-9	215	29	7	Rutgers
42	Anthony Mason	F	6-7	253	23	1	Tennessee State
34	Chris Morris	F	6-8	210	24	2	Auburn
7	Pete Myers	G-F	6-6	180	27	4	Arkansas-Little Rock
45	Purvis Short	F	6-7	220	33	12	Jackson State
—	Reggie Theus	G	6-7	213	33	12	Nevada-Las Vegas
—	Leon Wood	G	6-3	185	28	5	Cal-Fullerton

Rd.	Rookies	Sel. No.	Pos.	Ht.	Wt.	College
1	Derrick Coleman	1	F	6-10	235	Syracuse
1	Tate George	22	G	6-5	190	Connecticut
2	Jud Buechler	38	F	6-6	223	Arizona
2	*Michael Cutright	42	G	6-3	210	McNeese State

*Drafted by Nuggets in 1989

adequately. A statistical review is deceiving: the Nets averaged a league-high 16.6 offensive boards. But they also averaged a league-high 51.9 missed field goals a game. Throw in one night of Chris Dudley going to the foul line, and the Nets averaged about 70 misses a game. But here is where legitimate help is on the way. The Nets had the No. 1 pick in the draft and they selected Derrick Coleman of Syracuse, the leading rebounder in NCAA history.

OUTLOOK: Whenever the Nets are concerned, lottery status is virtually assured. This season should be no exception. But the Nets figure to show real, honest-to-goodness improvement on an 1989-90 season that was an utter disaster in every sense. A big key is the health of Hinson, whose knee woes limited him to 25 games. Another big element is that the Nets will embark on their second season under Fitch and should have a better grasp of his system. A 17-victory disgrace, the Nets could easily double that output and land again in the lottery, where the rebuilding could take another quantum leap.

NET PROFILES

ROY HINSON 29 6-9 215 — Forward-Center

Take my contract. Please... Has been in Cleveland and Philadelphia but never knew what hell was until coming to New Jersey in 1988 trade that made Mike Gminski a Sixer... Withstood the chaos for over two full seasons, now starting to wear down... Wasted season due to knee injury... Felt Nets played him too long with bum joint... Proven scorer and rebounder, superb shot-blocker... Has shown he can spell at center ... Looked like he'd flourish with Sam Bowie aboard but Nets will have to wait until this season to see... Played at Rutgers and was 20th overall pick in 1983 by Cavaliers... Went to Philly in 1986 for No. 1 pick in draft (Brad Daugherty)... Born May 2, 1961, in Trenton, N.J.... Made $800,000.

Year	Team	G	FG	FG Pct.	FT	FT Pct.	Reb.	Ast.	TP	Avg.
1983-84	Cleveland	80	184	.496	69	.590	499	69	437	5.5
1984-85	Cleveland	76	465	.503	271	.721	596	68	1201	15.8
1985-86	Cleveland	82	621	.532	364	.719	639	102	1606	19.6
1986-87	Philadelphia	76	393	.478	273	.758	488	60	1059	13.9
1987-88	Phil.-N.J.	77	453	.487	272	.775	517	99	1178	15.3
1988-89	New Jersey	82	495	.482	318	.757	522	71	1308	16.0
1989-90	New Jersey	25	145	.507	86	.869	172	22	376	15.0
	Totals	498	2756	.498	1653	.742	3433	491	7165	14.4

CHRIS MORRIS 24 6-8 210 — Forward

Right up there with Charlotte's Rex Chapman for worst shot selection in league... Selection has improved though, moving from abominable to simply abhorrent... A 42 percent shooter ... Absolutely phenomenal athletic talent... Needs tons of discipline in all aspects of game ... Suspended by coach Bill Fitch for calling the organization "——" among other choice words... Ball-handling a disaster, too. Led team in turnovers, which wouldn't be too bad if he were a point guard... Nets have preached patience, patience, patience since making Auburn product the No. 4 pick in 1988... Born Jan. 20, 1966, in Atlanta... Attitude and work ethic have been questioned since college, where some say he was more talented than Charles Barkley and Chuck Person . . . Made about $750,000.

Year	Team	G	FG	FG Pct.	FT	FT Pct.	Reb.	Ast.	TP	Avg.
1988-89	New Jersey......	76	414	.457	182	.717	397	119	1074	14.1
1989-90	New Jersey......	80	449	.422	228	.722	422	143	1187	14.8
	Totals	156	863	.438	410	.719	819	262	2261	14.5

SAM BOWIE 29 7-1 240   Center

Comeback of the Year, without question . . . NBA stopped giving out the award because it always went to a reformed druggie, but Bowie would have earned it in truest sense . . . Came to Nets with first-round pick in trade for Buck Williams in 1989 . . . Gave Nets legitimate inside help . . . Solid low-post player and good shot-blocker . . . Led team in boards (10.1) and blocks (1.78) . . . Of course, no Bowie season would be complete without injury: missed last six games with bone bruise in right foot . . . Injuries have dogged him since college career at Kentucky, where he missed two seasons with foot ailments . . . Dedicated sort who has come back from the dead more times than Dracula . . . Remember, he was the guy Portland drafted over Michael Jordan with No. 2 pick in 1984 draft . . . Born March 17, 1961, in Lebanon, Pa. . . . Good talker, nice man . . . Renegotiated contract into five-year, $13-million deal.

Year	Team	G	FG	FG Pct.	FT	FT Pct.	Reb.	Ast.	TP	Avg.
1984-85	Portland.........	76	299	.537	160	.711	656	215	758	10.0
1985-86	Portland.........	38	167	.484	114	.708	327	99	448	11.8
1986-87	Portland.........	5	30	.455	20	.667	33	9	80	16.0
1987-88	Portland.........					Injured				
1988-89	Portland.........	20	69	.451	28	.571	106	36	171	8.6
1989-90	New Jersey......	68	347	.416	294	.776	690	91	998	14.7
	Totals	207	912	.466	616	.730	1812	450	2455	11.9

REGGIE THEUS 33 6-7 213   Guard

From cover boy to traveling man . . . Handsome, once-prolific scorer joins fourth team in four years . . . Came to New Jersey from Orlando for second-round picks in 1993 and 1995 . . . Ranks sixth among active players in scoring . . . Drafted No. 9 as ''hardship'' in 1978 first round out of Nevada-Las Vegas by Chicago . . . Had two of his four 20-plus-average seasons with the Bulls . . . Traded for Steve Johnson and trio of second-round picks to Kings on Feb. 15, 1984 . . . Led team in assists four straight years, had two successive 20-plus seasons after Kings moved to Sacramento . . . Traded for Randy Wittman and first-round pick June 27, 1988, to Atlanta to "solve" Hawks' off-guard woes . . . Didn't . . . Expansion pick of Orlando . . . Had second-poorest shooting (.439) of career, but matched previous 11-year scoring average . . . Born Oct. 13, 1957, in Inglewood, Cal.

Year	Team	G	FG	FG Pct.	FT	FT Pct.	Reb.	Ast.	TP	Avg.
1978-79	Chicago	82	537	.480	264	.761	228	429	1338	16.3
1979-80	Chicago	82	566	.483	500	.838	329	515	1660	20.2
1980-81	Chicago	82	543	.495	445	.809	287	426	1549	18.9
1981-82	Chicago	82	560	.469	363	.808	312	476	1508	18.4
1982-83	Chicago	82	749	.478	434	.801	300	484	1953	23.8
1983-84	Chi.-K.C.	61	262	.419	214	.762	129	352	745	12.2
1984-85	Kansas City	82	501	.487	334	.863	270	656	1341	16.4
1985-86	Sacramento	82	546	.480	405	.827	304	788	1503	18.3
1986-87	Sacramento	79	577	.472	429	.867	266	692	1600	20.3
1987-88	Sacramento	73	619	.470	320	.831	232	463	1574	21.6
1988-89	Atlanta	82	497	.466	285	.851	242	387	1296	15.8
1989-90	Orlando	76	517	.439	378	.853	221	407	1438	18.9
	Totals	945	6474	.472	4371	.825	3120	6075	17505	18.5

CHRIS DUDLEY 25 6-11 242   Center

The Legend . . . Incredibly missed 18 of 19 free throws in game vs. Pacers on April 14, 1990 . . . Claimed he was trying new style . . . Hasn't tried blind-folded yet . . . Worst free-throw shooter in the galaxy . . . Well, at least worst free-throw shooter in league at .319 (58-of-182) . . . Has some pluses, though . . . Smart defender . . . Good, tough rebounder who unfortunately gets fouled a lot going back up with offensive boards . . . Third generation Yalie . . . Grandfather Guilford Dudley was ambassador to Denmark under Nixon and Ford . . . Sixth Yale grad ever drafted, only third ever to play . . . Cavs' fourth-round pick in 1987 . . . Born Feb. 22, 1965, in Stamford, Conn. . . . Keep those foul-shooting tips coming.

Year	Team	G	FG	FG Pct.	FT	FT Pct.	Reb.	Ast.	TP	Avg.
1987-88	Cleveland	55	65	.474	40	.563	144	23	170	3.1
1988-89	Cleveland	61	73	.435	39	.364	157	21	185	3.0
1989-90	Clev.-N.J.	64	146	.411	58	.319	423	39	350	5.5
	Totals	180	284	.430	137	.381	724	83	705	3.9

DERRICK GERVIN 27 6-8 215   Forward

Yep, he's George's brother. Just look at the shots and assists: 197 shots, eight assists... So what? Among virtually everything else, Nets needed points... And he brought them that, averaging a point a minute in his first 90 minutes... Showed nice knack for getting to the basket... Nets rescued him from CBA at midseason and after two 10-day contracts, signed him for remainder of season and next season. Will get in mid-$200,000s... Missed last 12 games with herniated disc... Obviously, offense oriented. Nicknamed, "Cool No D"... Born March 28, 1963, in Detroit... Went to Texas-San Antonio and was drafted by Philadelphia in fourth round (90th selection) in 1985... Did stints in CBA, Spain and Italy.

Year	Team	G	FG	FG Pct.	FT	FT Pct.	Reb.	Ast.	TP	Avg.
1989-90	New Jersey	21	93	.472	65	.730	65	8	251	12.0

LESTER CONNER 31 6-4 185   Guard

Sorry, he should not be an NBA starter... Was supposed to babysit Mookie Blaylock, but wound up starting bulk of games... Real inconsistent, disappointing season... Shot awful .414 and assists dropped from 604 to 385... Hey, but he's a nice guy... And he did manage 2.1 steals, eighth-best in league, and just 1.7 turnovers... No question, though, he's a backup, which is what Nets envision even if he doesn't... Born Sept. 17, 1959, in Memphis, Tenn.... Was drafted in 1982 on first round by Warriors out of Oregon State... Came to Nets from Rockets along with Joe Barry Carroll in 1988 for Frank Johnson, Tony Brown, Lorenzo Romar and Tim McCormick... Made $1 million.

Year	Team	G	FG	FG Pct.	FT	FT Pct.	Reb.	Ast.	TP	Avg.
1982-83	Golden State	75	145	.479	79	.699	221	253	369	4.9
1983-84	Golden State	82	360	.493	186	.718	305	401	907	11.1
1984-85	Golden State	79	246	.451	144	.750	246	369	640	8.1
1985-86	Golden State	36	51	.375	40	.741	62	43	144	4.0
1987-88	Houston	52	50	.463	32	.780	38	59	132	2.5
1988-89	New Jersey	82	309	.457	212	.788	355	604	843	10.3
1989-90	New Jersey	82	237	.414	172	.804	265	385	648	7.9
	Totals	488	1398	.455	865	.757	1492	2114	3683	7.5

MOOKIE BLAYLOCK 23 6-1 185   Guard

Made the trade of Buck Williams a little easier to digest . . . At least he's no Pearl Washington . . . Or so Nets hope . . . Was New Jersey's first-round (No. 12) pick in 1989 out of Oklahoma, where he became first player ever with more than 200 assists and 100 steals in successive seasons . . . Former Nets' GM Harry Weltman introduced him to media as "Mookie Wilson" . . . Welcome to New Jersey . . . Handed starting point-guard job on Jan. 3 and brought pretty good direction, averaging 12.5 points and over six assists . . . Then broke little finger on left hand and sat until four games remained . . . Some questioned his desire . . . Pushes ball well and is strong defender . . . Shot selection shaky at times . . . Born March 20, 1967, in Garland, Tex. . . . Made about $600,000 last year.

Year	Team	G	FG	FG Pct.	FT	FT Pct.	Reb.	Ast.	TP	Avg.
1989-90	New Jersey	50	212	.371	63	.778	140	210	505	10.1

ANTHONY MASON 23 6-7 253   Forward

A hulkster who could be stand-in for King Kong remake . . . Purely garbage-time performer, showed some skills around the basket . . . Cameoed for 108 minutes . . . Began season on injured list with summer-league stress fracture . . . Involved in infamous Atlanta limousine incident where he and teammates blew curfew, trashed limo and tried to stiff driver . . . Enough said about his smarts . . . Born Dec. 14, 1966, in Miami, Fla. . . . Tennessee State product drafted on third round by Portland in 1988 . . . Signed as free agent by Nets.

Year	Team	G	FG	FG Pct.	FT	FT Pct.	Reb.	Ast.	TP	Avg.
1989-90	New Jersey	21	14	.350	9	.600	34	7	37	1.8

JACK HALEY 26 6-10 240   Forward-Center

Married to an actress, has appeared in rock videos and commercials . . . Has even occasionally appeared in NBA games . . . Tough, no-nonsense, won't-back-down type . . . Once picked a fight with Charles Barkley . . . Showed guts, not smarts. Barkley then went off and tore Nets apart . . . In 56 games with Nets, grabbed 108 offensive rebounds . . . Good on glass, but not too hot on putting it back up . . . Shot just .398 overall, which isn't too great when you're 6-10 and an inside player . . . Perfect 12th man. Accepts role and hustles and bangs. Unfortunately, with Nets, he's more like eighth or ninth man . . . Born Jan. 27, 1964, in Seal Beach, Cal. . . . UCLA product was Chicago's fourth-round pick in 1987 before hitting the Europe trail for season . . . Waiver wire pickup by Nets.

Year	Team	G	FG	FG Pct.	FT	FT Pct.	Reb.	Ast.	TP	Avg.
1988-89	Chicago	51	37	.474	36	.783	71	10	110	2.2
1989-90	Chi.-N.J.	67	138	.398	85	.680	300	26	361	5.4
	Totals	118	175	.412	121	.708	371	36	471	4.0

PETE MYERS 27 6-6 180   Guard

Was waived by Bulls, Sixers and Knicks . . . And was absolutely stunned when Knicks released him on trade deadline day . . . Competitive, defensive specialist . . . Terrific in pressing situation . . . Was Michael Jordan's practice shadow for over year with Bulls. Claims that's where he learned "D" . . . Extremely limited offensive game. No range on shot, often poor shot selection . . . Knicks claimed he was locker-room disruption because he whined for more playing time and back-stabbed some starters . . . Nets overjoyed to get him . . . Born Sept. 15, 1963, in Mobile, Ala. . . . Arkansas-Little Rock product was sixth-round pick of Bulls in 1986 . . . Paid $175,000.

Year	Team	G	FG	FG Pct.	FT	FT Pct.	Reb.	Ast.	TP	Avg.
1986-87	Chicago	29	19	.365	28	.651	17	21	66	2.3
1987-88	San Antonio	22	43	.453	26	.667	37	48	112	5.1
1988-89	Phil.-NY	33	31	.425	33	.688	33	48	95	2.9
1989-90	N.Y.-N.J.	52	89	.396	66	.660	96	135	244	4.7
	Totals	136	182	.409	153	.665	183	252	517	3.8

PURVIS SHORT 33 6-7 220   Forward

Why didn't contenders go after this guy? . . . Can still contribute in proper situation with that pretty rainbow jumper . . . Played too many minutes (27.0 per) and legs gave out, especially defensively . . . Averaged 13.1 ppg, second-lowest total in 12-year career . . . But he passed 14,000-point mark and played in all 82 games . . . Played nine years in Golden State before trade to Houston for Dave Feitl and first-rounder... Never known for lateral quickness, so teams really go at him on defense... Signed free-agent contract with Nets for $500,000... Born July 2, 1957, in Hattiesburg, Miss.... Warriors made him fifth selection in 1978 after career at Jackson State.

Year	Team	G	FG	FG Pct.	FT	FT Pct.	Reb.	Ast.	TP	Avg.
1978-79	Golden State	75	369	.479	57	.671	347	97	795	10.6
1979-80	Golden State	62	461	.503	134	.812	316	123	1056	17.0
1980-81	Golden State	79	549	.475	168	.820	391	249	1269	16.1
1981-82	Golden State	76	456	.488	177	.801	266	209	1095	14.4
1982-83	Golden State	67	589	.487	255	.828	354	228	1437	21.4
1983-84	Golden State	79	714	.473	353	.793	438	246	1803	22.8
1984-85	Golden State	78	819	.460	501	.817	398	234	2186	28.0
1985-86	Golden State	64	633	.482	351	.865	329	237	1632	25.5
1986-87	Golden State	34	240	.479	137	.856	137	86	621	18.3
1987-88	Houston	81	474	.481	206	.858	222	162	1159	14.3
1988-89	Houston	65	198	.413	77	.865	179	107	482	7.4
1989-90	New Jersey	82	432	.455	198	.835	248	145	1072	13.1
	Totals	842	5934	.474	2614	.824	3625	2123	14607	17.3

MICHAEL CUTRIGHT 23 6-3 230   Guard

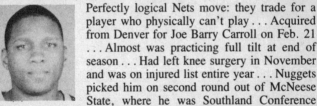

Perfectly logical Nets move: they trade for a player who physically can't play... Acquired from Denver for Joe Barry Carroll on Feb. 21 ... Almost was practicing full tilt at end of season... Had left knee surgery in November and was on injured list entire year... Nuggets picked him on second round out of McNeese State, where he was Southland Conference Player of the Year in 1988-89... Muscular two-guard who some compare to Vinnie Johnson... Minimum-wage earner at $125,000... Born May 10, 1967, in Zwolle, La.

THE ROOKIES

DERRICK COLEMAN 23 6-10 235   Forward

Somebody has to rebound all those missed Chris Dudley free throws... The No. 1 pick in the nation last June, the Syracuse consensus All-American was generally regarded as the plum of the draft... Scott Layden, Utah's director of player personnel, called Coleman "a young Karl Malone"... Set NCAA record with 1,537 career rebounds... Averaged career highs of 17.9 points, 12.1 rebounds as a senior... Potentially awesome low-post presence . . . Good shot-blocker . . . Handles ball exceptionally well for his size . . . Broke Sherman Douglas' Syracuse scoring record by amassing 2,143 points . . . Born June 21, 1967, in Detroit.

TATE GEORGE 22 6-5 190   Guard

Returns to scene of his "Meadowlands Miracle" shot that beat Clemson at final buzzer for Connecticut in NCAA East Regional . . . Nets made no bones why they picked him at No. 22 with slot obtained from Bulls for Dennis Hopson: "He's a happy guy, a cheerleader type. We need that kind of chemistry here," said coach Bill Fitch . . . Oh, and he can play . . . "He has good point-guard skills and defensive ability," endorsed superscout Marty Blake . . . An 11.5 ppg scorer as a senior on a team where offense took back seat to swarming, relentless defense.

JUD BUECHLER 22 6-6 223   Forward

A real steal . . . Nets picked him up from Seattle, which made him 38th pick, for agreeing not to draft Gary Payton with No. 1 pick . . . Nets weren't going to, anyway . . . Nothing flashy, just sound all-around smart player who averaged 14.9 points and 8.3 rebounds for Arizona while earning All-Pac 10 status . . . Born June 19, 1968.

COACH BILL FITCH: Figured the job would be tough, not 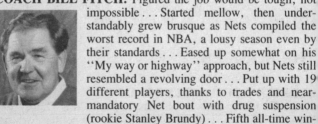 impossible . . . Started mellow, then understandably grew brusque as Nets compiled the worst record in NBA, a lousy season even by their standards . . . Eased up somewhat on his "My way or highway" approach, but Nets still resembled a revolving door . . . Put up with 19 different players, thanks to trades and near-mandatory Net bout with drug suspension (rookie Stanley Brundy) . . . Fifth all-time winningest coach with 779 regular-season victories . . . Two-time NBA Coach of the Year, with Cavs (1975-76) and with Celts (1979-80) . . . Led Celts to NBA title in 1980-81 . . . Entering 20th head coaching season. Figures to have a lot more say in franchise operations . . . College stints at alma mater Coe (Iowa) College,

North Dakota, Bowling Green and Minnesota . . . Assistant basketball and head baseball coach at Creighton, where he coached Hall of Fame pitcher Bob Gibson in both sports . . . Masters degree in educational psychology from Creighton . . . Born May 19, 1934, in Davenport, Iowa.

GREATEST REBOUNDER

Through their darkest days, Buck Williams was probably the Nets' lone link to respectability. And definitely their link to rebounding competitiveness.

Williams, now successfully plying his blue-collar trade in Portland, is one of only eight NBA players to grab 1,000 rebounds in each of his first four pro seasons. He completed his eight-year Net sentence as the greatest rebounder in franchise history. And by a lot.

His 7,576 Net rebounds (12.1 average) are more than double the second-best Net total of 3,671 by Mike Gminski. Still Maryland's second greatest rebounder (he left after his junior season), Williams owns a single-game NBA high of 27 boards.

ALL-TIME NET LEADERS

SEASON

Points: Rick Barry, 2,518, 1971-72 (ABA)
Assists: Kevin Porter, 801, 1977-78
Rebounds: Billy Paultz, 1,035, 1971-72 (ABA)

GAME

Points: Julius Erving, 63 vs. San Diego (4 OT), 2/14/75 (ABA)
Assists: Kevin Porter, 29 vs. Houston, 2/24/78
Rebounds: Billy Paultz, 33 vs. Pittsburgh, 2/17/71 (ABA)

CAREER

Points: Buck Williams, 10,440, 1981-89
Assists: Billy Melchionni, 2,251, 1969-75 (ABA)
Rebounds: Buck Williams, 7,576, 1981-89

NEW YORK KNICKS

TEAM DIRECTORY: Pres.: Richard Evans; VP-GM: Al Bianchi; Exec. VP/MSG Sports Group: Jack Diller; Dir. Administration: Hal Childs; Dir. Scouting Services: Dick McGuire; Dir. Communications: John Cirillo; Publicity Mgr.: Dennis D'Agostino; Coach: Stu Jackson; Asst. Coaches: Paul Silas, Ernie Grunfeld, Jeff Van Gundy. Arena: Madison Square Garden (18,212). Colors: Orange, white and blue.

First-team NBA doesn't say it all for Patrick Ewing.

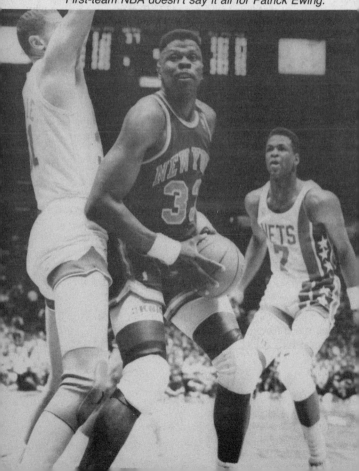

SCOUTING REPORT

SHOOTING: The highly respectable .484 team mark is deceiving. Take away Patrick Ewing's .551 stud marksmanship and the Knicks tumble down to .464. Take away Charles Oakley's .524 and the plunge is even more drastic. You get the picture: take the Knicks away from underneath and it gets ugly.

The perimeter game was as reliable as the weather. That had a lot to do with drafting of Jerrod Mustaf, whom the Knicks feel will develop into a reliable shooting small forward. Trent Tucker (.417) was a big disappointment and Gerald Wilkins (.457) was too inconsistent. Mark Jackson's .437 effort was one reason why he gave way to Maurice Cheeks at the point. The Knicks will need to replace the departed Johnny Newman's 12.9 average.

PLAYMAKING: The young, creative, crowd-pleasing whiz, Rod Strickland, is gone. Jackson is trying to return to being just that, but must remember substance comes before flash. And on hand to remind him is the wondrous veteran, Cheeks, whose very presence makes a team a better playmaking bunch.

Of course, creativity was a failed course for much of the year as the Knicks tried to go forward in a halfcourt game with running players. There are exceptions, but overall, the Knicks are simply not a good passing team. Those 17.2 turnovers per game—and remember, they spent much of the season in a set-it-up mode—are not the mark of a bunch of passing fancies.

DEFENSE: The Knicks' defense—like everything else—starts with the big guy in the middle, Ewing. The second most efficient shot-blocker in the league, Ewing forces dozens of alterations and causes teams to think thrice about attacking the middle. But give Ewing a rest or a third foul early and a neon "Welcome" sign flashes in the paint. Teams simply challenge with abandon.

Other areas of the Knick defensive game suffer, too. Newman was a generally underrated defender, but he could be bullied at small forward, as can Kenny Walker at the power slot when he fills in for Oakley. Simply, the Knicks must upgrade their transition and halfcourt defense if they expect to move up a level.

KNICK ROSTER

No.	Veterans	Pos.	Ht.	Wt.	Age	Yrs. Pro	College
1	Maurice Cheeks	G	6-1	180	34	12	West Texas State
33	Patrick Ewing	C	7-0	240	28	5	Georgetown
40	Stuart Gray	C	7-0	245	27	6	UCLA
13	Mark Jackson	G	6-3	205	25	3	St. John's
34	Charles Oakley	F	6-9	245	26	5	Virginia Union
23	Brian Quinnett	F	6-8	236	24	1	Washington State
6	Trent Tucker	G	6-5	200	30	8	Minnesota
55	Kiki Vandeweghe	F	6-8	220	32	10	UCLA
7	Kenny Walker	F	6-8	217	26	4	Kentucky
45	Eddie Lee Wilkins	F-C	6-10	220	28	5	Gardner-Webb
21	Gerald Wilkins	G	6-6	200	27	5	Tenn.-Chattanooga

Rd.	Rookies	Sel. No.	Pos.	Ht.	Wt.	College
1	Jerrod Mustaf	17	F	6-10	244	Maryland

REBOUNDING: When they're good, they're great. When they're not, they're horrid. With Ewing (10.9) and Oakley (11.9) up front, the Knicks had their first double-digit rebounding pair since Jerry Lucas and Dave DeBusschere turned the trick in 1971-72. And after Ewing and Oakley, there's er... there's um ... not a heckuva lot. At small forward, the Knicks were the worst rebounding team in the league with Newman and Kiki Vandeweghe turning in 1, 2 or 3 routinely. One offseason quest was to find size for the frontline and the search might take the Knicks to the trading deadline.

OUTLOOK: Stu Jackson's Knicks were not nearly as good as their record of 35-17 indicated at one point. Nor were they as bad as the 10-20 mark they posted at the finish. They underwent change of the first order: in coaches, in personnel, in lineups. With return visits to the up-tempo style to which they are infinitely more suited, with a force like Ewing in the middle and with residence in a division that has no clear-cut dominant power, the Knicks could again rise to the top of the Atlantic Division—especially if Vandeweghe can shed his injury problems. But unless some gaping holes are plugged, they will remain, at best, a second-round play-off team.

KNICK PROFILES

PATRICK EWING 28 7-0 240   Center

Bow head when name is mentioned in New York . . . Had sensational record-setting season that culminated with first-team All-NBA selection . . . Only player to rank in top 10 for scoring (28.6), rebounding (10.9), blocks (3.99) and field-goal percentage (.551) . . . His 2,347 points set club record . . . Scored 40 or better 11 times, rebounded 20 or better three times.
. . . Established single-game career high with 51 points vs. Celtics on March 24 . . . Starred in playoffs (29.4 ppg), but Knicks' slim second-round chances virtually ended when he was called for third foul early in second quarter of Game 4 . . . Constantly adding to offensive arsenal and developed almost unstoppable lefty hook . . . Is everything folks thought he'd be out of Georgetown, where he became College Player of the 1980s . . . True gentleman whose only aim is winning . . . At times last year he felt he had to do everything himself. That's because he very often had to . . . First-ever NBA lottery prize in '85 . . . Born Aug. 5, 1962, in Kingston, Jamaica . . . Was NBA's highest-paid last season at $4 million.

Year	Team	G	FG	FG Pct.	FT	FT Pct.	Reb.	Ast.	TP	Avg.
1985-86	New York	50	386	.474	226	.739	451	102	998	20.0
1986-87	New York	63	530	.503	296	.713	555	104	1356	21.5
1987-88	New York	82	656	.555	341	.716	676	125	1653	20.2
1988-89	New York	80	727	.567	361	.746	740	188	1815	22.7
1989-90	New York	82	922	.551	502	.775	893	182	2347	28.6
	Totals	357	3221	.536	1726	.741	3315	701	8169	22.9

MAURICE CHEEKS 34 6-1 180   Guard

Oh, to be his agent . . . Widespread talk of his retirement enhanced bargaining position after coming to Knicks from Spurs in the controversial swap for Rod Strickland on Feb. 21, 1990, as Knicks dealt youth for "maturity, experience and stability." . . . Longtime mainstay in Philadelphia before he was dealt to San Antonio on Aug. 8, 1989, in trade that left him bitter: he found out through media . . . Classy pro averaged 7.9 points and 4.9 assists in 31 games for New York as he ultimately supplanted Mark Jackson as starter . . . Turned in her-

oic 48-minute, 21-point effort in Game 5 upset of Celtics . . .
All-time NBA steals leader with 2,066 . . . Second-round pick of
Philly from West Texas State in '78 . . . Born Sept. 8, 1956, in
Chicago . . . Remarkable clutch player whose playoff scoring average
is three points higher than regular-season mark.

Year	Team	G	FG	FG Pct.	FT	FT Pct.	Reb.	Ast.	TP	Avg.
1978-79	Philadelphia	82	292	.510	101	.721	254	431	685	8.4
1979-80	Philadelphia	79	357	.540	180	.779	274	556	898	11.4
1980-81	Philadelphia	81	310	.534	140	.787	245	560	763	9.4
1981-82	Philadelphia	79	352	.521	171	.777	248	667	881	11.2
1982-83	Philadelphia	79	404	.542	181	.754	209	543	990	12.5
1983-84	Philadelphia	75	386	.550	170	.733	205	478	950	12.7
1984-85	Philadelphia	78	422	.570	175	.879	217	497	1025	13.1
1985-86	Philadelphia	82	490	.537	282	.842	235	753	1266	15.4
1986-87	Philadelphia	68	415	.527	227	.777	215	538	1061	15.6
1987-88	Philadelphia	79	428	.495	227	.825	253	635	1086	13.7
1988-89	Philadelphia	71	336	.483	151	.774	183	554	824	11.6
1989-90	S.A.-N.Y.	81	307	.504	171	.847	240	453	789	9.7
	Totals	934	4499	.526	2176	.794	2778	6665	11218	12.0

CHARLES OAKLEY 26 6-9 245   Forward

Who was that missed man? . . . Missed last 17
games with broken left hand, which he suffered
during game in which he had 19 rebounds . . .
The man is a terror on the boards . . . Grabbed
Knick career-high 20 rebounds in Game 3 victory
over Pistons in conference semis . . .
Above-average low-post defender, below-
average low-post scorer . . . Has range up to 18
feet, but shot selection is often disastrous . . . Averaged 2.7 turnovers,
most by any Eastern Conference power forward . . . Rapped
teammates for lack of defense in first two games of Boston series
in playoffs. Knicks responded, winning next three . . . A major
asset on any team, but forever feels unappreciated . . . Ninth overall
pick in 1985 out of Virginia Union, was traded by Cavs on
draft day to Bulls, who sent him to Knicks for Bill Cartwright on
eve of 1987 draft . . . Born Dec. 18, 1963, in Cleveland . . . A
bargain at $1 million.

Year	Team	G	FG	FG Pct.	FT	FT Pct.	Reb.	Ast.	TP	Avg.
1985-86	Chicago	77	281	.519	178	.662	664	133	740	9.6
1986-87	Chicago	82	468	.445	245	.686	1074	296	1192	14.5
1987-88	Chicago	82	375	.483	261	.727	1066	248	1014	12.4
1988-89	New York	82	426	.510	197	.773	861	187	1061	12.9
1989-90	New York	61	336	.524	217	.761	727	146	889	14.6
	Totals	384	1886	.491	1098	.720	4392	1010	4896	12.8

KIKI VANDEWEGHE 32 6-8 220   Forward

Will real Kiki stand up this year? Will his back let him?... Re-injured before training camp started and never got into flow... Back got better, then tendinitis flared in left foot... Lost about 20 pounds during rehab... All in all, it wasn't his best season... Played 22 regular-season games, but moved into starting lineup for final 13... Shot just .442... Had major trouble getting off shot vs. Dennis Rodman in playoffs... If health doesn't improve, he may retire... Eleventh overall pick by Dallas out of UCLA in 1980 draft... Did time in Denver and Portland before coming to Knicks for first-round pick on Feb. 23, 1989... Born Aug. 1, 1958, in Weisbaden, Germany to father, Ernie, former Knick, and mother Coleen, former Miss America... Made nearly $1.1 million.

Year	Team	G	FG	FG Pct.	FT	FT Pct.	Reb.	Ast.	TP	Avg.
1980-81	Denver	51	229	.426	130	.818	270	94	588	11.5
1981-82	Denver	82	706	.560	347	.857	461	247	1760	21.5
1982-83	Denver	82	841	.547	489	.875	437	203	2186	26.7
1983-84	Denver	78	895	.558	494	.852	373	238	2295	29.4
1984-85	Portland	72	618	.534	369	.896	228	106	1616	22.4
1985-86	Portland	79	719	.540	523	.869	216	187	1962	24.8
1986-87	Portland	79	808	.523	467	.886	251	220	2122	26.9
1987-88	Portland	37	283	.508	159	.878	109	71	747	20.2
1988-89	Port.-N.Y.	45	200	.469	80	.899	71	69	499	11.1
1989-90	New York	22	102	.442	44	.917	53	41	258	11.7
	Totals	627	5401	.530	3102	.871	2469	1476	14033	22.4

TRENT TUCKER 30 6-5 200   Guard

Never found his shot last season, which is not good when you are regarded first and foremost as a shooter... Misfired for career-low .417 ... Another rumored as expendable in potential Knick shakeup... Good defender, leader type ... Elder statesman on Knick roster after he was No. 6 overall pick in 1982 draft out of Minnesota... Solid bench player who has accepted role, but whose perimeter skills—he's a .408 career three-point shooter—have been eyed in places such as Atlanta, Cleveland and Los Angeles... Hit disputed three-pointer at :00.1 vs. Bulls on Jan. 15, 1990, forcing NBA to change rules regarding shots in final :00.3 . . . Earned $900,000 . . . Born Dec. 20, 1959, in Tarboro, N.C.

Year	Team	G	FG	FG Pct.	FT	FT Pct.	Reb.	Ast.	TP	Avg.
1982-83	New York	78	299	.462	43	.672	216	195	655	8.4
1983-84	New York	63	225	.500	25	.758	130	138	481	7.6
1984-85	New York	77	293	.483	38	.792	188	199	653	8.5
1985-86	New York	77	349	.472	79	.790	169	192	818	10.6
1986-87	New York	70	325	.470	77	.762	135	166	795	11.4
1987-88	New York	71	193	.424	51	.718	119	117	506	7.1
1988-89	New York	81	263	.454	43	.782	176	132	687	8.5
1989-90	New York	81	253	.417	66	.767	174	173	667	8.2
	Totals	598	2200	.461	422	.756	1307	1312	5262	8.8

EDDIE LEE WILKINS 28 6-10 220   Center-Forward

Finished a mere 1,118 assists behind John Stockton for assist lead. Passing is not his strong suit. Neither is looking to pass . . . Backup center to Patrick Ewing, his body and talents more suited to power-forward duty . . . Uncanny offensive rebounder. Averaged one every 8.5 minutes. Good for anybody, darned good for a sub . . . Likeable sort who has an ugly game with limited skills . . . Defensively, gets overpowered against frontline centers . . . A favorite of GM Al Bianchi, who matched offer sheet by Washington that brings Eddie Lee into his third year at $330,000 . . . Born May 7, 1962, in Cartersville, Ga. . . . Sixth-round choice of the Knicks in 1984 out of Gardner-Webb . . . Warm comeback story. Tore anterior cruciate in left knee in 1985, career seemed finished . . . But he rehabbed, went the CBA route and is back with pros.

Year	Team	G	FG	FG Pct.	FT	FT Pct.	Reb.	Ast.	TP	Avg.
1984-85	New York	54	116	.498	66	.541	262	16	298	5.5
1986-87	New York	24	56	.441	27	.466	107	6	139	5.8
1988-89	New York	71	114	.465	61	.550	148	7	289	4.1
1989-90	New York	79	141	.455	89	.605	265	16	371	4.7
	Totals	228	427	.467	243	.555	782	45	1097	4.8

MARK JACKSON 25 6-3 205   Guard

Bench Mark, Skid Mark, Trade Mark, Mark Down. He has heard them all . . . Maybe NBA's biggest flop last year when he averaged 9.9 points and almost as many weekly trade rumors . . . Lost starting job to Maurice Cheeks in March. Many felt he should have lost it to Rod Strickland in October . . . Reported out of shape after off-season of resting injured knee. Pulled groin muscle and season went downhill . . . But he's not a lost cause . . . Has shown he can play and perform in the clutch . . . If he returns to old form, he must do one thing: stop blaming others (coaches, media) for predicament and accept responsibility . . . Drafted 18th on first round out of St. John's by Knicks in 1987 and promptly won Rookie of Year award . . . Born April 1, 1965, in Queens, N.Y. . . . Earned $1.4 million.

Year	Team	G	FG	FG Pct.	FT	FT Pct.	Reb.	Ast.	TP	Avg.
1987-88	New York	82	438	.432	206	.774	396	868	1114	13.6
1988-89	New York	72	479	.467	180	.698	341	619	1219	16.9
1989-90	New York	82	327	.437	120	.727	318	604	809	9.9
	Totals	236	1244	.446	506	.734	1055	2091	3142	13.3

KENNY WALKER 26 6-8 217   Forward

Worst hairdo in league. Maybe on planet . . . Makes up for it with charming disposition and never has sour word for anyone . . . Work ethic probably kept him in New York through first 2½ dark seasons . . . Gained confidence and fan support with surprise victory in '89 Slam Dunk Contest . . . Settled into bench role and flourished, averaging 7.9 points and 5.0 rebounds in 23 minutes . . . Quality athlete who can jump to rafters and play strong defense . . . Against the big guys, though, can be muscled . . . Shot career-high .531 . . . Plagued by knee tendinitis and back strain and missed 14 games . . . Kentucky All-American was first-round pick (No. 5 overall) of '86 draft . . . Born Aug. 18, 1964, in Roberta, Ga. . . . Earned $660,000.

Year	Team	G	FG	FG Pct.	FT	FT Pct.	Reb.	Ast.	TP	Avg.
1986-87	New York	68	285	.491	140	.757	338	75	710	10.4
1987-88	New York	82	344	.473	138	.775	389	86	826	10.1
1988-89	New York	79	174	.489	66	.776	230	36	419	5.3
1989-90	New York	68	204	.531	125	.723	343	49	535	7.9
	Totals	297	1007	.491	469	.755	1300	246	2490	8.4

GERALD WILKINS 27 6-6 200   Guard

Terrific open-court player. Trouble was Knicks played mostly halfcourt game all season... When he's good, he's very good. When he's bad, it's enough to gag... The one Knick capable of breaking down defenses with speed and quickness... Has made vast strides in all-around game, but must improve his decision-making... Scorer's mentality. When he gets ball, team usually stands around and watches... Needs perimeter consistency... Averaged 14.5 points and career-high 4.5 rebounds... But was one of league leaders in turnovers (194)... Dominique's little brother who actually outplayed 'Nique in head-to-head matchups last year... Second-round pick (No. 37) in 1985 from Tennessee-Chattanooga... Born Sept. 11, 1963, in Baltimore... Made $750,000 base last season.

Year	Team	G	FG	FG Pct.	FT	FT Pct.	Reb.	Ast.	TP	Avg.
1985-86	New York	81	437	.468	132	.557	208	161	1013	12.5
1986-87	New York	80	633	.486	235	.701	294	354	1527	19.1
1987-88	New York	81	591	.446	191	.786	270	326	1412	17.4
1988-89	New York	81	462	.451	186	.756	244	274	1161	14.3
1989-90	New York	82	472	.457	208	.803	371	330	1191	14.5
	Totals	405	2595	.462	952	.721	1387	1445	6304	15.6

BRIAN QUINNETT 24 6-8 236   Forward

Carried all the bags and video equipment and all the good stuff that makes life as a rookie so enjoyable... Knicks are high on his skill, but want him to get tougher mentally... A small forward whom the Knicks tried at power slot, which screwed him up... Tremendous practice shooter. Game time? Well, he was only .328 in 193 minutes... Hero of Jan. 27 win in Denver when he came off 18-game Did Not Play streak and contributed with tough defense... Knicks' only pick of 1989 draft (No. 50 overall) out of Washington State... Born May 30, 1966, in Cheney, Wash.... Earned $125,000 minimum... Awed early on by NBA but he has a future.

Year	Team	G	FG	FG Pct.	FT	FT Pct.	Reb.	Ast.	TP	Avg.
1989-90	New York	31	19	.328	2	.667	28	11	40	1.3

Charles Oakley is supreme as Knick chairman of the board.

STUART GRAY 27 7-0 245   Center

Knicks sought his services for two seasons. One question: Why?...After they got him, they hardly played him...Played in 19 games for New York after he was acquired from Charlotte for 1991 second-rounder...No offense at all ...He's a big banger type, who'll stand his ground and ultimately foul out...Was out of shape when Knicks got him, probably because he was doing so much sitting with Hornets...Claims Mel Daniels taught him never to back down from anybody...Drafted on second round by Indiana in 1984 after bypassing senior season at UCLA...Born May 27, 1963, in the Panama Canal Zone...In high school, he, Patrick Ewing and Greg Dreiling were heralded as The Trio that would completely dominate in college and the pros. Didn't turn out that way, did it?

Year	Team	G	FG	FG Pct.	FT	FT Pct.	Reb.	Ast.	TP	Avg.
1984-85	Indiana.........	52	35	.380	32	.681	123	15	102	2.0
1985-86	Indiana.........	67	54	.500	47	.635	118	15	155	2.3
1986-87	Indiana.........	55	41	.406	28	.718	129	26	110	2.0
1987-88	Indiana.........	74	90	.466	44	.603	250	44	224	3.0
1988-89	Indiana.........	72	72	.471	44	.688	245	29	188	2.6
1989-90	Char.-N.Y.	58	42	.424	32	.681	145	19	116	2.0
	Totals	378	334	.448	227	.660	1010	148	895	2.4

THE ROOKIE

JERROD MUSTAF 21 6-10 244   **Forward**
Basketball babe . . . Left Maryland program destined for probation
after his sophomore season . . . Knicks sought size and felt that in
two more seasons, this guy would have gone in top three picks
. . . They're enamored of his shooting touch which projects him
as a 6-10 small forward . . . Figure he'll get some time at the four
spot, too . . . Nothing to write home about defensively—yet . . .
Averaged 18.5 points last season . . . Decent left hand, puts the
ball on the floor well . . . Born Oct. 28, 1969.

COACH STU JACKSON: In his words, Knicks went through
"some controversy, a nine-game winning
streak, a six-game losing streak, a major personnel move, changes in our starting lineup,
injuries, a player had a baby—and I had
twins." Other than that, it was a typically normal season in New York, where the media
turned on the microscope the minute he was
hired and never turned it off . . . Try to find a
nicer guy anywhere . . . Underwent a grueling
learning experience as youngest NBA coach in his rookie year . . .
Led Knicks to 47 victories in a season that could have hit 50 had
not Charles Oakley broken his hand . . . A proponent of the Rick
Pitino pressing style—he was Pitino's assistant at Providence and
with Knicks—Jackson led Knicks through a campaign designed
to improve the halfcourt game . . . According to Pistons' coach
Chuck Daly, Jackson "has the toughest job in all of basketball—
and he handled it well." . . . Has business background, working
for IBM after collegiate career at Oregon and Seattle . . . Wife Dr.
Janet Taylor is sister of former Knick Vince Taylor and a full-
fledged psychiatrist, which comes in handy for a New York coach
. . . Is the favorite son of Reading, Pa., where he was born Dec.
11, 1955.

GREATEST REBOUNDER

In their history, the Knicks have fielded some of the game's most feared rebounders: Dave DeBusschere, Jerry Lucas and now Charles Oakley. But one Knick towers above all others: Willis Reed. A Hall of Famer now serving as New Jersey's senior VP for basketball operations, Reed finished his 10 seasons in New York—three of them reduced by the knee injury that ended his career—as the greatest rebounder in team history.

Six times, "The Captain" grabbed over 1,000 to finish with 8,414. He produced five of the six greatest single-season rebound totals ever by a Knick—including 1,191 in 1968-69 and 1,175 in his 1964-65 rookie season. For his 650-game career, Reed averaged 12.9 rebounds per game.

ALL-TIME KNICK LEADERS

SEASON

Points: Patrick Ewing, 2,347, 1989-90
Assists: Mark Jackson, 868, 1987-88
Rebounds: Willis Reed, 1,191, 1968-69

GAME

Points: Bernard King, 60 vs. New Jersey, 12/25/85
Assists: Richie Guerin, 21 vs. St. Louis, 12/12/58
Rebounds: Harry Gallatin, 33 vs. Ft. Wayne, 3/15/53
　　　　　　　Willis Reed, 33 vs. Cincinnati, 2/2/71

CAREER

Points: Walt Frazier, 14,617, 1967-77
Assists: Walt Frazier, 4,791, 1967-77
Rebounds: Willis Reed, 8,414, 1964-74

PHILADELPHIA 76ERS

TEAM DIRECTORY: Owner: Harold Katz; GM: Gene Shue; Dir. Player Personnel: Bob Weinhauer; Dir. Pub. Rel.: Zack Hill; Coach: Jim Lynam; Asst. Coaches: Fred Carter, Bob Weinhauer, Buzz Braman. Arena: The Spectrum (18,168). Colors: Red, white and blue.

SCOUTING REPORT

SHOOTING: For the second straight season, the Sixers shot 49 percent, but this time it was much more effective because there was balance. The second-season emergence of Hersey Hawkins made the Sixers' inside game more devastating. He was, in Charles Barkley's estimation, "the key to our success."

Thus freed, Barkley shot a staggering .600, the second-best mark in the league. But where the Sixers fell far short—as they did in virtually every category—came in their bench production. Ron Anderson, streaky at best, hit .457 and after him, there was virtually nothing. The Sixers should continue at about the same pace but must come up with some bench help if they are to be taken as a threat to more than the division.

PLAYMAKING: The Sixers gambled, dealing away veteran Maurice Cheeks before last season, but it paid off as Johnny Dawkins smoothly moved in and assumed the point-guard chores after a rocky, turnover-laced start. By midseason, Dawkins was in control. Up front, Barkley burned all the doubling strategies and recorded over 300 assists for the fourth time in six NBA seasons.

The trade of scrappy Scott Brooks left backup point guard in doubt. But the Sixers hope second-round draft choice Brian Oliver of Georgia Tech can fill that role. They already like the leap in size at that spot, from the 5-11 of Brooks to the 6-4 of Oliver.

DEFENSE: This is where the Sixers made their biggest strides, and no doubt the arrival of Rick Mahorn had something to do with it. Mahorn, a fierce, often downright dirty, inside defender, makes opponents think six times before entering the lane. Consequently, Sixers' opponents shot .480, down from over 50 percent the previous season. And once again things should be looking up. And up. And . . . The arrival of Manute Bol, called by new GM Gene Shue "the best defender around, gives the Sixers another legiti-

To many, all-around Charles Barkley rated MVP award.

mate, if not bulky, inside terror. Mahorn's presence enables Barkley to move back to small forward, where he doesn't have to try to defend guys four inches taller.

Turnovers forced were a bit low (15.0), but the Sixers compensated with the third-lowest turnovers-committed pace in the league. And a big plus was the cerebral work of Mike Gminski

SIXER ROSTER

No.	Veterans	Pos.	Ht.	Wt.	Age	Yrs. Pro	College
20	Ron Anderson	F	6-7	215	31	6	Fresno State
34	Charles Barkley	F	6-5	252	27	6	Auburn
—	Manute Bol	C	7-7	225	27	5	Bridgeport
12	Johnny Dawkins	G	6-2	170	27	4	Duke
42	Mike Gminski	C	6-11	260	31	10	Duke
33	Hersey Hawkins	G	6-3	190	25	3	Bradley
44	Rick Mahorn	F-C	6-10	255	32	10	Hampton Institute
21	Kenny Payne	F	6-8	220	23	1	Louisville
18	Derek Smith	F-G	6-6	218	29	8	Louisville
23	Bob Thornton	F	6-10	225	28	5	Cal-Irvine

Rd.	Rookies	Sel. No.	Pos.	Ht.	Wt.	College
2	Brian Oliver	32	G	6-4	210	Georgia Tech
2	Derek Strong	47	F	6-7	222	Xavier

at center. Largely unheralded, Gminski usually kept opposing centers at or below their scoring averages.

REBOUNDING: Thump and Bump crashed and banged the boards all season, making the Sixers a formidable rebounding outfit. Toss in Gminski and the Sixer front line grabbed over 2,000 rebounds. Hawkins grabbed over 300. Not bad. But then, unfortunately, the Sixers had to go to their bench. And again, they usually came up empty. The Sixers' crying need, and one they must address this season, is the addition of a banging, rebounding reserve. Bob Thornton and Kurt Nimphius were not quite the answer.

OUTLOOK: In a weakened Atlantic Division, the Sixers very well could rise to the top of the heap again. Every team in the East is flawed and the Sixers may have enough starting talent to make it back-to-back Atlantic Division crowns. But they could also make it back-to-back early playoff exits unless additional help is found.

The backcourt of Hawkins and Dawkins should be even more fluid in their second season together. Barkley is Barkley. Mahorn will help in every way when healthy. Gminski will burn from the perimeter, play smart inside. But then what? A big reserve body was an imperative and they came up with Bol.

SIXER PROFILES

CHARLES BARKLEY 27 6-5 252　　　　　Forward

Sir Charles . . . And smile when you say that . . . Then again, he'll probably make you smile . . . One of the primo forces in the NBA . . . No one had more offensive rebounds than his 361 . . . With inside help supplied by Rick Mahorn, he moved back to small forward and was simply awesome . . . Majority of players felt he was the MVP . . . Averaged 25.2 points, missed third straight 2,000-point campaign by 11 . . . And he averaged less than 15 shots a game . . . NBA's second-best field-goal percentage at .600 . . . Averaged 25.4 ppg in playoffs with injured right shoulder . . . Says what he thinks and feels while management usually cringes . . . Was only player in league with back-to-back 20-plus rebound games . . . Eastern Conference All-Star starter . . . Gee, think Bobby Knight might take him for Olympic squad now? . . . Born Feb. 20, 1963, in Leeds, Ala. . . . Sixers made him fifth selection of 1984 draft out of Auburn as an undergraduate . . . Voted SEC Player of the Decade by panel of sportswriters and broadcasters . . . Earned $2.8 million . . . Entertained as analyst for ESPN during NBA Finals . . . One of most colorful characters in all of sports.

Year	Team	G	FG	FG Pct.	FT	FT Pct.	Reb.	Ast.	TP	Avg.
1984-85	Philadelphia	82	427	.545	293	.733	703	155	1148	14.0
1985-86	Philadelphia	80	595	.572	396	.685	1026	312	1603	20.0
1986-87	Philadelphia	68	557	.594	429	.761	994	331	1564	23.0
1987-88	Philadelphia	80	753	.587	714	.751	951	254	2264	28.3
1988-89	Philadelphia	79	700	.579	602	.753	986	325	2037	25.8
1989-90	Philadelphia	79	706	.600	557	.749	909	307	1989	25.2
	Totals	468	3738	.581	2991	.741	5569	1684	10605	22.7

RICK MAHORN 32 6-10 255　　　　Forward-Center

Was he Trump? Or Bump? Or both? . . . Along with Sir Charles, drove opponents daffy with muscular inside game . . . And kept NBA coffers filled with technical fines . . . Grabbed 568 rebounds, his most in five seasons . . . Freed from guard-run Piston offense, scoring increased to 10.8 ppg, highest since his third year in league . . . The ultimate Bad Boy . . . Got along famously with Barkley . . . A coach's dream. Supplies that mental toughness, dogged determination and locker-room leadership that's worth more than bevy of draft picks ... Three-time NAIA All-American at Hampton Institute ... Played through assorted injuries: chronic back, elbow, sciatic nerve—and still played his most minutes in six years ... Was picked up by Minnesota from Pistons as second overall pick in expansion draft. Refused to report. Wound up in Philly for a first-rounder and two second-rounders ... Born Sept. 21, 1958, in Hartford, Conn. ... Will earn base of $750,000 with incentives that make deal worth over $1 million.

Year	Team	G	FG	FG Pct.	FT	FT Pct.	Reb.	Ast.	TP	Avg.
1980-81	Washington	52	111	.507	27	.675	215	25	249	4.8
1981-82	Washington	80	414	.507	148	.632	704	150	976	12.2
1982-83	Washington	82	376	.490	146	.575	779	115	898	11.0
1983-84	Washington	82	307	.507	125	.651	738	131	739	9.0
1984-85	Washington	77	206	.499	71	.683	608	121	483	6.3
1985-86	Detroit	80	157	.455	81	.681	412	64	395	4.9
1986-87	Detroit	63	144	.447	96	.821	375	38	384	6.1
1987-88	Detroit	67	276	.574	164	.756	565	60	717	10.7
1988-89	Detroit	72	203	.517	116	.748	496	59	522	7.3
1989-90	Philadelphia	75	313	.497	183	.715	568	98	811	10.8
	Totals	730	2507	.502	1157	.685	5460	861	6174	8.5

JOHNNY DAWKINS 27 6-2 170   Guard

How do you follow Maurice Cheeks? Well, for starters, average 14.3 points, average over seven assists and less than 2.7 turnovers ... Came to Sixers from Spurs before 1989-90 season with Jay Vincent for Cheeks, Chris Welp and David Wingate ... Sixers ain't complaining ... Great leaper, great speed ... And showed great poise in playoffs, his first trip in postseason ... Still learning the point-guard position but got better and better as season progressed ... Began to understand when and where to deliver ball ... Duke grad, so you know he's been schooled ... Took Duke to 1986 NCAA championship game, where they lost to Louisville ... Spurs' first-round pick in '86 ... Born Sept. 28, 1963, in Washington, D.C. ... Earned $475,000.

Year	Team	G	FG	FG Pct.	FT	FT Pct.	Reb.	Ast.	TP	Avg.
1986-87	San Antonio	81	334	.437	153	.801	169	290	835	10.3
1987-88	San Antonio	65	405	.485	198	.896	204	480	1027	15.8
1988-89	San Antonio	32	177	.443	100	.893	101	224	454	14.2
1989-90	Philadelphia	81	465	.489	210	.861	247	601	1162	14.3
	Totals	259	1381	.468	661	.861	721	1595	3478	13.4

DEREK SMITH 29 6-6 218   Forward-Guard

Injury problems have always stunted him... And injury struck again last season, costing the Sixers dearly in playoffs... Plagued by tendinitis in left knee and was limited to one game in postseason—further depleting already shoddy Sixer bench... Tore left knee cartilege in '85, has never been the same player... Still, has value in Sixer system... Can swing between small forward and big guard... Intensely loyal to coach Jim Lynam, who had him in San Diego and again in Philly, twice rescuing him from scrap heap... Still gets to the basket but jumper is not what it used to be... Tough, in-your-gut defender... Born Nov. 1, 1961, in Morgansville, Ga.... Second-round pick by Golden State in 1982 out of Louisville... After tours with Clips and Kings, he was free-agent pickup in late 1988-89 by Sixers ... Earned $525,000.

Year	Team	G	FG	FG Pct.	FT	FT Pct.	Reb.	Ast.	TP	Avg.
1982-83	Golden State	27	21	.412	17	.680	38	2	59	2.2
1983-84	San Diego	61	238	.546	123	.755	170	82	600	9.8
1984-85	L.A. Clippers	80	682	.537	400	.794	427	216	1767	22.1
1985-86	L.A. Clippers	11	100	.552	58	.690	41	31	259	23.5
1986-87	Sacramento	52	338	.447	178	.781	182	204	863	16.6
1987-88	Sacramento	35	174	.478	87	.770	103	89	443	12.7
1988-89	Sac.-Phil.	65	216	.435	129	.686	167	128	568	8.7
1989-90	Philadelphia	75	261	.508	130	.699	172	109	668	8.9
	Totals	406	2030	.499	1122	.753	1300	861	5227	12.9

MIKE GMINSKI 31 6-11 260   Center

Flashy and exciting as mowing grass but he gets the job done... Ewing, Olajuwon and Robinson scored at or below their averages against Sixers, so he must be doing something right ... Superb perimeter shooter who caused match-up headaches for every team... Solid, competent, smart... Often drew coverage from small forward as centers played Rick Mahorn and power forwards went on Charles Barkley... Sixth straight season of 80 percent or better at foul line... Crossword puzzle whiz... One of driest wits in NBA... Great interview... Has fouled out once in career and that was in rookie season... Born Aug. 3, 1959, in Monroe, Conn.... Superb baseball player as a kid... Nets made him seventh pick in 1980 out of Duke... Came to Sixers with Ben Coleman from New Jersey in 1988 for Roy Hinson and Tim McCormick . . . Made $1.85 million last season.

Year	Team	G	FG	FG Pct.	FT	FT Pct.	Reb.	Ast.	TP	Avg.
1980-81	New Jersey	56	291	.423	155	.767	419	72	737	13.2
1981-82	New Jersey	64	119	.441	97	.822	186	41	335	5.2
1982-83	New Jersey	80	213	.500	175	.778	382	61	601	7.5
1983-84	New Jersey	82	237	.513	147	.799	433	92	621	7.6
1984-85	New Jersey	81	380	.465	276	.841	633	158	1036	12.8
1985-86	New Jersey	81	491	.517	351	.893	668	133	1333	16.5
1986-87	New Jersey	72	433	.457	313	.846	630	99	1179	16.4
1987-88	N.J.-Phil.	81	505	.448	355	.906	814	139	1365	16.9
1988-89	Philadelphia	82	556	.477	297	.871	769	138	1409	17.2
1989-90	Philadelphia	81	458	.457	193	.821	687	128	1112	13.7
	Totals	760	3683	.469	2359	.846	5621	1061	9728	12.8

RON ANDERSON 32 6-7 215   Forward

How do you spell Sixer bench? A-N-D-E-R-S-O-N . . . Unfortunately for him, Sixers needed to spell their small forward Charles Barkley about 600 fewer minutes . . . As a result of decreased time, he had erratic season . . . Shooting (.451) and scoring (11.9) were down . . . Typical streak-shooter, when he's good, he's terrific. When he's bad, push him off a cliff . . . Shot under 40 percent in nine playoff games . . . Born Oct. 15, 1958, in Chicago . . . Didn't play ball in high school. Was working as a supermarket stock manager when a friend talked him into playing junior college . . . Transferred to Fresno State and was 26 when he entered NBA with Cavs in 1984 . . . Played two years with Pacers, then stolen by Sixers for the unforgettable Everette Stephens in 1988 . . . Had $600,000 salary.

Year	Team	G	FG	FG Pct.	FT	FT Pct.	Reb.	Ast.	TP	Avg.
1984-85	Cleveland	36	84	.431	41	.820	88	34	210	5.8
1985-86	Clev.-Ind.	77	310	.494	85	.669	274	144	707	9.2
1986-87	Indiana	63	139	.473	85	.787	151	54	363	5.8
1987-88	Indiana	74	217	.498	108	.766	216	78	542	7.3
1988-89	Philadelphia	82	566	.491	196	.856	406	139	1330	16.2
1989-90	Philadelphia	78	379	.451	165	.838	295	143	926	11.9
	Totals	410	1695	.478	680	.798	1430	592	4078	9.9

HERSEY HAWKINS 25 6-3 190   Guard

See? Nobody could be as bad as he was in playoffs of rookie season in 1988-89, when he missed 21 of 24 shots . . . Came back in second year to shoot 46 percent, average 18.5 points and pour in 84 trifectas, easing inside doubling on Barkley . . . Sir Charles calls him "the difference" in team becoming Atlantic Division champs . . . Improved in playoffs with 23.5 ppg with a high of 39 vs. Cavs . . . Only Sixer to play all 82 games . . . Philly was 28-8 when he scored 20 . . . Scorer's mentality, but plays decent defense . . . Fifth all-time college scorer with 3,008 points . . . All-American at Bradley . . . Drafted by Clippers as sixth pick in 1988, came to Sixers in three-way deal with Sonics . . . Born Sept. 29, 1965, in Chicago . . . Paid $550,000.

Year	Team	G	FG	FG Pct.	FT	FT Pct.	Reb.	Ast.	TP	Avg.
1988-89	Philadelphia	79	442	.455	241	.831	225	239	1196	15.1
1989-90	Philadelphia	82	522	.460	387	.888	304	261	1515	18.5
	Totals	161	964	.458	628	.865	529	500	2711	16.8

BOB THORNTON 28 6-10 225   Forward

A journeyman named desire . . . Played a big part of Sixer bench, averaging over 10 minutes . . . Which says something about Sixer depth problems . . . Pretty much bench fodder since becoming Knicks' fourth-round pick out of Cal-Irvine back in 1984 . . . No natural talent to speak of . . . But he works as hard as anybody in the league . . . Very limited offensive game . . . Good practice player who'll bang and hustle and sweat . . . And that's why he's still in the league . . . Born July 10, 1962, in Los Angeles . . . Paid $210,000.

Year	Team	G	FG	FG Pct.	FT	FT Pct.	Reb.	Ast.	TP	Avg.
1985-86	New York	71	125	.456	86	.531	290	43	336	4.7
1986-87	New York	33	29	.433	13	.650	56	8	71	2.2
1987-88	N.Y.-Phil	48	65	.500	34	.618	112	15	164	3.4
1988-89	Philadelphia	54	47	.423	32	.533	92	15	127	2.4
1989-90	Philadelphia	56	48	.429	26	.510	133	17	123	2.2
	Totals	262	314	.452	191	.548	683	98	821	3.1

MANUTE BOL 28 7-7 225   Center

Golden State traded him in the summer for a Sixer first-round draft choice in 1991 . . . Had more than 200 rejections fourth straight year . . . But dropped from top of league to No. 4 in shot-blocking (3.17 a game) . . . Of course, he still doesn't have to leave feet . . . Born Oct. 16, 1962, in Gogrial, Sudan, where he was a Dinka Tribesman . . . Played at University of Bridgeport . . . Drafted No. 31 in second round of 1985 by Washington . . . After three seasons, was traded by Bullets to Warriors for Dave Feitl . . . Brightens locker rooms wherever he plays . . . Peers love his loose attitude more than coaches do . . . Thrills fans with a Tinkertoy construction of an off-the-shoulder, three-point shot.

Year	Team	G	FG	FG Pct.	FT	FT Pct.	Reb.	Ast.	TP	Avg.
1985-86	Washington......	80	128	.460	42	.488	477	23	298	3.7
1986-87	Washington......	82	103	.446	45	.672	362	11	251	3.1
1987-88	Washington......	77	75	.455	26	.531	275	13	176	2.3
1988-89	Golden State.....	80	127	.369	40	.606	462	27	314	3.9
1989-90	Golden State.....	75	56	.331	25	.510	276	36	146	1.9
	Totals	394	489	.412	178	.562	1852	110	1185	3.0

KENNY PAYNE 23 6-8 220   Forward

Who was that guy sitting on end of bench? . . . Played even fewer minutes (216) than George McCloud, Indiana's seldom-used first-round pick . . . Reportedly a shooting small forward, but didn't get enough time for anyone to judge . . . Sixers made him 19th pick in 1989 out of Louisville, where he played in shadow of Pervis Ellison . . . Doesn't create; catch-and-shoot type . . . Was regarded as one of best pure shooters in '89 draft . . . Has the physical build, but with Charles Barkley playing small forward, minutes were hard to come by . . . Born Nov. 25, 1966, in Laurel, Miss. . . . Got $430,000.

Year	Team	G	FG	FG Pct.	FT	FT Pct.	Reb.	Ast.	TP	Avg.
1989-90	Philadelphia	35	47	.435	16	.889	26	10	114	3.3

THE ROOKIES

BRIAN OLIVER 22 6-4 210   **Guard**

Nice pickup with the 32d pick on the season round . . . Duke coach Mike Krzyzewski called the Dennis Scott and Kenny Anderson-overshadowed guard at Georgia Tech "one of the best players" in the country . . . If he can stick, he'd be perfect for bench-poor Sixers . . . Played off-guard for Yellow Jackets last season, but was the point guard before Anderson arrived. Versatility a big asset and he's going to a team desperate for versatile athletes . . . Averaged 21.3 points as a senior . . . Born June 1, 1968.

DEREK STRONG 22 6-7 222   **Forward**

Went 47th in the draft . . . Stock plunged after his season-long collegiate listing of 6-10 size turned out to be a sham . . . Still, an impressive physical specimen . . . Real strong inside player who relies on muscle and position . . . Good defender, above-average shot-blocker . . . Teamed with Tyrone Hill at Xavier to stop Georgetown duo of Alonzo Mourning and Dikembe Mutombo in Midwest Regionals . . . Averaged 14.2 points and 9.9 boards . . . Born Feb. 9, 1968.

COACH JIM LYNAM: Not only is he good, but Charles Barkley loves him . . . Well-respected in NBA circles, a good communicator . . . A real get-in-your-face guy who has superb rapport with players . . . His two full seasons with Sixers have produced 99 victories . . . Overall head coaching record of 167-179, including two dreadful seasons with Clippers . . . Spent 10 years in college ranks at Fairfield, American and St. Joseph's (Pa.), his alma mater . . . Played at St. Joe's under Jack Ramsay in early 1960s, and later became an assistant under Ramsay at Portland . . . Born Sept. 15, 1941, in Philly . . . Entering second season of three-year deal that averages $200,000 per.

GREATEST REBOUNDER

In the history of the franchise, including the days in Syracuse, no player grabbed more rebounds than Dolph Schayes, who hauled in 11,256 in 996 regular-season games, an average of 11.3 per. But even Schayes' numbers have to take a backseat to a man who in five seasons earned the title of the greatest rebounder in franchise history. And that's simply because he was the greatest rebounder of all time, Wilt Chamberlain.

Chamberlain started his career in Philadelphia with the Warriors before they moved to San Francisco. But on his return trip as a Sixer, Wilt grabbed 6,632 boards in just 277 games, an average of 23.9 per. And those numbers leave Chamberlain fourth on the all-time Sixer list, behind Schayes, Johnny Kerr, and Billy Cunningham.

But for his career, "The Stilt" collected an all-time high 23,924 rebounds, a 22.9 average, another all-time mark.

ALL-TIME 76ER LEADERS

SEASON

Points: Wilt Chamberlain, 2,649, 1965-66
Assists: Maurice Cheeks, 753, 1985-86
Rebounds: Wilt Chamberlain, 1,957, 1966-67

GAME

Points: Wilt Chamberlain, 68 vs. Chicago, 12/16/67
Assists: Wilt Chamberlain, 21 vs. Detroit, 2/2/68
        Maurice Cheeks, 21 vs. New Jersey, 10/30/82
Rebounds: Wilt Chamberlain, 43 vs. Boston, 3/6/65

CAREER

Points: Hal Greer, 21,586, 1958-73
Assists: Maurice Cheeks, 6,212, 1978-89
Rebounds: Dolph Schayes, 11,256, 1948-64

WASHINGTON BULLETS

TEAM DIRECTORY: Pres.: Abe Pollin; Vice Chairman: Jerry Sachs; Exec. VP: Susan O'Malley; GM: John Nash; Dir. Pub. Rel.: Rick Moreland; Coach: Wes Unseld; Asst. Coaches: Bill Blair, Jeff Bzdelik. Arena: Capital Centre (18,756). Colors: Red, white and blue.

Adaptable Bernard King adds chapter to comeback legend.

SCOUTING REPORT

SHOOTING: All things considered, the Bullets' .475 shooting in their motion offense wasn't all that bad. Once John Williams went out with a ravaged knee after 18 games, Bernard King went back to working in the low post, forsaking a lot of the perimeter game he had promised. But that was a move of necessity.

The best shooter on the team, Jeff Malone, is gone as the Bullets had to deal something for the big man they so desperately need. So now Ledell Eackles, who has shown flashes of Vinnie Johnson-like streak shooting, must step in and move from the .439 performer he was to the .491 shooter Malone was.

PLAYMAKING: The Bullets are not a bad passing team, which of course helps when you run a motion offense like they do. Darrell Walker, the marvelous rebounding, workaholic point guard, finished 10th in the league with 8.0 assists per game and seven others had over 130 assists. But the Bullets are not a very creative team. They take what is there and rarely create for themselves or their teammates.

DEFENSE: If defense is 90 percent effort, then the Bullets were and will be a marvelous defensive team. Problem is, they're not, because the talent part counts for a lot more. Undermanned and undersized every night, the Bullets did the best they could with obviously lacking resources. Size simply gave them fits. Charles Jones, the aging defensive specialist inside, did his best but was overwhelmed by the stallions in the NBA center stables.

Eackles will have a big role to fill on the defensive side. And Malone's—generally underrated, though at times wimpy—defensive skills will be missed. Walker's pesky approach always ticks off opponents. But up front, the Bullets simply are not a good defensive bunch. But not from a lack of trying.

REBOUNDING: When a point guard leads a team in rebounding, it says something about that team. And last year, point guard Walker was the best boarder the Bullets could muster. True, Williams probably would have led if healthy, but this is an imperfect world and things don't always go as planned.

The Bullets must get a workhorse effort from Pervis Ellison, who can forget any of the early coddling he received in Sacramento. Harvey Grant has to bulk up and realize an outside touch is nice, but the Bullets need more inside work from him. Mark Alarie gives nice reserve board work and Walker will continue being Walker. Even if he doesn't lead the team again.

BULLET ROSTER

No.	Veterans	Pos.	Ht.	Wt.	Age	Yrs. Pro	College
31	Mark Alarie	F	6-8	225	26	4	Duke
20	Steve Colter	G	6-3	165	28	6	New Mexico State
21	Ledell Eackles	G	6-5	215	23	2	New Orleans
43	Pervis Ellison	C-F	6-9	210	23	1	Louisville
44	Harvey Grant	F	6-9	215	25	2	Oklahoma
12	Tom Hammonds	F	6-9	225	23	1	Georgia Tech
23	Charles Jones	C-F	6-9	225	33	7	Albany State
30	Bernard King	F	6-7	205	33	12	Tennessee
5	Darrell Walker	G	6-4	180	29	7	Arkansas
34	John Williams	F	6-9	235	24	4	LSU

Rd.	Rookies	Sel. No.	Pos.	Ht.	Wt.	College
2	Greg Foster	35	C	7-0	240	Texas-El Paso
2	A.J. English	37	G	6-3	175	Virginia Union

OUTLOOK: Look at the bright side: the Bullets, barring another disastrous dumb trade (which isn't likely with John Nash in as general manager) should have their own lottery pick in June. There are monstrous questions surrounding the team: how well will Ellison, after a washout rookie season in Sacramento, perform in the far more physical East? Can Eackles pick up the scoring and shooting slack created by the departure of Malone? Can Harvey Grant become a Horace Grant? How effective will Williams be after destroying his knee?

The Bullets will play hard and kick and scrape every night. Nothing less is to be expected of a Wes Unseld team. But the horses aren't there yet for legit playoff contention.

BULLET PROFILES

BERNARD KING 33 6-7 205   Forward

Played 82 games for first time since the 1978-79 season . . . So honestly, the knee is no longer a question . . . Name should forever be linked with "Comeback" . . . Changed game again. When he came back, he went from his fearsome low-post game to the perimeter. Last season saw a return to more of the low-post game . . . Greatest game face in league, perhaps in all of sports...One of game's greatest scorers...Once had back-to-back 50-point games with Knicks...Was NBA scoring champ in 1984-85...Had ninth full season averaging 20 points or better ...Explosiveness from the wing is gone, but his determination never left...Originally first-round pick of Nets out of Tennessee in 1977...Spent time in Utah, Golden State and New York... After 1980-81 season, was first player to win Comeback of Year Award...Born Dec. 4, 1956, in Brooklyn, N.Y....Brother Albert played with Nets, now in Europe...Has another year at $1.5 million left...Signed as free agent in 1987 after Knicks didn't match offer sheet, which they now must regret.

Year	Team	G	FG	FG Pct.	FT	FT Pct.	Reb.	Ast.	TP	Avg.
1977-78	New Jersey	79	798	.479	313	.677	751	193	1909	24.2
1978-79	New Jersey	82	710	.522	349	.564	669	295	1769	21.6
1979-80	Utah	19	71	.518	34	.540	88	52	176	9.3
1980-81	Golden State	81	731	.588	307	.703	551	287	1771	21.9
1981-82	Golden State	79	740	.566	352	.705	469	282	1833	23.2
1982-83	New York	68	603	.528	280	.722	326	195	1486	21.9
1983-84	New York	77	795	.572	437	.779	394	164	2027	26.3
1984-85	New York	55	691	.530	426	.772	317	204	1809	32.9
1985-86	New York					Injured				
1986-87	New York	6	52	.495	32	.744	32	19	136	22.7
1987-88	Washington	69	470	.501	247	.762	280	192	1188	17.2
1988-89	Washington	81	654	.477	361	.819	384	294	1674	20.7
1989-90	Washington	82	711	.487	412	.803	404	376	1837	22.4
	Totals	778	7026	.524	3550	.724	4665	2553	17615	22.6

DARRELL WALKER 29 6-4 180   Guard

Wes Unseld's kind of guy...A point guard leading the team in rebounding...Next thing you know, a small forward will be Defensive Player of the Year...If ever there was a Hubie Brown player, here he is...Of course, he and Hubie got along like brothers—Cain and Abel—when he was in New York...But that's history...Recent history sees him collecting triple-doubles like baseball cards. Had nine triples last season. Only Larry Bird and Magic Johnson had more...Sacrificed body for team. By 70th game, had little spring left in legs...Averaged career-high 8.8 rebounds. First time in Bullet history a guard led in boards...Shooting improved to point where you didn't cringe when he launched...Tough, in-your-gut defender, averaged 1.72 steals...A team player that every coach should have....Born March 9, 1961, in Chicago...Knicks' first-round pick out of

Arkansas in '83 ... Came from Denver as part of the Michael Adams deal.

Year	Team	G	FG	FG Pct.	FT	FT Pct.	Reb.	Ast.	TP	Avg.
1983-84	New York	82	216	.417	208	.791	167	284	644	7.9
1984-85	New York	82	430	.435	243	.700	278	408	1103	13.5
1985-86	New York	81	324	.430	190	.686	220	337	838	10.3
1986-87	Denver	81	358	.482	272	.745	327	282	988	12.2
1987-88	Washington	52	114	.392	82	.781	127	100	310	6.0
1988-89	Washington	79	286	.420	142	.772	507	496	714	9.0
1989-90	Washington	81	316	.454	138	.687	714	652	772	9.5
	Totals	538	2044	.438	1275	.732	2340	2559	5369	10.0

JOHN WILLIAMS 24 6-9 235   Forward

Star on the rise? ... Will we ever know? ... Was emerging as the stud Bullets hoped for when he left LSU after sophomore year in 1986 ... Then he wiped out knee on Dec. 5, 1989, tearing medical collateral ligament and partially tearing anterior cruciate ligament ... Only played in 18 games ... Was accepting team leadership baton from Bernard King when injury struck ... Was second on team in scoring, rebounds and assists ... Having lost most of baby fat that plagued him his first three seasons, he showed terrific development ... Good ball-handler, has played every position at one time or another ... Born Oct. 26, 1966, in Los Angeles, where he attended Crenshaw High (same as Darryl Strawberry) ... Awesome raw talent, Bullets made him No. 12 pick in '86 ... Earned $1.1 million.

Year	Team	G	FG	FG Pct.	FT	FT Pct.	Reb.	Ast.	TP	Avg.
1986-87	Washington	78	283	.454	144	.646	366	191	718	9.2
1987-88	Washington	82	427	.469	188	.734	444	232	1047	12.8
1988-89	Washington	82	438	.466	225	.776	573	356	1120	13.7
1989-90	Washington	18	130	.474	65	.774	136	84	327	18.2
	Totals	260	1278	.465	622	.729	1519	863	3212	12.4

HARVEY GRANT 25 6-9 215   Forward

Twin brother of Bulls' Horace ... And Horace is winning the race to legit pro status ... Started real strong, then tailed off ... A lot like his rookie season, which was disrupted by injury ... Averaged 13.3 points and 6.3 rebounds as a starter ... Not too effective underneath for a 6-9 guy ... Often too passive, tentative ... Has nice perimeter touch and Bullets encouraged him to put it on display more . . . Good, sound athletic type who needs sharpening and re-finishing . . . Defensively has the tools but needs to strengthen up . . . Born July 4, 1965, in Sparta, Ga. . . . Came out of Oklahoma in 1988 after leading Sooners to NCAA championship game . . . Bullets made him No. 12 pick of first round . . . Paid $300,000.

Year	Team	G	FG	FG Pct.	FT	FT Pct.	Reb.	Ast.	TP	Avg.
1988-89	Washington......	71	181	.464	34	.596	163	79	396	5.6
1989-90	Washington......	81	284	.473	96	.701	342	131	664	8.2
	Totals	152	465	.469	130	.670	505	210	1060	7.0

LEDELL EACKLES 23 6-5 215   Guard

Natural scorer . . . Resembles one of those pop 'em balloon dolls that always bounces back up . . . And this one would bounce back shooting . . . Instant offense off bench, adept at drawing contact and going to the foul line . . . Streak shooter, must improve consistency . . . And he must keep weight down . . . Was pretty much a balloon at New Orleans . . . Not a bad one-on-one defender but is prone to losing interest when he's away from ball . . . Had four three-pointers in one game vs. Miami . . . Was second-round steal (36th pick) by Bullets in 1988 draft . . . Born Nov. 24, 1966, in Baton Rouge, La. . . . Earned $250,000.

Year	Team	G	FG	FG Pct.	FT	FT Pct.	Reb.	Ast.	TP	Avg.
1988-89	Washington......	80	318	.434	272	.786	180	123	917	11.5
1989-90	Washington......	78	413	.439	210	.750	175	182	1055	13.5
	Totals	158	731	.437	482	.770	355	305	1972	12.5

CHARLES JONES 33 6-9 225   Center-Forward

Hey, C.J. Go stop Ewing. Then Akeem. Relax after that. It's only David Robinson . . . If you can't have the center you love, go with the one you've got . . . And that's what Bullets did with their stringbean veteran . . . Played all but one game, averaged 2.43 blocks, seventh-best in NBA . . . Offensively bankrupt. Had just 12 games of double-figure points. And he tied a personal high with six free throws in one game. That says enough about offensive game . . . Defensive all the way . . . Good weak-side help . . . Had 10 blocks at Orlando to tie career high . . . Real good back man in trapping defense . . . Would be a swell second-unit player for a contender. Born April 3, 1957, in McGehee,

Ark. . . . Was the 165th pick in 1979 draft by Phoenix . . . Came to Bullets as free agent in '85, signing a 10-day contract and then sticking . . . Contract re-done to pay him $650,000 this season.

Year	Team	G	FG	FG Pct.	FT	FT Pct.	Reb.	Ast.	TP	Avg.
1983-84	Philadelphia	1	0	.000	1	.250	0	0	1	1.0
1984-85	Chi.-Wash.	31	67	.528	40	.690	184	26	174	5.6
1985-86	Washington	81	129	.508	54	.628	321	76	312	3.9
1986-87	Washington	79	118	.474	48	.632	356	80	284	3.6
1987-88	Washington	69	72	.407	53	.707	325	59	197	2.9
1988-89	Washington	53	60	.480	16	.640	257	42	136	2.6
1989-90	Washington	81	94	.508	68	.648	504	139	256	3.2
	Totals	395	540	.483	280	.653	1947	422	1360	3.4

MARK ALARIE 26 6-8 225   Forward

Those who watch also serve . . . Went from Washington washout to solid role player . . . Has made good strides under Wes Unseld, becoming far more aggressive on the boards, especially on offensive end . . . Fundamentally sound, makes most of his skills . . . Nice touch, even if his .473 shooting percentage last season was career-low . . . His 60 steals more than doubled previous best . . . Good team player with good work ethic . . . Born Dec. 11, 1963, in Phoenix . . . Drafted No. 18 out of Duke by Denver in 1986, came to Bullets with Darrell Walker for Michael Adams and Jay Vincent in 1987 . . . Made $650,000.

Year	Team	G	FG	FG Pct.	FT	FT Pct.	Reb.	Ast.	TP	Avg.
1986-87	Denver	64	217	.490	67	.663	214	74	503	7.9
1987-88	Washington	63	144	.480	35	.714	160	39	327	5.2
1988-89	Washington	74	206	.478	73	.839	255	63	498	6.7
1989-90	Washington	82	371	.473	108	.812	374	142	860	10.5
	Totals	283	938	.479	283	.765	1003	318	2188	7.7

TOM HAMMONDS 23 6-9 223   Forward

Nice personality . . . Enough with the superlatives . . . Had a very disappointing rookie season . . . Ninth overall pick in last year's draft after starring at Georgia Tech, he only earned 805 minutes on a team desperate for help up front . . . Averaged 5.3 points and 2.8 rebounds . . . In-between size . . . Asked to change from his college inside game with less than spectacular results, much like early Kenny Walker days in New York . . . Lacking perimeter game . . . Good work ethic but encountered all the typical rookie adjustment problems... Born March 27, 1967, in Crestview, La.... Paid $850,000.

Year	Team	G	FG	FG Pct.	FT	FT Pct.	Reb.	Ast.	TP	Avg.
1989-90	Washington......	61	129	.437	63	.643	168	51	321	5.3

STEVE COLTER 28 6-3 165   Guard

Probably should be a lot better than he is... Isiah Thomas, for instance, says he hates to play against him... He's a good ball-handler, a good passer, a good jumper and a decent shooter... Very low in turnover area, too—38 in 977 minutes... No glaring weakness but no great strength, either... A nice backup... Deeply religious fellow... Some observers questioned whether sports is the most important thing in his life ... Second-round pick from New Mexico State by Portland in 1984... Signed with Bullets as free agent in 1987... Earned $350,000.

Year	Team	G	FG	FG Pct.	FT	FT Pct.	Reb.	Ast.	TP	Avg.
1984-85	Portland.........	78	216	.453	98	.754	150	243	556	7.1
1985-86	Portland.........	81	272	.456	135	.823	177	257	706	8.7
1986-87	Chi.-Phil........	70	169	.426	82	.766	108	210	424	6.1
1987-88	Phil.-Wash.......	68	203	.460	75	.789	173	261	484	7.1
1988-89	Washington......	80	203	.444	125	.749	182	225	534	6.7
1989-90	Washington......	73	142	.478	77	.811	176	148	361	4.9
	Totals	450	1205	.452	592	.781	966	1344	3605	6.8

PERVIS ELLISON 23 6-9 210   Center-Forward

Had reason as a rookie to drop the "Never" from Never Nervous Pervis nickname... A miserable debut... Chosen by Bill Russell, then the Kings' top basketball man, as the first overall pick in 1989... Now he'll be project of Wes Unseld as Bullets got him in pre-draft three-way deal which saw Jeff Malone go to Utah... Starred at Louisville, where he finished with 2,143 points... MVP in 1986 Final Four, leading Cardinals to championship... Born April 3, 1967, in Savannah, Ga... A controversial pick at No. 1, especially when it turned out later Russell apparently hadn't summoned the player for the usual round of personal, psychological, aptitude testing so common these days... Reported late in contract dispute and with unannounced carry-over injury... Made 22 of his 34 appearances as a starter and scared no one . . . His .442 rookie FG mark confirms previous beliefs that he's a clumsy shooter beyond dunking range.

Year	Team	G	FG	FG Pct.	FT	FT Pct.	Reb.	Ast.	TP	Avg.
1989-90	Sacramento	34	111	.442	49	.628	196	65	271	8.0

THE ROOKIES

GREG FOSTER 22 7-0 230   Center

A 7-footer who goes at No. 35 sort of tells you something right away . . . Averaged 10.6 points and 6.2 rebounds for Texas-El Paso . . . Mobility and athleticism not quite his strong points . . . But he is a 7-footer . . . No range at all. And he still only shot .459 . . . Bullets are desperate for big help and feel he is a project who could emerge . . . MVP of Western Athletic Conference tourney . . . Born Sept. 3, 1968.

A. J. ENGLISH 23 6-3 180   Guard

Known for his shotmaking and leadership, the 37th draft pick was NCAA Division II Player of the Year as a senior at Virginia Union, where he averaged 33.4 points last season . . . Born July 11, 1967, in Wilmington, Del.

COACH WES UNSELD: Did the best job possible with donut team: no center . . . Players love him due to his simple approach: work your butt off or I'll kick it to Havana . . . Treats 12th man the same as he treats the superstars and team responds . . . Not quite in top five of best-dressed coaches . . . But when you're Unseld's size, you wear what fits . . . Incredible Hall of Fame playing career. Undersized center and playoff MVP on Bullets' championship team of 1978 . . . Only he and Wilt Chamberlain won Rookie of the Year and MVP Awards in the same season . . . Eighth all-time rebounder . . . Has 2½-year coaching record of 101-118 . . . Yes, it's a losing mark but with he has had to work with, the record is terrific . . . Straightforward, no flash . . . Did tour of duty in Bullets' front office after retirement in 1980 . . . Returned to bench as assistant to Kevin Loughery in 1987 . . . Took over after 27 games of 1987-88 season . . . Born March 14, 1946, in Louisville, Ky. . . . Bullets made him the No. 2 overall pick in 1968 draft after starring at Louisville.

GREATEST REBOUNDER

He was the epitome of power: bone-jarring picks and outlet passes thrown like bullets. And rebounds that came in bunches through sweat, muscle and position.

At 6-7, Wes Unseld, now the coach of the team with whom he earned Hall of Fame status, used every millimeter of his height to reign as one of the game's premier rebounders for 13 seasons. Although he claimed only one NBA rebounding title—in 1974-75, when he averaged 14.8 boards—Unseld was a perennial top 10 finisher. He was second in the league in each of his first three seasons, but his 1,491 in 1968-69 after he was the second pick in the draft rank as the third-greatest total ever for a rookie.

While one-time Bullet teammate Elvin Hayes produced more lifetime boards, all of Unseld's came in a Bullet uniform. Hayes split his time with three teams. Unseld's 13,769 Bullet career rebounds translated to a 14.0 lifetime average. And he's eighth on the all-time NBA list.

ALL-TIME BULLET LEADERS

SEASON

Points: Walt Bellamy, 2,495, 1961-62
Assists: Kevin Porter, 734, 1980-81
Rebounds: Walt Bellamy, 1,500, 1961-62

GAME

Points: Earl Monroe, 56 vs. Los Angeles, 2/3/68
Assists: Kevin Porter, 24 vs. Detroit, 3/23/80
Rebounds: Walt Bellamy, 37 vs. St. Louis, 12/4/64

CAREER

Points: Elvin Hayes, 15,551, 1972-81
Assists: Wes Unseld, 3,822, 1968-81
Rebounds: Wes Unseld, 13,769, 1968-81

DALLAS MAVERICKS

TEAM DIRECTORY: Pres.: Donald Carter; Chief Oper. Off./GM: Norm Sonju; VP Basketball Oper.: Rick Sund; Dir. Communications: Allen Stone; Dir. Media Services: Kevin Sullivan; Coach: Richie Adubato; Asst. Coaches: Gar Heard, Bob Zuffelato. Arena: Reunion Arena (17,007). Colors: Blue and green.

Rolando Blackman eyes 10th straight 1,000-point season.

SCOUTING REPORT

SHOOTING: You can't make 'em if you can't see 'em. And for some reason the Mavericks always seem to be taking difficult shots. Maybe ex-Nugget Fat Lever will change that. Despite Derek Harper's experience at the point, no one ever seems to get a gimme in halfcourt sets. And the Mavs do slow it down. Slow? Give the crowd more barbecue, less Sominex.

Mavs look smooth when Rolando Blackman runs around three screens and pops out for a 20-footer. That's neat. And twice a quarter the ball goes low to James Donaldson, who looks around and usually throws it back out. Mavs start all over. Yawn.

Last year, Dallas had one player who made more shots than he missed: Donaldson. That's scary, and also no way to establish an offense. The Mavs held opponents to 102.2 points a game— and scored 102.2 points a game. Lever is charged with opening up things in this stagnant attack, which should get a boost from the newly-arrived Alex English.

PLAYMAKING: Harper and Blackman have been the backcourt starters here since January 1986. Hey, it's a tough job and these two have done it—with mixed results. Blackman managed his ninth straight season of 1,000-plus points last year and he should pass Mark Aguirre this season as the franchise's all-time scorer. Harper is probably a scoring guard masked in a point-guard's role, but it's too late to change now. Again, the arrival of Lever might open things in what has been a pass-it-in, kick-it-out, shoot-a-jumper offense.

DEFENSE: Richie Adubato used to play soda bottles vs. salt and pepper shakers, designing defenses, in roadside coffee shops after high-school games in the early part of his coaching career. Richie knows "D," which is how he got into the league at Dick Vitale's behest in Detroit, and which is why he was hired later in Dallas by John MacLeod. The addition of Rodney McCray, a solid rebounder and gritty defender, is a plus. The stealthiness of Harper, the intimidation in the middle by Donaldson and Roy Tarpley's aggressiveness are the keys to Dallas' defense, which keeps improving under Adubato.

REBOUNDING: The Mavs' small forwards always *look* so nice. Mostly because so many of them have liked taking that fadeaway jumper, hoping it swishes, while backpedaling the other way.

MAVERICK ROSTER

No.	Veterans	Pos.	Ht.	Wt.	Age	Yrs. Pro	College
2	Steve Alford	G	6-2	182	25	3	Indiana
22	Rolando Blackman	G	6-6	206	31	9	Kansas State
15	Brad Davis	G	6-3	183	34	13	Maryland
40	James Donaldson	C	7-2	280	33	10	Washington State
2	Alex English	F	6-7	190	36	13	South Carolina
12	Derek Harper	G	6-4	200	29	7	Illinois
—	Fat Lever	G	6-3	175	30	8	Arizona State
7	Bob McCann	F	6-6	240	26	1	Morehead State
—	Rodney McCray	F	6-8	235	29	7	Louisville
42	Roy Tarpley	F	7-0	250	25	4	Michigan
33	Randy White	F	6-8	250	23	1	Louisiana Tech
32	Herb Williams	F-C	6-11	242	32	9	Ohio State

Rd.	Rookies	Sel. No.	Pos.	Ht.	Wt.	College
2	Phil Henderson	49	G	6-4	170	Duke

Mark Aguirre was that way, so was Adrian Dantley (when not posted low), and so was Sam Perkins, who left for the Lakers in the offseason.

The Dallas centers do the dirty work, mostly on size and by assignment. However, the best rebounder, easily, is Tarpley, but he's not always around. The 7-0 Tarpley, a power forward, is terrific when sound. Make that more-than-terrific. But as a team, Dallas has remained a mediocre rebounding club at the contender level, and approached disgrace on the offensive boards—which explains, perhaps, the acquisition of McCray.

OUTLOOK: There's still no *there* there—whether the Mavs are cavorting in Reunion Arena or climbing walls in despair and occasional giddiness at foreign courts. The franchise has yet to have a winning road record. To use a boxing analogy, the Dallas basketball team is not one you want to look for a six- or eight-round bout. Adubato's corner work is going to keep the Texans close.

But in main-eventers—10, 12, 15 rounds—the Mavericks always have lacked the mark of a champion. They bruise you and scar you, and then watch the ref lift the other guy's hand in victory. Nice club fighters without a KO punch. Did Lever arrive with a roll of quarters clenched in his fist?

MAVERICK PROFILES

ROLANDO BLACKMAN 31 6-6 206   Guard

Mr. Maverick . . . The best and most consistently productive player in franchise history . . . Topped 1,000 points for ninth straight year . . . Check this combination: Averaged 36.7 minutes a game, about 60 seconds under his own club record, and didn't foul out all season; hasn't been disqualified in 710 games played . . . If he and newly acquired Fat Lever remain together, what happens to each player's All-Star ambitions? . . . Born Feb. 26, 1959, in Panama City, Panama . . . Moved to Brooklyn, N.Y., as a youngster . . . Three-time Big 8 Defensive Player of Year at Kansas State, was selected ninth in the first round of 1981 draft by Mavs . . . Had best shooting year (.498) in four seasons, but always has been around .500 in his excellent career . . . Serves as team's captain and Players Association rep.

Year	Team	G	FG	FG Pct.	FT	FT Pct.	Reb.	Ast.	TP	Avg.
1981-82	Dallas	82	439	.513	212	.768	254	105	1091	13.3
1982-83	Dallas	75	513	.492	297	.780	293	185	1326	17.7
1983-84	Dallas	81	721	.546	372	.812	373	288	1815	22.4
1984-85	Dallas	81	625	.508	342	.828	300	289	1598	19.7
1985-86	Dallas	82	677	.514	404	.836	291	271	1762	21.5
1986-87	Dallas	80	626	.495	419	.884	278	266	1676	21.0
1987-88	Dallas	71	497	.473	331	.873	246	262	1325	18.7
1988-89	Dallas	78	594	.476	316	.854	273	288	1534	19.7
1989-90	Dallas	80	626	.498	287	.844	280	289	1552	19.4
	Totals	710	5318	.502	2980	.834	2588	2243	13679	19.3

LAFAYETTE (FAT) LEVER 30 6-3 175   Guard

Finally going to have a paycheck to match his performance . . . What does he do? Just about everything . . . Last year for Denver, led team in scoring (18.3), rebounding (9.3), assists (6.5) . . . Became the ninth—and smallest—NBA player ever to pull off that trifecta for his team . . . Became known for versatility during collegiate career at Arizona State . . . The 11th pick of the 1982 draft by Portland . . . Taken for granted by Blazers, who included him in Calvin Natt, Wayne Cooper package for Kiki Vandeweghe after Lever's second season . . . Never had a bad season for Nuggets . . . Before last year, never earned much in way of national recognition beyond second team All-NBA (1987), second unit All-Defense following season . . . Always took the pressure shot or the beat-the-clock attempt for Nuggets, in part accounting for career sub-50 percent FG mark . . . Placed second in league (10-5) to Magic Johnson in triple-doubles last year.

Year	Team	G	FG	FG Pct.	FT	FT Pct.	Reb.	Ast.	TP	Avg.
1982-83	Portland	81	256	.431	116	.730	225	426	633	7.8
1983-84	Portland	81	313	.447	159	.743	218	372	788	9.7
1984-85	Denver	82	424	.430	197	.770	411	613	1051	12.8
1985-86	Denver	78	468	.441	132	.725	420	584	1080	13.8
1986-87	Denver	82	643	.469	244	.782	729	654	1552	18.9
1987-88	Denver	82	643	.473	248	.785	665	639	1546	18.9
1988-89	Denver	71	558	.457	270	.785	662	559	1409	19.8
1989-90	Denver	79	568	.443	271	.804	734	517	1443	18.3
	Totals	636	3873	.452	1637	.772	4064	4364	9502	14.9

ROY TARPLEY 25 7-0 250   Forward

Marvelous talent . . . Sensational future ahead of him—if he keeps his head straight . . . Is among the league's elite big men . . . Ferocious style . . . Born Nov. 28, 1964, in Detroit . . . Played on successive Big 10 champions at Michigan . . . Was seventh pick in first round of 1986 by Dallas . . . Won the league's "6th Man" award in 1987-88 . . . Quick hands and feet make him a threat to block shots or steal ball . . . Runs floor superbly but has a junior-high-level jumper . . . He's always among NBA leaders in rebounds secured per minute.

Year	Team	G	FG	FG Pct.	FT	FT Pct.	Reb.	Ast.	TP	Avg.
1986-87	Dallas	75	233	.467	94	.676	533	52	561	7.5
1987-88	Dallas	81	444	.500	205	.740	959	86	1093	13.5
1988-89	Dallas	19	131	.541	66	.688	218	17	328	17.3
1989-90	Dallas	45	314	.451	130	.756	589	67	758	16.8
	Totals	220	1122	.483	495	.724	2299	222	2740	12.5

DEREK HARPER 29 6-4 200   Guard

Watch your program and cup of soda . . . Blink and they're gone around this swift-handed point guard . . . Was fifth in league in steals last year . . . Had twice as many as any Mav, and for the sixth straight season broke his own team record . . . Still, you're never quite sure what he's going to do in the BIG game . . . Should actually be better at running the club—which is why Mavs went out and acquired Fat Lever . . . Born Oct. 13, 1961, in Elberton, Ga. . . . He left Illinois after junior year . . . Was the 11th pick in the 1983 first round by Mavs . . . He's missed only nine games in seven seasons . . . Last year had more assists than next two teammates combined . . . Has eclectic offcourt tastes: jazz and soap operas.

Year	Team	G	FG	FG Pct.	FT	FT Pct.	Reb.	Ast.	TP	Avg.
1983-84	Dallas	82	200	.443	66	.673	172	239	469	5.7
1984-85	Dallas	82	329	.520	111	.721	199	360	790	9.6
1985-86	Dallas	79	390	.534	171	.747	226	416	963	12.2
1986-87	Dallas	77	497	.501	160	.684	199	609	1230	16.0
1987-88	Dallas	82	536	.459	261	.759	246	634	1393	17.0
1988-89	Dallas	81	538	.477	229	.806	228	570	1404	17.3
1989-90	Dallas	82	567	.488	250	.794	244	609	1473	18.0
	Totals	565	3057	.488	1248	.753	1514	3437	7722	13.7

RODNEY McCRAY 29 6-8 235   Guard

Made impressive comeback physically and statistically in second full season with Kings . . . And now he's a Maverick, traded for one of Dallas' No. 1 picks prior to the 1990 draft . . . Led league in minutes played last year with 3,238 . . . Played all 82 games for third time in his seven pro years . . . Has missed one game twice, more than three only in 1988-89 . . . A stamina-sapping, weight-adding condition was traced to a colon blockage that needed surgical correction . . . Born Aug. 29, 1961, in Mt. Vernon, N.Y. . . . Member of Louisville's 1980 NCAA champions . . . 1980 Olympian . . . The No. 3 pick in 1983 draft by Houston . . . Never met offensive expectations there . . . First NBA All-Defensive Team in 1987-88 . . . Traded to Kings with Jim Petersen by Houston on Oct. 11, 1988, for Otis Thorpe . . . A career .513 FG shooter . . . With one-game high of 30 last season, his 16.6-point average was four above career norm.

Year	Team	G	FG	FG Pct.	FT	FT Pct.	Reb.	Ast.	TP	Avg.
1983-84	Houston	79	335	.499	182	.731	450	176	853	10.8
1984-85	Houston	82	476	.535	231	.738	539	355	1183	14.4
1985-86	Houston	82	338	.537	171	.770	520	292	847	10.3
1986-87	Houston	81	432	.552	306	.779	578	434	1170	14.4
1987-88	Houston	81	359	.481	288	.785	631	264	1006	12.4
1988-89	Sacramento	68	340	.466	169	.722	514	293	854	12.6
1989-90	Sacramento	82	537	.515	273	.784	669	377	1358	16.6
	Totals	555	2817	.513	1620	.762	3901	2191	7271	13.1

ALEX ENGLISH 36 6-7 190   Forward

Eighth-highest scorer in NBA history, unhappy with Doug Moe in Denver, signed estimated $1.5 million, free-agent contract with Mavs . . . Born Jan. 5, 1954, in Columbia, S.C. . . . Set South Carolina career scoring record, finished with 1,000-plus rebounds . . . He's since left most board work to others, and done quite nicely as a pro . . . Milwaukee selected him 23rd with second-round 1976 pick . . . Underutilized by Bucks, for whom in two seasons he had his only sub-10-point seasons . . . Traded to Denver, he was always as graceful as a mile-high cumulus cloud . . . Actor, writer and poet . . . Subtleties of his game lost favor with meat-and-potatoes lover Doug Moe . . . If not scoring 26-to-28-points a game, his "deficiencies are exposed," according to ex-teammate and Nugget broadcaster Dan Issel . . . Production? Scored 21,018 points in decade commencing Jan. 1, 1980, ending Dec. 31, 1989.

Year	Team	G	FG	FG Pct.	FT	FT Pct.	Reb.	Ast.	TP	Avg.
1976-77	Milwaukee	60	132	.477	46	.767	168	25	310	5.2
1977-78	Milwaukee	82	343	.542	104	.727	395	129	790	9.6
1978-79	Indiana	81	563	.511	173	.752	655	271	1299	16.0
1979-80	Ind.-Den.	78	553	.501	210	.789	605	224	1318	16.9
1980-81	Denver	81	768	.494	390	.850	646	290	1929	23.8
1981-82	Denver	82	855	.551	372	.840	558	433	2082	25.4
1982-83	Denver	82	959	.516	406	.829	601	397	2326	28.4
1983-84	Denver	82	907	.529	352	.824	464	406	2167	26.4
1984-85	Denver	81	939	.518	383	.829	458	344	2262	27.9
1985-86	Denver	81	951	.504	511	.862	405	320	2414	29.8
1986-87	Denver	82	965	.503	411	.844	344	422	2345	28.6
1987-88	Denver	80	843	.495	314	.828	373	377	2000	25.0
1988-89	Denver	82	924	.491	325	.858	326	383	2175	26.5
1989-90	Denver	80	635	.491	161	.880	286	225	1433	17.9
	Totals	1114	10337	.509	4158	.831	6284	4246	24850	22.3

RANDY WHITE 23 6-8 250   Forward

Handled himself pretty well as a rookie in difficult set of circumstances . . . How difficult? He came out of the same college as Karl Malone and drew endless and unfair comparisons . . . And Dallas had passed on Malone, now merely a superstar . . . Then he arrives in football-crazed Dallas, where one of the most famous Cowboys had been a guy by the name of Randy

White . . . Born Nov. 4, 1967, in Shreveport, La. . . . Played tight end and defensive end first two seasons at Huntington High in his hometown . . . Then concentrated on hoops . . . Finished third in career scoring, fourth in rebounding at Louisiana Tech . . . Dallas made him the No. 8 pick in 1989 draft . . . Earned two starts in 55 games, shot poorly from field, terribly from foul line.

Year	Team	G	FG	FG Pct.	FT	FT Pct.	Reb.	Ast.	TP	Avg.
1989-90	Dallas	55	93	.369	50	.562	173	21	237	4.3

BRAD DAVIS 34 6-3 183   Guard

No one has worked harder to make a career than this example of doggedness . . . After all these years, he can still contribute . . . Born Dec. 17, 1955, in Monaca, Pa. . . . Went into 1977 draft under the old "hardship" rules after his junior year at Maryland . . . Picked 15th in first round by the Lakers, with whom he lasted only one season . . . Had mini-runs with Indiana and Utah and was in CBA three different times . . . Signed as free agent by Dallas and he's the only remaining member of franchise's first team—though technically not an "original" Mav . . . One of league's oldest players in both age and length of service . . . Once made 10 consecutive three-pointers, and his .337 mark last season was better than his career mark . . . Coach Richie Adubato calls him "one of the most incredible performers" he's ever seen.

Year	Team	G	FG	FG Pct.	FT	FT Pct.	Reb.	Ast.	TP	Avg.
1977-78	Los Angeles	33	30	.417	22	.759	35	83	82	2.5
1978-79	L.A.-Ind.	27	31	.564	16	.696	17	52	78	2.9
1979-80	Ind.-Utah	18	35	.556	13	.813	17	50	83	4.6
1980-81	Dallas	56	230	.561	163	.799	151	385	626	11.2
1981-82	Dallas	82	397	.515	185	.804	226	509	993	12.1
1982-83	Dallas	79	359	.572	186	.845	198	565	915	11.6
1983-84	Dallas	81	345	.530	199	.836	187	561	896	11.1
1984-85	Dallas	82	310	.505	158	.888	193	581	825	10.1
1985-86	Dallas	82	267	.532	198	.868	146	467	764	9.3
1986-87	Dallas	82	199	.456	147	.860	114	373	577	7.0
1987-88	Dallas	75	208	.501	91	.843	102	303	537	7.2
1988-89	Dallas	78	183	.483	99	.805	108	242	497	6.4
1989-90	Dallas	73	179	.490	77	.770	93	242	470	6.4
	Totals	848	2773	.517	1554	.832	1587	4413	7343	8.7

JAMES DONALDSON 33 7-2 280   Center

Made a remarkable physical recovery to play in 73 games last year . . . A huge man, he had ruptured patellar tendon in his right knee on March 10, 1989 . . . Worked out in a rehabilitation program and now is planning his own sports-medicine clinic . . . Born Aug. 16, 1957, in Heacham, England, while his father was there in military service . . . Not much of a high-school player, had only two scholarship offers . . . Got a sociology degree and not a lot of basketball headlines at Washington State . . . Afterthought 73d pick by Seattle in 1979's fourth round . . . Despite moves from Sonics to Clippers to Mavericks, once went 586 games without missing an appearance . . . Shot .539 from floor last season against his prior career .587 . . . Stubborn or superstitious? Hasn't attempted a three-pointer under any circumstance in his 10 seasons.

Year	Team	G	FG	FG Pct.	FT	FT Pct.	Reb.	Ast.	TP	Avg.
1980-81	Seattle	68	129	.542	101	.594	309	42	359	5.3
1981-82	Seattle	82	255	.609	151	.629	490	51	661	8.1
1982-83	Seattle	82	289	.583	150	.688	501	97	728	8.9
1983-84	San Diego	82	360	.596	249	.761	649	90	969	11.8
1984-85	L.A. Clippers	82	351	.637	227	.749	668	48	929	11.3
1985-86	LAC-Dal.	83	256	.558	204	.803	795	96	716	8.6
1986-87	Dallas	82	311	.586	267	.812	973	63	889	10.8
1987-88	Dallas	81	212	.558	147	.778	755	66	571	7.0
1988-89	Dallas	53	193	.573	95	.766	570	38	481	9.1
1989-90	Dallas	73	258	.539	149	.700	630	57	665	9.1
	Totals	768	2614	.582	1740	.735	6340	648	6968	9.1

HERB WILLIAMS 32 6-11 242   Forward-Center

On the way down . . . Four times among league's top 10 shot-blockers, but not last year—his first full season as a Mav . . . Holds a bundle of career records for Pacers, who drafted him No. 14 in 1981 . . . Born Feb. 16, 1958, in Columbus, Ohio . . . Topped 2,000 points, 1,000 rebounds during his college career at Ohio State . . . Played seven-plus steady but unspectacular seasons in Indiana . . . Compiled a 7.7 rebounding average during Pacer stay . . . Had been an annual double-figure scorer until drifting to 8.6 last year . . . Made the second-luckiest heave in NBA history on Jan. 8, 1988—an 81-footer.

Year	Team	G	FG	FG Pct.	FT	FT Pct.	Reb.	Ast.	TP	Avg.
1981-82	Indiana	82	407	.477	126	.670	605	139	942	11.5
1982-83	Indiana	78	580	.499	155	.705	583	262	1315	16.9
1983-84	Indiana	69	411	.478	207	.702	554	215	1029	14.9
1984-85	Indiana	75	575	.475	224	.657	634	252	1375	18.3
1985-86	Indiana	78	627	.492	294	.730	710	174	1549	19.9
1986-87	Indiana	74	451	.480	199	.740	543	174	1101	14.9
1987-88	Indiana	75	311	.425	126	.737	469	98	748	10.0
1988-89	Ind.-Dal.	76	322	.436	133	.686	593	124	777	10.2
1989-90	Dallas	81	295	.444	108	.679	391	119	700	8.6
	Totals	688	3979	.472	1572	.702	5082	1557	9536	13.9

STEVE ALFORD 25 6-2 182   Guard

Second time around with Dallas . . . Last season wasn't much more fun than the first stop . . . A 19.5-point collegiate career scorer and .533 shooter in four years under Bobby Knight . . . Led nation in free-throw shooting with .913 as freshman before playing on 1984 Olympic team and the Indiana NCAA champs of 1987 . . . Mavs chose him in second round (26th) of 1987 draft . . . Made scant appearances as a rookie and then split 1988-89 between Dallas and Golden State . . . Born Nov. 23, 1964, in Franklin, Ind.

Year	Team	G	FG	FG Pct.	FT	FT Pct.	Reb.	Ast.	TP	Avg.
1987-88	Dallas	28	21	.382	16	.941	23	23	59	2.1
1988-89	Dal.-G.S.	66	148	.457	50	.820	72	92	366	5.5
1989-90	Dallas	41	63	.457	35	.946	25	39	168	4.1
	Totals	135	232	.449	101	.878	120	154	593	4.4

THE ROOKIE

PHIL HENDERSON 22 6-4 170   Guard

A plugger, but an erratic shooter . . . Earned a spot on All-NCAA Final Four team last spring despite Duke's blowout loss in finals to UNLV . . . Would you nightly put your life in these hands? Year-by-year FG shooting: .556, .429, .525, .473 . . . "He should shoot any time he has an open shot,'' says Duke coach Mike Krzyzewski . . . Guard-rich Dallas, without a first-round pick, gave him a look at No. 49 in second round . . . Born April 17, 1968, in University Park, Ill.

COACH RICHIE ADUBATO: Patience, patience, patience . . . Trying to make it permanent after a second shot as a quick-fill, interim coach . . . This time has a much better chance of sticking . . . Born Nov. 23, 1937, in East Orange, N.J. . . . A longtime member of North Jersey high-school coaching fraternity that has advanced to top level . . . Peers include college coaches Rollie Massimino and Lou Campanelli, veteran pro assistant Herman Kull, TV analysts Hubie Brown and Dick Vitale . . . Had his first experience as head man in Detroit . . . Was hired as assistant by Vitale, and took over after Vitale was fired 12 games into the 1979-80 season . . . Richie left soon after, went into scouting . . . Hired by John MacLeod as No. 1 aide and defensive specialist in 1986 . . . Influence was measurable: Mavs in four years dropped points-allowed average from 114.2 to 110.4 to 104.9 to club-record 104.7 . . . Mavs were 5-6 when MacLeod was dismissed Nov. 29 . . . Club finished 42-29 under Adubato, who had contract extended for three years as season was ending . . . Hoops aside, Adubato (you pronounce it ''Ab-duh-bah-doe'') is consumed in offseason by ravioli, tennis and the theater.

GREATEST REBOUNDER

Choose by totals and Mark Aguirre (yes!) is still the No. 1 guy in Dallas rebounding. Go by average/potential, it has to be Roy Tarpley. But on consistent production your man is James Donaldson, a quietly efficient professional who has spent roughly half his 10-year career with the Mavs after stints with Seattle and the L.A. Clippers.

The 7-2 Donaldson never has had a 1,000-rebound season, but Aguirre boarded only on occasional whim before his trade. Sam Perkins? He was rarely much more than an eight-rebounds-per-game, perimeter-shooting forward.

Lurking is Tarpley—a gifted, 7-foot problem child. With continuing effort—he has a 10.5 average over two full seasons and bits of two others—he could move into most-favored boardman status.

ALL-TIME MAVERICK LEADERS

SEASON

Points: Mark Aguirre, 2,330, 1983-84
Assists: Derek Harper, 634, 1987-88
Rebounds: James Donaldson, 973, 1986-87

GAME

Points: Mark Aguirre, 49 vs. Philadelphia, 1/28/85
Assists: Derek Harper, 18 vs. Boston, 12/29/88
Rebounds: James Donaldson, 27 vs. Portland (3 OT), 12/29/89

CAREER

Points: Mark Aguirre, 13,930, 1981-89
Assists: Brad Davis, 4,228, 1980-90
Rebounds: Sam Perkins, 3,767, 1984-90

DENVER NUGGETS

TEAM DIRECTORY: Owners: Bertram M. Lee, Pete C. Bynoe, Robert Wussler; Pres.: Carl Scheer; GM: Bernie Bickerstaff; Asst. to Pres.: Dan Issel; Dir. Pub. Rel.: Jay Clark; Coach: Paul Westhead. Arena: McNichols Sports Arena (17,022). Colors: White, blue, green, yellow, red, purple and orange.

Walter Davis carries 19.9 average into 14th season.

SCOUTING REPORT

SHOOTING: This is playground heaven for guys who love to launch it. If you promise to make four passes a game—two if you're a non-starter—you apparently may put up a shot every other time you touch the ball. That includes inbound passes, by the way. Wrong? The Nuggets led the league in shots attempted last year (no, this is not a recording).

Unfortunately for Denver, 22 teams in the NBA managed a better field-goal percentage. And while only the Clippers, with nine, had more players average double-figure scoring than the Nuggets, not one Denver player—not Alex English (now in Dallas), not Walter Davis—shot 50 percent.

The cast of characters has changed this season. You bet it has! Start with the biggest character of all, Doug Moe, replaced after a decade by Paul Westhead. But will the offensive philosophy change? No way. "We'll have the fastest-paced game in basketball," promises Westhead. "It's going to knock your socks off. If you wear a neck brace, you won't last through any of our games."

PLAYMAKING: What's it tell you when your leading scorer and rebounder is also your No. 1 assist man? Well, it either means that Magic Johnson slipped across the Rockies unannounced or that Fat Lever did all the work. And *did* is the operative word here. Lever's gone, moved on to Dallas, and Denver apparently will be going with a backcourt of a 6-1 (sure!) rookie, Chris Jackson, at the point, and 5-10 (equally sure!) Michael Adams at off-guard. Well, maybe not all the time, but frequently enough to raise the spirits of WBL hopefuls everywhere.

In the so-called passing-game offense that Moe so cherished, there was not a whole lot of playmaking involved. Pass the ball, go away; pass the ball, go away. Someone finally is left alone, and he shoots. Having someone in addition to Davis able to shoot well would help. Maybe that someone is Orlando Woolridge, late of the Los Angeles Lakers..

DEFENSE: Don't laugh. The Nuggets play defense. Fullcourt sometimes, halfcourt sometimes, no court sometimes. They're a strange team when the other club has the ball. Denver gambles on the perimeter and smothers inside. It's when the Nuggets try to do both at the same time that they get in trouble, which is often. Moe's club was first in steal-to-turnover ratio. And—surprise—

NUGGET ROSTER

No.	Veterans	Pos.	Ht.	Wt.	Age	Yrs. Pro	College
14	Michael Adams	G	5-10	165	27	5	Boston College
6	Walter Davis	G	6-6	200	36	13	North Carolina
23	T.R. Dunn	G	6-4	192	35	13	Alabama
24	Bill Hanzlik	F	6-7	200	32	10	Notre Dame
35	Jerome Lane	F	6-6	232	23	2	Pittsburgh
21	Todd Lichti	G	6-4	205	23	1	Stanford
41	Blair Rasmussen	C	7-0	260	27	5	Oregon
0	Orlando Woolridge	F	6-9	215	30	9	Notre Dame

Rd.	Rookies	Sel. No.	Pos.	Ht.	Wt.	College
1	Chris Jackson	34	G	6-1	170	Louisiana State
1	*Terry Mills	16	F	6-10	230	Michigan
2	Marcus Liberty	42	F	6-8	205	Illinois

*Drafted by Bucks, traded to Nuggets; signed to play in Greece

Lever had a lot to do with both numbers. He hiked the former, lowered the latter. Isolated, Denver's big people traditionally have been vulnerable. Westhead says his Nuggets will play a full-court pressure defense.

REBOUNDING: About a month after the draft, the Denver roster still seemed ready to compete in one of those 6-foot-8 and under summer leagues. Small, small guards they had. Forwards, also small or contact-shy, they also had—in abundance. Centers? Well, Danny Schayes was the best they had, and now he's in Milwaukee. And Terry Mills, the 6-10 rookie for whom Schayes was traded, signed for big bucks to play in Greece.

Jerome Lane should be able to help. In a rapidly changing, well-muscled Western Conference, the Nuggets are notably lacking the beef.

OUTLOOK: Can Westhead make the difference? This much is safe to say: the future is not now. The Nuggets almost certainly will fall below .500 this year and will only sniff at a playoff spot for several more seasons. Denver had to make changes, but the personnel moves came much too late. Not months late, years late. The sacrificial moving of Lever was reflective of the shakiness in the front office. While Moe always managed to make things exciting, the patience limit of Denver fans was severely stretched. It was time for a change.

NUGGET PROFILES

WALTER DAVIS 36 6-6 200   Guard-Forward

Chronologically, "The Greyhound" is long in the tooth... Defensively, for opponents, he's more of a toothache... It's almost hard to believe that 14 years ago he was a U.S. Olympian ... Or that it was 1978 when he was NBA Rookie of Year with Phoenix... His playing skills have held up remarkably, but he's more proud of off-floor life... Twice a hospitalized abuser of illegal substances, he's been model citizen since celebrated "second strike" in Phoenix... Born Sept. 9, 1954, in Pineville, N.C.... Honed skills under Dean Smith at North Carolina... Phoenix took him with fifth pick in 1977 draft... Only twice, in 1978 and '79, has he even made All-NBA second team ... Spent first 11 seasons as a Sun before signing with Denver as a free agent July 6, 1988... Still a remarkable scorer (17.5)... Came off bench in all 69 appearances and was being sought by other clubs through mid-summer.

Year	Team	G	FG	FG Pct.	FT	FT Pct.	Reb.	Ast.	TP	Avg.
1977-78	Phoenix	81	786	.526	387	.830	484	273	1959	24.2
1978-79	Phoenix	79	764	.561	340	.831	373	339	1868	23.6
1979-80	Phoenix	75	657	.563	299	.819	272	337	1613	21.5
1980-81	Phoenix	78	593	.539	209	.836	200	302	1402	18.0
1981-82	Phoenix	55	350	.523	91	.820	103	162	794	14.4
1982-83	Phoenix	80	665	.516	184	.818	197	397	1521	19.0
1983-84	Phoenix	78	652	.512	233	.863	202	429	1557	20.0
1984-85	Phoenix	23	139	.450	64	.877	35	98	345	15.0
1985-86	Phoenix	70	624	.485	257	.843	203	361	1523	21.8
1986-87	Phoenix	79	779	.514	288	.862	244	364	1867	23.6
1987-88	Phoenix	68	488	.473	205	.887	159	278	1217	17.9
1988-89	Denver	81	536	.498	175	.879	151	190	1267	15.6
1989-90	Denver	69	497	.481	207	.912	179	155	1207	17.5
	Totals	916	7530	.516	2939	.848	2802	3685	18140	19.8

MICHAEL ADAMS 27 5-10 165   Guard

Don't blink, or he's gone... A loose toy cannon in now ex-coach Doug Moe's open offense ... What position does he play, anyway?... Only shot better than .433 once in five-year career... But quickness (you can't guard him too close), three-point shooting make him a constant pest... Born Jan. 19, 1963, in Hartford, Conn.... Productive career at Boston College, but pros were scared off by size, matchup problems ... Taken 66th in third round of 1985 draft by Sacramento ... Funny game, pro hoops: Couldn't make it with Kings or Washington Bullets, but has started since then-assistant Allan Bristow persuaded Moe to deal for him in 1987 ... Had spent 38 games in CBA with, aptly, the Bay State Bombardiers ... Last year, pushed up 432 three-pointers, fell eight short of matching own NBA record with 158 makes (.368).

Year	Team	G	FG	FG Pct.	FT	FT Pct.	Reb.	Ast.	TP	Avg.
1985-86	Sacramento	18	16	.364	8	.667	6	22	40	2.2
1986-87	Washington	63	160	.407	105	.847	123	244	453	7.2
1987-88	Denver	82	416	.449	166	.834	223	503	1137	13.9
1988-89	Denver	77	468	.433	322	.819	283	490	1424	18.5
1989-90	Denver	79	398	.402	267	.850	225	495	1221	15.5
	Totals	319	1458	.424	868	.833	860	1754	4275	13.4

BILL HANZLIK 32 6-7 200　　　　Guard-Forward

Became 10-year man last season ... Earnest, competent overachiever ... Never a very good shooter ... Made a career by doing the tough dirty work ... Has guarded everyone from 6-footers to Kareem Abdul-Jabbar ... And he even drove Kareem to frustration ... Born Dec. 6, 1957, in Middletown, Ohio ... He was "that other guy," on Notre Dame team that included higher-scoring pros Kelly Tripucka, Orlando Woolridge ... Lifelong regret is summer of 1980, when he was on the Olympic team that boycotted the Games ... Taken with 20th pick in first round of 1980 by Seattle ... After two years with SuperSonics, spent eight straight seasons with Denver ... Second-unit NBA All-Defensive team in 1986 ... Since then has twice come back from back surgery ... Was constant target of barbs from Doug Moe, who said he was a 100-percent shooter—75 percent in practice, 25 percent in games.

Year	Team	G	FG	FG Pct.	FT	FT Pct.	Reb.	Ast.	TP	Avg.
1980-81	Seattle	74	138	.478	119	.793	153	111	396	5.4
1981-82	Seattle	81	167	.468	138	.784	266	183	472	5.8
1982-83	Denver	82	187	.428	125	.781	236	268	500	6.1
1983-84	Denver	80	132	.431	167	.807	205	252	434	5.4
1984-85	Denver	80	220	.421	180	.756	207	210	621	7.8
1985-86	Denver	79	331	.447	318	.785	264	316	988	12.5
1986-87	Denver	73	307	.412	316	.786	256	280	952	13.0
1987-88	Denver	77	109	.380	129	.791	171	166	350	4.5
1988-89	Denver	41	66	.437	68	.782	93	86	201	4.9
1989-90	Denver	81	179	.452	136	.743	207	186	500	6.2
	Totals	748	1836	.434	1696	.781	2058	2058	5414	7.2

JEROME LANE 23 6-6 232   Forward

Beginning third NBA season, but still an undefined talent... Might have groomed himself for a more promising pro career had he been able to stand one more year in college... This is a player who has played point guard—and led the NCAA in rebounding as a sophomore with 13.5 a game at Pitt... But still doesn't know how to make free throws on anything near a consistent basis... Born Dec. 4, 1966, in Akron, Ohio... Left Pittsburgh in 1988 after junior year... Nuggets made him the 23d choice in the first round... Missed six weeks of rookie year with sprained ankle... Strong offensive rebounder... Shot only .469 last season in an offense designed for good opportunities... Pencil him in as a future factor in the All-Star Weekend dunk contest.

Year	Team	G	FG	FG Pct.	FT	FT Pct.	Reb.	Ast.	TP	Avg.
1988-89	Denver	54	109	.426	43	.384	200	60	261	4.8
1989-90	Denver	67	145	.469	44	.367	361	105	334	5.0
	Totals	121	254	.450	87	.375	561	165	595	4.9

TODD LICHTI 23 6-4 205   Guard

Painful range of emotions last year... A mid-first-round pick in the 1989 draft... But not even Stanford prepares you for personal tragedy... Less than a year after the draft, his girl friend was killed in an auto accident... A passenger in the car, Lichti was fortunate to escape only with a foot injury that required surgical repair... Born Jan. 8, 1967, in Walnut Creek, Cal.... Averaged exactly 20.1 points through each of final two seasons, 66 games for Stanford... Quickness fell into question for some reason... Estimates of his draft spot ranged from lottery to early second round... Denver, recalling he'd been high-school sprinter, made him No. 15... More a scorer than shooter, he doesn't really have three-point range... Adept on fast-break wing and gets to foul line—usually positive career indicators in young players.

Year	Team	G	FG	FG Pct.	FT	FT Pct.	Reb.	Ast.	TP	Avg.
1989-90	Denver	79	250	.486	130	.747	151	116	630	8.0

ORLANDO WOOLRIDGE 30 6-9 215   Forward

'O' Wow... Was Lakers' best off-the-bench scorer before coming to Nuggets in August trade... Learned "new" game after joining Lakers two years ago... Didn't fit comfortably into offensive scheme until last season... Had been suspended from league for substance abuse early in 1987-88 season, second with Nets... Born Dec. 16, 1959, in Bernice, La.... In 1981, Chicago grabbed him out of Notre Dame with sixth pick in first round... Did zilch his rookie year, but went over 20-plus points in three of next five years... Cost the Nets a No. 1 pick to take him from Bulls... Not much loved in Meadowlands because of that and subsequent drug suspension... Scary dunker off the drive, when he doesn't drift away from hoop to be cute... After much urging and coaching, he controlled jumper last season and his .556 FG percentage was fifth-best in league.

Year	Team	G	FG	FG Pct.	FT	FT Pct.	Reb.	Ast.	TP	Avg.
1981-82	Chicago	75	202	.513	144	.699	227	81	548	7.3
1982-83	Chicago	57	361	.580	217	.638	298	97	939	16.5
1983-84	Chicago	75	570	.525	303	.715	369	136	1444	19.3
1984-85	Chicago	77	679	.554	409	.785	435	135	1767	22.9
1985-86	Chicago	70	540	.495	364	.788	350	213	1448	20.7
1986-87	New Jersey	75	556	.521	438	.777	367	261	1551	20.7
1987-88	New Jersey	19	110	.445	92	.708	91	71	312	16.4
1988-89	L.A. Lakers	74	231	.468	253	.738	270	58	715	9.7
1989-90	L.A. Lakers	62	306	.556	176	.733	185	96	788	12.7
	Totals	584	3555	.525	2396	.742	2592	1148	9512	16.3

BLAIR RASMUSSEN 27 7-0 260   Center-Forward

The player with whom just about every other NBA player shares a love-hate relationship... All but the super-paid superstars liked the size of the contract he got last year... What peers didn't appreciate was that before theirs did, this (then) fourth-year non-factor's salary went through the roof—seven years for an estimated $17.5-million... Born Nov. 13, 1962, in Auburn, Wash.... MVP at Oregon final three seasons... Never averaged more than 16.6 in college... In 1985, Denver made him the 15th pick overall... Has had two double-figure scoring seasons in pros (including last year's 12.4)... Started 55 times... Teammates called him "Cashmussen"... At an unskinny 7-0, he was second rebounder in Denver to 6-3 Fat Lever and specialized in fallaway or stepback jumpers... What hath Jack Sikma wrought?

Year	Team	G	FG	FG Pct.	FT	FT Pct.	Reb.	Ast.	TP	Avg.
1985-86	Denver	48	61	.407	31	.795	97	16	153	3.2
1986-87	Denver	74	268	.470	169	.732	465	60	705	9.5
1987-88	Denver	79	435	.492	132	.776	437	78	1002	12.7
1988-89	Denver	77	257	.445	69	.852	287	49	583	7.6
1989-90	Denver	81	445	.497	111	.828	594	82	1001	12.4
	Totals	359	1466	.477	512	.782	1880	285	3444	9.6

T.R. DUNN 35 6-4 192   Guard

Good extra hand to have around on deep team... Scouts always loved his desire and athleticism more than his skills... Born Feb. 1, 1955, in Birmingham, Ala.... He's only averaged double-figure scoring twice since high school—in his sophomore and senior seasons at Alabama... Chosen 41st in the 1977 second round by Portland... Traded after three years with Trail Blazers to Denver, where he missed only four games in next eight seasons... Defensive specialist... Most he's ever averaged over a season is 8.2 points in his second year as a Nugget... Free agent, went to Phoenix for a year... Returned last season to Nuggets to help off-the-bench... Still one of best backcourt defenders in NBA.

Year	Team	G	FG	FG Pct.	FT	FT Pct.	Reb.	Ast.	TP	Avg.
1977-78	Portland	63	100	.417	37	.661	147	45	237	3.8
1978-79	Portland	80	246	.448	122	.772	344	103	614	7.7
1979-80	Portland	82	240	.436	84	.757	324	147	564	6.9
1980-81	Denver	82	146	.412	79	.653	301	81	371	4.5
1981-82	Denver	82	258	.512	153	.712	559	188	669	8.2
1982-83	Denver	82	254	.482	119	.730	615	189	627	7.6
1983-84	Denver	80	174	.470	106	.731	574	228	454	5.7
1984-85	Denver	81	175	.489	84	.724	385	153	434	5.4
1985-86	Denver	82	172	.454	68	.773	377	171	412	5.0
1986-87	Denver	81	118	.428	36	.655	265	147	272	3.4
1987-88	Denver	82	70	.449	40	.769	240	87	180	2.2
1988-89	Phoenix	34	12	.343	9	.750	60	25	33	1.0
1989-90	Denver	65	44	.454	26	.667	138	43	114	1.8
	Totals	976	2009	.457	963	.724	4329	1607	4981	5.1

Michael Adams and the three-point shot are synonymous.

THE ROOKIES

CHRIS JACKSON 21 6-1 170   Guard

Quick, flashy and creative . . . Also: Small, weak defensively and suspect physical strength . . . Not a surprise that he was encouraged to come out of LSU after only two years . . . But a huge surprise that he went as high as No. 3 overall by Nuggets . . . Assumption of supporters is that his weaknesses will be masked in passing-game offense and help-out defense . . . Entertaining player who led SEC in scoring both college seasons . . . Netted 30 or more points in 28 of 64 contests, notching 50 three times . . . Afflicted with Tourette's Syndrome, a neurological condition often manifesting itself in facial twitching, and blackouts . . . Born March 9, 1969, in Gulfport, Miss.

MARCUS LIBERTY 22 6-8 205 **Forward**
Played two collegiate seasons . . . Ineligible as freshman and passed up senior year at Illinois . . . Led team in rebounds and shot-blocking and his 50.8 percent shooting and 17.8-point average last year were second only to Kendall Gill . . . Has nice range near three-point line, but don't ever ask him to make a pass . . . Born Oct. 27, 1968, in Chicago.

COACH PAUL WESTHEAD: Replacing colorful, controversial Doug Moe, he returns to the NBA after five seasons at Loyola Marymount, where his teams set NCAA scoring records . . . "People who know me realize I stood for fast-break basketball long before I got into the NBA," he says . . . Born Feb. 21, 1939, in Malverne, Pa., he played at St. Joseph's . . . Coached nine years at LaSalle (142-105) before joining the Lakers as an assistant to Jack McKinney in 1979 . . . Was the toast of Tinseltown in the spring of 1980 when he guided the Lakers to the NBA championship after taking over for McKinney, who was forced to step down after a bizarre bicycle accident . . . In 1980-81, the Lakers won the Pacific Division title but lost in the playoffs . . . Was fired 11 games into the 1981-82 season after criticism of his offense by Magic Johnson . . . Coached the Chicago Bulls for just one season, 1982-83, when they were 28-54 . . . Overall NBA record is 140-104 . . . Is a Shakespearean scholar.

GREATEST REBOUNDER

George McGinnis holds the franchise's single-season record (864) but based on production and longevity the honor goes to Dan Issel, who had been a pro for six seasons before the merger with the ABA brought the former Kentucky star and Denver into the NBA.

Issel led the club six times in rebounding—including 1983-84, when he was 36. The most amazing Denver rebounder was the now-departed 6-3 Fat Lever, whose 734 boards last year led the Nuggets for the fourth straight time.

Also, don't forget a fellow named Spencer Haywood, who at age 20 merely averaged 19.5 rebounds while becoming both the 1969-70 ABA Rookie of the Year and the league MVP in his only season with Denver.

ALL-TIME NUGGET LEADERS

SEASON

Points: Spencer Haywood, 2,519, 1969-70 (ABA)
        Alex English, 2,414, 1985-86
Assists: Lafayette Lever, 664, 1986-87
Rebounds: Spencer Haywood, 1,637, 1969-70 (ABA)
        George McGinnis, 864, 1978-79

GAME

Points: David Thompson, 73 vs. Detroit, 4/9/78
Assists: Larry Brown, 23 vs. Pittsburgh, 2/20/72 (ABA)
        Lafayette Lever, 23 vs. Golden State, 4/21/89
Rebounds: Spencer Haywood, 31 vs. Kentucky, 11/13/69 (ABA)
        Dan Issel, 24 vs. Phoenix, 10/25/78
        George McGinnis, 24 vs. San Antonio, 1/24/81

CAREER

Points: Alex English, 21,645, 1979-90
Assists: Alex English, 3,679, 1979-90
Rebounds: Dan Issel, 6,630, 1975-85

GOLDEN STATE WARRIORS

TEAM DIRECTORY: Owner: Jim Fitzgerald; Pres.: Daniel Finane; GM-Coach: Don Nelson; Dir. Player Personnel: Sam Schuler; Dir. Scouting: Ed Gregory; Asst. Coaches: Donn Nelson, Garry St. Jean; Dir. Media Rel.: Julie Marvel. Arena: Oakland Coliseum (15,025). Colors: Gold and blue.

Chris Mullin's .536 FG pct. was best in his five seasons.

SCOUTING REPORT

SHOOTING: Chris Mullin put together another impressive season—seventh in the league in scoring, eighth in FT percentage, 11th in FG percentage. But he's still a big guard playing small forward. The big guard isn't bad, either. Mitch Richmond doesn't shoot it quite as pretty as does Mullin, but Mitch showed that his rookie toughness was no one-year fling.

Following Richmond's pace—although he was not named Rookie of the Year because of a tall fellow named Robinson down Texas way—Tim Hardaway was the league's best first-year playmaker, and his 14.7 ppg were second only to the Spurs' Mr. Robinson. Mullin is 6-7, Richmond 6-4, Hardaway maybe 6-0. Golden State still has one of the league's taller benches—and no inside game on the floor.

PLAYMAKING: Despite the emergence of Hardaway, the Warriors were a sad 24th in assist-turnover ratio, mostly because in addition to the three dominant players, only Sarunas Marciulionis apparently can catch a pass and turn it into a basket. Coach Don Nelson has used variations of his brewed-in-Milwaukee point-forward offense, but with mixed results. Assists are hard to come by when there's no dependable low-post person working for position to receive the ball.

DEFENSE: Golden State will jump out in halfcourt traps and try to create confusion by swarming. But this is not a very good fundamental defensive club—and 119.4 points allowed per game last season seems to support the suggestion. It won't get any better now that 7-7 Manute Bol has taken his shot-blocking skills to Philadelphia. He was responsible for 238 of the team's blocked shots.

REBOUNDING: Alton Lister, a risky pickup last year by Don Nelson, went down early with an injury that cost him all but 40 minutes last season. The veteran Lister had been counted on as the main board man, and no one ever really picked up for him. Mullin, of all people, was the team's leading rebounder. Bol had all of 33 offensive rebounds in 1989-90. There were substitute small forwards in the league last year—Indiana's Mike Sanders, Clipper Jeff Martin, for two quick examples—who doubled that number in roughly similar minutes.

WARRIOR ROSTER

No.	Veterans	Pos.	Ht.	Wt.	Age	Yrs. Pro	College
5	Tim Hardaway	G	6-0	175	24	1	Texas-El Paso
22	Rod Higgins	F	6-7	205	30	8	Fresno State
53	Alton Lister	C-F	7-0	240	32	8	Arizona State
13	Sarunas Marciulionis	G	6-5	200	26	1	Lithuania
17	Chris Mullin	F	6-7	215	27	5	St. John's
43	Jim Petersen	C-F	6-10	235	28	6	Minnesota
23	Mitch Richmond	G	6-5	215	25	2	Kansas State
52	Mike Smrek	C	7-0	260	28	5	Canisius
20	Terry Teagle	F-G	6-5	195	30	8	Baylor
3	Tom Tolbert	F	6-7	240	25	2	Arizona

Rd.	Rookies	Sel. No.	Pos.	Ht.	Wt.	College
1	Tyrone Hill	11	F	6-10	243	Xavier
2	Les Jepsen	28	C	7-0	237	Iowa
2	Kevin Pritchard	34	G	6-3	180	Kansas

OUTLOOK: Record crowds are rushing out to see Nelson's Grand Experiment of sending all these mis-sized guys scurrying about. But positive results have been slow to come. How Xavier's 6-10 Tyrone Hill, the first draft pick at No. 11, affects this potpourri is unpredictable. Last year's 45 losses might look good this time next spring.

WARRIOR PROFILES

CHRIS MULLIN 27 6-7 215   Guard-Forward

Has solidly made himself one of league's top 20 players . . . An argument could be made for top 10 . . . Seems to have beaten an alcohol addiction problem that became public in third pro season . . . Born July 30, 1963, in Brooklyn, N.Y. . . . Renowned gym rat . . . A marvelously adaptable player at St. John's . . . Averaged 19.5 points and shot .550 over four-year career . . . A 1984 Olympian . . . First-round (No. 7) choice in 1985 by Warriors . . . Pro scoring escalated each of first four seasons, starting with 14.0 as rookie . . . He "dropped" from 26.5 to 25.1 last year—but 1989-90 was his best as a pro . . . Set NBA record with combined .536 FG and .889 FT . . . Also became first Warrior to lead team in scoring and rebounding since Nate Thurmond in 1964-65.

Year	Team	G	FG	FG Pct.	FT	FT Pct.	Reb.	Ast.	TP	Avg.
1985-86	Golden State	55	287	.463	189	.896	115	105	768	14.0
1986-87	Golden State	82	477	.514	269	.825	181	261	1242	15.1
1987-88	Golden State	60	470	.508	239	.885	205	290	1213	20.2
1988-89	Golden State	82	830	.509	493	.892	483	415	2176	26.5
1989-90	Golden State	78	682	.536	505	.889	463	319	1956	25.1
	Totals	357	2746	.511	1695	.879	1447	1390	7355	20.6

MITCH RICHMOND 25 6-5 215   Guard

Suspicion prevails that he was 25 years old at birth . . . Came into the league two seasons ago and absolutely bullied many veteran players . . . Clear-shot Rookie of the Year, and evidently not a one-season flash . . . Born June 30, 1965, in Fort Lauderdale, Fla. . . . Prepared two years at Moberly Area (Mo.) JC before starring at Kansas State, averaging 20.7 ppg . . . The No. 5 pick in 1988 by Golden State . . . A defender's nightmare: He'll launch a three-pointer, drive on you or post you up—and bruise your body in the process . . . Last season he became the first player since Jamaal Wilkes (1974-75) to improve Rookie of the Year figures in scoring, FG and FT percentage.

Year	Team	G	FG	FG Pct.	FT	FT Pct.	Reb.	Ast.	TP	Avg.
1988-89	Golden State	79	649	.468	410	.810	468	334	1741	22.0
1989-90	Golden State	78	640	.497	406	.866	360	223	1720	22.1
	Totals	157	1289	.482	816	.837	828	557	3461	22.0

TERRY TEAGLE 30 6-5 195   Forward-Guard

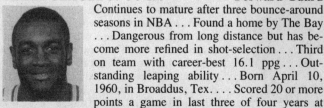

Continues to mature after three bounce-around seasons in NBA . . . Found a home by The Bay . . . Dangerous from long distance but has become more refined in shot-selection . . . Third on team with career-best 16.1 ppg . . . Outstanding leaping ability . . . Born April 10, 1960, in Broaddus, Tex. . . . Scored 20 or more points a game in last three of four years at Baylor . . . Houston tabbed him 16th, expecting big-time shooting immediately . . . Didn't happen . . . Shot .428 FG as a rookie and minutes were sliced by one-third in second season . . . Spent 1984-

85 changing uniforms at Detroit (Pistons and Spirits of CBA) and Golden State.

Year	Team	G	FG	FG Pct.	FT	FT Pct.	Reb.	Ast.	TP	Avg.
1982-83	Houston	73	332	.428	87	.696	194	150	761	10.4
1983-84	Houston	68	148	.470	37	.841	78	63	340	5.0
1984-85	Det.-G.S.	21	74	.540	25	.714	43	14	175	8.3
1985-86	Golden State	82	475	.496	211	.796	235	115	1165	14.2
1986-87	Golden State	82	370	.458	182	.778	175	105	922	11.2
1987-88	Golden State	47	248	.454	97	.802	81	61	594	12.6
1988-89	Golden State	66	409	.476	182	.809	263	96	1002	15.2
1989-90	Golden State	82	538	.480	244	.830	367	155	1323	16.1
	Totals	521	2594	.470	1065	.793	1436	759	6282	12.1

TIM HARDAWAY 24 6-0 175   Guard

Marvelous addition last year by Golden State ... Performed like a pro almost from first day ... Warriors made him No. 14 pick in 1989 draft ... When needed, he's a scorer without being a great shooter ... Started 78 of 79 games he was able to play ... As expected, experienced defensive problems because of size ... But he led NBA rookies in assists and was second only to David Robinson in first-year-player scoring ... Born Sept. 12, 1966, in Chicago ... The Western Athletic Conference Player of the Year as a senior ... Sparked Texas-El Paso into NCAA tournament his final year with speed and leadership ... Polished his credentials in the tryout "classics" at both Portsmouth and Orlando.

Year	Team	G	FG	FG Pct.	FT	FT Pct.	Reb.	Ast.	TP	Avg.
1989-90	Golden State	79	464	.471	211	.764	310	689	1162	14.7

ROD HIGGINS 30 6-7 205   Guard-Forward

Versatile fellow ... Strange composition of last year's Warriors had him playing power forward and center at times ... He's become a wily veteran, respected for his consistency ... Must be defended when he slips out to three-point arc ... If you don't pay strict attention, he'll kill you on offensive boards ... Born Jan. 31, 1960, in Monroe, La. ... Drafted in second round at No. 31 out of Fresno State by Chicago in 1982 ... Joined Warriors in 1986-87, making it five NBA teams (and one CBA club) for his career ... In 1985-86, donned uniforms of Seattle,

San Antonio, New Jersey, Chicago—in one season . . . Averaging double-figures last three seasons.

Year	Team	G	FG	FG Pct.	FT	FT Pct.	Reb.	Ast.	TP	Avg.
1982-83	Chicago	82	313	.448	209	.792	366	175	848	10.3
1983-84	Chicago	78	193	.447	113	.724	206	116	500	6.4
1984-85	Chicago	68	119	.441	60	.667	147	73	308	4.5
1985-86	Sea.-S.A.-N.J.-Chi	30	39	.368	19	.704	51	24	98	3.3
1986-87	Golden State	73	214	.519	200	.833	237	96	631	8.6
1987-88	Golden State	68	381	.526	273	.848	293	188	1054	15.5
1988-89	Golden State	81	301	.476	188	.821	376	160	856	10.6
1989-90	Golden State	82	304	.481	234	.821	422	129	909	11.1
	Totals	562	1864	.477	1296	.803	2098	961	5204	9.3

SARUNAS MARCIULIONIS 26 6-5 200   Guard

Greatest NBA player ever produced by Lithuania . . . Also the first . . . Born June 13, 1964, in Kaunas, Lithuania . . . Through vagaries of NBA international agreements, Golden State got him for a relative pittance—discarding a transfer fee to his Eastern Bloc club team and a decent salary . . . Don Nelson's son, Donn, was gung-ho over him and became one of his best friends . . . It's worn-out already, but the comparison remains: a Gail Goodrich play-alike . . . Not yet as efficient a left-handed shooter as Goodrich, but stronger and a better passer . . . Started three of the 75 games of his rookie season and figures to get better and better.

Year	Team	G	FG	FG Pct.	FT	FT Pct.	Reb.	Ast.	TP	Avg.
1989-90	Golden State	75	289	.519	317	.787	221	121	905	12.1

ALTON LISTER 32 7-0 240   Center-Forward

A plodding, no-headlines type of guy . . . In first eight seasons as a pro at Milwaukee and Seattle he had missed 13 of 656 games . . . So, picked up by Warriors in a move for center stability, went down and out for season with bad leg injury after hobbling through 40 minutes in three games . . . Don Nelson would have preferred playing with him than without him, but admits: "He's not an All-Star center, not a Messiah." . . . Born Oct. 1, 1958, in Dallas . . . Played a season at San Jacinto (Tex.) JC before going on to Arizona State and 1980 Olympic team . . . Drafted 21st on first round in 1981 by Milwaukee, where he played under Nelson . . . Traded after five seasons to Seattle as part of Jack Sikma deal.

Year	Team	G	FG	FG Pct.	FT	FT Pct.	Reb.	Ast.	TP	Avg.
1981-82	Milwaukee	80	149	.519	64	.520	387	84	362	4.5
1982-83	Milwaukee	80	272	.529	130	.537	568	111	674	8.4
1983-84	Milwaukee	82	256	.500	114	.626	603	110	626	7.6
1984-85	Milwaukee	81	322	.538	154	.588	647	127	798	9.9
1985-86	Milwaukee	81	318	.551	160	.602	592	101	796	9.8
1986-87	Seattle	75	346	.504	179	.675	705	110	871	11.6
1987-88	Seattle	82	173	.504	114	.606	627	58	461	5.6
1988-89	Seattle	82	271	.499	115	.646	545	54	657	8.0
1989-90	Golden State	3	4	.500	4	.571	8	2	12	4.0
	Totals	646	2111	.519	1034	.604	4682	757	5257	8.1

TOM TOLBERT 25 6-7 240   Forward

"Find of the year," according to Don Nelson . . . Where Warriors "found" him was on waiver wire . . . Born Oct. 16, 1965, in Long Beach, Cal. . . . Attended three colleges . . . Started at UC-Irvine, moved after two seasons to Cerritos College for a year, averaged 14.0 ppg with Arizona from 1986 to 1988 . . . Didn't make it with Charlotte, which had taken him No. 34 in 1988 draft . . . Hornets gave him 117 minutes, he scored 40 points . . . Was signed by Warriors, for whom he started 21 times in 70 games and bumped people around.

Year	Team	G	FG	FG Pct.	FT	FT Pct.	Reb.	Ast.	TP	Avg.
1988-89	Charlotte	14	17	.459	6	.500	21	7	40	2.9
1989-90	Golden State	70	218	.493	175	.726	363	58	616	8.8
	Totals	84	235	.491	181	.715	384	65	656	7.8

JIM PETERSEN 28 6-10 235   Center-Forward

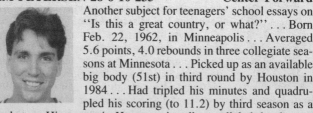

Another subject for teenagers' school essays on "Is this a great country, or what?" . . . Born Feb. 22, 1962, in Minneapolis . . . Averaged 5.6 points, 4.0 rebounds in three collegiate seasons at Minnesota . . . Picked up as an available big body (51st) in third round by Houston in 1984 . . . Had tripled his minutes and quadrupled his scoring (to 11.2) by third season as a Rocket . . . His ascent in Houston virtually paralleled the descent of Ralph Sampson, who was making about 10 times more a year guaranteed . . . Slowed way down before being traded to Sacramento, where he was not sensational except on the new salary chart . . . After being moved to Golden State last year (for Sampson, ironically) he played in only 43 games, started 19, scored 4.0 points . . . ''He struggled,'' said Don Nelson, terming 1989-90 a ''wasted year.''

Year	Team	G	FG	FG Pct.	FT	FT Pct.	Reb.	Ast.	TP	Avg.
1984-85	Houston	60	70	.486	50	.758	147	29	190	3.2
1985-86	Houston	82	196	.477	113	.706	396	85	505	6.2
1986-87	Houston	82	386	.511	152	.727	557	127	924	11.3
1987-88	Houston	69	249	.510	114	.745	436	106	613	8.9
1988-89	Sacramento	66	278	.459	115	.747	413	81	671	10.2
1989-90	Golden State	43	60	.426	52	.712	160	23	172	4.0
	Totals	402	1239	.487	596	.731	2109	451	3075	7.6

MIKE SMREK 28 7-0 260   Center

Amiable journeyman . . . Never has stolen a paycheck . . . Limited skills, but work ethic and size will always land him a job somewhere . . . Born Aug. 31, 1962, in Welland, Ont. . . . Yes, his first sport was ice hockey . . . Moved across border to play basketball at Canisius . . . Portland took him 25th in 1985, then promptly traded his rights to Chicago . . . Bulls waived him after one season . . . Free agent ended up with two championship rings as a Laker sub before moving on to San Antonio and Golden State . . . Got 21 points in 107 minutes last season as Warrior non-factor.

Year	Team	G	FG	FG Pct.	FT	FT Pct.	Reb.	Ast.	TP	Avg.
1985-86	Chicago	38	46	.377	16	.552	110	19	108	2.8
1986-87	L.A. Lakers	35	30	.500	16	.640	37	5	76	2.2
1987-88	L.A. Lakers	48	44	.427	44	.667	85	8	132	2.8
1988-89	San Antonio	43	72	.471	49	.645	129	12	193	4.5
1989-90	Golden State	13	10	.417	1	.167	34	1	21	1.6
	Totals	177	202	.437	126	.624	395	45	530	3.0

THE ROOKIES

TYRONE HILL 22 6-10 243   Forward

Hard worker with limited scoring ability off own moves . . . Still he was Player of Year in Midwestern Collegiate Conference and averaged 20.2 points for Xavier (Ohio) . . . Was the fourth-leading rebounder in nation (12.2) last season after ranking second as a junior with same average... "Great rebounders go after every rebound, and that's what Tyrone does," said Xavier coach Pete Gillen... Shot 57.8 percent over career... Born March 17, 1968, in Cincinnati.

LES JEPSEN 23 7-0 237   Center

Big-time happenings draft day at the Tough Luck cafe/bar when this project was picked at No. 28... Tough Luck is in Bowbells, N.D., where Jepsen was born June 24, 1967... Scored 189 points first three years at Iowa, 417 as a senior (14.9 avg.)... Third-team All-Big 10 in final season when he was second in FG shooting, third in rebounding, fourth in blocked shots in conference ... First pick of second round, fourth center chosen overall... Uh, Golden State coach Don Nelson also went to Iowa.

KEVIN PRITCHARD 23 6-3 180   Guard

All-Big 8 guard last season... Member of Kansas' 1988 NCAA championship team... Last year led Jayhawks in scoring, assists, steals, FT shooting... Twice made conference All-Defensive team... Played both guard spots in college... Will have to earn backup spot at point behind Tim Hardaway to stick with Golden State, which chose him at No. 34.

COACH DON NELSON: He's a wizard, a master, a good ol'  farm boy strutting the sidelines in taped-up sneaks... He knows his hoops and sometimes, as a powerful executive, puts people through his own hoops... Widely respected as a judge of talent, he's been an innovator on the court (e.g. Manute Bol away from the hoop, no-center lineups)... He's also become increasingly powerful in using his influence to direct players and aspiring assistant coaches... Born May 15, 1949, in Muskegon, Mich.... He starred at Iowa before beginning a 14-year NBA career, mostly for Boston, for whom his last-second shot clinched a championship-deciding game at Los Angeles... Produced seven division titles, six 50-plus win years in 10 seasons at Milwaukee before complicated set of circumstances left him first as part-owner and desk man, then also floor coach of Warriors. Twice he has been named Coach of the Year

... Won a lot of friends nationally with sincere, hands-on support of Farm Aid ... Warriors' 37-45 year in 1989-90 was only Nelson's third loser in 13 NBA seasons.

GREATEST REBOUNDER

Nate Thurmond is the best center many fans of the "NBA—It's Fantastic!" generation never saw.

The 6-11 strongman from Bowling Green labored 11 of 14 pro years in the Bay Area, often overlooked. At a time the NBA West was a late-night rumor anywhere east of Reno, he vied with media-centers-of-attractions Bill Russell, Wilt Chamberlain, Willis Reed and that skinny Alcindor kid from UCLA.

Thurmond once grabbed 18 boards in a quarter, 24 in a half. His 42 rebounds in a game is second only to the franchise-best 55 Wilt hauled in as a Philadelphia Warrior.

ALL-TIME WARRIOR LEADERS

SEASON

Points: Wilt Chamberlain, 4,029, 1961-62
Assists: Eric Floyd, 848, 1986-87
Rebounds: Wilt Chamberlain, 2,149, 1960-61

GAME

Points: Wilt Chamberlain, 100 vs. New York, 3/2/62
Assists: Guy Rodgers, 28 vs. St. Louis, 3/14/63
Rebounds: Wilt Chamberlain, 55 vs. Boston, 11/24/60

CAREER

Points: Wilt Chamberlain, 17,783, 1959-65
Assists: Guy Rodgers, 4,845, 1958-70
Rebounds: Nate Thurmond, 12,771, 1963-74

HOUSTON ROCKETS

TEAM DIRECTORY: Chairman: Charlie Thomas; Pres.: Ray Patterson; GM: Steve Patterson; Dir. Media Inf.: Jay Goldberg; Coach: Don Chaney; Asst. Coaches: Carroll Dawson, Rudy Tomjanovich, Calvin Murphy, John Killilea. Arena: The Summit (16,279). Colors: Red and gold.

SCOUTING REPORT

SHOOTING: Hard to believe, but statistically the Rockets shot the ball better last year than they had the season before. And they won four more games than the 41-41 of 1989-90. But coach Don Chaney still only has two dependable percentage shooters—the terribly over-burdened Akeem Olajuwon and hard-working Otis Thorpe. The latter was No. 8 in the NBA in FG percentage.

Buck Johnson, a reluctant shooter early in his career, threw up more attempts than anyone on the team except Akeem, and fell under .500 markmanship. Ohio U. rookie Dave Jamerson, acquired in a draft-day trade with Miami for Alec Kessler, might be the intermediate threat eventually to relieve doubling on Olajuwon. The Sleepy Floyd-Mitchell Wiggins-Vernon Maxwell backcourt triumvirate is competent at best.

PLAYMAKING: Floyd was 20th in the league in three-point shooting and placed 17th among the assist leaders, but he still hasn't won a fan club among point-guard aficionados. The Rockets could make things so much easier on themselves if they would capitalize better on Olajuwon's hard work on the defensive boards and then bust out on the break. Houston can be scary when the ball is pushed up the court on transition. Why don't the Rockets do that more often? Most likely it's because their guards often forget the old maxim about the shortest distance between two points being a straight line.

DEFENSE: Too often, a Rocket makes a dubious stab at a steal and then looks over his shoulder, expecting Olajuwon to pick up and cover. That's fine, except that is the way Akeem likes to play, too. Somehow that produced the NBA's fifth-best defense (by FG percentage) last season. It probably helped that Olajuwon, again the league leader in blocked shots, also was eighth in steals. Thorpe always has been a decent defender when he doesn't go for shoulder

Akeem Olajuwon led league in blocked shots and rebounds.

and ball fakes, and Johnson—overmatched in some situations—
has surprised scouts with his defensive potential.

REBOUNDING: Of course it comes as no surprise to learn that
Olajuwon led the NBA in board work. He scored an 850 in the
defensive part of the exam, which is merely the highest total of
any player in a decade—since Swen Nater hauled in 864 for the
San Diego Clippers in 1979-80.

You'd figure that with Akeem collecting 14 a game and Thorpe
taking 9.0 (with a one-game high of 26), the Rockets would be
in position to win a lot more than 41 games. But with the Rockets,
you just can't figure.

ROCKET ROSTER

No.	Veterans	Pos.	Ht.	Wt.	Age	Yrs. Pro	College
44	Adrian Caldwell	F	6-8	266	26	1	Lamar
4	Byron Dinkins	G	6-1	170	23	1	NC-Charlotte
21	Eric Floyd	G	6-3	183	30	8	Georgetown
1	Buck Johnson	F	6-7	206	26	4	Alabama
5	John Lucas	G	6-2	180	37	14	Maryland
11	Vernon Maxwell	G	6-5	185	25	2	Florida
40	Tim McCormick	C	7-0	237	28	6	Michigan
34	Akeem Olajuwon	C	7-0	258	27	6	Houston
13	Larry Smith	F	6-8	251	32	10	Alcorn State
33	Otis Thorpe	F	6-10	246	28	6	Providence
15	Mitchell Wiggins	G	6-4	199	31	5	Florida State
10	David Wood	F	6-9	228	25	1	Nevada-Reno
42	Mike Woodson	G	6-5	200	32	10	Indiana

Rd.	Rookies	Sel. No.	Pos.	Ht.	Wt.	College
1	Dave Jamerson	15	G	6-5	192	Ohio
2	Carl Herrera	30	F	6-9	215	Houston

OUTLOOK: Olajuwon has such a marvelous posture and stately carriage that it is going to be doubly sad when he is forced to retire because of chronic stoop-shoulderness. The guy's got the weight of the entire franchise on one shoulder and his personal ambition/frustration on the other. He's the team's best scorer, rebounder, shot-blocker, stealer—and one of a handful of Rockets who appear to take winning and losing seriously. With a talent of these dimensions you'd think management's search for a supporting cast would not end with Thorpe and the constantly perplexing Floyd.

ROCKET PROFILES

AKEEM OLAJUWON 27 7-0 258   Center

If you still believe he's a 7-footer, let us introduce you to 6-4 Muggsy Bogues . . . Whatever his real size, Olajuwon's one of league's most athletic players . . . Since Kareem Abdul-Jabbar, current centers are measured against him—without a tape measure . . . Born Jan. 21, 1963, at Lagos, Nigeria . . . NCAA's Most Outstanding Player in 1983 for University of Hous-

ton . . . Rockets couldn't and didn't miss with 1984's overall No. 1 pick . . . Runs, jumps, shoots, steals, blocks, scowls at All-Pro level . . . Last year became first man in 10 seasons since Swen Nater to grab 800 defensive rebounds . . . Also was first in 13 seasons, since Bill Walton, to lead league in rebounds, blocked shots . . . Missed back-to-back 2,000-point seasons by five . . . Was eighth in NBA steals, ninth in scoring, led team in minutes played . . . Doomed to become hoop's Ernie Banks, never getting to Championship Series?

Year	Team	G	FG	FG Pct.	FT	FT Pct.	Reb.	Ast.	TP	Avg.
1984-85	Houston	82	677	.538	338	.613	974	111	1692	20.6
1985-86	Houston	68	625	.526	347	.645	781	137	1597	23.5
1986-87	Houston	75	677	.508	400	.702	858	220	1755	23.4
1987-88	Houston	79	712	.514	381	.695	959	163	1805	22.8
1988-89	Houston	82	790	.508	454	.696	1105	149	2034	24.8
1989-90	Houston	82	806	.501	382	.713	1149	234	1995	24.3
	Totals	468	4287	.515	2302	.678	5826	1014	10878	23.2

OTIS THORPE 28 6-10 246   Forward

Tenth of 12 children, he's never needed an alarm clock to get to work on time . . . He's there every night . . . In 1989-90, second season with Houston, competed in all 82 games for fifth time in six-season career . . . Born Aug. 5, 1962, in Boynton Beach, Fla. . . . By time he had left Providence, he was Big East career-rebound leader and only Chris Mullin had scored more points . . . Drafted No. 9 by Kings in 1984, when club was still in Kansas City . . . Lost seven games to knee strain after franchise moved to Sacramento . . . Since then, including move to Houston in 1988 for Rodney McCray and Jim Petersen, he's played 378 without a miss . . . Shot .548 FG last season, about career average, to place No. 8 in league . . . Second on team in rebounding only to Akeem Olajuwon . . . At least as good as many more publicized power forwards.

Year	Team	G	FG	FG Pct.	FT	FT Pct.	Reb.	Ast.	TP	Avg.
1984-85	Kansas City	82	411	.600	230	.620	556	111	1052	12.8
1985-86	Sacramento	75	289	.587	164	.661	420	84	742	9.9
1986-87	Sacramento	82	567	.540	413	.761	819	201	1547	18.9
1987-88	Sacramento	82	622	.507	460	.755	837	266	1704	20.8
1988-89	Houston	82	521	.542	328	.729	787	202	1370	16.7
1989-90	Houston	82	547	.548	307	.688	734	261	1401	17.1
	Totals	485	2957	.546	1902	.713	4153	1125	7816	16.1

Reliable Otis Thorpe has played in 378 consecutive games.

BUCK JOHNSON 26 6-7 206   Forward

Gradual, steady improvement became a mini-explosion last year . . . All of a sudden, he's a player . . . Scoring had gotten slightly better each of first three seasons . . . But last year he became dependable mid-double-figure contributor . . . Also a stern defender . . . Born Jan. 3, 1964, in Birmingham, Ala. . . . Helped get Alabama to four straight NCAA visits . . . Houston took him with 20th pick in 1986 draft . . . Terrible three-point shooter at small forward/big guard . . . Fouled out of eight games while making 104 steals—second on team to Akeem Olajuwon . . . Rockets still believe he can be an Alex English-type but that's being very optimistic.

Year	Team	G	FG	FG Pct.	FT	FT Pct.	Reb.	Ast.	TP	Avg.
1986-87	Houston	60	94	.468	40	.690	88	40	228	3.8
1987-88	Houston	70	155	.520	67	.736	168	49	378	5.4
1988-89	Houston	67	270	.524	101	.754	286	126	642	9.6
1989-90	Houston	82	504	.495	205	.759	381	252	1215	14.8
	Totals	279	1023	.503	413	.747	923	467	2463	8.8

ERIC (SLEEPY) FLOYD 30 6-3 183   Guard

Dropped from sixth to 16th in NBA assists last year . . . It's an old theme, but this player has never been a creative, give-it-up point guard . . . Must have had a pocket computer working last season: Finished at exactly 600 assists, 1,000 points . . . Had his best shooting season in three years, if you call .451 a best . . . Born in Gastonia, N.C., March 6, 1960 . . . Leading scorer in Georgetown history when he left and was drafted No. 13 by New Jersey in 1982 . . . In his third season with Rockets after five years at Golden State and rookie campaign with Nets . . . Came to Houston with Joe Barry Carroll in blockbuster trade for Ralph Sampson and Steve Harris on Dec. 12, 1987 . . . Set an NBA playoff record with 29 points in fourth quarter of 1987 series vs. Lakers, while with Golden State . . . Started 73 of 82 appearances last year in Houston, where he still hasn't solved team's backcourt deficiencies.

Year	Team	G	FG	FG Pct.	FT	FT Pct.	Reb.	Ast.	TP	Avg.
1982-83	N.J.-G.S.	76	226	.429	150	.833	137	138	612	8.1
1983-84	Golden State	77	484	.463	315	.816	271	269	1291	16.8
1984-85	Golden State	82	610	.445	336	.810	202	406	1598	19.5
1985-86	Golden State	82	510	.506	351	.796	297	746	1410	17.2
1986-87	Golden State	82	503	.488	462	.860	268	848	1541	18.8
1987-88	G.S.-Hou.	77	420	.433	301	.850	296	543	1155	15.0
1988-89	Houston	82	396	.443	261	.845	306	709	1162	14.2
1989-90	Houston	82	362	.451	187	.806	198	600	1000	12.2
	Totals	640	3511	.459	2363	.828	1975	4260	9769	15.3

MIKE WOODSON 32 6-5 200   Guard

Tick-tock, tick-tock . . . Another clock running down . . . He's been with five teams in workmanlike 10-season career . . . Hadn't scored as few points as he did last year since he was a rookie; hadn't shot as poorly (.395) ever . . . Once was a deadeye shooter . . . Born March 24, 1958, in Indianapolis . . . MVP when Indiana won the 1980 NIT championship . . . Drafted 12th in first round later that spring by New York . . . Knicks only used him one season before sending him, through New Jersey, to K.C. Kings . . . Best years actually were spent later, leading Clippers in scoring two years in a row . . . Besides having lost his shot, limping, and being unable to defend anyone, career prospects are swell.

Year	Team	G	FG	FG Pct.	FT	FT Pct.	Reb.	Ast.	TP	Avg.
1980-81	New York.......	81	165	.442	49	.766	97	75	380	4.7
1981-82	N.J.-K.C........	83	538	.503	221	.773	247	222	1304	15.7
1982-83	Kansas City......	81	584	.506	298	.790	248	254	1473	18.2
1983-84	Kansas City......	71	389	.477	247	.818	175	175	1027	14.5
1984-85	Kansas City......	78	530	.496	264	.800	198	143	1329	17.0
1985-86	Sacramento......	81	510	.475	242	.837	226	197	1264	15.6
1986-87	L.A. Clippers.....	74	494	.437	240	.828	162	196	1262	17.1
1987-88	L.A. Clippers.....	80	562	.445	296	.868	190	273	1438	18.0
1988-89	Houston........	81	410	.438	195	.823	194	206	1046	12.9
1989-90	Houston........	61	160	.395	62	.721	88	66	394	6.5
	Totals	771	4342	.468	2114	.812	1825	1807	10917	14.2

MITCHELL WIGGINS 31 6-4 199   Guard

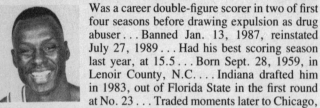

Was a career double-figure scorer in two of first four seasons before drawing expulsion as drug abuser... Banned Jan. 13, 1987, reinstated July 27, 1989... Had his best scoring season last year, at 15.5... Born Sept. 28, 1959, in Lenoir County, N.C.... Indiana drafted him in 1983, out of Florida State in the first round at No. 23... Traded moments later to Chicago, where he started 40 games as a rookie... He's been with Houston on and off since... Had best free-throw season last year... Pass? Mitchell will pass on that option... Placed eighth last year on a team that had a shared abhorrence for the assist.

Year	Team	G	FG	FG Pct.	FT	FT Pct.	Reb.	Ast.	TP	Avg.
1983-84	Chicago	82	399	.448	213	.742	328	187	1018	12.4
1984-85	Houston........	82	318	.484	96	.733	235	119	738	9.0
1985-86	Houston........	78	222	.454	86	.729	159	101	531	6.8
1986-87	Houston........	32	153	.437	49	.754	133	76	355	11.1
1989-90	Houston........	66	416	.488	192	.810	286	104	1024	15.5
	Totals	340	1508	.466	636	.759	1141	587	3666	10.8

LARRY SMITH 32 6-8 251   Forward

Age and years of toil are catching (have caught?) up with him... And it showed last year... Terrific competitor... Probably the best career offensive rebounder of the '80s... Born Jan. 18, 1958, in Rolling Fork, Miss. ... Played at Alcorn State and was 1980 second-round choice (24th) by Golden State... Has faded badly, sadly... Until last season a career .539 FG shooter, most of them put-backs, he fell to .474 in 1989-90 as a 74-game sub...Except for checking him out, opponents no longer even attempt to defend him away from post, which in Houston belongs to Akeem Olajuwon...Even his horrendous free-throw shooting continued to get worse, with third straight season under 41 percent.

Year	Team	G	FG	FG Pct.	FT	FT Pct.	Reb.	Ast.	TP	Avg.
1980-81	Golden State.....	82	304	.512	177	.588	994	93	785	9.6
1981-82	Golden State.....	74	220	.534	88	.553	813	83	528	7.1
1982-83	Golden State.....	49	180	.588	53	.535	485	46	413	8.4
1983-84	Golden State.....	75	244	.560	94	.560	672	72	582	7.8
1984-85	Golden State.....	80	366	.530	155	.605	869	96	887	11.1
1985-86	Golden State.....	77	314	.536	112	.493	856	95	740	9.6
1986-87	Golden State.....	80	297	.546	113	.574	917	95	707	8.8
1987-88	Golden State.....	20	58	.472	11	.407	182	25	127	6.4
1988-89	Golden State.....	80	219	.552	18	.310	652	118	456	5.7
1989-90	Houston.........	74	101	.474	20	.364	452	69	222	3.0
	Totals.........	691	2303	.535	841	.544	6892	792	5447	7.9

ADRIAN CALDWELL 24 6-8 266   Forward

Rockets signed him in 1989 after he impressed at rookie camp...Had only 331 minutes playing time...Has to be more consistent in rebounding and defense...Born July 4, 1966, in Corpus Christi, Tex...Starred at Navarro JG, then had a year at SMU and a year at Lamar, where he led the 1988-89 Cardinals in scoring, rebounding and FG pct.

Year	Team	G	FG	FG Pct.	FT	FT Pct.	Reb.	Ast.	TP	Avg.
1989-90	Houston.........	51	42	.553	13	.464	109	7	97	1.9

BYRON DINKINS 22 6-1 170   Guard

Is North Carolina-Charlotte's fourth all-time scorer, but as a rookie he discovered he'll have to improve his shooting...And the Rockets want him to show more leadership qualities...Was first UNCC scholarship signee by coach and former NBA star Jeff Mullins...Twice won university's Jesse Owens Award as top black student-athlete...Born Sept. 12, 1965, in Gainesville, Fla.

Year	Team	G	FG	FG Pct.	FT	FT Pct.	Reb.	Ast.	TP	Avg.
1989-90	Houston.........	33	44	.404	26	.867	40	75	115	3.5

TIM McCORMICK 28 7-0 237   Center

Seemed to be a better-than nice prospect coming out of college . . . Now his credentials are more suited as travel agent . . . Born March 10, 1962, in Detroit . . . Had a knee operation following freshman season at Michigan . . . Declared for early-entry in 1984 after solid back-to-back seasons in Big 10 . . . Selected 12th by Cleveland, beginning whirlwind tour that has taken him (or at least his rights in trade) to Washington, Seattle, Philadelphia, New Jersey, and then Houston . . . Most productive years (two) have been in Atlantic Division as a 76er and Net . . . Has been either hurt or unproductive as a two-season Rocket fizzle.

Year	Team	G	FG	FG Pct.	FT	FT Pct.	Reb.	Ast.	TP	Avg.
1984-85	Seattle	78	269	.557	188	.715	398	78	726	9.3
1985-86	Seattle	77	253	.570	174	.713	403	83	681	8.8
1986-87	Philadelphia	81	391	.545	251	.719	611	114	1033	12.8
1987-88	Phil-N.J.	70	348	.537	145	.647	467	118	841	12.0
1988-89	Houston	81	169	.481	87	.674	261	54	425	5.2
1989-90	Houston	18	10	.345	10	.526	27	3	30	1.7
	Totals	405	1440	.539	855	.701	2167	450	3736	9.2

VERNON MAXWELL 25 6-5 185   Guard

His basketball skills keep coaches drooling . . . But he has some, uh, personality problems . . . Often forgets he's not best (or only) player on floor . . . Born Sept. 12, 1965, in Gainesville, Fla. . . . Stayed local to attend Florida . . . Drafted 47th in 1988 by Denver, which promptly traded his rights for a 1989 second-rounder . . . Lasted one full season in San Antonio before Houston bought his rights on Feb. 21, 1990 . . . Promptly played in 30 straight, started final 10 . . . You'd like to think, though, that an off-guard scoring 11.7 and 9.0 in his first two years might want to shoot better than .435.

Year	Team	G	FG	FG Pct.	FT	FT Pct.	Reb.	Ast.	TP	Avg.
1988-89	San Antonio	79	357	.432	181	.745	202	301	927	11.7
1989-90	S.A.-Hou.	79	275	.439	136	.645	228	296	714	9.0
	Totals	158	632	.435	317	.698	430	597	1641	10.4

THE ROOKIES

DAVE JAMERSON 23 6-5 192   **Guard**
Highly lauded shooter . . . Rockets acquired his rights (No. 15)
and those of Carl Herrera (30) from Miami by drafting 6-11 Alec
Kessler at No. 12 and then trading in pre-arranged deal . . . Averaged 31.2 points as Ohio U. senior and was third-leading scorer
in nation . . . A career .846 FT mark . . . Born Aug. 13, 1967, in
Stow, Ohio . . . Missed his sophomore year, redshirting medically
after knee surgery.

CARL HERRERA 23 6-9 215   **Forward**
Keep a steady radar track on this one . . . Born Dec. 14, 1966, in
Caracas, Venezuela . . . Showed up at Jacksonville (Tex.) JC, and
averaged 20.1 points, 11.3 rebounds as a freshman . . . His second
year, he scored 25.5, boarded at 13.2, and was co-JUCO Player
of Year with Larry Johnson, the staying-in-school UNLV sensation
. . . Southwest Conference Newcomer of Year last season, ranking
in Top 10 in five categories for Houston . . . Rockets went for him
despite pre-draft reports he had agreed to play in Europe.

COACH DON CHANEY: He's done a nice job re-establishing
stability on the floor, but now needs some front-
office support if Rockets are going to keep pace
in the ever-improving Western Conference . . .
Did well to mask Houston deficiencies and
make playoff appearance against Lakers briefly
interesting . . . No one knows more than he that
the team is predictable in halfcourt sets, de-
pendent as it has become on Akeem Olajuwon
. . . That's where front office has to help . . .
Born March 22, 1946, in New Orleans . . . Played at University
of Houston, where he broke color barrier with Elvin Hayes before
embarking on 11-year NBA career . . . Possesses solid reputation
around league . . . Was an assistant at Detroit, San Diego/L.A.
Clippers and Atlanta before coaching the Clippers for parts of the
three seasons (53-132). A dead-even .500 last year has him at 86-
78 in two Houston seasons.

GREATEST REBOUNDER

It's between the ex-pupil and onetime mentor, but Akeem Olajuwon has passed Moses Malone as greatest rebounder in Houston history. Maybe Moses will understand.

No quarrel with the three MVP awards and six NBA rebounding championships won by Malone, who had at least 1,180 boards in each of his four completely healthy seasons in Houston. Of course, Moses bulked up on so many of his offensive boards by playing pattycake with his own misses.

Meanwhile, Olajuwon's rebounding prowess has often been obscured by his staggering score-steal-block figures. But Olajuwon has improved his board scores successively the last four years. And he averaged 14.0 last season while taking his second straight rebounding title.

ALL-TIME ROCKET LEADERS

SEASON

Points: Moses Malone, 2,520, 1980-81
Assists: John Lucas, 768, 1977-78
Rebounds: Moses Malone, 1,444, 1978-79

GAME

Points: Calvin Murphy, 57 vs. New Jersey, 3/18/78
Assists: Art Williams, 22 vs. San Francisco, 2/14/70
            Art Williams, 22 vs. Phoenix, 12/28/68
Rebounds: Moses Malone, 37 vs. New Orleans, 2/9/79

CAREER

Points: Calvin Murphy, 17,949, 1970-83
Assists: Calvin Murphy, 4,402, 1970-83
Rebounds: Elvin Hayes, 6,974, 1968-72, 1981-84

LOS ANGELES CLIPPERS

TEAM DIRECTORY: Owner: Donald T. Sterling; Exec. VP/GM: Elgin Baylor; Exec. VP/Business Oper.: Andy Roeser; Dir. Pub. Rel.: Bill Kreifeldt; Coach: Mike Schuler; Asst. Coaches: Alvin Gentry, John Hammond; Arena: Los Angeles Sports Arena (15,350). Colors: Red, white and blue.

Danny Manning came back from surgery better than ever.

SCOUTING REPORT

SHOOTING: One moment, Ron "Hollywood" Harper had arrived from Cleveland in exchange for the signing rights to Danny Ferry, the recalcitrant draft pick, and L.A.'s *other team* sparkled offensively—actually winning as often as it lost. The next eye blink, and Harper was down and most of the Clippers' explosiveness had vanished with him.

After knee surgery even more severe than Danny Manning's the year before, Harper is expected back for most of 1990-91. Don't dismiss this team's scoring ability. Manning was 13th league-wide in FG percentage and Benoit Benjamin 17th last year. Limited to 44 games because of his injury, Gary Grant was No. 5 in assists per game.

Charles Smith and Ken Norman are scoring-hungry youngsters. Now the club also has added 1987 NBA Coach of the Year Mike Schuler with his fastbreak/scoring style, and Bo Kimble, the nation's leading collegiate scorer and local hero from Loyola Marymount.

PLAYMAKING: Grant, who is quicker and almost as well-muscled as Portland's Terry Porter, was an alert passer in former coach Don Casey's patient attack. Now he'll be able to show what he can do in the open floor. Schuler will let Grant and his young friends run. "Our main goals are to make the playoffs and lead the NBA in scoring," said Schuler, whose early Portland teams finished 1st and 2nd successively in scoring. Complementary backcourters are Winston Garland and Tom Garrick. Manning is a marvelous passer from the high post, but the team was 23rd in assists-to-turnovers.

DEFENSE: When Benjamin manages to keep his concentration and not sulk, he is a threatening presence around the lane—fifth in shot-blocks last season. Only Manning, Grant and Garrick are serious steal threats and, individually, few Clipper forwards are gifted defensively. Still, Casey managed to coax a No. 13 rating out of these people in defense against FG shooting. Announced as the new coach, Schuler came out of the chute immediately, promising the Clippers would press "a lot."

REBOUNDING: Benjamin has another chance to become a legitimate star—and make a bundle of money in his contract-ending season—if only . . . But everyone's heard that before. The team's second choice in last June's draft, Loy Vaught, also is in a fa-

CLIPPER ROSTER

No.	Veterans	Pos.	Ht.	Wt.	Age	Yrs. Pro	College
51	Ken Bannister	C-F	6-9	260	30	4	St. Augustine
00	Benoit Benjamin	C	7-0	275	25	5	Creighton
3	Jay Edwards	G	6-4	205	21	1	Indiana
11	Winston Garland	G	6-2	170	25	3	SW Missouri State
22	Tom Garrick	G	6-2	195	24	2	Rhode Island
23	Gary Grant	G	6-3	196	25	2	Michigan
4	Ron Harper	G-F	6-6	198	26	4	Miami (Ohio)
5	Danny Manning	F	6-10	230	24	2	Kansas
15	Jeff Martin	G-F	6-5	195	23	1	Murray State
33	Ken Norman	F	6-8	219	26	3	Illinois
54	Charles Smith	F	6-10	238	25	2	Pittsburgh
24	Joe Wolf	C-F	6-10	235	25	3	North Carolina

Rd.	Rookies	Sel. No.	Pos.	Ht.	Wt.	College
1	Bo Kimble	8	G	6-3	197	Loyola Marymount
1	Loy Vaught	13	F	6-9	230	Michigan

vorable position to help. Charles Smith, who is not the best professional forward in Los Angeles only because James Worthy also plays there, is at his best when inclined to attack the offensive boards.

OUTLOOK: After you get past making easy jokes about this traditionally mismanaged franchise and get down to the player part, you're operating at a different level. Last year the Clippers scored 103.8 points a game, which isn't great, but showed their potential while the defensive-oriented Casey tried to bring some restraint and consistency in his first full year. Player pettiness and the owner's famous impatience forced him out. Schuler is stepping into a super situation, and knows it.

CLIPPER PROFILES

DANNY MANNING 24 6-10 230   Forward

Mr. Versatility . . . Literally played each position (at least for a set or two) last year . . . Came back from injury that required reconstructive right knee surgery after scoring double-figures in all but three of first 26 games as rookie . . . Born May 17, 1966, in Hattiesburg, Miss. . . . His father, NBA stalwart Ed, coached him (as an assistant) at Kansas . . . Led Jayhawks to

1988 NCAA championship... Member of Olympic team that summer and became No. 1 overall draftee by Clips... A public relations major at Kansas, he could have done a better job blunting players' undercutting of later-ousted coach Don Casey... Most accurate FG shooter (.533), second in steals and third on team in scoring (16.3) last year.

Year	Team	G	FG	FG Pct.	FT	FT Pct.	Reb.	Ast.	TP	Avg.
1988-89	L.A. Clippers	26	177	.494	79	.767	171	81	434	16.7
1989-90	L.A. Clippers	71	440	.533	274	.741	422	187	1154	16.3
	Totals	97	617	.521	353	.746	593	268	1588	16.4

RON HARPER 26 6-6 198   Guard-Forward

Looked to be a legitimate All-Star candidate after arriving from Cleveland in trade for negotiating rights to Danny Ferry... Then one of those things that happens to the Clippers so often, happened... Tore apart knee cartilage and ligaments in a no-contact play and will miss first few months of 1990-91 play... Born Jan. 20, 1964, in Dayton, Ohio... Drafted No. 8 by Cleveland in first round of 1986 out of Miami (Ohio)... Flamboyant performer, enjoys taking part in offseason charity games and once long-jumped over three provocatively kneeling Lakers Girls en route to slamming the hoop in a dunk contest after Magic Johnson's benefit game for United Negro College Fund... Had a high-point game of 39 while averaging 22.9 points in 28 starts with Clips last year... His quick, full return to good health is imperative in team's hoped-for turnaround.

Year	Team	G	FG	FG Pct.	FT	FT Pct.	Reb.	Ast.	TP	Avg.
1986-87	Cleveland	82	734	.455	386	.684	392	394	1874	22.9
1987-88	Cleveland	57	340	.464	196	.705	223	281	879	15.4
1988-89	Cleveland	82	587	.511	323	.751	409	434	1526	18.6
1989-90	Clev.-LAC	35	301	.473	182	.788	206	182	798	22.8
	Totals	256	1962	.475	1087	.723	1230	1291	5077	19.8

KEN NORMAN 26 6-8 219   Forward

Shame on "The Snake" for still being a dreadful free-thrower... But shame-shame-shame on many higher-profile, higher-paid pals on this team who should blush watching this guy bust it nightly... Born Sept. 5, 1964, in Chicago ... Rough, unpolished gem out of Illinois after beginning collegiate career at world-famed Wabash... Nice 1987 pick in first round at No.

9 by Clips . . . Tentative defender away from low box but aggressive inside . . . Not unwilling to unleash a jumper or two, he had a 35-point game and finished with more than 1,000 points second straight season . . . A certifiably lousy free-thrower, he again threw bricks from foul line. How certifiably bad? Last year he shot .632, a career best, and he's now at .601 over three seasons.

Year	Team	G	FG	FG Pct.	FT	FT Pct.	Reb.	Ast.	TP	Avg.
1987-88	L.A. Clippers	66	241	.482	87	.512	263	78	569	8.6
1988-89	L.A. Clippers	80	638	.502	170	.630	667	277	1450	18.1
1989-90	L.A. Clippers	70	484	.510	153	.632	470	160	1128	16.1
	Totals	216	1363	.501	410	.601	1400	515	3147	14.6

WINSTON GARLAND 25 6-2 170   Guard

Nice supporting-role player . . . Spent two-thirds of last year with Golden State before joining Clippers . . . Started 15 times in 28 games . . . Maintained decent assist-turnover ratio . . . Oddly, still not much of a percentage shooter (.428 as a Clipper) but became team's best three-point threat and averaged 10.9 for L.A. . . . Born Dec. 19, 1964, in Gary, Ind. . . . Second-round pick (No. 40) by Milwaukee in 1987 out of Southwest Missouri State after transferring from Southeastern (Iowa) Community College . . . Cut by Bucks, he averaged 13.5 in two full seasons at Golden State.

Year	Team	G	FG	FG Pct.	FT	FT Pct.	Reb.	Ast.	TP	Avg.
1987-88	Golden State	67	340	.439	138	.879	227	429	831	12.4
1988-89	Golden State	79	466	.434	203	.809	328	505	1145	14.5
1989-90	G.S.-LAC	79	230	.401	102	.836	214	303	574	7.3
	Totals	225	1036	.428	443	.836	769	1237	2550	11.3

CHARLES SMITH 25 6-10 238   Forward

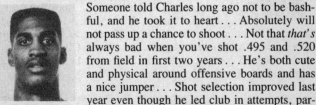

Someone told Charles long ago not to be bashful, and he took it to heart . . . Absolutely will not pass up a chance to shoot . . . Not that *that's* always bad when you've shot .495 and .520 from field in first two years . . . He's both cute and physical around offensive boards and has a nice jumper . . . Shot selection improved last year even though he led club in attempts, particularly after Ron Harper went down . . . Born July 16, 1965, in Bridgeport, Conn. . . . He was third player picked in 1988's first round . . . Former Pitt star landed in Los Angeles via a draft-day trade with Philadelphia for Hersey Hawkins and a 1989 first-round pick . . . It has become fashionable among some scouts to mention he might in the long run be a better player than Danny Manning, his more touted peer and former Olympic teammate.

Year	Team	G	FG	FG Pct.	FT	FT Pct.	Reb.	Ast.	TP	Avg.
1988-89	L.A. Clippers.....	71	435	.495	285	.725	465	103	1155	16.3
1989-90	L.A. Clippers.....	78	595	.520	454	.794	524	114	1645	21.1
	Totals	149	1030	.509	739	.766	989	217	2800	18.8

TOM GARRICK 24 6-2 195   Guard

Should have long pro career . . . Not a star, but a strong-willed player . . . A leader and keeper . . . Born July 7, 1966, in West Warwick, R.I. . . . Captain at Rhode Island, where he set other people up and managed a 50-point game . . . Brilliant in 1988 postseason play . . . Selected No. 45 by Clippers that summer . . . Made 10 starts in final 11 games of rookie year . . . Shot .494 last season and made 22 of his 73 appearances as a starter.

Year	Team	G	FG	FG Pct.	FT	FT Pct.	Reb.	Ast.	TP	Avg.
1988-89	L.A. Clippers.....	71	176	.490	102	.803	156	243	454	6.4
1989-90	L.A. Clippers.....	73	208	.494	88	.772	162	289	508	7.0
	Totals	144	384	.492	190	.788	318	532	962	6.7

GARY GRANT 25 6-3 196   Guard

Suffered fractured and dislocated ankle and missed just about half the season . . . Had averaged 13.1 points, starting each of 44 games . . . Finished season with 139 more assists than nearest teammate . . . Didn't quite make All-Media-Relations Team with unprovoked shove of reporter in locker room . . . Born April 21, 1965, in Parson, Kan. . . . Big 10 Defensive Player of Year as junior at Michigan . . . Consensus All-American senior year . . . A 1988 draft-day deal sent him to Clippers as first-rounder (No. 15 overall) . . . Put up 22 points, 11 rebounds, 17 assists on Jan. 30, 1990, vs. Lakers.

Year	Team	G	FG	FG Pct.	FT	FT Pct.	Reb.	Ast.	TP	Avg.
1988-89	L.A. Clippers.....	71	361	.435	119	.735	238	506	846	11.9
1989-90	L.A. Clippers.....	44	241	.466	88	.779	195	442	575	13.1
	Totals	115	602	.447	207	.753	433	948	1421	12.4

BENOIT BENJAMIN 25 7-0 275   Center

Big Ben/Gentle Ben/Perplexing Ben . . . Remains an enigma after five full seasons . . . Too many times Clips look better without him . . . It's never been a question of talent . . . Skill he's got, but will? . . . Born Nov. 12, 1964, in Monroe, La. . . . Picked No. 3 overall by Clippers in 1985 out of Creighton . . . "Put me at the bottom of the list of Benjamin fans," former Philly GM John Nash said early last season, scanning about-to-be free agents. "My opinion is, he's one of the most lackluster names out there. For a handful of games he played well at the end of the [1988-89] season, realizing his contract was up. He appears to be an immense talent, whose play has been sporadic, with a questionable work ethic." . . . Scoring average dropped last season from 16.4 to 13.5 . . . Had as many turnovers (187) as blocks.

Year	Team	G	FG	FG Pct.	FT	FT Pct.	Reb.	Ast.	TP	Avg.
1985-86	L.A. Clippers	79	324	.490	229	.746	600	79	878	11.1
1986-87	L.A. Clippers	72	320	.449	188	.715	586	135	828	11.5
1987-88	L.A. Clippers	66	340	.491	180	.706	530	172	860	13.0
1988-89	L.A. Clippers	79	491	.541	317	.744	696	157	1299	16.4
1989-90	L.A. Clippers	71	362	.526	235	.732	657	159	959	13.5
	Totals	367	1837	.502	1149	.731	3069	702	4824	13.1

JEFF MARTIN 23 6-5 195   Guard-Forward

Got minutes last year perhaps even he didn't expect . . . Does he fit into a running game? His high school was named Cross Country . . . Voted Ohio Valley Conference Player of Year in 1989 . . . Averaged 25.6 points, 5.2 rebounds as a senior at Murray State . . . Left there with 12 school records, missed only one of 117 possible games and was invited to Olympic Trials . . . A second-round (No. 31) choice in 1989 by Clippers . . . Team circumstances and his hard work earned him 69 appearances and 23 starts . . . Shot only .411 but will again get a long look . . . Born Jan. 14, 1967, in Cherry Valley, Ark.

Year	Team	G	FG	FG Pct.	FT	FT Pct.	Reb.	Ast.	TP	Avg.
1989-90	L.A. Clippers	69	170	.411	91	.705	159	44	433	6.3

JAY EDWARDS 21 6-4 205   Guard

Still learning what pro hoops and life are all about . . . Played in as many games last season as he lost (four) in entire high-school career . . . Born Jan. 13, 1969, in Muncie, Ind. . . . Teamed with Lyndon Jones on three straight Indiana state championship teams (85-4) at Marion High . . . Made All-Big 10 and a few All-American teams . . . Left Indiana U. after two seasons . . . Picked by Clippers in second round (No. 33) in 1989 . . . Saw only 26 minutes of playing time as rookie.

Year	Team	G	FG	FG Pct.	FT	FT Pct.	Reb.	Ast.	TP	Avg.
1989-90	L.A. Clippers	4	3	.429	1	.333	2	4	7	1.8

JOE WOLF 25 6-10 235   Forward-Center

Important career year personally for the former North Carolina standout . . . He's shot .407, .423 and now .395 in his first three years . . . Born Dec. 17, 1964, in Kohler, Wis. . . . The Clippers selected him at the 13th spot of the first round in 1987 . . . His soft touch and confidence at long distance seemed a bonus in a player of his size at North Carolina, where he had shot .571 and averaged 15.2 ppg as a senior for Dean Smith . . . But he can't shoot over people as easily in the pros and still seems reluctant to power ball to hoop . . . Shot fewer than one free throw per game in 77 appearances, 19 starts last season . . . Minutes per game could drop under new coach Mike Schuler.

Year	Team	G	FG	FG Pct.	FT	FT Pct.	Reb.	Ast.	TP	Avg.
1987-88	L.A. Clippers	42	136	.407	45	.833	187	98	320	7.6
1988-89	L.A. Clippers	66	170	.423	44	.688	271	113	386	5.8
1989-90	L.A. Clippers	77	155	.395	55	.775	232	62	370	4.8
	Totals	185	461	.409	144	.762	690	273	1706	5.8

KEN BANNISTER 30 6-9 260   Center-Forward

Career backup man . . . Made one start in 52 games last year . . . Not bad as a buying-time spot player, behind true big-timer, which he was to Pat Ewing, isn't to Benoit Benjamin . . . Quiet guy off floor, likes chess and works with underprivileged and handicapped . . . A tight end in high school, but a career brick-tosser at NBA foul line, making 47.3 percent last season

... Born April 1, 1960, in Baltimore ... Knicks picked him 156th on seventh round in 1984 out of St. Augustine's (N.C.) College ... Became known as "The Animal" for his crude style of play ... After two seasons in N.Y., he drifted about, was with Wichita Falls and Rockford in CBA ... Signed as free agent with Clippers April 5, 1989.

Year	Team	G	FG	FG Pct.	FT	FT Pct.	Reb.	Ast.	TP	Avg.
1984-85	New York	75	209	.470	91	.474	330	39	509	6.8
1985-86	New York	70	235	.491	131	.526	322	42	601	8.6
1988-89	L.A. Clippers	9	22	.611	30	.566	33	3	74	8.2
1989-90	L.A. Clippers	52	77	.478	52	.473	112	18	206	4.0
	Totals	206	543	.484	304	.503	797	102	1390	6.7

THE ROOKIES

GREG (BO) KIMBLE 24 6-3 197   Guard
This Bo knows something ... A long-range threat with muscle and playground smarts to overpower people inside ... Won nationally televised One-on-One contest and $100,000 days before Clips made him No. 8 pick ... Leading scorer in nation last season (35.3), picking up reins of Loyola Marymount after on-court fatal seizure of high-school teammate and closest pal, Hank Gathers ... Says if he wasn't picked in two first spots, he wanted to be chosen by Clippers ... Born April 9, 1966, in Philadelphia.

LOY VAUGHT 23 6-9 230   Forward
GM Elgin Baylor and Mike Schuler, the first-year coach, insist that this is the guy they coveted at No. 13, unless Felton Spencer slipped that far ... At Michigan, Vaught twice led Big 10 in FG percentage (career 61.7 percent) ... A shot-blocker of some potential, he could play some center when run-minded Clippers decide to go with small lineup ... Born Feb. 27, 1967, in Grand Rapids, Mich.

COACH MIKE SCHULER: He has to win, and win big, soon ... Like this season, his first ... Donald T. Sterling, the team's flamboyant, flighty owner, put the pressure on weeks before making the hiring official ... The annual lawn party at Sterling's Beverly Hills estate on a brilliant spring Sunday was titled a "Farewell to the Lottery Draft" gathering ... Schuler lives X's and O's, which wouldn't be too bad if he didn't also dream about X's and O's ... NBA Coach of the Year at Portland, in 1986-87 . . . Had 127-83, .605 record before top players (Hello, Clyde) got him dumped in February 1989 . . . Assistant at Golden State when L.A. job opened . . . Not a "players coach," inherits youngish players, many of whom insist on being coddled . . . Born Sept. 23, 1940, in Portsmouth, Ohio.

GREATEST REBOUNDER

Five years into his career, Benoit Benjamin should be the headline. But no matter the varied home ports of the Clippers—embarked long ago from Buffalo—fulfillment rarely matches promise.

Three straight team-leading totals—including his league-leading 1,155 in 1974-75—earns the dock manager's nod for then-Brave Bob McAdoo.

Benoit? In his best years combined in Los Angeles, he totaled 1,353 boards. With 1,184, Elmore Smith led Buffalo in 1971-72. Swen Nater got 1,216 in a year (1979-80), and two other times in San Diego topped 1,000. In 1987-88 in L.A., Michael Cage had an asterisk-adorned 13.03 average to lead the league, playing catch/miss/catch with himself on the season's final day.

ALL-TIME CLIPPER LEADERS

SEASON

Points: Bob McAdoo, 2,831, 1974-75
Assists: Norm Nixon, 914, 1983-84
Rebounds: Swen Nater, 1,216, 1979-80

GAME

Points: Bob McAdoo, 52 vs. Seattle, 3/17/76
          Bob McAdoo, 52 vs. Boston, 2/22/74
Assists: Ernie DiGregorio, 25 vs. Portland, 1/1/74
Rebounds: Swen Nater, 32 vs. Denver, 12/14/79

CAREER

Points: Randy Smith, 12,735, 1971-79, 1982-83
Assists: Randy Smith, 3,498, 1971-79, 1982-83
Rebounds: Bob McAdoo, 4,229, 1972-76

LOS ANGELES LAKERS

TEAM DIRECTORY: Owner: Jerry Buss; GM: Jerry West; Dir. Pub. Rel.: John Black; Coach: Mike Dunleavy; Asst. Coaches: Bill Bertka, Randy Pfund. Arena: The Great Western Forum (17,505). Colors: Royal purple and gold.

Magic Johnson took MVP honors for third time in four years.

SCOUTING REPORT

SHOOTING: This might not have struck you as you watched on TV as they missed CYO-YMHA junior league layup after layup in last spring's playoff debacle against Phoenix (or Houston, for that matter): The Lakers are still an excellent point-producing team.

They are older. They are slower. But Magic Johnson never claimed to be swift. And last year they got smarter. Too late, they got smarter. It probably wasn't until about, oh, the third period of Detroit's repeat-clinching win over Portland, that collectively it sank in that they had, in fact, missed Kareem Abdul-Jabbar. Not his prime-of-career scoring, but his physical presence.

Sixty-three wins and a .490 FG percentage mask a lot of problems in a regular season. By playoff time, James Worthy was being doubled, not the low post (Mychal Thompson). Guards were not dropping off Byron Scott to shield the low post (Vlade Divac). New coach Mike Dunleavy's tough job includes chasing the ghost of Kareem out of this club's halfcourt mindset. Free-agent signee Sam Perkins from Dallas should help.

PLAYMAKING: If there's a problem on this once-great team, we can skip on to the next category because this is not a trouble area. In his time, at his size, Bob Cousy was as flashy. But no one ever has been able to deliver the ball to a player in scoring position as well and as consistently as Magic. He always seems to have an idea in mind on the break and possesses the skill to complete the play. In halfcourt sets, with Abdul-Jabbar gone, he is creating from the point position and from the power forward side and from the center's hole. The general pro-level ability—competently adequate—of his teammates pales in comparison.

DEFENSE: Abdul-Jabbar had masked several individual weaknesses of teammates as they won five NBA titles in the 1980s. The Lakers were risk-takers at times, knowing the 7-2 center lurked behind. Last year opponents attacked the middle and found it soft. At times, Pat Riley made excellent use of a halfcourt zone trap.

Whether Dunleavy, his successor, will further exploit that tactic might depend on how much has gone from the legs of his guard and small forward chasers—and the dubious defensive court sense displayed by the exciting Divac in his rookie season. Replacing the departed Michael Cooper will be one of Dunleavy's biggest tasks.

LAKER ROSTER

No.	Veterans	Pos.	Ht.	Wt.	Age	Yrs. Pro	College
12	Vlade Divac	C	7-1	248	22	1	Yugoslavia
10	Larry Drew	G	6-2	190	32	9	Missouri
45	A.C. Green	F	6-9	224	27	5	Oregon State
32	Earvin (Magic) Johnson	G	6-9	220	31	11	Michigan State
31	Mark McNamara	C	6-11	235	31	7	California
14	Sam Perkins	F-C	6-9	235	29	5	North Carolina
4	Byron Scott	G	6-4	193	29	7	Arizona State
43	Mychal Thompson	C	6-10	235	35	11	Minnesota
42	James Worthy	F	6-9	225	29	8	North Carolina

Rd.	Rookies	Sel. No.	Pos.	Ht.	Wt.	College
1	Elden Campbell	27	F-C	6-11	215	Clemson
2	Tony Smith	51	G	6-4	190	Marquette

REBOUNDING: Perhaps you could spell that word for the Lakers? Except for A.C. (Always Coming) Green, most of these people have a regal disdain for the backboard. Magic is an opportunistic rebounder, an effective one at times. But when he's playing the point and also crashing the offensive boards, the opponents usually have a clear run to the other end.

Before the Dunleavy-for-Riley move at season's end, a decision had been made to start Divac, the 7-1 Yugoslavian import, and return the 6-10 Thompson to a come-off-the-bench role. Divac, however, is foul-prone. And while Thompson maintains his gladiator-pretty upper-body musculature, he has very old and sore feet.

OUTLOOK: No longer the "cream of the crop"—as Dunleavy characterizes the status of this club—the Lakers remain formidable and will be so as long as Magic is allowed to bring along four friends and a basketball every night. But unless they find a way to rest Magic without games falling to pieces in a matter of seconds, discover better and more consistent off-guard play, enjoy continuing improved scoring from Worthy, and find instant maturity for the young Divac, there will be earlier and earlier beach time for the once dominant Pacific Division powers.

LAKER PROFILES

EARVIN (MAGIC) JOHNSON 31 6-9 220   Guard

Named MVP second year in a row, narrowly beating out Philadelphia's Charles Barkley and Chicago's Michael Jordan in the closest voting in the 10 years that balloting has been done by a media panel . . . "Earvin is the smartest player in the league, a true genius in the game," tributed Pat Riley . . . He led the league with 11 triple-doubles and topped the Lakers with a 22.3 ppg, 18th in the NBA . . . Ranked second behind Utah's John Stockton in assists and his free-throw percentage was seventh . . . Had his most three-point field goals ever (106 of 276) . . . Quickness and hand-eye coordination still make him NBA's most dangerous man in the middle of fastbreaks . . . Born Aug. 14, 1959, in Lansing, Mich. . . . Led Michigan State to 1979 NCAA title over Larry Bird and Indiana State . . . No. 1 overall pick by Lakers when he came out after soph year.

Year	Team	G	FG	FG Pct.	FT	FT Pct.	Reb.	Ast.	TP	Avg.
1979-80	Los Angeles	77	503	.530	374	.810	596	563	1387	18.0
1980-81	Los Angeles	37	312	.532	171	.760	320	317	798	21.6
1981-82	Los Angeles	78	556	.537	329	.760	751	743	1447	18.6
1982-83	Los Angeles	79	511	.548	304	.800	683	829	1326	16.8
1983-84	Los Angeles	67	441	.565	290	.810	491	875	1178	17.6
1984-85	L.A. Lakers	77	504	.561	391	.843	476	968	1406	18.3
1985-86	L.A. Lakers	72	483	.526	378	.871	426	907	1354	18.8
1986-87	L.A. Lakers	80	683	.522	535	.848	504	977	1909	23.9
1987-88	L.A. Lakers	72	490	.492	417	.853	449	858	1408	19.6
1988-89	L.A. Lakers	77	579	.509	513	.911	607	988	1730	22.5
1989-90	L.A. Lakers	79	546	.480	567	.890	522	907	1765	22.3
	Totals	795	5608	.525	4269	.841	5825	8932	15708	19.8

JAMES WORTHY 29 6-9 225   Forward

Wondering where James went during the playoffs? So is James . . . No. 10 in career postseason shooting, he couldn't buy a hoop . . . Missed layups, missed three-foot swoop-hooks, with both hands against Phoenix in deciding games of Western semis . . . Later, he resembled straight-A student who, on graduation, accidentally had tipped over the tables stacked with diplomas . . . Still is pivotal to Lakers . . . When he's on his game, the team is unstoppable . . . Class act on and off floor and a worthy All-Star four straight years... Born Feb. 27, 1961, in Gastonia, N.C.... Star at North Carolina and named Most Outstanding Player as a junior in 1982 NCAA Tournament... An early entry, he was first player taken that June in draft... Married to college sweetheart, Angela, and both have made TV appearances—he more reluctantly than she, an aspiring model/actress ... Private person with a give-you-quivers singing voice.

Year	Team	G	FG	FG Pct.	FT	FT Pct.	Reb.	Ast.	TP	Avg.
1982-83	Los Angeles	77	447	.579	138	.624	399	132	1033	13.4
1983-84	Los Angeles	82	495	.556	195	.759	515	207	1185	14.5
1984-85	L.A. Lakers	80	610	.572	190	.776	511	201	1410	17.6
1985-86	L.A. Lakers	75	629	.579	242	.771	387	201	1500	20.0
1986-87	L.A. Lakers	82	651	.539	292	.751	466	226	1594	19.4
1987-88	L.A. Lakers	75	617	.531	242	.796	374	289	1478	19.7
1988-89	L.A. Lakers	81	702	.548	251	.782	489	288	1657	20.5
1989-90	L.A. Lakers	80	711	.548	248	.782	478	288	1685	21.1
	Totals	632	4862	.555	1798	.759	3619	1832	11542	18.3

BYRON SCOTT 29 6-4 193　　　　　Guard

Nagging injuries—or something—seemed to have him off stride almost all last season... Had poorest shooting year (.470) in seventh season... Oddly, he placed fifth in NBA with .423 marksmanship from three-point land... Born March 28, 1961, in Ogden, Utah... Grew up and went to school blocks from Forum and used to sneak into Laker games... Set school scoring mark in three seasons at Arizona State... San Diego Clippers made him fourth player (and first guard overall) in 1983... Traded before season began to Lakers for Norm Nixon, Eddie Jordan and two future picks... Deal was abhorred initially by Laker fans and most players, but it was an inspired move... In 1987-88 became only sixth single-season scoring leader of Lakers in 30 years (Baylor, West, Goodrich, Abdul-Jabbar, Magic)... Awesome distance-shooter in pre-practice H-O-R-S-E contests... Goes from midcourt to behind sideline seats.

Year	Team	G	FG	FG Pct.	FT	FT Pct.	Reb.	Ast.	TP	Avg.
1983-84	Los Angeles	74	334	.484	112	.806	164	177	788	10.6
1984-85	L.A. Lakers	81	541	.539	187	.820	210	244	1295	16.0
1985-86	L.A. Lakers	76	507	.513	138	.784	189	164	1174	15.4
1986-87	L.A. Lakers	82	554	.489	224	.892	286	281	1397	17.0
1987-88	L.A. Lakers	81	710	.527	272	.858	333	335	1754	21.7
1988-89	L.A. Lakers	74	588	.491	195	.863	302	231	1448	19.6
1989-90	L.A. Lakers	77	472	.470	160	.766	242	274	1197	15.5
	Totals	545	3706	.503	1288	.833	1726	1706	9053	16.6

A.C. GREEN 27 6-9 224   Forward

Son of a preacher man . . . Devoutly religious but his cheek only turns so far . . . Second dedication: Hit the offensive board, very hard . . . Was among several key Lakers who claimed to have become "confused" about roles assigned by then-coach Pat Riley one-third into season . . . Born Oct. 4, 1963, in Portland . . . Everyone except Laker GM Jerry West apparently thought he was all effort and no pro skills at Oregon State . . . West got him with 23d pick in 1985 . . . Has missed only three games in career (all in second season to injury) . . . Current 321 consecutive-game streak is second only to Houston's Otis Thorpe at 378.

Year	Team	G	FG	FG Pct.	FT	FT Pct.	Reb.	Ast.	TP	Avg.
1985-86	L.A. Lakers	82	209	.539	102	.611	381	54	521	6.4
1986-87	L.A. Lakers	79	316	.538	220	.780	615	84	852	10.8
1987-88	L.A. Lakers	82	322	.503	293	.773	710	93	937	11.4
1988-89	L.A. Lakers	82	401	.529	282	.786	739	103	1088	13.3
1989-90	L.A. Lakers	82	385	.478	278	.751	712	90	1061	12.9
	Totals	407	1633	.514	1175	.755	3157	424	4459	11.0

MYCHAL THOMPSON 35 6-10 235   Center

After 2½ years as "The Man Behind Kareem Abdul-Jabbar," he became Lakers' second starting center since, it seems, the Korean War . . . Didn't like starting all that much, and his body agreed with the mind . . . Missed 12 games with assorted bumps, especially nagging foot injuries that persist . . . "If there was a tax on pain, I'd be collecting a lot of money from this old body," he said as summer began . . . Quick-witted and glib . . . And an excellent, self-contained veteran player who is still a reasonable scorer, smart defender, so-so rebounder . . . Born Jan. 30, 1955, in Nassau, Bahamas . . . Attended high school in Miami before playing four years and averaging 20.5 points at Minnesota . . . Portland used No. 1 pick overall in 1978 draft to get him . . . Made NBA All-Rookie team but broken leg cost him a full season during eight-year stay with Trail Blazers . . . Traded to Spurs, he spent half-season in San Antonio before being swapped to Lakers for Frank Brickowski and Petur Gudmundsson and two draft picks on Feb. 13, 1987 ... Has two championship rings with Los Angeles.

Year	Team	G	FG	FG Pct.	FT	FT Pct.	Reb.	Ast.	TP	Avg.
1978-79	Portland	73	460	.490	154	.572	604	176	1074	14.7
1979-80	Portland					Injured				
1980-81	Portland	79	569	.494	207	.641	686	284	1345	17.0
1981-82	Portland	79	681	.523	280	.628	921	319	1642	20.8
1982-83	Portland	80	505	.489	249	.621	753	380	1259	15.7
1983-84	Portland	79	487	.524	266	.667	688	308	1240	15.7
1984-85	Portland	79	572	.515	307	.684	618	205	1451	18.4
1985-86	Portland	82	503	.498	198	.641	608	176	1204	14.7
1986-87	S.A.-LAL	82	359	.450	219	.737	412	115	938	11.4
1987-88	L.A. Lakers	80	370	.512	185	.634	489	66	925	11.6
1988-89	L.A. Lakers	80	291	.559	156	.678	467	48	738	9.2
1989-90	L.A. Lakers	70	281	.500	144	.706	477	43	706	10.1
	Totals	863	5078	.504	2365	.653	6723	2120	12522	14.5

VLADE DIVAC 22 7-1 248   Center

Statistically at least, the best 26th pick of past decade ... You could look it up, and go beyond a decade ... Except assists, had numerical superiority in every category ... Born Feb. 2, 1968, in Prijepolje, Yugoslavia ... Left home with parental approval at age 12 to hone skills for pro hoops career ... Pro center at age 16 for club team ... Gold medalist for nation's junior Olympic team in 1985 World University Games ... Played for Partizan and Yugoslavian National team ... Lakers took him with their only pick in 1989 draft ... Clumsy in low-post defense ... Has inside and outside moves ... Runs and even handles ball on the break ... Outgoing personally and favorite of fans and teammates ... He'd be starting at forward had arrival preceded Kareem Abdul-Jabbar's retirement.

Year	Team	G	FG	FG Pct.	FT	FT Pct.	Reb.	Ast.	TP	Avg.
1989-90	L.A. Lakers	82	274	.499	153	.708	512	75	701	8.5

SAM PERKINS 29 6-9 235   Forward-Center

After six seasons with Dallas, which made him fourth overall pick in the 1984 draft, he signed a multiyear contract with the Lakers in August ... Always has you thinking he'll explode to superstar level but never quite comes through ... He's big enough and strong enough to defend against some of the biggest centers and offensively he's a threat in the low post ...

Doesn't have that great ego that goes into the making of the great ones, but he always helped carry the Mavs when the going got tough... Born June 14, 1961, in New York City... Was MVP of the NCAA Final Four in 1983 when North Carolina won the title... College teammate of Michael Jordan and co-captain of the 1984 gold-medal U.S. Olympic team.

Year	Team	G	FG	FG Pct.	FT	FT Pct.	Reb.	Ast.	TP	Avg.
1984-85	Dallas	82	347	.471	200	.820	605	135	903	11.0
1985-86	Dallas	80	458	.503	307	.814	685	153	1234	15.4
1986-87	Dallas	80	461	.482	245	.828	616	146	1186	14.8
1987-88	Dallas	75	394	.450	273	.822	601	118	1066	14.2
1988-89	Dallas	78	445	.464	274	.833	688	127	1171	15.0
1989-90	Dallas	76	435	.493	330	.778	572	175	1206	15.9
	Totals	471	2540	.477	1629	.814	3767	854	6766	14.4

MARK McNAMARA 31 6-11 235   Center

Veteran bench-sitter... Played key role off floor last season, becoming big brother/translator for Vlade Divac... Knowledge of Italian and his European playing experience gave the Yugoslavian rookie someone to gab with... Born June 8, 1959, in San Jose, Cal.... Began career at Santa Clara, transferred after two seasons to California... Averaged 19.6 points, 11.6 rebounds in two years at Cal and led nation as senior with .702 FG... Philadelphia took him 22d on first round of 1982... Deep sub on 1983 NBA champion 76ers... Including European stops, he'd been with San Antonio, Kansas City, Philadelphia again before signing with L.A.... Started only one of his 33 games last year... Surfer, volleyball player, and costumed role as "Wookie" in *Return of the Jedi*... His Northern California hillside property was severely damaged by 1989 earthquake.

Year	Team	G	FG	FG Pct.	FT	FT Pct.	Reb.	Ast.	TP	Avg.
1982-83	Philadelphia	36	29	.453	20	.444	76	7	78	2.2
1983-84	San Antonio	70	157	.621	74	.471	317	31	388	5.5
1984-85	S.A.-K.C.	45	40	.526	32	.516	74	6	112	2.5
1986-87	Philadelphia	11	14	.467	7	.368	36	2	35	3.2
1987-88	Philadelphia	42	52	.391	48	.727	157	18	152	3.6
1988-89	L.A. Lakers	39	32	.500	49	.628	100	10	113	2.9
1989-90	L.A. Lakers	33	38	.442	26	.650	63	3	102	3.1
	Totals	276	362	.513	256	.548	823	77	980	3.6

Vlade Divac bounded from Belgrade to All-Rookie Team.

LARRY DREW 32 6-2 190   Guard

Personally disappointing year... First real chance to play for title contender... But things never quite meshed... Got three emergency starts in 80 games... Born April 2, 1958, in Kansas City, Kan.... Drafted 17th out of Missouri in 1980 on the first round by Detroit... Traded after rookie year to Kansas City... Had best season in 1982-83, averaging 20.1, and was on a run of five straight double-figure campaigns when traded to Clippers before 1986-87 season... Spent two years there, bolted to Europe... Signed as a free agent by Lakers to understudy Magic Johnson... Shot .444 in regular season... Non-factor in playoffs.

Year	Team	G	FG	FG Pct.	FT	FT Pct.	Reb.	Ast.	TP	Avg.
1980-81	Detroit	76	197	.407	106	.797	120	249	504	6.6
1981-82	Kansas City	81	358	.473	150	.794	149	419	874	10.8
1982-83	Kansas City	75	599	.492	310	.820	207	610	1510	20.1
1983-84	Kansas City	73	474	.462	243	.776	146	558	1194	16.4
1984-85	Kansas City	72	457	.501	154	.794	164	484	1075	14.9
1985-86	Sacramento	75	376	.485	128	.795	125	338	890	11.9
1986-87	L.A. Clippers	60	295	.432	139	.837	103	326	741	12.4
1987-88	L.A. Clippers	74	328	.456	83	.769	119	383	765	10.3
1989-90	L.A. Lakers	80	170	.444	46	.767	98	217	418	5.2
	Totals	666	3254	.468	1359	.798	1231	3584	7971	12.0

THE ROOKIES

ELDEN CAMPBELL 22 6-11 215   Forward-Center

Another in a series of rabbit-out-of-the-hat tricks by Lakers GM Jerry West?... Campbell was born almost up the street from the Forum, played at Morningside High, where Byron Scott had come to fame... Leading career scorer in history at Clemson, where he led ACC in blocked shots as a senior... Only Tree Rollins rejected more shots at Clemson than he did... Claims his "look" scared off scouts, mistaking his stoic manner for lack of intensity... Born July 23, 1968, in Inglewood, Cal.

TONY SMITH 22 6-4 190   Guard

Does not—repeat, does not—figure to become this season's Vlade Divac... Chosen at No. 51 by Lakers, who do need a support shooting guard... He's probably not the answer... Born June

4, 1968, in East Wauwatosa, Wis., and was star of 24-1 team s senior at East Wauwatosa High... An engineering major at Marquette, where his coach says he was "strong, quick and athetic."... Averaged 23.8 points in final year, despite shooting 41 ercent from floor... An .856 free-thrower.

COACH MIKE DUNLEAVY: Succeeded last year's Coach of the Year, Pat Riley, who resigned early in June after the Lakers had been eliminated in conference semifinals by Phoenix... Lakers had won four of their five titles in the 1980s under Riley, who left with NBA history's highest winning percentages in both regular season (.733) and playoffs (.694, including record 102 wins)... Mike performed competitively as recently as last season—in five games of emergency service he made a pair of three-pointers for Milwaukee, where he had been an assistant coach for three years... Born March 21, 1954, in Brooklyn, N.Y., he became a 6-3 playmaking, scoring guard at South Carolina... He was a sixth-round pick by the 76ers in 1976, seeing limited action, and landed with the Houston Rockets for a four-year stay... Had a year with San Antonio and filled in for an injury-depleted Bucks' squad late in the 1983-84 season... Faces enormous pressure with "Showime" at the Forum.

GREATEST REBOUNDER

From Minnesota's 10,000 lakes to the Pacific shore, this franchise has been blessed by three of the game's greatest centers.

Beginning at the NBA's start, when George Mikan keyed Minneapolis, through Wilt Chamberlain and Kareem Abdul-Jabbar in L.A., the Lakers have won 11 league championships. And their centers have taken six rebounding titles.

Pressed, Mikan might mention he was the 1952-53 board leader and his team won five NBA titles—after having dominated the NBL. Abdul-Jabbar, rebounding leader in 1975-76, can point to six league title rings—five as a Laker. Wilt? He's the all-time career boardman, leading the league six times with Philadelphia, once at San Francisco, four as a Laker.

ALL-TIME LAKER LEADERS

SEASON

Points: Elgin Baylor, 2,719, 1962-63
Assists: Earvin (Magic) Johnson, 988, 1988-89
Rebounds: Wilt Chamberlain, 1,712, 1968-69

GAME

Points: Elgin Baylor, 71 vs. New York, 11/15/60
Assists: Jerry West, 23 vs. Philadelphia, 2/1/67
　　　　　Earvin (Magic) Johnson, 23 vs. Seattle, 2/21/84
Rebounds: Wilt Chamberlain, 42 vs. Boston, 3/7/69

CAREER

Points: Jerry West, 25,192, 1960-74
Assists: Earvin (Magic) Johnson, 8,932, 1980-90
Rebounds: Elgin Baylor, 11,463, 1958-72

MINNESOTA TIMBERWOLVES

TEAM DIRECTORY: Owners: Harvey Ratner, Marv Wolfenson; Pres.: Bob Stein; VP/Marketing, Sales: Tim Leiweke; Dir. Player Personnel: Billy McKinney; Dir. Media Rel.: Bill Robertson; Coach: Bill Musselman; Asst. Coaches: Tom Thibodeau, Eric Musselman. Arena: Target Center (18,500). Colors: Blue, green and silver.

Out of Laker captivity, Tony Campbell unleashed a 23.2 ppg.

SCOUTING REPORT

SHOOTING: If he is nothing else—and he is a whole lot else—Bill Musselman is insistent that his teams take good shots, and a good shot to Musselman is anything from, say, five feet to a dunk. Tony Campbell has never seen a shot from anywhere that he didn't like, and the two—who go back to the CBA—compromised last year. Top Cat had an excellent scoring year (23.2).

The expansionists had four other double-figure scorers, the highest of whom was Tyrone Corbin (14.7). Combined, the Timberwolves could produce only 95.2 ppg. Of course, some of that is Musselman's approach. But things will have to loosen up. Sidney Lowe, for instance, was third in the league in assist/turnover ratio, but the last time Lowe took a chance with the ball it probably was to bounce it while Musselman was calling a play.

PLAYMAKING: Rookie Pooh Richardson had a nice break-in season, eliminating a lot of erraticism from his game and pushing the ball when allowed to by his cautious coach. Gerald Glass of Mississippi, one of Minnesota's two first-rounders last June, might help in the backcourt—not as a passer, but as an easer of pressure. Unleashed slowly, Richardson could crack the top 15 in assists if the Timberwolves come up with some people who can lift the shooting percentage above last year's awful .446.

DEFENSE: This has always been the mark of a Musselman team—college, CBA, wherever—and it will be here, too. He doesn't have enough athletes to play the single-up style he loves, but the team-help concept was assimilated so well last year that the rag-tag Wolves limited opponents to just 99.4 points a game. Randy Breuer, acquired from Milwaukee, led Minnesota in blocked shots in 51 games. Strangely, the Wolves were only 18th in defense against FG percentage. That's a mark of physical deficiency, not attention to detail.

REBOUNDING: Breuer will have to stick closer to the hoop if Minnesota is to pick up its offensive board work. Top pick Felton Spencer of Louisville will be expected to do a lot of dirty work early. The team's best pure athlete, Corbin has been underappreciated through his career. He was second in the league in the steal-to-turnover category, and led the club in rebounds. Sam Mitchell, a free-agent rookie whose path had crossed Musselman's in the CBA, was the fourth-best rebounder among last year's rookies as well being the Class of 1989-90's No. 5 scorer.

TIMBERWOLF ROSTER

No.	Veterans	Pos.	Ht.	Wt.	Age	Yrs. Pro	College
45	Randy Breuer	C	7-3	258	30	7	Minnesota
1	Scott Brooks	G	5-11	165	25	2	Cal-Irvine
19	Tony Campbell	F-G	6-7	231	28	6	Ohio State
23	Tyrone Corbin	F	6-6	222	27	5	DePaul
52	Gary Leonard	C	7-0	246	23	1	Missouri
35	Sidney Lowe	G	6-0	203	30	4	North Carolina State
42	Sam Mitchell	F	6-7	214	27	1	Mercer
4	Tod Murphy	F	6-10	222	26	2	Cal-Irvine
24	Jerome Richardson	G	6-1	180	24	1	UCLA
5	Doug West	F-G	6-6	200	23	1	Villanova

Rd.	Rookies	Sel. No.	Pos.	Ht.	Wt.	College
1	Felton Spencer	6	C	7-0	265	Louisville
1	Gerald Glass	20	G-F	6-6	221	Mississippi

OUTLOOK: Minnesota is probably a half-decade at best away from playoff contention, but this will be a contentious pack of Timberwolves during the regular season as long as Musselman doesn't push them over the edge. Not even all his 1988-89 careful preparation during the team's year-in-waiting period could have averted a 22-60 debut, but the coach does not take losing easily. Of his final 105 CBA games, his teams won 91 times.

TIMBERWOLF PROFILES

TYRONE CORBIN 27 6-6 222   Forward

Not a star, but a true pro . . . Slipped away from front offices that usually do better . . . Born Dec. 31, 1962, in Columbia, S.C. . . . Drafted in 1985 out of DePaul by San Antonio in second round (35th) . . . Hobbled by knee as rookie, he was waived by Spurs, signed by Cleveland . . . Despite being a tough player in clutch, he was sent with Kevin Johnson in trade to Phoenix for Larry Nance and Mike Sanders (draft picks spiced the deal) . . . Exposed to expansion by the Suns after one full season—numerically his best and Suns' turnaround campaign . . . Last year, had first double-figure scoring season (14.7) and leading steal-turnover ratio (1.22) in West . . . Best all-around player on team.

Year	Team	G	FG	FG Pct.	FT	FT Pct.	Reb.	Ast.	TP	Avg.
1985-86	San Antonio	16	27	.422	10	.714	25	11	64	4.0
1986-87	S.A.-Clev.	63	156	.409	91	.734	215	97	404	6.4
1987-88	Clev.-Phoe.	84	257	.490	110	.797	350	115	625	7.4
1988-89	Phoenix	77	245	.540	141	.788	398	118	631	8.2
1989-90	Minnesota.	82	521	.481	161	.770	604	216	1203	14.7
	Totals	322	1206	.481	513	.773	1592	557	2927	9.1

TONY CAMPBELL 28 6-7 231   Forward-Guard

Inch for inch, "Blumpy" is player-coach-captain of All-Ego Team . . . He knew he was good about 25 years ago . . . Born May 7, 1962, in Teaneck, N.J. . . . First-round pick (No. 20) out of Ohio State in 1984 by Detroit . . . Released after three years by Pistons . . . CBA's No. 1 success story . . . With coach Bill Musselman at Albany in 1987, he led league in FG and FT shooting, was third in scoring . . . He'd already been signed by Lakers when CBA named him Player and Newcomer of Year . . . Despite scoring skill and one good game in 1989 Finals vs. Pistons, he popped off once too often for Laker GM Jerry West, who released him . . . Voted third most-improved player in league last season . . . Started 81 of 82 games, averaged 39 minutes, 23.2 points—and had a negative 213-251 assist-turnover ratio.

Year	Team	G	FG	FG Pct.	FT	FT Pct.	Reb.	Ast.	TP	Avg.
1984-85	Detroit	56	130	.496	56	.800	89	24	316	5.6
1985-86	Detroit	82	294	.484	58	.795	236	45	648	7.9
1986-87	Detroit	40	57	.393	24	.615	58	19	138	3.5
1987-88	L.A. Lakers	13	57	.564	28	.718	27	15	143	11.0
1988-89	L.A. Lakers	63	158	.458	70	.843	130	47	388	6.2
1989-90	Minnesota.	82	723	.457	448	.787	451	213	1903	23.2
	Totals	336	1419	.466	684	.784	991	363	3536	10.5

JEROME (POOH) RICHARDSON 24 6-1 180   Guard

Surprising, surprised, surprise . . . Unexpectedly went 10th in last year's draft . . . Unexpectedly stayed cool when Bill Musselman was reluctant to let him run club on floor . . . Unexpectedly curbed natural push-it-up instincts when he became a full-timer and finished with seventh-best (3.93) assist-to-turnover ratio in league . . . Born May 4, 1966, in Philadelphia

. . . Made All-PAC 10 three years for UCLA and broke conference career assist mark . . . Determined effort produced 56 percent FG senior season and eased some scouts' doubts . . . Among late-summer gym rats who competed with/against Magic Johnson at UCLA.

Year	Team	G	FG	FG Pct.	FT	FT Pct.	Reb.	Ast.	TP	Avg.
1989-90	Minnesota.	82	426	.461	63	.589	217	554	938	11.4

SAM MITCHELL 27 6-7 214   Forward

Just after you've enunciated your 8,796th argument against expansion, paused for a breath, along comes a Sam Mitchell . . . Born Sept. 9, 1963, in Columbus, Ga. . . . Played at lightly scouted Mercer (Ga.) College . . . Not selected in 1986 draft until third round (54th) by Houston . . . Kissed bon voyage by Rockets, Mitchell played in France his first year out of college before becoming a CBA wanderer through three clubs . . . Hooked up with—surprise!—Bill Musselman and was on Rapid City's 1987 champions . . . Third-leading scorer on team last year, his 1,012 points were fifth in rookie scoring, and he trailed only David Robinson, J.R. Reid, Vlade Divac in first-year rebounding.

Year	Team	G	FG	FG Pct.	FT	FT Pct.	Reb.	Ast.	TP	Avg.
1989-90	Minnesota.	80	372	.446	268	.768	462	89	1012	12.7

RANDY BREUER 30 7-3 258   Center

Among NBA superstars' personal favorite players . . . Not just because he's a nice fellow . . . But if Breuer gets $960,000, reasoning goes, what's a good player worth? . . . Born Oct. 11, 1960, in Lake City, Minn. . . . Was 1983 first-round (18th) pick out of Minnesota by Bucks . . . Had one double-figure scoring season in six unfulfilling years as a Buck . . . Had 47 starts in 51 games with T-Wolves after they traded Brad Lohaus for him on Jan. 4, 1990 . . . Produced a 40-point game, but averaged 10.2, pulled 5.7 boards, and shot a dead-awful .416 . . . Earned spot in trivia annals in 1988 when he guarded Kareem Abdul-Jabbar the night his streak of 787 straight double-figure scoring games ended.

Year	Team	G	FG	FG Pct.	FT	FT Pct.	Reb.	Ast.	TP	Avg.
1983-84	Milwaukee	57	68	.384	32	.696	109	17	168	2.9
1984-85	Milwaukee	78	162	.511	89	.701	256	40	413	5.3
1985-86	Milwaukee	82	272	.477	141	.712	458	114	685	8.4
1986-87	Milwaukee	76	241	.485	118	.584	350	47	600	7.9
1987-88	Milwaukee	81	390	.495	188	.657	551	103	968	12.0
1988-89	Milwaukee	48	86	.480	28	.549	135	22	200	4.2
1989-90	Mil.-Minn.	81	298	.428	126	.653	417	97	722	8.9
	Totals	503	1517	.471	722	.655	2276	440	3756	7.5

SCOTT BROOKS 25 5-11 165   Guard

Traded by Sixers for second-round draft choice . . . Scrappy player with all the apparent athletism of an ice cube . . . But there will always be a place for his hustle . . . Scott Skiles type . . . Tenacious defender who'll work until he drops and come back for more . . . His .431 shooting percentage is somewhat misleading because almost one-third of his shots came from three-point range, where he shot 39 percent . . . Didn't do much in playoffs, though . . . Good ball-handler and can pick your pocket on defense . . . Born July 31, 1965, in Lathrop, Cal. . . . Cal-Irvine product who signed with Sixers as free agent for 1988-89 after they dropped him previous season . . . Earned $275,000.

Year	Team	G	FG	FG Pct.	FT	FT Pct.	Reb.	Ast.	TP	Avg.
1988-89	Philadelphia	82	156	.420	61	.884	94	306	428	5.2
1989-90	Philadelphia	72	119	.431	50	.877	64	207	319	4.4
	Totals	154	275	.425	111	.881	158	513	747	4.9

TOD MURPHY 26 6-9 222   Forward

Workaholic and overachiever . . . Maybe that explains why he's "lost" an inch between scouting measurements and signing on here? . . . Must be used to being short-changed, having been born in Lakewood, Cal., on Christmas Eve, 1963 . . . Drafted almost as a 6-10 afterthought (No. 53) by Seattle out of Cal-Irvine in 1986 . . . Cut by Sonics, played in Italy . . . Made one-game 1987 appearance with Clippers before going

CBA route . . . Naturally, he played there for Bill Musselman— and was 1987-88 MVP of Championship Series . . . Nice shooter . . . Spent 1988-89 in Spain, hustled through tryout camps to sign with Minnesota last year . . . Started 55 games, played all 82, was team's No. 2 rebounder.

Year	Team	G	FG	FG Pct.	FT	FT Pct.	Reb.	Ast.	TP	Avg.
1987-88	L.A. Clippers	1	1	1.000	3	.750	2	2	5	5.0
1989-90	Minnesota	82	260	.471	144	.709	564	106	680	8.3
	Totals	83	261	.472	147	.710	566	108	685	8.3

SIDNEY LOWE 30 6-0 203   Guard

Aging man on a short leash . . . Enjoyed enormous minor-league success with Bill Musselman, directing coach's do-as-I-say offense . . . Point guard on three CBA champs . . . Born Jan. 21, 1960, in Washington, D.C. . . . Made the All-Final Four team after helping North Carolina State win 1983 NCAA title . . . Drafted in second round (No. 25) that summer by Chicago . . . Minnesota is his fifth NBA team—and second successive expansion club . . . Played 14 games in Charlotte's initial season . . . Last year he shot .319 FG, attempted nine 3-pointers (made a pair) . . . Cautious style allowed him to rank third in NBA assist-to-turnover ratio (5.35).

Year	Team	G	FG	FG Pct.	FT	FT Pct.	Reb.	Ast.	TP	Avg.
1983-84	Indiana	78	107	.413	108	.777	122	269	324	4.2
1984-85	Det.-Atl.	21	10	.370	8	1.000	16	50	28	1.3
1988-89	Charlotte	14	8	.320	7	.636	34	93	23	1.6
1989-90	Minnesota	80	73	.319	39	.722	163	337	187	2.3
	Totals	193	198	.367	162	.764	335	749	562	2.9

DOUG WEST 23 6-6 200   Forward-Guard

At his peak, an excellent young player . . . Unfortunately, his peak appears to have been reached, if not almost attained, about five years ago . . . Born May 27, 1967, in Altoona, Pa. . . . Highly recruited out of high school, he was MVP in Dapper Dan Classic of 1986 in Pittsburgh . . . Reliable, four-year starter at Villanova but never became a program-maker . . . Taken in second round (No. 38) last year by Minnesota . . . Hasn't shown enough moves to hoop to be a small forward, doesn't seem able to drill it well enough to be an off-guard.

Year	Team	G	FG	FG Pct.	FT	FT Pct.	Reb.	Ast.	TP	Avg.
1989-90	Minnesota.......	52	53	.393	26	.813	70	18	135	2.6

GARY LEONARD 23 7-0 246 — Center

In urban-renewal parlance, here is the most basic of projects... Didn't become a full-time starter at Missouri until senior year... Averaged 10.4 points, 5.5 rebounds in final collegiate season... Passed into second round, he was drafted No. 34 by Timberwolves... Says he likes horses and playing the guitar... Didn't start once in rookie season for center-poor club ... During 22 mostly very brief appearances he shot almost as poorly from foul line (.429) as he did from the floor (.419)... Born Feb. 16, 1967, in St. Louis, Mo.

Year	Team	G	FG	FG Pct.	FT	FT Pct.	Reb.	Ast.	TP	Avg.
1989-90	Minnesota.......	22	13	.419	6	.429	27	1	32	1.5

THE ROOKIES

FELTON SPENCER 22 7-0 265 — Center

Let's see... This guy used to be the backup at Louisville to Pervis Ellison, who was such a successful No. 1 pick a year ago that he was traded away less than 365 days later by Sacramento... The "best" of three centers taken in the first round, at No. 6... Never averaged more than 8.2 points, 5.1 rebounds until senior year's 14.9 and 8.5... He'll stay out of the way on offense under Bill Musselman, who will make him concentrate on boards and improve man-to-man defense... Born Jan. 5, 1968, in Louisville, he made a good showing last spring in Orlando (tryout) Classic.

GERALD GLASS 21 6-6 221 — Guard-Forward

Second-leading scorer (2,813 points) in NCAA over past five years behind La Salle's Lionel Simmons... Timberwolves picked Mississippi star at No. 20 in first round... Played at Amada Elzy High in Greenwood, Miss., before averaging 19.5 a game in two seasons at Division II Delta State... After sitting out one year, he put up 28.0 and 24.1 at Mississippi and induced LSU's Dale

Brown to predict a Glass appearance in NBA All-Star Game "within the next three years." . . . Born Nov. 12, 1968.

COACH BILL MUSSELMAN: Tough, chesty guy . . . First-year team reflected his personality . . . Chest-to-chest defenders, inaugural Timberwolves were tough to score upon . . . They didn't win much (22-60) but opponents didn't have much fun . . . Trailed only Pistons in points-allowed . . . Took job Aug. 23, 1988, a year in advance of club's expansion debut . . . Personally scouted everyone in NBA, including refs, scoring tables, visitors' dressing rooms in 1988-89 season . . . Every night, he seemed to be everywhere a ball was being bounced . . . Born Aug. 13, 1940, in Wooster, Ohio . . . Coached at every level . . . Tough? His 1968-69 Ashland team set NCAA Division II record, allowing 33.9 points a game . . . After .811 winning percentage in six Ashland seasons, won Big 10 in first of four years at Minnesota . . . Spent a year and change (27-67, 1980-82) with then chaotic Cleveland Cavaliers . . . Only man ever to coach in four U.S. pro leagues—ABA, WBA, CBA, NBA . . . Won four straight CBA championships 1985-88, was twice Coach of Year.

GREATEST REBOUNDER

Well, you've got to play by the rules, and the editor says to pick one guy. So Tod Murphy is runnerup; he gets a silver-plated asterisk. And—drum roll, please—the greatest-ever Timberwolves rebounder is . . . Tyrone Corbin.

No one in Minnesota's storied annals ever got to the offensive boards more often (219), crashed the defensive glass better (385), totaled more rebounds (604) than did the heavily traveled, 6-6 Corbin last year.

OK. It was the first year for the expansionist Timberwolves. But who's counting?

Corbin was the fourth player picked in the expansion draft. Murphy earns mention because the 6-9 center/forward/afterthought was second to Corbin (7.4-6.9 per game) and played 500 fewer minutes.

Wolves' Pooh Richardson made the NBA All-Rookie Team.

ALL-TIME TIMBERWOLF LEADERS

SEASON

Points: Tony Campbell, 1,903, 1989-90
Assists: Jerome Richardson, 554, 1989-90
Rebounds: Tyrone Corbin, 604, 1989-90

GAME

Points: Tony Campbell, 44 vs. Boston, 2/2/90
Assists: Sidney Lowe, 17 vs. Golden State, 3/20/90
Rebounds: Todd Murphy, 20 vs. L.A. Clippers, 1/2/90

CAREER

Points: Tony Campbell, 1,903, 1989-90
Assists: Jerome Richardson, 554, 1989-90
Rebounds: Tyrone Corbin, 604, 1989-90

ORLANDO MAGIC

TEAM DIRECTORY: General Partner: William duPont III; Pres./ GM: Pat Williams; Dir. Scouting: John Gabriel; Dir. Publicity/ Media Rel.: Alex Martins; Coach: Matt Guokas; Asst. Coaches: John Gabriel, Brian Hill. Arena: Orlando Arena (15,500). Colors: Electric blue, quick silver and magic black.

Terry Catledge made the most of expansion opportunity.

SCOUTING REPORT

SHOOTING: In their first year of existence, the Magic expected less than perfection. Needless to say, they expected right. They ran but they did not shoot very well. How bad was Orlando's offensive proficiency? Let's put it this way: If Akeem Olajuwon had played 82 games against this club, he might have grabbed 1,800 defensive rebounds, not the mere 850 he had for Houston against all comers last season.

While scoring an entertaining 110.9 points a game, the Magic shot only .459 from the floor. Fortunately, the two guys closest to 50 percent were a pair of rookies: Nick Anderson (.494) and Michael Ansley (.497). The best producers of points were veterans Terry Catledge, Reggie Theus (now gone to the Nets) and Otis Smith, each acquired in the expansion draft. Dennis Scott, the 6-8 scorer from Georgia Tech, will get a lot of chances, immediately, to fill it up.

PLAYMAKING: Matt Guokas, a pass-first guard during his journeyman playing career and a balanced-attack coach at Philadelphia, unleashed these guys last year. An 18-64 record was about what could be expected. You knew this was a team in trouble when the leading assist man was Theus. You can't compete in this league without a more-than-dependable point guard and center. The Magic have neither.

DEFENSE: As blessed as the meek who shall inherit the earth are the Magic, who wouldn't impede your path to the hoop if your or their lives depended upon it. Opponents made 49.8 percent of their shots against Orlando. So? So this: Only one team in the league—Utah, .505—shot better than 49.8 over the course of the season, and everyone did it against the munchkin Magic. Lack of a defensive center left open a toll-free lane to the hoop, and all summer long Guokas was desperately searching for a roadblock.

REBOUNDING: The season-ending injury of veteran Dave Corzine—able to play only six games—crushed the team's easily bruised physical makeup. Corzine is a physical presence on defense and a reasonably efficient rebounder. Somehow, forwards Catledge and Sidney Green enabled Orlando to finish the season with a numerical advantage in rebounds (3,769-3,742). But then the porous Magic defense didn't force very many stops to miss and board opportunities were relatively rare at that end of the floor.

MAGIC ROSTER

No.	Veterans	Pos.	Ht.	Wt.	Age	Yrs. Pro	College
42	Mark Acres	F-C	6-11	225	28	3	Oral Roberts
25	Nick Anderson	F	6-6	205	22	1	Illinois
45	Michael Ansley	F	6-7	225	23	1	Alabama
33	Terry Catledge	F	6-8	230	27	5	South Alabama
40	Dave Corzine	C	6-11	260	34	12	DePaul
21	Sidney Green	F	6-9	220	29	7	Nevada-Las Vegas
—	Greg Kite		6-11	250	30	7	Brigham Young
35	Jerry Reynolds	C-F	6-8	206	27	5	Louisiana State
4	Scott Skiles	G	6-1	180	26	4	Michigan State
32	Otis Smith	G-F	6-5	210	26	4	Jacksonville
31	Jeff Turner	F	6-9	240	28	4	Vanderbilt
11	Sam Vincent	G	6-2	192	27	5	Michigan State
20	Morlon Wiley	G	6-4	192	24	2	Long Beach State

Rd.	Rookies	Sel. No.	Pos.	Ht.	Wt.	College
1	Dennis Scott	4	G-F	6-8	229	Georgia Tech

OUTLOOK: On its face, this seems to be a team destined in the near future to remain forward-dominated. And forward-oriented expansion teams do not have neither a rich nor lengthy tradition of success. Scott, whose offensive skills are unquestioned, could be positioned at off-guard.

But expansion teams typically struggle until they have wangled a floor leader at the point and have stumbled upon the right big body to fill the middle. There's this, though: The Magic are rarely dull. Which to eager-to-be-pleased, unsophisticated new audiences often is enough in the short haul. The NBA, it's fantastic.

MAGIC PROFILES

TERRY CATLEDGE 27 6-8 230   Forward

Backbone of club in first year . . . Former first-round pick (21st) out of South Alabama by Philadelphia in 1985 . . . Born Aug. 22, 1963, in Houston, Miss. . . . Had two progressively nice seasons with 76ers in which scoring and rebounding virtually doubled with increased playing time . . . Dealt with Moses Malone and two No. 1s on draft day 1986 to Washington for Jeff Ruland (since retired) and ever-injured Cliff Robinson . . .

Was exposed to expansion draft despite two good years with Bullets, including 18.3 points, 8.1 rebounds in 1987 playoffs... Started 72 of 74 games for Magic... Calls himself "Cadillac" because he's "big, black and lovely."

Year	Team	G	FG	FG Pct.	FT	FT Pct.	Reb.	Ast.	TP	Avg.
1985-86	Philadelphia	64	202	.469	90	.647	272	21	494	7.7
1986-87	Washington	78	413	.495	199	.594	560	56	1025	13.1
1987-88	Washington	70	296	.506	154	.655	397	63	746	10.7
1988-89	Washington	79	334	.490	153	.602	572	75	822	10.4
1989-90	Orlando	74	546	.474	341	.702	563	72	1435	19.4
	Totals	365	1791	.486	937	.647	2364	287	4522	12.4

SIDNEY GREEN 29 6-9 220   Forward

Still managing to keep up his board scores... Top pick last year (from New York) in the expansion draft, he returned favor with team-best 588 rebounds for Magic... Had second double-figure scoring season of career at 10.4 ... Best was 13.5 in 1985-86, last of three seasons with Chicago before spending one year at Detroit... Born Jan. 4, 1961, in Brooklyn, N.Y... Never really has performed at level of a No. 5 pick, which Bulls made him in 1983 out of Nevada-Las Vegas... Had played back-to-back 82-game seasons as a Knick sub before being put on expansion list... Made 31 starts in 73 appearances with Orlando and was third in minutes played.

Year	Team	G	FG	FG Pct.	FT	FT Pct.	Reb.	Ast.	TP	Avg.
1983-84	Chicago	49	100	.439	55	.714	174	25	255	5.2
1984-85	Chicago	48	108	.432	79	.806	246	29	295	6.1
1985-86	Chicago	80	407	.465	262	.782	658	139	1076	13.5
1986-87	Detroit	80	256	.472	119	.672	653	62	631	7.9
1987-88	New York	82	258	.441	126	.663	642	93	642	7.8
1988-89	New York	82	194	.460	129	.759	394	76	517	6.3
1989-90	Orlando	73	312	.468	136	.651	588	99	761	10.4
	Totals	494	1635	.458	906	.721	3355	523	4177	8.5

SCOTT SKILES 26 6-1 180   Guard

Settling down to become decent pro... Made All-American at Michigan State in 1986 *Sporting News* vote... Some thought, however, he was overrated as pro prospect... Compounded the exposure with personal and legal problems ... Born March 5, 1964, in LaPorte, Ind.... Selected on 1986 first round (No. 22) by Milwaukee... Sat a lot for Bucks, who traded him

after one year to Indiana for a second-rounder... Tough guy...
Overcame ankle, knee and back problems and self-induced pressure to have nice year with Pacers before put up for expansion
... Started 32 of 70 appearances with Orlando... Shot a mere
.409 from floor, but led Magic in three-point shooting with 52-of-132.

Year	Team	G	FG	FG Pct.	FT	FT Pct.	Reb.	Ast.	TP	Avg.
1986-87	Milwaukee	13	18	.290	10	.833	26	45	49	3.8
1987-88	Indiana	51	86	.411	45	.833	66	180	223	4.4
1983-89	Indiana	80	198	.448	130	.903	149	390	546	6.8
1989-90	Orlando	70	190	.409	104	.874	159	334	536	7.7
	Totals	214	492	.418	289	.878	400	949	1354	6.3

OTIS SMITH 26 6-5 210   Guard-Forward

Prototype player for what the World Basketball
League had in mind... But he's never settled
for a 6-5-and-under format... Wants to, and
does, mix it up with the big boys... Born Jan.
30, 1964, in Jacksonville, Fla.... All-Sun Belt
Conference four years at Jacksonville...
Drafted 41st (second round) in 1986 by Denver
... Played little as rookie for Nuggets with bad
left knee and was sold next season in rare NBA cash deal to Golden
State... Had a pair of double-figure scoring seasons with Warriors
... Suspect shooting off-guard and undersized small forward...
Good rejector for his size, deft stealer... Started 35 of 65 games
with Magic... His 13.5-point scoring was career best.

Year	Team	G	FG	FG Pct.	FT	FT Pct.	Reb.	Ast.	TP	Avg.
1986-87	Denver	28	33	.418	12	.571	34	22	78	2.8
1987-88	Den.-G.S.	72	325	.491	178	.777	247	155	841	11.7
1988-89	Golden State	80	311	.435	174	.798	330	140	803	10.0
1989-90	Orlando	65	348	.492	169	.761	300	147	875	13.5
	Totals	245	1017	.470	533	.772	911	464	2597	10.6

JERRY REYNOLDS 27 6-8 206   Center-Forward

Multi-positional player still seeking niche in
sixth season as pro... Led expansion team in
blocks and steals... Depends on defensive versatility to mask offensive limitations... Born
Dec. 23, 1962, in Brooklyn, N.Y.... New
York Prep Player of Year in 1980-81... Made
SEC All-Freshman team at Louisiana State...
Led team three years and league once in

steals... "Hardship" first-round pick (22d) by Milwaukee in 1985... Is called "Ice" once he got cold shoulder from then-Milwaukee coach Don Nelson... Traded by Bucks for a second-rounder to Seattle after three-year contract expired... Started 40 of 67 games with Orlando... Had one-game high of 36 points.

Year	Team	G	FG	FG Pct.	FT	FT Pct.	Reb.	Ast.	TP	Avg.
1985-86	Milwaukee	55	72	.444	58	.558	80	86	203	3.7
1986-87	Milwaukee	58	140	.393	118	.641	173	106	404	7.0
1987-88	Milwaukee	62	188	.449	119	.773	160	104	498	8.0
1988-89	Seattle	56	149	.417	127	.760	100	62	428	7.6
1989-90	Orlando	67	309	.417	239	.742	323	180	858	12.8
	Totals	298	858	.422	661	.710	836	538	2391	8.0

MORLON WILEY 24 6-4 192   Guard

Third pro year and no one seems certain where to play him... Shooting guard in high school and college... Prep whiz at Long Beach Poly, led team to California State High School title ... Helped Long Beach State break string of six losing seasons in his senior year... Dallas picked him 46th in second round of 1988... Got little time behind Rolando Blackman-Derek Harper-Brad Davis troika... Used only 40 times (twice as a starter) last season by Magic, who got him in expansion... Even here, he'll have to shoot a lot better than .442 to make the point.

Year	Team	G	FG	FG Pct.	FT	FT Pct.	Reb.	Ast.	TP	Avg.
1988-89	Dallas	51	46	.404	13	.813	47	76	111	2.2
1989-90	Orlando	40	92	.442	28	.737	52	114	229	5.7
	Totals	91	138	.429	41	.759	99	190	340	3.7

NICK ANDERSON 22 6-6 205   Forward

The first-ever draft pick of Orlando... Magic made him the 11th choice in 1989 first round ... Born Jan. 20, 1968, in Chicago... Played with budding legend Ben Wilson at Simeon High before latter was slain in random shooting ... Became Mr. Illinois High School basketball player... Helped Illinois reach Final Four before losing to Big 10 rival Michigan... Wears No. 25 in memory of Wilson... Used as starter only nine times, but played in 81 games in rookie season . . . A classic tweener . . . Too small to play most forwards, so his future seems as two-guard.

Year	Team	G	FG	FG Pct.	FT	FT Pct.	Reb.	Ast.	TP	Avg.
1989-90	Orlando	81	372	.494	186	.705	316	124	931	11.5

MICHAEL ANSLEY 23 6-7 225   Forward

''Baby Face'' . . . Played a lot tougher at times than his schoolboy nickname . . . But must get stronger, quicker . . . Born Feb. 8, 1967, in Birmingham, Ala. . . . Played at Alabama and was taken in second round (37th) of 1989 draft . . . Made five starts in his 72 rookie appearances . . . Shot .497 from field, working within limited range . . . Decent free-thrower, but didn't even attempt a three-pointer . . . Magic have to be encouraged by his ranking as No. 2 on team in offensive rebounding despite being 10th in minutes played.

Year	Team	G	FG	FG Pct.	FT	FT Pct.	Reb.	Ast.	TP	Avg.
1989-90	Orlando	72	231	.497	164	.722	362	40	626	8.7

MARK ACRES 27 6-11 225   Center-Forward

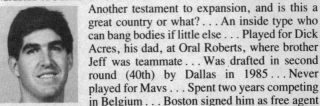

Another testament to expansion, and is this a great country or what? . . . An inside type who can bang bodies if little else . . . Played for Dick Acres, his dad, at Oral Roberts, where brother Jeff was teammate . . . Was drafted in second round (40th) by Dallas in 1985 . . . Never played for Mavs . . . Spent two years competing in Belgium . . . Boston signed him as free agent and he spent two years as a bench-sitter with Celtics . . . Picked by Orlando in expansion draft . . . Started 50 of his 80 games, averaging 4.5 points . . . Born Nov. 15, 1962, in Inglewood, Cal.

Year	Team	G	FG	FG Pct.	FT	FT Pct.	Reb.	Ast.	TP	Avg.
1987-88	Boston	79	108	.532	71	.640	270	42	287	3.6
1988-89	Boston	62	55	.482	26	.542	146	19	137	2.2
1989-90	Orlando	80	138	.484	83	.692	431	67	362	4.5
	Totals	221	301	.500	180	.645	847	128	786	3.6

SAM VINCENT 27 6-2 192   Guard

Owns a championship ring . . . Also owns reputation as often being out of control at the point, where control is the point . . . Born May 18, 1963, in Lansing, Mich. . . . Followed his brother, Jay, and idol Magic Johnson to Michigan State . . . Was a teammate of Scott Skiles with Spartans . . . Drafted 20th in 1985 first round by Boston . . . Rookie sub on Celtics' 1985-86 NBA champs . . . Found lacking in niceties of the profession by Boston, Seattle and Chicago . . . Benched by Bulls and later exposed to expansion draft . . . About to become an unrestricted free agent, he was signed to three-year deal before last season by Magic . . . Made 45 starts in 63 games and almost doubled his first four years' scoring average of 6.1.

Year	Team	G	FG	FG Pct.	FT	FT Pct.	Reb.	Ast.	TP	Avg.
1985-86	Boston	57	59	.364	65	.929	48	69	184	3.2
1986-87	Boston	46	60	.441	51	.927	27	59	171	3.7
1987-88	Sea.-Chi.	72	210	.456	145	.868	152	381	573	8.0
1988-89	Chicago	70	274	.484	106	.822	190	335	656	9.4
1989-90	Orlando	63	258	.457	188	.879	194	354	705	11.2
	Totals	308	861	.456	555	.874	611	1198	2289	7.4

JEFF TURNER 28 6-9 240   Forward

Bags are always packed . . . Born April 9, 1962, in Bangor, Me. . . . Played high school ball in Brandon, Fla . . . Recruited to Vanderbilt, where he was twice Southeast Conference All-Academic . . . Was on Bobby Knight's 1984 Olympic team . . . Drafted 17th in first round of 1984 by New Jersey . . . Played a lot of games but not many minutes after rookie year for Nets, who released him after three seasons . . . Competed two years in Italy before signing with Magic as free agent in summer of 1989 . . . Made 15 starts in 60 appearances . . . Career backup type at power forward and spot center.

Year	Team	G	FG	FG Pct.	FT	FT Pct.	Reb.	Ast.	TP	Avg.
1984-85	New Jersey	72	171	.454	79	.859	218	108	421	5.8
1985-86	New Jersey	53	84	.491	58	.744	137	14	226	4.3
1986-87	New Jersey	76	151	.465	76	.731	197	60	378	5.0
1989-90	Orlando	60	132	.429	42	.778	227	53	308	5.1
	Totals	261	538	.456	255	.777	779	235	1333	5.1

DAVE CORZINE 34 6-11 260   Center

Journeyman might have reached end of the NBA journey . . . Born April 25, 1956, in Chicago . . . Stayed home to attend DePaul . . . Played first two years sparingly with Washington, which drafted him 18th in 1978 first round . . . Broke into double figures two years at San Antonio before moving on to Chicago . . . Steady, unsensational performer with Bulls, who traded him to Magic for pair of second-round picks . . . ''He's the Lou Gehrig of basketball,'' crowed Magic GM Pat Williams in anticipation last fall as Corzine once played 480 straight games before breaking a hand. ''All he does is play 80 games a year for you, 20 to 24 minutes.'' . . . Alas, he went down early, played in only 79 minutes of six games, and future is uncertain.

Year	Team	G	FG	FG Pct.	FT	FT Pct.	Reb.	Ast.	TP	Avg.
1978-79	Washington	59	63	.534	49	.778	147	49	175	3.0
1979-80	Washington	78	90	.417	45	.662	270	63	225	2.9
1980-81	San Antonio	82	366	.490	125	.714	636	117	857	10.5
1981-82	San Antonio	82	336	.519	159	.746	629	130	832	10.1
1982-83	Chicago	82	457	.497	232	.720	717	154	1146	14.0
1983-84	Chicago	82	385	.467	231	.840	575	202	1004	12.2
1984-85	Chicago	82	276	.486	149	.745	422	140	701	8.5
1985-86	Chicago	67	255	.491	127	.743	433	150	640	9.6
1986-87	Chicago	82	294	.475	95	.736	540	209	683	8.3
1987-88	Chicago	80	344	.481	115	.752	527	154	804	10.1
1988-89	Chicago	81	203	.461	71	.740	315	103	479	5.9
1989-90	Orlando	6	11	.379	0	.000	18	2	22	3.7
	Totals	863	3080	.484	1398	.749	5229	1473	7568	8.8

THE ROOKIE

DENNIS SCOTT 22 6-8 229   Guard-Forward

Line 'em up, knock 'em down . . . His backers insist he is the rarest of modern players: Someone who can actually shoot the ball with consistent success from outside . . . Then you look at his .452 FG career . . . But scouts remind you to look at his range and degree of difficulty . . . Others say, when he's in playing shape, Scott can not only shoot, but SCORE. There's a fine-line difference . . . ACC Player of Year at Georgia Tech as a junior, he averaged

27.7 points last year . . . Born Sept. 5, 1968 . . . Honed his high-school academics at Flint Hill Prep, in Reston, Va.

COACH MATTY GUOKAS: His dad's son through and through . . . Born Feb. 25, 1944, in Philadelphia . . . Matt, Jr. had a brilliant high school career in Philly, finished his collegiate days as an All-American at St. Joseph's, where his dad had made the alma mater famous a generation before with the Mighty Mites . . . Got drafted to play with the hometown pro team, just as his dad had—the Warriors way back then, the 76ers when it was his turn . . . Member of Philadelphia's 1966-67 NBA champions . . . Played 10 pro seasons with six franchises . . . Involved in trades with two players who also later became NBA head coaches—Bob Weiss and Dave Wohl . . . Began broadcasting career after playing days, doing color/play-by-play on 76ers games . . . Appointed assistant coach of 76ers by Billy Cunningham to replace Chuck Daly . . . Compiled 119-88 record as head coach in Philadelphia . . . Hired on June 1, 1988, to become first coach of Magic by GM/president Pat Williams, former 76ers GM . . . Finished last (18-64) in Central Division of Eastern Conference in debut.

GREATEST REBOUNDER

With the team's sorry shape at center as it enters its second year, Terry Catledge and Sidney Green will have a few seasons more to work out the "greatest ever" problem themselves.

Meanwhile, a coin flip and the trusted COCPM evaluative measurement (cop-out, caroms per minute) gives temporary possession of the crown to Green, who had 41 fewer starts and three-quarters of Catledge's minutes played, but still had an edge in totals (588-563) and average (8.1-7.6).

Green (from New York) was the first player taken in the expansion draft; Catledge (Washington) was No. 5.

ALL-TIME MAGIC LEADERS

SEASON

Points: Reggie Theus, 1,438, 1989-90
Assists: Reggie Theus, 407, 1989-90
Rebounds: Sidney Green, 588, 1989-90

GAME

Points: Terry Catledge, 49 vs. Golden State, 1/13/90
Assists: Sam Vincent, 17 vs. Indiana, 1/30/90
　　　　Scott Skiles, 17 vs. New York, 3/20/90
Rebounds: Sidney Green, 19 vs. Chicago, 2/14/90

CAREER

Points: Reggie Theus, 1,438, 1989-90
Assists: Reggie Theus, 407, 1989-90
Rebounds: Sidney Green, 588, 1989-90

PHOENIX SUNS

TEAM DIRECTORY: Pres.-CEO: Jerry Colangelo; VP-Dir. Pub. Rel.: Tom Ambrose; Dir. Media Rel.: Barry Ringel; Dir. Player Personnel-Coach: Cotton Fitzsimmons; Asst. Coaches: Paul Westphal, Lionel Hollins. Arena: Veterans Memorial Coliseum (14,471). Colors: Purple, orange and copper.

Tom Chambers' 27.2 ppg was tops in nine-year career.

SCOUTING REPORT

SHOOTING: Bombs away! We're talking versatile point-production here. Tom Chambers was fourth, Kevin Johnson 15th in NBA scoring—four others averaged double-figures, and still four others had at least one 20-point game. The Suns shot .496 and outscored opponents by seven points a game.

The lowest-scoring starter, center Mark West, for whom Phoenix runs no plays, was so offended that he became the only player in the league to shoot better than 60 percent (.625). Jeff Hornacek (11th) and Eddie Johnson (19th) provide three-point threats on a team that also gets to the free-throw line frequently and shoots well there. K. Johnson trailed only John Stockton and Magic Johnson in assists.

PLAYMAKING: KJ, whose brightest moments unfortunately did not come against Portland, normally passes well off the dribble. His assists in the halfcourt offense come off two-man games, or isolation plays from which he can line-drive passes to the weakside on the few occasions when he hasn't defeated his man for a layup.

Hornacek at last has shaken the tag of best-guard-no-one-knows, and he can adequately play the point when KJ needs a rest or is injured. KJ missed eight full games in 1989-90 and Hornacek easily was the team's No. 2 feeder over the season's course.

DEFENSE: This is another team-defense operation, with much of the action directed toward West, a hard worker who also was the eighth best shot-rejector in the league. The Lakers went into a horrible shooting slump against this team in the Western semis, but not enough credit was given Phoenix for its part. In the off-season, the Suns added Ed Nealy, giving them more muscle (with Kurt Rambis and West).

REBOUNDING: West, No. 17 in the NBA with 728 rebounds, is the main boarder, but three teammates (Dan Majerle, Chambers and Rambis) also produced 100-plus offensive rebounds. When it comes to scoring and second chances to score, these people get quite serious. In the draft, Phoenix went for St. John's power forward Jayson Williams with its top pick, at No. 21. Williams is coming off a foot injury, however.

SUN ROSTER

No.	Veterans	Pos.	Ht.	Wt.	Age	Yrs. Pro	College
3	Kenny Battle	F	6-6	211	26	1	Illinois
17	Rickey Blanton	F-G	6-7	215	24	1	Louisiana State
24	Tom Chambers	F	6-10	230	31	9	Utah
14	Jeff Hornacek	G	6-4	190	27	4	Iowa State
8	Eddie Johnson	F-G	6-7	215	31	9	Illinois
7	Kevin Johnson	G	6-1	190	24	3	California
28	Andrew Lang	C	6-11	250	24	2	Arkansas
9	Dan Majerle	G-F	6-6	220	25	2	Central Michigan
32	Mike Morrison	G	6-4	195	23	1	Loyola-Maryland
45	Ed Nealy	F	6-7	240	30	7	Kansas State
34	Tim Perry	F	6-9	220	25	2	Temple
31	Kurt Rambis	F	6-8	213	32	9	Santa Clara
41	Mark West	C	6-10	246	29	7	Old Dominion

Rd.	Rookies	Sel. No.	Pos.	Ht.	Wt.	College
1	Jayson Williams	21	F	6-10	240	St. John's
2	Negele Knight	31	G	6-1	182	Dayton
2	Cedric Ceballos	48	F	6-6	210	Cal-Fullerton
2	Stefano Rusconi	52	F	6-9	230	Varese (Italy)

OUTLOOK: Cotton Fitzsimmons liked the looks of this team so much last year—despite a flameout in the Western Conference finals—that he cancelled whatever thoughts he might have been entertaining of allowing Paul Westphal to take over the coaching while he went back to the front office. Despite the NBA Finals appearance of Portland and the lurking threat of the Lakers, many people think the Suns and Spurs are *the* Western teams to watch through the early '90s.

SUN PROFILES

KEVIN JOHNSON 24 6-1 190   **Guard**

A little magic/Magic here . . . Surrenders eight inches in height to the L.A.'s Johnson, but nothing when measuring will to win . . . They don't, actually, but it seems Suns score every time they clear side for KJ in two-man game . . . Born March 4, 1966, in Sacramento . . . Played at California and was seventh pick in 1987 by Cleveland . . . Spent two 1986 games at shortstop for Modesto in Class A after Oakland drafted him in 23d round . . . Logjam behind Mark Price helped inspire trade that sent K J, Tyrone Corbin and Mark West to Phoenix for Larry Nance and Mike Sanders in February 1988 . . . Second-team All-NBA and Most Improved Player in 1989, his first full season as Sun . . . Averaged 22.5 points, trailed only John Stockton and Magic in 1989-90 assists with 11.4 average.

Year	Team	G	FG	FG Pct.	FT	FT Pct.	Reb.	Ast.	TP	Avg.
1987-88	Clev.-Phoe.	80	275	.461	177	.839	191	437	732	9.2
1988-89	Phoenix	81	570	.505	508	.882	340	991	1650	20.4
1989-90	Phoenix	74	578	.499	501	.838	270	846	1665	22.5
	Totals	235	1423	.494	1186	.856	801	2274	4047	17.2

TOM CHAMBERS 31 6-10 230   Forward

Coming off best season of an under-appreciated career . . . Helped the Suns advance to Western Conference finals . . . Posted personal-high 27.2-point average, including a 60-point game . . . High on the list of blunders by Clippers, who let him go via a trade after two years . . . Scored a lot of points at Seattle—and was All-Star Game MVP in 1987 . . . Had been criticized for selfishness but has become ultimate team man with Phoenix, which signed him as an unrestricted free agent in July 1988 . . . He played collegiately at Utah and was drafted No. 8 by San Diego Clippers in 1981 . . . Dangerous outside shooter and explosive dunker . . . Last year, led team in games and starts (81), was second in rebounding and free-throwing (at .861 to Kevin Johnson's .917) . . . Born June 21, 1959, in Ogden, Utah.

Year	Team	G	FG	FG Pct.	FT	FT Pct.	Reb.	Ast.	TP	Avg.
1981-82	San Diego	81	554	.525	284	.620	561	146	1392	17.2
1982-83	San Diego	79	519	.472	353	.723	519	192	1391	17.6
1983-84	Seattle	82	554	.499	375	.800	532	133	1483	18.1
1984-85	Seattle	81	629	.483	475	.832	579	209	1739	21.5
1985-86	Seattle	66	432	.466	346	.836	431	132	1223	18.5
1986-87	Seattle	82	660	.456	535	.849	545	245	1909	23.3
1987-88	Seattle	82	611	.448	419	.807	490	212	1674	20.4
1988-89	Phoenix	81	774	.471	509	.851	684	231	2085	25.7
1989-90	Phoenix	81	810	.501	557	.861	571	190	2201	27.2
	Totals	715	5543	.479	3853	.804	4912	1690	15097	21.1

JEFF HORNACEK 27 6-4 190   Guard

Sure, NOW everyone says what a fine player he is...On the list of every knowledgeable observer's most-underrated list even before breakthrough 1989-90 season...Suns took him 46th out of Iowa State in 1986...Academic All-American in college, he was too smart to listen to those who said he wouldn't make it as pro...Can shoot, drive, pass, play both guard spots...Made some crunch-time shots from No. 2 spot and also spelled Kevin Johnson at point as Suns eliminated Lakers in Western semis...Hard-nosed defender led club in steals ...Placed 11th in league in three-point accuracy, 12th in FG percentage, and just missed top 20 at foul line...Born April 3, 1963, in Elmhurst, Ill.

Year	Team	G	FG	FG Pct.	FT	FT Pct.	Reb.	Ast.	TP	Avg.
1986-87	Phoenix	80	159	.454	94	.777	184	361	424	5.3
1987-88	Phoenix	82	306	.506	152	.822	262	540	781	9.5
1988-89	Phoenix	78	440	.495	147	.826	266	514	1054	13.5
1989-90	Phoenix	67	483	.536	173	.856	313	337	1179	17.6
	Totals	307	1388	.506	566	.825	1025	1703	3438	11.2

DAN MAJERLE 25 6-6 220   Guard-Forward

All that's missing from his game is a reliable one-step-shoot jumper...Tireless enough to (gasp!) inspire John Havlicek comparison in style...He's more muscled, tanner, but not nearly the scoring threat of Boston's Hall of Famer...Born Sept. 9, 1965, in Traverse City, Mich....Three-time All-Mid-American Conference pick at Central Michigan... Earned close pro attention in postseason tryouts...Portsmouth Classic MVP...Played on 1988 U.S. Olympic team...Phoenix made him a first-round pick (14th) and he faded with mono second month in pros...Made 23 starts last year, but might be better suited to (and more productive) coming off bench...In any scenario, needs to master the "J."

Year	Team	G	FG	FG Pct.	FT	FT Pct.	Reb.	Ast.	TP	Avg.
1988-89	Phoenix	54	181	.419	78	.614	209	130	467	8.6
1989-90	Phoenix	73	296	.424	198	.762	430	188	809	11.1
	Totals	127	477	.422	276	.713	639	318	1276	10.0

EDDIE JOHNSON 31 6-7 215   Forward-Guard

Offensive machine whose scoring memory function again was zapped from computer during playoffs ... Suns basically beat Lakers in Western semis with little help from NBA's 1988-89 "Sixth Man" winner ... After having shot .453 and scored 16.9 in regular season, he was .377 and 9.5 anchor against Portland ... Had come up way short 12 months before when Phoenix was swept by L.A. ... Has had three 20-point seasons in nine-year career since Kansas City made him 29th pick, out of Illinois, in 1981 second round ... Second at foul line last season to Larry Bird, .930 to .917 ... Still capable of 20-plus quarters if not defended nostril-to-nostril ... Born May 1, 1959, in Chicago.

Year	Team	G	FG	FG Pct.	FT	FT Pct.	Reb.	Ast.	TP	Avg.
1981-82	Kansas City	74	295	.459	99	.664	322	109	690	9.3
1982-83	Kansas City	82	677	.494	247	.779	501	216	1621	19.8
1983-84	Kansas City	82	753	.485	268	.810	455	296	1794	21.9
1984-85	Kansas City	82	769	.491	325	.871	407	273	1876	22.9
1985-86	Sacramento	82	623	.475	280	.816	419	214	1530	18.7
1986-87	Sacramento	81	606	.463	267	.829	353	251	1516	18.7
1987-88	Phoenix	73	533	.480	204	.850	318	180	1294	17.7
1988-89	Phoenix	70	608	.497	217	.868	306	162	1504	21.5
1989-90	Phoenix	64	411	.453	188	.917	246	107	1080	16.9
	Totals	690	5275	.480	2095	.828	3327	1808	12905	18.7

ANDREW LANG 24 6-11 250   Center

Not exactly most aggressive player in NBA history ... Hired to board, not score, he managed to play 1,011 minutes in 74 games and come away with all of 83 offensive rebounds ... Hey, the Suns shoot the ball pretty well, but there were still a few misses available ... Averaged 6.9 points, 5.7 rebounds in four-year career at Arkansas ... Eventual wife Bronwyn played for Lady Razorbacks ... He was the 28th pick of Phoenix in 1988 ... Got the dunk down fairly well (a two-season .540 FG mark), but he's .652 from foul line ... And that's an improvement on old college times ... Born June 28, 1966, in Pine Bluff, Ark.

Year	Team	G	FG	FG Pct.	FT	FT Pct.	Reb.	Ast.	TP	Avg.
1988-89	Phoenix	62	60	.513	39	.650	147	9	159	2.6
1989-90	Phoenix	74	97	.557	64	.653	271	21	258	3.5
	Totals	136	157	.540	103	.652	418	30	417	3.1

KEN BATTLE 26 6-6 211   Forward

Hard-working guy and a decent shooter... Nice pickup by Phoenix in 1989 draft-day deal with Detroit... Leading scorer in nation as a freshman at Northern Illinois... Transferred to Illinois and averaged 19.9 in two seasons, the last ending in Final Four... Suns got him and Michael Williams from Detroit in exchange for draft rights to Arizona's Anthony Cook...

Earned eight rookie starts in 59 appearances... Seems to have secured a future in league... But he'll be an off-the-bench cog for now with increasingly deep Suns... Born Oct. 10, 1964, in Aurora, Ill.

Year	Team	G	FG	FG Pct.	FT	FT Pct.	Reb.	Ast.	TP	Avg.
1989-90	Phoenix	59	93	.547	55	.671	124	38	242	4.1

KURT RAMBIS 32 6-8 213   Forward

"Superman" lives, but couldn't fly Suns past Portland and into NBA Finals... Clark Kent with muscles... Veteran acquired from Charlotte in midwinter... Move was just what a sun-and-fun person as well as Suns needed... Born Feb. 25, 1958, in Cupertino, Cal. ... Doesn't do anything halfway... Pushed himself to fine career at Santa Clara... Drafted

1980 third round at No. 58 by New York, but never played there ... Competed in Greece before signing with Lakers... Earned four championship rings and became expendable... Nice raise as free-agent signee of Charlotte and had only career double-figure scoring season... Helped make Suns believe in themselves when he arrived... Infectious hustler.

Year	Team	G	FG	FG Pct.	FT	FT Pct.	Reb.	Ast.	TP	Avg.
1981-82	Los Angeles	64	118	.518	59	.504	348	56	295	4.6
1982-83	Los Angeles	78	235	.569	114	.687	531	90	584	7.5
1983-84	Los Angeles	47	63	.558	42	.636	266	34	168	3.6
1984-85	L.A. Lakers	82	181	.554	68	.660	528	69	430	5.2
1985-86	L.A. Lakers	74	160	.595	88	.721	517	69	408	5.5
1986-87	L.A. Lakers	78	163	.521	120	.764	453	63	446	5.7
1987-88	L.A. Lakers	70	102	.548	73	.785	268	54	277	4.0
1988-89	Charlotte	75	325	.518	182	.734	703	159	832	11.1
1989-90	Char.-Phoe.	74	190	.509	82	.646	525	135	462	6.2
	Totals	642	1537	.539	828	.691	4139	729	3902	6.1

ED NEALY 30 6-7 240   Forward

Surprising sixth man... At year's end, was getting standing ovations from appreciative Chicago crowds... And now he's signed as an unrestricted free agent with the Suns... An improbable story... A model in hustle and determination... Can't run. Can't shoot. Can't jump. Got spot duty and simply made the most of it... Tremendous Game 4 effort in playoffs vs. Sixers filling in for injured Scottie Pippen... Phil Jackson called him a ''genius'' for his ability to do the right thing... A coach on the court... Michael Jordan loves him because he sets best picks on team... Didn't even figure to be in NBA last year. Bulls did Suns a favor and took him off their hands in preseason ... Gets good position, will bang and do the dirty things... Knows limitations, which puts him a leg up on a lot of guys in league... Earned $150,000 minimum... Born Feb. 19, 1960, in Pittsburg, Kan.... Had two tours with Bulls. Traded in 1988 for Craig Hodges... Was eighth-round pick in 1982 by Kansas City out of Kansas State.

Year	Team	G	FG	FG Pct.	FT	FT Pct.	Reb.	Ast.	TP	Avg.
1982-83	Kansas City......	82	147	.595	70	.614	485	62	364	4.4
1983-84	Kansas City......	71	63	.500	48	.800	222	50	174	2.5
1984-85	Kansas City......	22	26	.591	10	.526	44	18	62	2.8
1986-87	San Antonio	60	84	.438	51	.739	284	83	223	3.7
1987-88	San Antonio	68	50	.459	41	.651	222	49	142	2.1
1988-89	Chi.-Phoe.......	43	13	.361	4	.444	78	14	30	0.7
1989-90	Chicago	46	37	.529	30	.732	138	28	104	2.3
	Totals	392	420	.510	254	.677	1473	304	1099	2.8

MARK WEST 29 6-10 246   Center

An extremely tall tortoise... Came out of his shell late in career and outlasted more publicized peers... Dominated young (Vlade Divac) and old centers (Mychal Thompson) against Lakers in playoffs... Plays within limits and won't force a shot... But set loose underneath, it's slam after slam... Taken out of Old Dominion as a stab with 30th pick in 1983 by Dallas... Stopped at Milwaukee and Cleveland before arriving in Phoenix with Kevin Johnson in February 1988 Larry Nance trade... Has a great glower on floor and temper to match... Punched out a door window in dressing room last season after homecourt loss to Chicago . . . Born Nov. 5, 1960, in Petersburg, Va.

Year	Team	G	FG	FG Pct.	FT	FT Pct.	Reb.	Ast.	TP	Avg.
1983-84	Dallas	34	15	.357	7	.318	46	13	37	1.1
1984-85	Mil.-Clev.	66	106	.546	43	.494	251	15	255	3.9
1985-86	Cleveland	67	113	.541	54	.524	322	20	280	4.2
1986-87	Cleveland	78	209	.543	89	.514	339	41	507	6.5
1987-88	Clev.-Phoe.	83	316	.551	170	.596	523	74	802	9.7
1988-89	Phoenix	82	243	.653	108	.535	551	39	594	7.2
1989-90	Phoenix	82	331	.625	199	.691	728	45	861	10.5
	Totals	492	1333	.578	670	.578	2760	247	3336	6.8

TIM PERRY 25 6-9 220   Forward

Time to put up or move on . . . Has yet to make work ethic pay off in pros as it did in college . . . Says he studies tape diligently . . . Watches James Worthy for offensive moves, Dennis Rodman for defensive tips . . . Better, suggested a Los Angeles curmudgeon, he should focus on Tyrone Corbin, the hard-working former Phoenix power forward whose spot he was supposed to fill . . . Born June 4, 1965, in Freehold, N.J. . . . An eye-opening No. 7 pick out of Temple in 1988 by Phoenix . . . Shot .513, scored 4.2 in 60 games but lost occasional starting position when Phoenix got veteran Kurt Rambis.

Year	Team	G	FG	FG Pct.	FT	FT Pct.	Reb.	Ast.	TP	Avg.
1988-89	Phoenix	62	108	.537	40	.615	132	18	257	4.1
1989-90	Phoenix	60	100	.513	53	.589	152	17	254	4.2
	Totals	122	208	.525	93	.600	284	35	511	4.2

THE ROOKIES

JAYSON WILLIAMS 22 6-10 240   Forward

Elevator man . . . His production and intensity went up and down during college career at St. John's . . . Suns' pick at No. 21 . . . Might wean him into backup role . . . Academically ineligible as a freshman, he was a 9.9-point contributor as a soph, starting 13 of 28 games . . . Had best year as a junior—shot .573 and averaged 19.6 . . . MVP for NIT champion Redmen . . . Senior year (14.6 points, .534 FG, 7.8 rebounds) ended after 13 games with broken right foot . . . Born Feb. 22, 1968, in New York City.

NEGELE KNIGHT 23 6-1 182   Guard

Dayton's all-time assist leader and sixth all-time scorer . . . Ineffective as a freshman, he missed all of 1986-87 with bone spurs in both ankles . . . Played well as soph and junior, then had super senior season . . . Averaged 29.7 last five weeks of season, while going .703 from three-point line . . . Big games in ''big games'' made him appealing (No. 31) to Phoenix . . . Born March 6, 1967, in Dayton, Ohio.

CEDRIC CEBALLOS 21 6-6 210   Forward

Reinforced his questioned credentials in Orlando All-Star Classic last spring . . . Was a prep prospect at L.A.'s Dominguez High before helping Ventura JC to California state championship in second season . . . Scored heavily in both years at Cal-State Fullerton, but it was his rebounding (16.3 in three games against UNLV) that led Phoenix to take a closer look at No. 48 . . . Born Aug. 2, 1969.

COACH COTTON FITZSIMMONS: No, even his *best* coaching pals don't call him ''Lowell,'' which he was christened after being born Oct. 7, 1931, in Hannibal, Mo. . . . And don't get him started on his fabulous career at Hannibal-LeGrange JC and Midwestern (Mo.) State . . . He's an X-and-O man on the bench and when given space and freedom (as he's had with Phoenix) he's pretty close to a personnel genius in the office . . . As a glorified scout, he quietly rebuilt the Suns—and then in 1988-89 coached Phoenix to a 55-27 record . . . That was the second-best mark in franchise history and it was an improvement of 27 wins over previous year . . . Coach of the Year that season, 10 years after winning same honor in 1979 at Kansas City . . . Before Suns beat Lakers last spring in Game 1 of Western semifinals, he'd lost 37 (yes, as in 37) straight at the Forum . . . Topped that off by advancing past L.A. on the same floor four games later.

GREATEST REBOUNDER

He was powerful, intelligent, indefatigable, dedicated and precise. But what Paul Silas definitely was not during 16 NBA seasons was "delicate."

Out of Creighton in 1964, he never topped 6-7 and never asked, "May I, please?" when chasing missed shots—more than a few of which were his own. He shot .432 for his career, averaging under double figures in scoring and playing in only two All-Star Games.

But from start (age 21) to finish (37) he averaged 9.9 boards a game. In his second year as a Sun, 1970-71, he produced the first of his four career 1,000-board seasons. Silas was with Phoenix only three years, averaging 12.1 rebounds a contest, before moving on to Boston, Denver and Seattle.

ALL-TIME SUN LEADERS

SEASON

Points: Tom Chambers, 2,201, 1989-90
Assists: Kevin Johnson, 991, 1988-89
Rebounds: Paul Silas, 1,015, 1970-71

GAME

Points: Tom Chambers, 60 vs. Seattle, 3/24/90
Assists: Gail Goodrich, 19 vs. Philadelphia, 10/22/69
Rebounds: Paul Silas, 27 vs. Cincinnati, 1/18/71

CAREER

Points: Walter Davis, 15,666, 1977-88
Assists: Alvan Adams, 4,012, 1975-88
Rebounds: Alvan Adams, 6,937, 1975-88

PORTLAND TRAIL BLAZERS

TEAM DIRECTORY: Chairman: Paul Allen; Pres.: Harry Glickman; Dir. Media Services: John Lashway; Coach: Rick Adelman; Asst. Coaches: Jack Schalow, John Wetzel. Arena: Memorial Coliseum (12,884). Colors: Red, black and white.

Buck Williams discovered there is life after New Jersey.

SCOUTING REPORT

SHOOTING: Returning to the Finals for the first time since the too-brief glory days, the Trail Blazers went down in flames to the Pistons. But all guns were firing; mostly blanks, but firing. During a season in which Portland improved from 39 to 59 wins, each starter scored comfortably in double-figures.

While Clyde Drexler again was the best producer of points (13th in the NBA), Buck Williams brought along his promised consistency in his first season away from the Meadowlands and the dreadful Nets. Buck was 10th in the league in FG percentage. Jerome Kersey had many more good games than poor ones, and could be on the verge of a breakout season. The only serious three-point threats were point guard Terry Porter and second-year Yugoslavian Drazen Petrovic, but Danny Ainge may help out here.

PLAYMAKING: Porter, the league's sixth-best free-thrower, was ranked eighth in assists. Except for Drexler—and backup point guard Danny Young—no one else is all that adept at tossing the ball to someone wearing the same color jersey.

The Trail Blazers score a lot of baskets on breakaways and Drexler, in particular, is capable of making his own plays off the dribble in halfcourt sets. Too often, however—and this was critical in the Finals against Detroit—Portland has a tendency to stand around and then rush to beat the 24-second clock.

DEFENSE: Rick Adelman's first year as head coach produced enough discipline to make the Trail Blazers the fourth-most difficult team in the league against which to make a field goal. That's part tribute to him, with equal shares to the general athleticism of his players and the attitude inspired by Williams. How rookie Alaa Abdelnaby, the 6-10 Duke forward-center, will fare in this mix remains to be determined.

REBOUNDING: Williams pulled in an even 800 boards and was 10th in the league. As a team, Portland had a comfortable 3,907-3,412 margin on the boards during the regular season. (That, too, wouldn't hold up against Detroit, alas.) Kersey and Williams are eager workers on the offensive boards, and the Blazers got some nice help from Cliff Robinson. The latter, who had dropped in drafting clubs' favor last spring, was a pleasant and often aggressive surprise. Kevin Duckworth, who flattened out in the regular season, was hurt early in postseason and when healed was generally ineffective.

TRAIL BLAZER ROSTER

No.	Veterans	Pos.	Ht.	Wt.	Age	Yrs. Pro	College
9	Danny Ainge	G	6-5	185	31	9	Brigham Young
2	Mark Bryant	F	6-9	245	25	2	Seton Hall
42	Wayne Cooper	C	6-10	220	33	12	New Orleans
22	Clyde Drexler	G	6-7	215	28	7	Houston
00	Kevin Duckworth	C	7-0	270	26	4	Eastern Illinois
25	Jerome Kersey	F	6-7	225	28	6	Longwood
44	Drazen Petrovic	G	6-5	195	26	1	Yugoslavia
30	Terry Porter	G	6-3	195	27	5	Wis.-Stevens Pt.
3	Cliff Robinson	F	6-10	225	23	1	Connecticut
52	Buck Williams	F	6-8	225	30	9	Maryland
21	Danny Young	G	6-4	175	28	6	Wake Forest

Rd.	Rookies	Sel. No.	Pos.	Ht.	Wt.	College
1	Alaa Abdelnaby	25	F	6-10	240	Duke

OUTLOOK: The Blazers became for real in their own minds and to opponents with a 10-game winning streak in early March. Now, where this team goes is in either of two directions: forward, pumped by its November-through-May success; or stuck at the "almost" level, spirit sapped by the blowout in the Finals. Adelman is convinced the groundwork is permanently placed and his team will remain an ongoing contender.

TRAIL BLAZER PROFILES

CLYDE DREXLER 28 6-7 215   Guard

Couldn't get his team a title but converted some disbelievers in Finals... Averaged 23.3 points during regular season, played strong complementary role in Western playoffs, then shot .543 FG, averaged 26.4 points vs. Pistons... Born June 22, 1962, in New Orleans... Founding member of Houston's Phi Slamma Jamma... One of game's great leapers, jumped from school early and was 14th pick as an undergrad in 1983 by Trail Blazers... Forget his 7.7-point rookie-year debut ...In the six years since, he's averaged 22.5 points... "Clyde the Glide"... Everybody knows the nickname but it doesn't tell the whole story... Second on team in steals last season.

Year	Team	G	FG	FG Pct.	FT	FT Pct.	Reb.	Ast.	TP	Avg.
1983-84	Portland	82	252	.451	123	.728	235	153	628	7.7
1984-85	Portland	80	573	.494	223	.759	476	441	1377	17.2
1985-86	Portland	75	542	.475	293	.769	421	600	1389	18.5
1986-87	Portland	82	707	.502	357	.760	518	566	1782	21.7
1987-88	Portland	81	849	.506	476	.811	533	467	2185	27.0
1988-89	Portland	78	829	.496	438	.799	615	450	2123	27.2
1989-90	Portland	73	670	.494	333	.774	507	432	1703	23.3
	Totals	551	4422	.493	2243	.779	3305	3109	11187	20.3

TERRY PORTER 27 6-3 195   Guard

Had a marvelous regular season and playoffs until Finals... Averaged 19 points, eight assists, but Pistons held him to sub-40-percent shooting... In Western Conference's rich pool of backcourt leaders, he ranks with best—although he might be better off the ball... An excellent defender who is showing more and more offensive ability... Born April 8, 1963, in Milwaukee... Turned out to be marvelous steal out of tiny Wisconsin-Stevens Point in 1986 by Portland, which got him 24th in first round... Built like a strong safety, he dabbles at golf in offseason... Placed eighth in NBA assists... "Terry Porter's raised my game a coupla notches," said Buck Williams during his first season at Portland... Holds club's one-season and single-game marks in feeds.

Year	Team	G	FG	FG Pct.	FT	FT Pct.	Reb.	Ast.	TP	Avg.
1985-86	Portland	79	212	.474	125	.806	117	198	562	7.1
1986-87	Portland	80	376	.488	280	.838	337	715	1045	13.1
1987-88	Portland	82	462	.519	274	.846	378	831	1222	14.9
1988-89	Portland	81	540	.471	272	.840	367	770	1431	17.7
1989-90	Portland	80	448	.462	421	.892	272	726	1406	17.6
	Totals	402	2038	.483	1372	.853	1471	3240	5666	14.1

JEROME KERSEY 28 6-7 225   Forward

That "other guy" in Portland... Helped enhance his league-wide reputation, but he's got critics closer to home... Made 82 starts for first time in six-year career... Also led Trail Blazers in minutes played... One of best dunkers in the game... Born June 26, 1962, in Clarksville, Va.... Drafted by Portland with 46th pick in 1984 out of Longwood College, in his hometown... Small-town guy beginning to emerge...

Fifth in NBA Most Improved Player voting in 1987-88 . . . Scoring dropped off mildly second year in row after three seasons of upward movement . . . But his overall play improved . . . Second on team in offensive rebounds, although he fouled out seven times.

Year	Team	G	FG	FG Pct.	FT	FT Pct.	Reb.	Ast.	TP	Avg.
1984-85	Portland	77	178	.478	117	.646	206	63	473	6.1
1985-86	Portland	79	258	.549	156	.681	293	83	672	8.5
1986-87	Portland	82	373	.509	262	.720	496	194	1009	12.3
1987-88	Portland	79	611	.499	291	.735	657	243	1516	19.2
1988-89	Portland	76	533	.469	258	.694	629	243	1330	17.5
1989-90	Portland	82	519	.478	269	.690	690	188	1310	16.0
	Totals	475	2472	.492	1353	.700	2971	1014	6310	13.3

KEVIN DUCKWORTH 26 7-0 270   Center

Has he reached a plateau already? . . . After removing a short ton of excess weight, he developed remarkably in second and third seasons . . . Started every game last year but reverted occasionally to erratic play . . . Born April 1, 1964, at Dolton, Ill. . . . San Antonio gambled, took him out of Eastern Illinois with 33d pick in second round in 1986 . . . That was good news for the Spurs. The bad news was they traded him to Portland for the recalcitrant Walter Berry . . . Ran away with Most Improved Player Award in 1987-88 . . . You could feed a small village with the fat he's lost, float a ship with sweat he's shed in offseasons . . . Rival vets admire his work ethic, frown at his on-court sulks . . . Hand injury hampered him in playoffs, although he started final 11 games.

Year	Team	G	FG	FG Pct.	FT	FT Pct.	Reb.	Ast.	TP	Avg.
1986-87	S.A.-Port.	65	130	.476	92	.687	223	29	352	5.4
1987-88	Portland	78	450	.496	331	.770	576	66	1231	15.8
1988-89	Portland	79	554	.477	324	.757	635	60	1432	18.1
1989-90	Portland	82	548	.478	231	.740	509	91	1327	16.2
	Totals	304	1682	.482	978	.750	1943	246	4342	14.3

BUCK WILLIAMS 30 6-8 225   Forward

Free at last! . . . His first pro season away from Nets was not his best statistically . . . But it was his longest and most satisfying . . . Bounced back from low-rebounding mark of career with team-best 9.8, 10th in league . . . Born March 8, 1960, in Rocky Mount, N.C. . . . Came out of Maryland as undergrad in 1981 and Nets made him third player chosen . . . Was Rookie of Year in 1981-82 and he stayed eight seasons on a treadmill with New Jersey . . . Last few years were ''an ordeal,'' he admits . . . Always one of league's most consistent, persistent offensive boardmen . . . Absence of Kevin Duckworth seemed to wear him down as playoffs advanced, but still led with 9.2 rebounds . . . Greatly respected by playing peers.

Year	Team	G	FG	FG Pct.	FT	FT Pct.	Reb.	Ast.	TP	Avg.
1981-82	New Jersey	82	513	.582	242	.624	1005	107	1268	15.5
1982-83	New Jersey	82	536	.588	324	.620	1027	125	1396	17.0
1983-84	New Jersey	81	495	.535	284	.570	1000	130	1274	15.7
1984-85	New Jersey	82	577	.530	336	.625	1005	167	1491	18.2
1985-86	New Jersey	82	500	.523	301	.676	986	131	1301	15.9
1986-87	New Jersey	82	521	.557	430	.731	1023	129	1472	18.0
1987-88	New Jersey	70	466	.560	346	.668	834	109	1279	18.3
1988-89	New Jersey	74	373	.531	213	.666	696	78	959	13.0
1989-90	Portland	82	413	.548	288	.706	800	116	1114	13.6
	Totals	717	4394	.550	2764	.654	8376	1092	11554	16.1

DANNY AINGE 31 6-5 185   Guard

 Crybaby or wimp? . . . Clarifies his image problem this way: "I have this reputation as a complainer. Actually, I'm a whiner, not a complainer." . . . Shooting dropped way off pre-1989-90 career .484 and Sacramento shipped him up to Portland for Byron Irvin and two draft picks . . . Produced Kings' only triple-double last season—27 points, 11 rebounds, 13 assists vs. Milwaukee, Dec. 5, 1989 . . . Born Feb. 17, 1959, in Eugene, Ore. . . . Two-sport BYU star began pro career in baseball with Toronto Blue Jays . . . Played first eight NBA years with Boston . . . Won two NBA titles there . . . Traded to the Kings in 1989 with Brad Lohaus for Joe Kleine and Ed Pinckney. Still does some critical, unwanted cross-continental GM-ing of Celtics.

Year	Team	G	FG	FG Pct.	FT	FT Pct.	Reb.	Ast.	TP	Avg.
1981-82	Boston	53	79	.357	56	.862	56	87	219	4.1
1982-83	Boston	80	357	.496	72	.742	214	251	791	9.9
1983-84	Boston	71	166	.460	46	.821	116	162	384	5.4
1984-85	Boston	75	419	.529	118	.868	268	399	971	12.9
1985-86	Boston	80	353	.504	123	.904	235	405	855	10.7
1986-87	Boston	71	410	.486	148	.897	242	400	1053	14.8
1987-88	Boston	81	482	.491	158	.878	249	503	1270	15.7
1988-89	Bos.-Sac.	73	480	.457	205	.854	255	402	1281	17.5
1989-90	Sacramento	75	506	.438	222	.831	326	453	1342	17.9
	Totals	659	3252	.476	1148	.855	1961	3062	8166	12.4

WAYNE COOPER 33 6-10 220 Center-Forward

Journeyman center nearing the end of journey? . . . Not quite yet, though . . . Hasn't done badly for a one-time second-rounder who isn't strong enough to be play middle, isn't quick enough to be a potent forward . . . After all these years, people still don't think he can stick the 16-footer, but he does . . . Used to drive Kareem Abdul-Jabbar bonkers . . . Born Nov. 16, 1956, in Milan, Ga. . . . Second-round pick (40th) by Golden State out of University of New Orleans in 1978 . . . Traded four times in career, all within Western Conference . . . Signed as free agent in July 1989 by Portland . . . Called upon in 79 games last year by Rick Adelman . . . Led Blazers in regular season with 95 blocks . . . Didn't cover himself with glory in playoffs, however, and minutes dropped.

Year	Team	G	FG	FG Pct.	FT	FT Pct.	Reb.	Ast.	TP	Avg.
1978-79	Golden State	65	128	.437	41	.672	280	21	297	4.6
1979-80	Golden State	79	367	.489	136	.751	507	42	871	11.0
1980-81	Utah	71	213	.452	62	.689	440	52	489	6.9
1981-82	Dallas	76	281	.420	119	.744	550	115	682	9.0
1982-83	Portland	80	320	.443	135	.685	611	116	775	9.7
1983-84	Portland	81	304	.459	185	.804	476	76	793	9.8
1984-85	Denver	80	404	.472	161	.685	631	86	969	12.1
1985-86	Denver	78	422	.466	174	.795	610	81	1021	13.1
1986-87	Denver	69	235	.448	79	.725	473	68	549	8.0
1987-88	Denver	45	118	.437	50	.746	270	30	286	6.4
1988-89	Denver	79	220	.495	79	.745	619	78	520	6.6
1989-90	Portland	79	138	.454	25	.641	339	44	301	3.8
	Totals	882	3150	.458	1246	.736	5806	809	7553	8.6

DRAZEN PETROVIC 26 6-5 195 Guard

Became first Yugoslavian to play in NBA Championship Series . . . Scored 10 points in four appearances . . . Averaged 13 minutes in 77 regular-season games as rookie . . . Born Oct. 22, 1964, in Zagreb, Yugoslavia . . . Drafted with 60th pick in third round back in 1986 . . . Legal complications delayed the signing . . . Star on Yugoslavian National team and was silver medalist on his country's silver-medal team in 1988 Olympics . . . Has never seen—or heard in any language—a shot he didn't like . . . Scored 63 points in 1989 European Cup for Real Madrid . . . Had to buy out his Spanish League commitment with Real Madrid for reported $1.15 million . . . Playing time should increase this year, perhaps in a quick lineup moving Clyde Drexler occasionally to forward.

Year	Team	G	FG	FG Pct.	FT	FT Pct.	Reb.	Ast.	TP	Avg.
1989-90	Portland	77	207	.485	135	.844	111	116	583	7.6

CLIFF ROBINSON 23 6-10 225　　　　　　Forward

One of the best picks in the 1989 draft, as it turned out . . . Hard work and improved attitude made him a contributor as a rookie . . . Born Dec. 16, 1966, in Buffalo, N.Y. . . . Played at Connecticut four years and was leading scorer three seasons . . . MVP for NIT champ Huskies . . . Suspect shooting, approach to game combined to drop in pre-draft evaluations . . . Slipped to second round and Portland took him with 36th choice . . . Played in each regular-season game, got enough time to average 9.1 points and foul out four times . . . A natural forward, he started in all but one game at center for injured Kevin Duckworth in seven-game Western semis against San Antonio . . . A lousy free-throw shooter, he also needs work working away from basket . . . But Blazers love his potential.

Year	Team	G	FG	FG Pct.	FT	FT Pct.	Reb.	Ast.	TP	Avg.
1989-90	Portland	82	298	.397	138	.550	308	72	746	9.1

MARK BRYANT 25 6-9 245　　　　　　Forward

Has he gotten the message yet? . . . Club's sending you some kind of message, Mark, when a first-round pick gets 803 minutes as a rookie and drops to 562 in second season . . . Especially on a team increasingly deep in forwards . . . Born April 25, 1965, in Glen Ridge, N.J. . . . Made a mark in Big East and was in middle of Seton Hall's first-ever NCAA tourney bid . . . Portland felt fortunate that summer to land him in first round at No. 21 . . . Found out quickly it's not easy to bully pros if you're not quick enough to find someone's body to bump with yours . . . Watched most of Finals against Detroit from bench. Sweated nine minutes in two games.

Year	Team	G	FG	FG Pct.	FT	FT Pct.	Reb.	Ast.	TP	Avg.
1988-89	Portland	56	120	.486	40	.580	179	33	280	5.0
1989-90	Portland	58	70	.458	28	.560	146	13	168	2.9
	Totals	114	190	.475	68	.571	325	46	448	3.9

DANNY YOUNG 28 6-4 175   Guard

A survivor . . . Played every game . . . Made eight regular-season starts . . . Seventh among NBA players in steal-turnover ratio, but role diminished in playoffs . . . Born July 26, 1962, in Raleigh, N.C. . . . The 39th pick in second round of 1984 out of Wake Forest by Seattle . . . After brief look, played most of first pro year with Wyoming in CBA . . . Sonics then kept him for three full seasons before cutting him . . . Portland signed him as a free agent as protection for Terry Porter . . . Sound understanding of game but a mechanical player.

Year	Team	G	FG	FG Pct.	FT	FT Pct.	Reb.	Ast.	TP	Avg.
1984-85	Seattle	3	2	.200	0	.000	3	2	4	1.3
1985-86	Seattle	82	227	.506	90	.849	120	303	568	6.9
1986-87	Seattle	73	132	.458	59	.831	113	353	352	4.8
1987-88	Seattle	77	89	.408	43	.811	75	218	243	3.2
1988-89	Portland	48	115	.460	50	.781	74	123	297	6.2
1989-90	Portland	82	138	.421	91	.813	122	231	383	4.7
	Totals	365	703	.456	333	.820	507	1230	1847	5.1

THE ROOKIE

ALAA ABDELNABY 22 6-10 240   Forward

Began blossoming in senior season at Duke, then flowered in post-tournament sightings by scouts . . . Scored more points (572, 15.1 ppg) in final year with Blue Devils than he had accumulated in first three . . . Nice, soft touch along baseline . . . Shot .625 FG last two seasons . . . Whether he can get low-post position against pros in another question . . . Selected at No. 25 by a team with a promising stable of young forwards . . . Born June 24, 1968 . . . Played high school ball in Bloomfield, N.J.

COACH RICK ADELMAN: An original Trail Blazer, team's first captain and in his first full season as head coach he directed Portland to Western Conference crown . . . Both he and his players were overmatched, however, in Finals against Detroit . . . Losing three straight games at home to Pistons didn't particularly embellish his late-game coaching credentials . . . A so-called ''players' coach,'' he replaced Mike Schuler in mid-1988-89, took the job full-time on May 11,

1989 as franchise's seventh head coach . . . Born June 16, 1946, at Lynwood, Cal., he went from Pius X High in Downey, Cal., to set a since-obliterated career scoring record at what is now called Loyola Marymount . . . Has earned both a bachelor's and master's degree from Loyola . . . Played seven NBA seasons with five franchises.

GREATEST REBOUNDER

Healthy, he was "Great Red." Hobbled, he was just another 6-11 Grateful Dead confidant. And Jerry Garcia never broke as many guitar strings as Bill Walton lost games to injury.

Walton's Portland stay lasted five seasons. He played in 209 games, missed 201. Big Red was the original Bad Foot. In 13 years as a pro, he made 468 games, missed 598. Still, he's the best the Trail Blazers have ever had.

His third year (1976-77) was magical. The only time Walton was fit enough to play 2,000 minutes, the former UCLA star was the NBA shot-block (3.24) and rebound (14.4) champ. That was when he led the Trail Blazers to the title and was playoff MVP. In healthy parts of four years in Portland, he averaged 13.5 boards a game.

ALL-TIME TRAIL BLAZER LEADERS

SEASON

Points: Clyde Drexler, 2,185, 1987-88
Assists: Terry Porter, 831, 1987-88
Rebounds: Lloyd Neal, 967, 1972-73

GAME

Points: Geoff Petrie, 51 vs. Houston, 2/16/73
          Geoff Petrie, 51 vs. Houston, 1/20/73
Assists: Terry Porter, 19 vs. Utah, 4/14/88
Rebounds: Sidney Wicks, 27 vs. Los Angeles, 2/26/75

CAREER

Points: Clyde Drexler, 11,187, 1984-90
Assists: Clyde Drexler, 3,109, 1984-90
Rebounds: Mychal Thompson, 4,878, 1978-86

SACRAMENTO KINGS

TEAM DIRECTORY: Managing General Partner: Gregg Lukenbill; Pres.: Rick Benner; Dir. Player Personnel: Jerry Reynolds; Coach: Dick Motta; Dir. Pub. Rel.: Julie Fie. Arena: ARCO Arena (17,014); Colors: Red, white and blue.

SCOUTING REPORT

SHOOTING: Well, at least most of the players will *look* different this year. The Kings have been mostly clown princes from the

Wayman Tisdale posted career highs in ppg and FG pct.

floor recently—but without providing commensurate laughs to the ARCO Arena faithful who sell out the building with shocking frequency. Only one incumbent King made more shots than he missed last year. That's Wayman Tisdale, whose .525 was 18th in the league while he was placing just inside the Top 20 in scoring.

This club has no three-point threat, which it is going to need, because Dick Motta is a firm believer in the pound-it-inside philosophy. The corollary to that approach, of course: Someone better nail an outside shot once in a while or the center and power forward are going to be strangled. Whether LaSalle's Lionel Simmons, the consensus college Player of the Year and Sacramento's initial first-round draft pick (of four), will be able to get his own shot at this level is a concern. Whether he has an outside shot is of even more concern.

PLAYMAKING: The Kings didn't have a point guard last year, although both Danny Ainge and Vinnie Del Negro (now in Italy) were among those playing at the position. Sacramento seemed to have gotten an out-and-out theft with Bimbo Coles at No. 40, but Motta and personnel man Jerry Reynolds opted to trade him to Miami for the aging Rory Sparrow. With Ainge traded to Portland for Byron Irvin, it's up to Sparrow—or possibly newcomer Travis Mays—to run the offense. Bobby Hansen from Utah can offset the loss of Ainge's off-guard abilities.

DEFENSE: In a pre-draft move, the Kings traded their best inside defender, Rodney McCray, to Dallas and secured another early selection position. Pervis Ellison, the disappointing No. 1 pick of the 1989 draft, wasn't very good even after recovering from early-season surgery. Ralph Sampson got little exposure, which considering his recent level of play, probably was a charitable decision by Motta.

Ellison is gone, traded, and Sampson, who at mid-summer seemed eager to attempt to play, waits out his guaranteed contract. Their standing-water-slow offense rather than defensive skill allowed Kings to be within 101.7-106.8 of opponents last season. Will the new faces change that a great deal? Probably not.

REBOUNDING: Sacramento was crushed by more than 300 rebounds over the length of the season. And the best individual board man was the since-traded McCray. Duane Causwell, who did not complete his final year of playing eligibility at Temple because of an academic problem, should get a long look as a short-term reliever at the center spot. He's got pro size and has shown willingness to work on his game.

KING ROSTER

No.	Veterans	Pos.	Ht.	Wt.	Age	Yrs. Pro	College
35	Antoine Carr	F	6-9	265	29	6	Wichita State
20	Bobby Hansen	G	6-6	200	29	7	Iowa
—	Byron Irvin	G	6-5	190	23	1	Missouri
45	Eric Leckner	C	6-11	265	24	2	Wyoming
21	Harold Pressley	F-G	6-7	210	27	4	Villanova
50	Ralph Sampson	C	7-4	250	30	7	Virginia
2	Rory Sparrow	G	6-2	175	32	10	Villanova
23	Wayman Tisdale	F	6-9	260	26	4	Oklahoma
4	Henry Turner	F	6-7	200	24	1	Cal-Fullerton
—	Bill Wennington	C	7-0	250	27	5	St. John's

Rd.	Rookies	Sel. No.	Pos.	Ht.	Wt.	College
1	Lionel Simmons	7	F	6-8	210	La Salle
1	Travis Mays	14	G	6-2	190	Texas
1	Duane Causwell	18	C	7-0	240	Temple
1	Anthony Bonner	23	F	6-8	225	St. Louis

OUTLOOK: Motta, who took over during the 1989-90 season, apparently hadn't tossed away any notebooks while fishing and broadcasting after leaving coaching and the Dallas Mavericks. Whoever guides the offense will have to force the ball to Tisdale for easy six-footers, run double-screens for his small forward (if Simmons can shoot the J), and run the off-guard off-back screens. The other rookies—Mays and Anthony Bonner—could become important factors, particularly the former. Well, at least the Kings won't look the same.

KING PROFILES

WAYMAN TISDALE 26 6-9 260   Forward

Dick Motta thinks he's more Clydesdale than bow-wow . . . His 22.3-point average was easily best of his career . . . Shot personal best from floor with .525 . . . Both marks placed him 18th in league . . . Three times an All-American at Oklahoma . . . Leading rebounder on 1984 Olympic gold-medal winners . . . No. 2 pick overall as undergraduate in 1985 draft by In-

diana (behind Patrick Ewing to New York) . . . Criticized as being too soft, but shows up for work . . . Never missed more than three games in a pro season . . . Traded with draft pick by Pacers to Kings in February 1989 for LaSalle Thompson, Randy Wittman . . . Born June 9, 1964, in Tulsa, Okla. . . . Father's a minister . . . A published song writer and recorded musician.

Year	Team	G	FG	FG Pct.	FT	FT Pct.	Reb.	Ast.	TP	Avg.
1985-86	Indiana.	81	516	.515	160	.684	584	79	1192	14.7
1986-87	Indiana.	81	458	.513	258	.709	475	117	1174	14.5
1987-88	Indiana.	79	511	.512	246	.783	491	103	1268	16.1
1988-89	Ind.-Sac.	79	532	.514	317	.773	609	128	1381	17.5
1989-90	Sacramento.	79	726	.525	306	.783	595	108	1758	22.3
	Totals	399	2743	.516	1287	.751	2754	535	6773	17.0

RALPH SAMPSON 30 7-4 250   Center

Both his knees are almost as bad as his recent press clippings . . . Seems like a zillion years ago since he was effective . . . Kings face the dilemma of having on hand a wounded warrior whose rocket has long since burst (weak double pun, alas, intended) . . . And they've got to pay him a king's ransom whether they can/will use him or not . . . Born July 7, 1960, in Harrisonburg, Va. . . . First pick of the 1983 draft by Houston . . . Three-time All-American at Virginia . . . *Sporting News* Collegiate Player of Year in 1982 . . . NBA Rookie of Year in 1984 and MVP of 1985 NBA All-Star Game . . . Averaged 20.7 points, 10.9 rebounds first three years but hasn't been able to do anything close to that since . . . Moved by Rockets with Steve Harris to Golden State in December 1987 for Joe Barry Carroll and Sleepy Floyd . . . Couldn't play and then wasn't used by Don Nelson in 1988-89, and was shipped to Sacramento.

Year	Team	G	FG	FG Pct.	FT	FT Pct.	Reb.	Ast.	TP	Avg.
1983-84	Houston	82	716	.523	287	.661	913	163	1720	21.0
1984-85	Houston	82	753	.502	303	.676	853	224	1809	22.1
1985-86	Houston	79	624	.488	241	.641	879	283	1491	18.9
1986-87	Houston	43	277	.489	118	.624	372	120	672	15.6
1987-88	Hou.-G.S..	48	299	.438	149	.760	462	122	749	15.6
1988-89	Golden State	61	164	.449	62	.653	307	77	393	6.4
1989-90	Sacramento.	26	48	.372	12	.522	84	28	109	4.2
	Totals	421	2881	.489	1172	.666	3870	1017	6943	16.5

ANTOINE CARR 29 6-9 265   Forward

Finally living up to great expectations? . . . Lifted seasonal average into double figures (12.3) first time in sixth year as pro . . . Produced 18.6 ppg in 33 games, mostly as a sub, with Kings . . . Detroit made the former Wichita State star the No. 8 overall pick in 1983 . . . Spent first pro year in Italy . . . Traded to Hawks with Cliff Levingston and draft picks for a washed-up Dan Roundfield . . . Never matched billing with Hawks and was usually injured or overweight . . . "He's so wide, it's a 24-second violation to go around him," says Lakers announcer Chick Hearn . . . Traded by Atlanta on Feb. 13, 1990 to Kings with Sedric Toney and a 1991 second-round pick for Kenny Smith and Mike Williams . . . Born July 23, 1961, in Oklahoma City . . . Made $529,000 before trade.

Year	Team	G	FG	FG Pct.	FT	FT Pct.	Reb.	Ast.	TP	Avg.
1984-85	Atlanta	62	198	.528	101	.789	232	80	499	8.0
1985-86	Atlanta	17	49	.527	18	.667	52	14	116	6.8
1986-87	Atlanta	65	134	.506	73	.709	156	34	342	5.3
1987-88	Atlanta	80	281	.544	142	.780	289	103	705	8.8
1988-89	Atlanta	78	226	.480	130	.855	274	91	582	7.5
1989-90	Atl.-Sac.	77	356	.494	237	.795	322	119	949	12.3
	Totals	379	1244	.509	701	.788	1325	441	3193	8.4

HAROLD PRESSLEY 27 6-7 210   Forward-Guard

Still seeking an identity in pros after four full seasons with this franchise . . . First-round draft pick (17th) by Sacramento in 1986 . . . He starred at Villanova in a step-by-step offense . . . Performed with versatility on 1985 NCAA title team after four multi-position years of Big East play . . . Born July 14, 1963, in Uncasville, Conn. . . . Swing man with passable passing skills in pros . . . Good offensive rebounding instincts also leave him vulnerable in open-court defense . . . Eighth in three-point percentage in 1988-89 (119-295 for .403), he was 46-148 for .311 from long distance last season.

Year	Team	G	FG	FG Pct.	FT	FT Pct.	Reb.	Ast.	TP	Avg.
1986-87	Sacramento	67	134	.423	35	.729	176	120	310	4.6
1987-88	Sacramento	80	318	.453	103	.792	369	185	775	9.7
1988-89	Sacramento	80	383	.439	96	.780	485	174	981	12.3
1989-90	Sacramento	72	240	.424	110	.780	309	149	636	8.8
	Totals	299	1075	.437	344	.778	1339	628	2702	9.0

BOBBY HANSEN 29 6-6 200   Guard

Adds veteran experience to Kings after seven years with Utah... Staggering to the mind, however, is how such an otherwise sound, if limited, player can continue to fare so poorly at the foul line... Clanked them up at .516 last year... An aversion to free-throw shooting may help explain his growing inclination to loft medium jumpers instead of looking for drives, potential fouls... Started 81 games last year... Not the quickest off-guard, but willing to mix it up defensively, bump taller back-courtmen... Born Jan. 18, 1961, in Des Moines, Iowa... Utah's third-round pick (54th) in 1983.

Year	Team	G	FG	FG Pct.	FT	FT Pct.	Reb.	Ast.	TP	Avg.
1983-84	Utah	55	65	.448	18	.643	48	44	148	2.7
1984-85	Utah	54	110	.489	40	.556	70	75	261	4.8
1985-86	Utah	82	299	.476	95	.720	244	193	710	8.7
1986-87	Utah	72	272	.453	136	.760	203	102	696	9.7
1987-88	Utah	81	316	.517	113	.743	187	175	777	9.6
1988-89	Utah	46	140	.467	42	.560	128	50	341	7.4
1989-90	Utah	81	265	.467	33	.516	229	149	617	7.6
	Totals	471	1467	.477	477	.679	1109	788	3550	7.5

ERIC LECKNER 24 6-11 265   Center

Usually plays within his limitations, which are many... Did a competent job as backup for Jazz, who sent him to Sacramento in a three-way trade involving Washington two days before the 1990 draft... Could get good shot at increased playing time here... Born May 27, 1966, in Inglewood, Cal.... Played four seasons at Wyoming... Won three straight MVP honors at WAC tourney... Chosen by Jazz 17th in 1988 draft... Good low-post shooter in college and pros—when he's real, real low... Had career scoring high (21) in final game of rookie season against Golden State.

Year	Team	G	FG	FG Pct.	FT	FT Pct.	Reb.	Ast.	TP	Avg.
1988-89	Utah	75	120	.545	79	.699	199	16	319	4.3
1989-90	Utah	77	125	.563	81	.743	192	19	331	4.3
	Totals	152	245	.554	160	.721	391	35	650	4.3

BYRON IRVIN 23 6-5 190 Guard

Comes to Kings in Danny Ainge trade after spending rookie season in Portland . . . Earned a pair of starts and appeared in 50 games as a rookie . . . Played for three coaches during college career at Arkansas and Missouri . . . Transferred from former after two seasons and made All-Big Eight senior season, when Tigers reached NCAA Final 16 . . . Born Dec. 2, 1966, in LaGrange, Ill. . . . Portland took him at No. 22 in first round of 1989 draft after obtaining pick from New York in Kiki Vandeweghe trade . . . And they liked his shooting (.532 FG, .348 three-pointers as a senior) . . . Didn't play in NBA Finals.

Year	Team	G	FG	FG Pct.	FT	FT Pct.	Reb.	Ast.	TP	Avg.
1989-90	Portland	50	96	.473	61	.670	74	47	258	5.2

RORY SPARROW 32 6-2 175 Guard

Still a card-carrying member of Bricklayers of America . . . Shot dismal .412 last year for Miami, which traded him to the Kings for the rights to Bimbo Coles (No. 40 in the draft) . . . Signed by Heat two days before 1988-89 season as unrestricted free agent and began year as starting point guard . . . But his minutes have steadily decreased . . . Good ball-handling skills, tough against pressure . . . One of most community-minded athletes in all of sport . . . Started Rory Sparrow Foundation for underprivileged kids . . . Born June 12, 1958, in Suffolk, Va. . . . First black athlete to graduate from Villanova engineering school . . . Originally drafted 75th overall by Nets in 1980 . . . Earned $350,000.

Year	Team	G	FG	FG Pct.	FT	FT Pct.	Reb.	Ast.	TP	Avg.
1980-81	New Jersey	15	22	.349	12	.750	18	32	56	3.7
1981-82	Atlanta	82	366	.501	124	.838	224	424	857	10.5
1982-83	Atl.-N.Y.	81	392	.484	147	.739	230	397	936	11.6
1983-84	New York	79	350	.474	108	.824	189	539	818	10.4
1984-85	New York	79	326	.492	122	.865	169	557	781	9.9
1985-86	New York	74	345	.477	101	.795	170	472	796	10.8
1986-87	New York	80	263	.446	71	.798	115	432	608	7.6
1987-88	N.Y.-Chi.	58	117	.399	24	.727	72	167	260	4.5
1988-89	Miami	80	444	.452	94	.879	216	429	1000	12.5
1989-90	Miami	82	210	.412	59	.766	138	298	487	5.9
	Totals	710	2835	.465	862	.807	1541	3747	6599	9.3

BILL WENNINGTON 25 7-0 250   Center

Finds himself a King after five "so-what?" years with Dallas...Career backup man... Got two starts, 814 minutes (in 60 games) last season with Mavs...Born Dec. 26, 1964, in Montreal...Once a hockey player, now an off-season water skier...Physical presence and jump-shooter at St. John's...Member of Canada's 1984 Olympic team...Still inexplicable pick at No. 16 by Dallas in 1986...Saved from expansion draft of 1988 when Mavs gave rights of Arvid Kramer to Miami, insuring he would not be taken by Heat.

Year	Team	G	FG	FG Pct.	FT	FT Pct.	Reb.	Ast.	TP	Avg.
1985-86	Dallas	56	72	.471	45	.726	132	21	189	3.4
1986-87	Dallas	58	56	.424	45	.750	129	24	157	2.7
1987-88	Dallas	30	25	.510	12	.632	39	4	63	2.1
1988-89	Dallas	65	119	.433	61	.744	286	46	300	4.6
1989-90	Dallas	60	105	.449	60	.800	198	41	270	4.5
	Totals	269	377	.447	223	.748	784	136	979	3.6

THE ROOKIES

LIONEL SIMMONS 21 6-8 210   Forward

Consensus Player of Year in college ball last spring for LaSalle ...Born Nov. 14, 1968, in Philadelphia...Stayed local to become all-time leader at LaSalle in scoring, shots blocked and steals ...Averaged 24.6 points in a four-year career and is third on NCAA's all-time scoring list...Scored 20 or more in 47 of last 50 collegiate games...Reportedly turned down rich offers to stay in school after 28.4-point scoring year as junior...Needs time to get off outside jumper, and he'll be meeting equally strong people inside at this level on a night-to-night basis.

TRAVIS MAYS 22 6-2 190   Guard

A scoring point guard whose figures escalated each of his four seasons at Texas...Finished as leading scorer in Southwest Conference history...High-school star at Vanguard in Ocala, Fla., before being recruited to Texas...Not much of a passer, which could be a problem with Dick Motta's inside-oriented plans, but Kings picked him at No. 14...Born June 19, 1968.

DUANE CAUSWELL 22 7-0 240   **Center**

Nation's No. 2 shot-blocker as a junior . . . Forced to withdraw
from school 12 games into final year at Temple . . . Had been
averaging 11.3 points, 8.3 rebounds, 4.0 blocks . . . Spent endless
hours later with veteran coach Jack McKinney honing his
game . . . "I see Patrick Ewing in him. I'm serious," said Billy
McKinney, who wasn't serious enough to draft him instead of
Felton Spencer at No. 6 for Minnesota . . . Sacramento took him
at 18 . . . Born May 31, 1968, in New York.

ANTHONY BONNER 22 6-8 225   **Forward**

Best player on a St. Louis team that, ignored by swollen NCAA
field, reached NIT championship game twice in a row . . . Born
June 8, 1968, in St. Louis . . . Averaged 11 rebounds a game in
his career and topped all NCAA boarders as a senior with 13.8 a
game . . . Limited range, but can handle the ball well and is alert
defensively . . . Contender for spot with Kings, who selected him
23rd.

COACH DICK MOTTA: Sassy as ever, he's back . . .
"Retired" at Dallas in 1987 after 19 NBA sea-

sons . . . Found a new challenge . . . At Chicago
he had inherited a 29-game winner in 1969 and
by 1971 the Bulls won 51 and he was Coach
of the Year . . . Led Washington to successive
finals while operatic fat ladies waited to sing,
won the 1978 championship . . . Later led Dallas from expansion to decency, improving
Mavs four straight years . . . Worn down by
player sniping, he retired with 808 NBA wins . . . Born Sept. 3,
1931, in Medvale, Utah, he was cut from Jordan (Utah) High
team, didn't compete at Utah State . . . After 1987, when not fishing, camping, or manufacturing chocolate, he was TV analyst on
Detroit games . . . Kings were 7-21 last Jan. 4 when he was
hired . . . "He's got more than 800 wins, so he's proven he can
win," grinned Danny Ainge, once a King. "But he's also got
more than 700 losses, so he's proven he can lose, too." . . . Early
on, Motta decided: "I think my main job right now is to sell

enthusiasm, to be positive and look for all the good things we do.'' . . . Under him, Kings went 16-48, and are still looking for good things.

GREATEST REBOUNDER

Move to Cincinnati from Rochester, hop to a Kansas City/Omaha duplex, then on to Sacramento, and it's a fair guess fortune has not over-burdened you with tall superstars.

Field a plus-.500 club four times in 24 years, win 1,591 of 3,400 games in 42 seasons and go winless in the postseason since 1981, you are not being hassled daily for fiscal upgrades by pivot men.

Which is why three 1,000-plus rebound years (1973-75) put Sam Lacey, a competent, 6-10 journeyman, snugly ahead of more famous Royals/Kings—including Hall of Famers Jerry Lucas and Oscar Robertson—on franchise board scores.

ALL-TIME KING LEADERS

SEASON

Points: Nate Archibald, 2,719, 1972-73
Assists: Nate Archibald, 910, 1972-73
Rebounds: Jerry Lucas, 1,688, 1965-66

GAME

Points: Jack Twyman, 59 vs. Minneapolis, 1/15/60
Assists: Phil Ford, 22 vs. Milwaukee, 2/21/79
         Oscar Robertson, 22 vs. New York, 3/5/66
         Oscar Robertson, 22 vs. Syracuse, 10/29/61
Rebounds: Jerry Lucas, 40 vs. Philadelphia, 2/29/64

CAREER

Points: Oscar Robertson, 22,009, 1960-70
Assists: Oscar Robertson, 7,721, 1960-70
Rebounds: Jerry Lucas, 8,831, 1963-69

SAN ANTONIO SPURS

TEAM DIRECTORY: Chairman: Red McCombs; Pres.: Gary Woods; Asst. to Chairman/Pres.: Bob Bass; Exec. VP: Russ Bookbinder; Dir. Pub. Rel.: Wayne Witt; Media Services Mgr.: Matt Sperisen; Coach: Larry Brown; Asst. Coaches: Gregg Popovich, R.C. Buford. Arena: HemisFair Arena (15,910). Colors: Metallic silver and black.

Worth waiting for, David Robinson was Rookie of the Year.

SCOUTING REPORT

SHOOTING: The Spurs shot a very warm .484 from the floor last year, and gave every indication that the pot had not even approached the boiling point. First, Sean Elliott will do better than his rookie .481. Second, when Willie Anderson becomes merely a two-position player (settle on off-guard and small forward, forget the point) he is going to become a true piece of work. And, third and best of all, the sensational first year of David Robinson assuredly was no aberration.

Except for backup forward-center Frank Brickowski, who is now with Milwaukee, no one on this club shot better than Mr. Robinson. His quickness was expected, but Robinson also brought pro-level strength and a dazzling deftness in his rookie bag of tricks. Oh, and the team's single-game high of 52 points was produced by Terry Cummings, the dependable power forward.

PLAYMAKING: Ah, there's the rub. Coach Larry Brown, after essentially trading youngish Johnny Dawkins for oldish Maurice Cheeks, switched plans in midstream. To New York went Maurice—never a truly happy Spur—and at the Riverwalk arrived Rod Strickland, a flashy talent with a passion to be a starter. Playing under control and thinking feed-David-first, then-take-an-option, Strickland could make this club a conference favorite this season. A key addition could be swingman Paul Pressey, who came from Milwaukee in the Brickowski deal.

DEFENSE: The presence of Robinson, who is quick enough to be active on either side of the lane, allows incredible freedom to gamble by perimeter defenders. David may not actually be everywhere, but he sure gives opponents that impression. Examples: He blocked 319 shots and scared away about half that many; San Antonio was sixth in steal-to-turnover ratio, and only Detroit and Utah were more successful in lowering opponents' FG percentage. Forget their misadventure in the playoffs. Defense will have this team back again and again.

REBOUNDING: Robinson, in his first year, trailed only Houston's Akeem Olajuwon in board work. And with the help of Cummings and occasional bursts from the wings by Anderson and Elliott, the Spurs usually accumulated three more boards a game than did their foes. So many problems does Robinson present under the board that while people are busy checking him out, he

SPUR ROSTER

No.	Veterans	Pos.	Ht.	Wt.	Age	Yrs. Pro	College
40	Willie Anderson	G-F	6-7	190	23	2	Georgia
34	Terry Cummings	F	6-9	240	29	8	DePaul
32	Sean Elliott	G-F	6-8	205	22	1	Arizona
—	David Greenwood	F	6-9	225	33	11	UCLA
20	Mike Mitchell	F	6-7	225	34	10	Auburn
00	Johnny Moore	G	6-3	185	32	9	Texas
14	Zarko Paspalj	F	6-9	220	24	1	Partizan Belgrad
—	Paul Pressey	G-F	6-5	203	31	8	Tulsa
50	David Robinson	C	7-1	235	25	1	Navy
1	Rod Strickland	G	6-3	175	24	2	DePaul
2	Reggie Williams	F	6-7	195	26	3	Georgetown
25	David Wingate	G	6-5	185	26	4	Georgetown

Rd.	Rookies	Sel. No.	Pos.	Ht.	Wt.	College
1	Dwayne Schintzius	24	C	7-1	293	Florida
2	Tony Massenburg	43	F	6-9	230	Maryland
2	Sean Higgins	54	F	6-9	195	Michigan

slips away often enough to double the ball—and he led the team in steals.

OUTLOOK: It is going to take a devastating injury or someone's fantastic blunder in judgment to mess up this team's track to the championship level. And what a nice situation for Dwayne Schintzius, if the controversial rookie brings a professional attitude along with his 7-1 wide body and 24th-pick money.

Informally, Brown and Robinson may have already discussed specific situations in which David might shift over to small forward, with Cummings at power forward and the massive Schintzius in the middle. If they haven't, they should. You're welcome.

SPUR PROFILES

DAVID ROBINSON 25 7-1 235   Center

Was he worth waiting for, or what?... No "what?" involved... In his rookie year he missed by 17 boards and seven points of posting a 2,000-point, 1,000-rebound season... Born Aug. 6, 1965, in Key West, Fla.... Entered the Naval Academy as a gangly 6-6 forward from Osbourn Park High in Manassas, Va., and left as a 7-1 All-American possessing 33 Academy records and a bachelor's degree in mathematics . . . The overall No. 1 pick in 1987 by San Antonio . . . Fulfilled two-year military obligation and played in 1988 Olympics before officially joining Spurs in May 1989 . . . Dazzled onlookers with foot speed, rejections and offensive moves in Southern California Pro Summer League and in other offseason competition . . . Started all but one game, led team in scoring, rebounding, blocked shots, minutes played . . . Tenth-leading scorer in league, second only to Akeem Olajuwon in rebounding (14.0-12.0), third to Olajuwon and Patrick Ewing in blocked shots.

Year	Team	G	FG	FG Pct.	FT	FT Pct.	Reb.	Ast.	TP	Avg.
1989-90	San Antonio	82	690	.531	613	.732	983	164	1993	24.3

WILLIE ANDERSON 23 6-7 190   Guard-Forward

Terrific young talent . . . Can play three positions but is better off avoiding the point spot, where Larry Brown once thought Willie would end up . . . Born Jan. 8, 1967, in Greenville, S.C. . . . Spurs took him 10th out of Georgia, where he had been All-Southeastern Conference as a senior . . . In 1988-89, led the team in scoring (18.6) as a rookie—a first in franchise's history . . . Named to the league's All-Rookie team . . . Call him "Chill" but not AWOL . . . He's missed only one game in his first two years . . . Again shot better than 49 percent and averaged 15.7 points while ranking second on club in assists.

Year	Team	G	FG	FG Pct.	FT	FT Pct.	Reb.	Ast.	TP	Avg.
1988-89	San Antonio	81	640	.498	224	.775	417	372	1508	18.6
1989-90	San Antonio	82	532	.492	217	.748	372	364	1288	15.7
	Totals	163	1172	.495	441	.762	789	736	2796	17.2

TERRY CUMMINGS 29 6-9 240   Forward

Mr. Consistency as a pro, and his numbers tell it every year . . . He's missed all of 25 games in eight NBA seasons . . . A pro's pro . . . Brought to San Antonio from Milwaukee before last season in trade for Spur star Alvin Robertson and the young forward-center Greg Anderson . . . Born March 15, 1961, in Chicago, Ill., and attended DePaul . . . Passed up final college season and was the second player taken overall (behind

James Worthy, ahead of Dominique Wilkins) in 1982 by San Diego . . . Spent two years with Clippers before being dealt to Milwaukee . . . Kept pace with career numbers as a Spur—22 points and more than eight rebounds . . . Pentecostal minister and evangelist, a composer and singer.

Year	Team	G	FG	FG Pct.	FT	FT Pct.	Reb.	Ast.	TP	Avg.
1982-83	San Diego	70	684	.523	292	.709	744	177	1660	23.7
1983-84	San Diego	81	737	.494	380	.720	777	139	1854	22.9
1984-85	Milwaukee	79	759	.495	343	.741	716	228	1861	23.6
1985-86	Milwaukee	82	681	.474	265	.656	694	193	1627	19.8
1986-87	Milwaukee	82	729	.511	249	.662	700	229	1707	20.8
1987-88	Milwaukee	76	675	.485	270	.665	553	181	1621	21.3
1988-89	Milwaukee	80	730	.467	362	.787	650	198	1829	22.9
1989-90	San Antonio	81	728	.475	343	.780	677	219	1818	22.4
	Totals	631	5723	.490	2504	.718	5511	1564	13977	22.2

SEAN ELLIOTT 22 6-8 205   Guard-Forward

Wasn't quite the immediate superstar some had him pre-labeled when San Antonio made him the third player picked last year . . . He'll get better and better, though . . . Debuting simultaneously with David Robinson took off a lot of the potential pressure . . . Clippers had shied away from picking him even higher because they apparently feared a long-healed knee injury . . . Started in 69 games and only missed one appearance while shooting a decent .481 and averaging 10 points a game . . . Born Feb. 2, 1968, at Tucson, Ariz., and was four times MVP at Arizona . . . Pac-10 Player of Year back-to-back and broke conference scoring record of UCLA's Lew Alcindor.

Year	Team	G	FG	FG Pct.	FT	FT Pct.	Reb.	Ast.	TP	Avg.
1989-90	San Antonio	81	311	.481	187	.866	297	154	810	10.0

ROD STRICKLAND 24 6-3 175   Guard

The young sparkplug who was supposed to put some speed into the San Antonio attack . . . Perhaps it will work out eventually . . . Was unhappy sitting on the bench . . . Made unforgivable no-look pass in final seconds of Game 7 in conference final against Portland that blew it for Spurs . . . Was unhappy sitting on the bench at New York behind Mark Jackson after a fairly productive rookie season . . . Questionable work habits prompted Knicks to send him west in exchange for Maurice Cheeks last February... Got there quickly enough not to miss a game, and he earned 24 starts as a Spur after being a sub 51 times in New York... People still question his strength and dedication... He's tired noticeably at end of first two seasons and he still is not always the most punctual guy known to man... Born July 11, 1966, in Bronx, N.Y.... Left school a year early and was drafted No. 19 by New York in 1988.

Year	Team	G	FG	FG Pct.	FT	FT Pct.	Reb.	Ast.	TP	Avg.
1988-89	New York	81	265	.467	172	.745	160	319	721	8.9
1989-90	N.Y.-S.A.	82	343	.454	174	.626	259	468	868	10.6
	Totals	163	608	.460	346	.680	419	787	1589	9.7

ZARKO PASPALJ 24 6-9 220   Forward

The pizza king of Pljevlja... He loves fast food, especially cheese and tomato pies with all the toppings... Born March 27, 1966, at Pljevlja, Montenegro, Yugoslavia... He speaks Serbian (except when ordering food, of course) and is mastering English well enough to get off on soul music and American movie comedies... An undrafted free agent, was signed by the Spurs in 1989 and became the first Yugoslavian officially under NBA contract... Big-time scorer for Partizan Belgrade and the Yugoslavian National Team... Member of his country's 1988 Olympic squad... Averaged 20 points as captain of team that won 1989 European Cup... Made one start in 28 appearances in rookie year but his .342 FG percentage earned him mostly bench time in playoffs.

Year	Team	G	FG	FG Pct.	FT	FT Pct.	Reb.	Ast.	TP	Avg.
1989-90	San Antonio	28	27	.342	18	.818	30	10	72	2.6

JOHNNY MOORE 32 6-3 185   Guard

Courageous veteran whose time may have run out... Made a comeback after spending much of two years battling a brain-affecting form of fever... Born March 3, 1958, in Altoona, Pa. ... Played at Texas and was drafted No. 43 in the second round by Seattle in 1979... Waived from the Northwest, he spent seven full seasons as a Spur... Four times in a row he averaged double-figure scoring while feeding Alvin Robertson and Mike Mitchell often enough to maintain a high-ranking assist-turnover ratio ... Felled by his illness, he was never quite the same upon return ... Played briefly with New Jersey in 1987-88 ... Re-signed by San Antonio last season, he got into 53 games, eight as a starter, but labored even worse than .373 FG, .593 FT and 2.2 ppg indicates.

Year	Team	G	FG	FG Pct.	FT	FT Pct.	Reb.	Ast.	TP	Avg.
1989-81	San Antonio	82	249	.479	105	.610	196	373	604	7.4
1981-82	San Antonio	79	309	.463	122	.670	275	762	741	9.4
1982-83	San Antonio	77	394	.468	148	.744	277	753	941	12.2
1983-84	San Antonio	59	231	.446	105	.755	178	566	595	10.1
1984-85	San Antonio	82	416	.457	189	.762	378	816	1046	12.8
1985-86	San Antonio	28	150	.495	59	.686	86	252	363	13.0
1986-87	San Antonio	55	198	.442	56	.800	100	250	474	8.6
1987-88	S.A.-N.J.	5	4	.400	0	.000	6	12	8	1.6
1989-90	San Antonio	53	47	.373	16	.593	52	82	118	2.2
	Totals	520	1998	.460	800	.712	1548	3866	4890	9.4

REGGIE WILLIAMS 26 6-7 195   Guard

A Georgetown enigma ... Born March 5, 1964, in Baltimore and heavily recruited at that city's famed Dunbar High ... As a freshman at Georgetown, he was Final Four MVP on the Hoya team that won the 1984 NCAA title ... Starred four years for John Thompson ... By end of career he was third in school scoring (to Patrick Ewing, Sleepy Floyd), rebounds and steals ... First-round pick (No. 4) in 1987 by Clippers ... Hurt most of rookie year and missed 13 games second season, averaging 10 points each time ... But shot horribly (40 percent) and his attitude was awful ... Shipped to Cleveland last season before moving on to Spurs, with whom he earned 68 minutes, no starts in 10 games ... Career FG percentage continues to plummet.

Year	Team	G	FG	FG Pct.	FT	FT Pct.	Reb.	Ast.	TP	Avg.
1987-88	L.A. Clippers	35	152	.356	48	.727	118	58	365	10.4
1988-89	L.A. Clippers	63	260	.438	92	.754	179	103	642	10.2
1989-90	LAC-Clev.-S.A.	47	131	.388	52	.765	83	53	320	6.8
	Totals	145	543	.400	192	.750	380	214	1327	9.2

PAUL PRESSEY 31 6-5 203   Guard-Forward

The glue began losing some stick'um... Long the irreplaceable element of Milwaukee's sophisticated system, he struggled all year and wound up being traded to the Spurs for Frank Brickowski... Had to accept bench role... Played 700 less minutes than previous season, fewest of career... All sorts of injuries, but biggest problem was left calf muscle......

Popularized the point-forward role under Don Nelson... Marvelous defender, good team player, generally overlooked in his career... Two-time All-Defensive first team, twice second team ... All-time leading Bucks' assist man with 3,272... Second in steals with 894... Born Dec. 24, 1958, in Richmond, Va.... Played at Tulsa and was 20th pick in 1982 draft by Bucks... Paid $800,000.

Year	Team	G	FG	FG Pct.	FT	FT Pct.	Reb.	Ast.	TP	Avg.
1982-83	Milwaukee	79	213	.457	105	.597	281	207	532	6.7
1983-84	Milwaukee	81	276	.523	120	.600	282	252	674	8.3
1984-85	Milwaukee	80	480	.517	317	.758	429	543	1284	16.1
1985-86	Milwaukee	80	411	.488	316	.806	399	623	1146	14.3
1986-87	Milwaukee	61	294	.477	242	.738	296	441	846	13.9
1987-88	Milwaukee	75	345	.491	285	.798	375	523	983	13.1
1988-89	Milwaukee	67	307	.474	187	.776	262	439	813	12.1
1989-90	Milwaukee	57	239	.472	144	.758	172	244	628	11.0
	Totals	580	2565	.490	1716	.745	2496	3272	6906	11.9

DAVID WINGATE 26 6-5 185   Guard

Another Georgetown product... Role player and occasional star for Hoyas... Born Dec. 15, 1963, in Baltimore... Chosen by Philadelphia at the No. 44 position in second round of the 1986 draft... Spent three full seasons with 76ers, mostly on the bench... Games played, minutes and scoring dropped each year... Sent with Maurice Cheeks to San Antonio in the trade for Johnny Dawkins... Made two starts in 78 games for

Spurs and averaged 6.8 points . . . Perfect bomb from three-point line: 0-for-13.

Year	Team	G	FG	FG Pct.	FT	FT Pct.	Reb.	Ast.	TP	Avg.
1986-87	Philadelphia	77	259	.430	149	.741	156	155	680	8.8
1987-88	Philadelphia	61	218	.400	99	.750	101	119	545	8.9
1988-89	Philadelphia	33	54	.470	27	.794	37	73	137	4.2
1989-90	San Antonio	78	220	.448	87	.777	195	208	527	6.8
	Totals	249	751	.428	362	.756	489	555	1889	7.6

THE ROOKIES

DWAYNE SCHINTZIUS 22 7-1 293   Center
Starting his pro career carrying heavy baggage . . . Oh, that's his waist and rump? . . . Born Oct. 14, 1968, and a prep star at Brandon, Fla., Schintzius became the so-called Brian Bosworth of college basketball because of his hair style (that's a style?) and independent thinking processes . . . Gifted prospect . . . Run-ins with coach at Florida, resignation from team and overweight appearance in postseason look-sees dropped him way down in draft . . . Among coaches claiming not to have had problems with him are USC's George Raveling and Larry Brown . . . The latter made him San Antonio's choice at No. 24.

TONY MASSENBURG 23 6-9 230   Forward
Bob Bass, the Spurs' personnel man, likes the well-built prospect's potential post-up skills . . . Larry Brown might have done a little political paying off here to buddy Gary Williams by opting to pick the second-team All-ACC teamer from Maryland this high (No. 43) . . . He was recruited from Sussex High in Richmond, Va. . . . Averaged 18.0 points, 10.1 rebounds as a senior, and left school with a degree . . . Born July 31, 1967.

SEAN HIGGINS 21 6-9 195   Forward
Early-entry candidate, and the final player selected in second round . . . Played only 72 collegiate games at Michigan . . . Might better have served himself by waiting another year . . . Ineligible after a

dozen freshman-season games, scored 12.4 and 14.0 in final two seasons . . . Reliable free-thrower, good FG shooter (.448 from three-point land) . . . Born Dec. 30, 1968, in Los Angeles, and nationally recruited at Fairfax High.

COACH LARRY BROWN: Mr. Everywhere . . . Has found a  home in San Antonio—or as long as Lt. Robinson wants to stay there? . . . Takes a bad rap in the sense that he's not the only guy who's jumped around from job to job . . . But no one's done it in more spectacular fashion or to and from more prestigious positions . . . Born Sept. 14, 1940, in Brooklyn, N.Y. . . . Played at North Carolina, in AAU ball, in the Olympics, was once MVP in an ABA All-Star Game . . . He's coached for two ABA teams, three NBA teams, been at UCLA, and didn't move to Spurs until completing five seasons at Kansas with an NCAA championship (1988) . . . After horrendous, franchise-worst 21-61 season in debut, rode/drove rookie David Robinson and rebuilt starting unit to 56-26 mark . . . NBA coaching record is 294-245 . . . Will he make Spurs even better? Will he be there when Spurs get championship-level better? Only L.B. knows.

GREATEST REBOUNDER

It's Swen Nater, that's who. So please don't pick a tiresome ABA-NBA quarrel. No bickering about what Artis Gilmore *might have* done had he spent his entire career here, what David Robinson *probably will* do in metallic silver and black.

Gilmore glommed his gaudiest stats (five straight 1,000-plus board seasons in the ABA, three more with Chicago's Bulls) before grabbing 984 here in 1982-83. That was his first (and best) as a Spur—but only one more than rookie Robinson clawed last year.

Still, Nater gave San Antonio two Swensational ABA years: he averaged 13.6 rebounds a game in 1973-74 and 16.4 in 1974-75. And got traded.

ALL-TIME SPUR LEADERS

SEASON

Points: George Gervin, 2,585, 1979-80
Assists: Johnny Moore, 816, 1984-85
Rebounds: Swen Nater, 1,279, 1974-75 (ABA)

GAME

Points: George Gervin, 63 vs. New Orleans, 4/9/78
Assists: John Lucas, 24 vs. Denver, 4/15/84
Rebounds: Manny Leaks, 35 vs. Kentucky, 11/27/70 (ABA)

CAREER

Points: George Gervin, 23,602, 1974-85
Assists: Johnny Moore, 3,663, 1980-87
Rebounds: George Gervin, 4,841, 1974-85

SEATTLE SUPERSONICS

TEAM DIRECTORY: Chairman: Barry Ackerley; Pres.: Bob Whitsitt; Dir. Pub. Rel.: Jim Rupp; Coach: K.C. Jones; Asst. Coaches: Bob Kloppenburg, Kip Motta. Arena: Seattle Center Coliseum (14,250). Colors: Green and yellow.

Sonics count on Xavier McDaniel's scoring and rebounding.

SCOUTING REPORT

SHOOTING: The decision seasons ago not to re-sign then-free-agent Tom Chambers looms larger and larger every year. Dale Ellis—who nearly killed himself in a car crash last season—still has the prettiest jumper in the league. But shot opportunities never seem to come so easily for him—or Xavier McDaniel, for that matter—as they did when Chambers was around either augmenting or leading that scoring troika.

Derrick McKey has legitimized his scoring credentials, but the Sonic guards have such a tough time getting the ball to Ellis and The X-Man that McKey has to settle for sloppy leftovers. The team almost always makes more errors than its foes (23rd in assists-to-turnovers) although Dana Barros was fourth in rookie assists and Nate McMillan finished 18th overall in feeds.

PLAYMAKING: Oregon State's Gary Payton, for all his flamboyance and preening, was the correct pick for this team at the No. 2 spot in the draft. Except for solid Sedale Threatt, virtually every Seattle point guard in the past half-dozen or so years has deferred to the demands of Ellis and McDaniel (and Chambers). Payton seems tough enough to run the show, and new head coach K.C. Jones is expected to give him backing.

DEFENSE: One very fine reason why this once-so-recently contending team dropped from 47 to 41 wins last season was because the Sonics simply did not play very well when the other team had the ball. Twenty-first in defense against FG shooting, Seattle also no longer had a protective shot-blocker after passing away Alton Lister. McKey is marvelously versatile—hedging against forwards, overpowering guards, out-quicking some centers. But most of the others too easily get caught up in you-against-me thinking and forget team concepts.

REBOUNDING: Almost four times out of 10, when Seattle misses a shot, the Sonics get another try. The official percentage of success in offensive-board chances in 1989-90 was .375. That was best in the league. (For comparison sake: the Lakers, granted a better shooting team, finished at only .328.) Michael Cage is the numerically best; the muscular forward also got help from McKey, Olden Polynice and Sean Kemp, the 20-year-old wonder child of last season.

SONIC ROSTER

No.	Veterans	Pos.	Ht.	Wt.	Age	Yrs. Pro	College
11	Dana Barros	G	5-11	163	23	1	Boston College
44	Michael Cage	C	6-9	230	28	6	San Diego State
20	Quintin Dailey	G	6-2	207	29	8	San Francisco
3	Dale Ellis	G	6-7	215	30	7	Tennessee
21	Jim Farmer	G	6-4	203	26	3	Alabama
15	Avery Johnson	G	5-11	175	25	2	Southern
40	Shawn Kemp	F	6-10	240	20	1	Trinity JC
34	Xavier McDaniel	F	6-7	205	27	5	Wichita State
31	Derrick McKey	F	6-9	210	24	3	Alabama
10	Nate McMillan	G	6-5	195	26	4	North Carolina State
50	Scott Meents	F	6-10	235	26	1	Illinois
23	Olden Polynice	C	7-0	242	25	3	Virginia
4	Sedale Threatt	G	6-2	177	29	7	W. Virginia Tech

Rd.	Rookies	Sel. No.	Pos.	Ht.	Wt.	College
1	Gary Payton	23	G	6-4	190	Oregon State
2	Abdul Shamsid-Deen	53	C	6-10	230	Providence

OUTLOOK: How smooth will be the transition from Bernie Bickerstaff, the former coach who brought in K.C. Jones as top assistant, then moved to the front office—and then split completely with Seattle to join Denver? The combination of ''rookie'' coach Jones, the Boston Hall-of-Famer, and rookie leader Payton could re-charge these still-young, but fully accredited underachievers. Jones also could make Payton and Kemp personal projects. For a youngster who never played a collegiate game, Kemp is enormously gifted in raw skill.

SUPERSONIC PROFILES

DALE ELLIS 30 6-7 215   Guard

Lucky to be alive...Racked up his 1989 Mercedes in an alcohol-related car accident last season...Missed 17 games, most while recovering from crash...Born Aug. 6, 1960, in Marietta, Ga....Starred at Tennessee and was the ninth player taken in first round by Dallas in 1983...A single-digit scorer for Mavs, who used him as a small forward off the bench... Traded to Seattle for Al Wood after 1986 season in one of most lopsided deals in NBA history...Scored 24.9 a game for Sonics in first year as starting off-guard and was NBA "Most Improved Player"... Improved average next two seasons before dropping to 23.5 last year despite one-game high of 53... Always one of league's most dangerous three-point launchers... Set NBA mark by playing 69 minutes in five-OT game vs. Milwaukee in November 1989... One of prettiest jumpers in league and especially lethal coming off screens.

Year	Team	G	FG	FG Pct.	FT	FT Pct.	Reb.	Ast.	TP	Avg.
1983-84	Dallas	67	225	.456	87	.719	250	56	549	8.2
1984-85	Dallas	72	274	.454	77	.740	238	56	667	9.3
1985-86	Dallas	72	193	.411	59	.720	168	37	508	7.1
1986-87	Seattle	82	785	.516	385	.787	447	238	2041	24.9
1987-88	Seattle	75	764	.503	303	.767	340	197	1938	25.8
1988-89	Seattle	82	857	.501	377	.816	342	164	2253	27.5
1989-90	Seattle	55	502	.497	193	.818	238	110	1293	23.5
	Totals	505	3600	.491	1481	.784	2023	858	9249	18.3

DANA BARROS 23 5-11 163   Guard

Didn't shoot well as a rookie (.405) but put some zip in Sonics in backcourt... Born April 13, 1967, in Boston... Something of a cult hero at Boston College, where he averaged 22 points a game his last two years... Despite (lack of) size he actually was the off-guard for Sonics on many occasions... Finished his collegiate career with a string intact of 70 games in which he'd made at least one three-pointer... Surprising No. 16 pick by Seattle in 1989... Got 25 starts and played in all but one game... Third on team in assists... Still shoots better off screens, but that's Dale Ellis' play.

Year	Team	G	FG	FG Pct.	FT	FT Pct.	Reb.	Ast.	TP	Avg.
1989-90	Seattle	81	299	.405	89	.809	132	205	782	9.7

XAVIER McDANIEL 27 6-7 205   Forward

Mean, artificially bald scoring machine... There's no X-factor (as in question mark) about his scoring... Should have been "official" Rookie of Year with 17.1 ppg in 1985-86... Since then, for four straight seasons he's never been below 20.5... Born June 4, 1963, in Columbia, S.C.... In 1984-85 at Wichita State, became only second man ever to lead NCAA Division I in scoring and rebounding... Was No. 4 pick overall in 1985 by Seattle . . . Explosive dunker . . . Still has most of 42-inch vertical leap despite knee surgery two summers ago . . . Lean in to fend off his deadly jumper and he'll spin, drive and dunk . . . Played 68 minutes vs. Bucks in last November's five-overtimer . . . Teammates call him "Half Dead." . . . You shouldn't.

Year	Team	G	FG	FG Pct.	FT	FT Pct.	Reb.	Ast.	TP	Avg.
1985-86	Seattle	82	576	.490	250	.687	655	193	1404	17.1
1986-87	Seattle	82	806	.509	275	.696	705	207	1890	23.0
1987-88	Seattle	78	687	.488	281	.715	518	263	1669	21.4
1988-89	Seattle	82	677	.489	312	.732	433	134	1677	20.5
1989-90	Seattle	69	611	.496	244	.733	447	171	1471	21.3
	Totals	393	3357	.495	1362	.713	2758	968	8111	20.6

OLDEN POLYNICE 25 7-0 242   Center

Olden, pal, it's getting to be a tired golden oldie routine . . . Triple-P package: power, Polynice, potential . . . Has yet to advance beyond club's own proclaimed super-prospect stage . . . Born Nov. 21, 1964, in Port-Au-Prince, Haiti . . . Played high-school ball in the Bronx, New York . . . Finished college shopping at Virginia, where he was successor to Ralph Sampson . . .
Left school after three years and completed for Rimini in Italy . . . Chicago's pick at No. 8 as 1987 undergrad . . . His and other draft rights were shipped to Seattle by Bulls for rights to Scottie Pippen . . . Hard worker earned seven starts in 79 games last season and lifted shooting to .540 FG . . . Without a clue at foul line . . . Still young but should be better at this stage.

Year	Team	G	FG	FG Pct.	FT	FT Pct.	Reb.	Ast.	TP	Avg.
1987-88	Seattle	82	118	.465	101	.639	330	33	337	4.1
1988-89	Seattle	80	91	.506	51	.593	206	21	233	2.9
1989-90	Seattle	79	156	.540	47	.475	300	15	360	4.6
	Totals	241	365	.505	199	.580	836	69	930	3.9

AVERY JOHNSON 25 5-11 175   Guard

Swift, pesky guard who knows the game . . . Size and defense probably too much to overcome, though . . . Born March 25, 1965, in New Orleans . . . Attended New Mexico JC and Cameron College in Oklahoma before starring two seasons at Southern University . . . Led Division I in assists both years . . . Unselected in 1988 draft . . . Free agent made Seattle roster in

successive camps . . . A terrible shooter . . . But he has neat career
assist-turnover ratio of 235-66.

Year	Team	G	FG	FG Pct.	FT	FT Pct.	Reb.	Ast.	TP	Avg.
1988-89	Seattle	43	29	.349	9	.563	24	73	68	1.6
1989-90	Seattle	53	55	.387	29	.725	43	162	140	2.6
	Totals	96	84	.373	38	.679	67	235	208	2.2

MICHAEL CAGE 28 6-9 230 — Forward

Played mostly at center last season after five
years at power forward—four for Clippers and
one with Sonics . . . Admits he had "a hard
time" adjusting but can rebound with anyone
. . . Mr. Muscle . . . A health-food nut who has
one of NBA's best-sculpted bodies . . . Only
SuperSonic to start 82 games last season . . .
Shot .504, right around his career FG percent-
age . . . His 10 rebounds a game placed him ninth in NBA after
having been 10th and first previous two years . . . Born Jan. 28,
1962, in West Memphis, Ark. . . . All-time scoring and rebounding
leader when he left San Diego State . . . The 14th player taken in
the first round of 1984 draft by the Clippers.

Year	Team	G	FG	FG Pct.	FT	FT Pct.	Reb.	Ast.	TP	Avg.
1984-85	L.A. Clippers	75	216	.543	101	.737	392	51	533	7.1
1985-86	L.A. Clippers	78	204	.479	113	.649	417	81	521	6.7
1986-87	L.A. Clippers	80	457	.521	341	.730	922	131	1255	15.7
1987-88	L.A. Clippers	72	360	.470	326	.688	938	110	1046	14.5
1988-89	Seattle	80	314	.498	197	.743	765	126	825	10.3
1989-90	Seattle	82	325	.504	148	.698	821	70	798	9.7
	Totals	467	1876	.501	1226	.709	4255	569	4978	10.7

DERRICK McKEY 24 6-9 210 — Forward

Best all-around player on Sonics for two seasons now . . . Not bad for a player without a
position . . . Actually, he's got a lot of positions—both forward spots on offense, and center and big guard on defense . . . Born Oct. 10,
1966, in Meridian, Miss. . . . Early entry in
1987 after improving his numbers and game
each of three years at Alabama . . . Seattle took
him at No. 9 . . . Didn't miss a game first two seasons and started
80 last year . . . More ardent boosters insist he's a taller Dennis
Rodman who can score . . . He always shoots around 50 percent
from field and is more than respectable at foul line . . . Denial isn't

strongest part of his defense yet, but he'll gamble for steals and also block shots.

Year	Team	G	FG	FG Pct.	FT	FT Pct.	Reb.	Ast.	TP	Avg.
1987-88	Seattle	82	255	.491	173	.772	328	107	694	8.5
1988-89	Seattle	82	487	.502	301	.803	464	219	1305	15.9
1989-90	Seattle	80	468	.493	315	.782	489	187	1254	15.7
	Totals	244	1210	.496	789	.787	1281	513	3253	13.3

SHAWN KEMP 20 6-10 240   Forward-Center

Mobile behemoth . . . Became first NBA teenager since Cliff Robinson left USC early to play for Nets in 1979 . . . Born Nov. 26, 1969, in Elkhart, Ind. . . . Grew four inches between eighth and ninth grades . . . Altogether, grew 13 inches in 15 months . . . Target of Indiana-Kentucky recruiting war . . . Opted for latter but then dropped out . . . Played very little for Trinity Valley (Tex.) JC . . . Seattle picked him 17th as a roll of the dice in 1989 first round . . . Played 81 games for Sonics, fouled out five times, but showed raw interior skills and nice outside touch . . . Blocked 70 shots, second on club to Derrick McKey's 81.

Year	Team	G	FG	FG Pct.	FT	FT Pct.	Reb.	Ast.	TP	Avg.
1989-90	Seattle	81	203	.479	117	.736	346	26	525	6.5

QUINTIN DAILEY 29 6-2 207   Guard

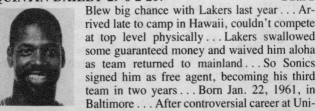

Blew big chance with Lakers last year . . . Arrived late to camp in Hawaii, couldn't compete at top level physically . . . Lakers swallowed some guaranteed money and waived him aloha as team returned to mainland . . . So Sonics signed him as free agent, becoming his third team in two years . . . Born Jan. 22, 1961, in Baltimore . . . After controversial career at University of San Francisco, was chosen seventh by Chicago in the first round of 1982 . . . Now he's just hanging on . . . Proven scorer (15.3 career before last season), he missed six of every 10 shots for Seattle and averaged 8.2 points in 30 games, two of them starts . . . Due to past drug and other problems, his dependability factor has frustrated coaches, management and fellow players.

Year	Team	G	FG	FG Pct.	FT	FT Pct.	Reb.	Ast.	TP	Avg.
1982-83	Chicago	76	470	.466	206	.730	260	280	1151	15.1
1983-84	Chicago	82	583	.474	321	.811	235	254	1491	18.2
1984-85	Chicago	79	525	.473	205	.817	208	191	1262	16.0
1985-86	Chicago	35	203	.432	163	.823	68	67	569	16.3
1986-87	L.A. Clippers	49	200	.407	119	.768	83	79	520	10.6
1987-88	L.A. Clippers	67	328	.434	243	.776	154	109	901	13.4
1988-89	L.A. Clippers	69	448	.465	217	.759	204	154	1114	16.1
1989-90	Seattle	30	97	.404	52	.788	51	34	247	8.2
	Totals	487	2854	.455	1526	.784	1263	1168	7255	14.9

NATE McMILLAN 26 6-5 195   Guard

Given a reasonable shot at running Sonics, but wasn't answer to lead-guard spot . . . Shows flashes of great ability with quickness and long arms . . . A nice enough fellow, after four NBA seasons he's still just a "nice" player . . . Born Aug. 3, 1964, in Raleigh, N.C. . . . Split collegiate career between Chowan (N.C.) College and N.C. State . . . Second-round choice at No. 30 by Seattle in 1986 . . . After being ranked seventh, sixth and fifth in league assists first three seasons, was 18th in 1989-90 . . . Team co-captain . . . Diligent defender and opportunistic rebounder . . . Hasn't approached 50 percent from field in a season since second year at Chowan College.

Year	Team	G	FG	FG Pct.	FT	FT Pct.	Reb.	Ast.	TP	Avg.
1986-87	Seattle	71	143	.475	87	.617	331	583	373	5.3
1987-88	Seattle	82	235	.474	145	.707	338	702	624	7.6
1988-89	Seattle	75	199	.410	119	.630	388	696	532	7.1
1989-90	Seattle	82	207	.473	98	.641	403	598	523	6.4
	Totals	310	784	.456	449	.653	1460	2579	2052	6.6

SEDALE THREATT 29 6-2 177   Guard

Ongoing personal success story . . . Never going to be a superstar, but he's already carved out a fine, seven-year pro career . . . Born Sept. 10, 1961, in Atlanta . . . Labored almost anonymously at West Virginia Institute of Technology . . . There were 158 players tapped in 1983 before Philadelphia named him in sixth round . . . Wherever he's been—Philly, Chicago, Seattle—club usually contends for playoff spot . . . A no-

nonsense defender ... Averaged double-figure scoring last season for first time ... Not much flair, but makes the basic plays and keeps turnovers within reason.

Year	Team	G	FG	FG Pct.	FT	FT Pct.	Reb.	Ast.	TP	Avg.
1983-84	Philadelphia	45	62	.419	23	.821	40	41	148	3.3
1984-85	Philadelphia	82	188	.452	66	.733	99	175	446	5.4
1985-86	Philadelphia	70	310	.453	75	.833	121	193	696	9.9
1986-87	Phil.-Chi.	68	239	.448	95	.798	108	259	580	8.5
1987-88	Chi.-Sea.	71	216	.508	57	.803	88	160	492	6.9
1988-89	Seattle	63	235	.494	63	.818	117	238	544	8.6
1989-90	Seattle	65	303	.506	130	.828	115	216	744	11.4
	Totals	464	1553	.473	509	.805	688	1282	3650	7.9

JIM FARMER 26 6-4 203   Guard

Makings of a journeyman ... Nothing flashy, just a decent fundamental performer ... Born Sept. 23, 1964, in Dothan, Ala. ... Starred at Alabama and opened eyes of pro scouts at the Aloha Classic ... Dallas made him the 20th player taken in first round of 1987 ... Waived by Mavs after unproductive rookie season, signed following November as free agent with Utah ... Jazz put him on expansion list after 412 minutes, 152 points ... Charlotte claimed him, didn't use him, and it was off to Seattle ... Next stop?

Year	Team	G	FG	FG Pct.	FT	FT Pct.	Reb.	Ast.	TP	Avg.
1987-88	Dallas	30	26	.377	9	.900	18	16	61	2.0
1988-89	Utah	37	57	.401	29	.707	55	28	152	4.1
1989-90	Seattle	38	89	.438	57	.713	43	25	243	6.4
	Totals	105	172	.415	95	.725	116	69	456	4.3

THE ROOKIES

GARY PAYTON 22 6-4 190   Guard

His middle name is not Bashful ... Took second place (to Bo Kimble) in last June's TV One-on-One contest, earned $50,000— and called it "chump change" for summer ... Frequently irritated Pac-10 fans and Oregon State opponents with cocky attitude ... More often than not backed up his flamboyance, although he and team faltered late in senior year ... Second on NCAA list for career steals and assists ... Seattle made him the No. 2 pick and probably will immediately put him at the point . . . Born July 23, 1968, in Oakland.

ABDUL SHAMSID-DEEN 22 6-10 230   Center

Penultimate pick by Seattle at No. 53 . . . He only made the varsity two years in high school, and if Shamsid-Deen makes THIS club, the SuperSonics are in deep trouble . . . In a center-poor draft, he didn't get a line in an extensive NBA pre-selection media guide . . . Born Aug. 1, 1968, in Tottenville, N.Y. . . . Shot .508 at Providence, where his one-game highs were 16 points, 15 rebounds, five blocks . . . Drew attention at Portsmouth Invitation tryout week, averaging 16 points and 16.5 boards.

COACH K.C. JONES: Player, coach, champion, saloon singer . . . Replaces old buddy, ex-employer/employee, Bernie Bickerstaff . . . Born May 25, 1932, in San Francisco . . . Guard on Bill Russell's USF 1955-56 NCAA champs . . . Olympic gold medal in 1956 . . . Celtics won NBA title eight times in second-round pick's nine years . . . Had first taste of coaching in 1968 at Brandeis University . . . Spent a year with ABA's San Diego Conquistadors before becoming bench boss of then-NBA Capital Bullets, where he hired Bickerstaff as assistant . . . Eventually took over at Boston, where he won NBA championship in his first year . . . "Retiring" from coaching several years ago under pressure, he became a Boston front-office nobody . . . Summoned by offer to become "consultant" on Aug. 15, 1989, by his pal, Bickerstaff, nine months later he became boss following Bernie's stress-related resignation . . . Was assistant to Bill Sharman in 1971 when 33-straight-win Lakers took NBA title.

GREATEST REBOUNDER

For long moments during special nights—of which he had many—he ruled the sky. Spencer Haywood often was a functioning Stealth Bomber.

Signed by the ABA after 24 games at the University of Detroit, he was a 6-9, 20-year-old terror in 1969-70 for Denver. He averaged 30 points and 19.5 boards, both league bests. He was Rookie of the Year and league MVP.

He jumped immediately to the NBA, eventually playing 12 seasons for five teams. Beginning at Seattle, he led the club in scoring and rebounding four successive times. And only Marvin Webster and Jack Sikma have had seasons remotely close to Haywood's three-year 13.0 average starting in 1971-72.

ALL-TIME SUPERSONIC LEADERS

SEASON

Points: Spencer Haywood, 2,251, 1972-73
Assists: Lenny Wilkens, 766, 1971-72
Rebounds: Jack Sikma, 1,038, 1981-82

GAME

Points: Fred Brown, 58 vs. Golden State, 3/23/74
Assists: Nate McMillan, 25 vs. LA Clippers, 2/23/87
Rebounds: Jim Fox, 30 vs. Los Angeles, 12/26/73

CAREER

Points: Fred Brown, 14,018, 1971-84
Assists: Fred Brown, 3,160, 1971-84
Rebounds: Jack Sikma, 7,729, 1977-86

UTAH JAZZ

TEAM DIRECTORY: Owner: Larry H. Miller; Pres.: Frank Layden; GM: R. Tim Howells; Dir. Player Personnel: Scott Layden; VP/Pub. Rel.: David Allred; Dir. Media Services: Kim Turner; Coach: Jerry Sloan; Asst. Coaches: Phil Johnson, Scott Layden, David Fredman, Gordon Chiesa. Arena: Salt Lake Palace (12,444). Colors: Purple, gold and green.

Karl Malone had a 61-point game and career-high 31 ppg.

SCOUTING REPORT

SHOOTING: What should happen when you have a guy who's tall enough to dunk on tippy-toes and another mobile mass of muscle so dependable that people with long, distorted memories of a once-efficient Postal Service call him Mailman because he delivers, and also have the league's best pure passer? You should shoot, oh, about .505 as a team. Which the Jazz—yawn—did last year, the best mark in the league.

For his career, Mark Eaton had shot something around .440. Last year it was .527. Why? Maybe because, at 7-4, he managed to put up all of 3.7 shots a game. The Mailman of course is Karl Malone, who scored 61 points in a game last winter but again didn't win the scoring championship because Michael Jordan is a contemporary. John Stockton isn't as inventive as Magic Johnson, nor is he as flashy off the dribble as Kevin Johnson. But no one throws a more catchable, score-producing pass.

PLAYMAKING: See above. That's no joke. The Jazz trying to get a decent shot without Stockton on the floor? Now, there's a joke. Utah, which goes about 7½ players deep on most nights, produced 2,212 assists collectively last season. Stockton's share was 1,134. If the NBA were a bread line and Stockton called in sick, 11 teammates would starve to death.

DEFENSE: With Eaton—who in his best years is an illegal defense—the Jazz play sideways defense, attempting to make every drive an adventure into Mark Lane. Twice the NBA Defensive Player of the Year, Eaton blocked only 201 shots last season. But small forwards and shooting guards know he's there and pull up for off-balance jumpers. Few power forwards or centers can overwhelm him with force.

Result: Opponents shot .455 FG against Utah last year; only Detroit, using a different style, did better. Of the teams annually mentioned for possible championship play, this is probably the slowest of foot. A quicker supporting cast, knowing Eaton is behind and waiting, wouldn't be ranked 20th in steals-to-turnovers.

REBOUNDING: Probably the most skilled player of his size in the league, Malone does most of Utah's important rebounding. Eaton mostly stands around and collects loose change, which is

JAZZ ROSTER

No.	Veterans	Pos.	Ht.	Wt.	Age	Yrs. Pro	College
41	Thurl Bailey	F	6-11	232	29	7	North Carolina St.
40	Mike Brown	F	6-9	260	27	4	George Washington
43	Raymond Brown	F	6-8	230	25	1	Idaho
53	Mark Eaton	C	7-4	290	33	8	UCLA
30	Theodore Edwards	G	6-5	200	25	1	East Carolina
35	Darrell Griffith	G	6-4	195	32	10	Louisville
15	Eric Johnson	G	6-2	205	24	1	Nebraska
24	Jeff Malone	G	6-4	205	29	7	Mississippi State
32	Karl Malone	F	6-9	256	27	5	Louisiana Tech
11	Delaney Rudd	G	6-2	195	28	1	Wake Forest
12	John Stockton	G	6-1	175	28	6	Gonzaga

Rd.	Rookies	Sel. No.	Pos.	Ht.	Wt.	College
2	Walter Palmer	33	C	7-1	215	Dartmouth

not a bad way to get it done. Mike Brown, who refuses to be outworked despite a lack of basic talent, is the most tenacious board cleaner among some impressive company. Bereft of first-round picks, Jerry Sloan selected Walter Palmer with the 33d pick in the draft. Palmer, of course, is the greatest 7-2 center in Dartmouth history.

OUTLOOK: Sloan coaxed four more wins out of this club than it had produced the previous year, when he had picked up the reins early in the season after Frank Layden's resignation to become a full-time golfer/humorist and part-time check-collector. But the Jazz flamed out in the playoffs—again. Too slow, too slow, too slow.

Also, Thurl Bailey looked better coming off the bench and the Jazz are still uncertain at off-guard. Someone has to pull the trigger here and infuse some new blood. Allow Stockton and Malone to run the floor at will and not have to pull up, waiting for Eaton to join the fun or posture himself near the scorer's table, signaling for an illegal-defense call because people for some reason refuse to guard him a half-mile from the hoop.

JAZZ PROFILES

KARL MALONE 27 6-9 256   Forward

Needs a new personal marketing manager... The "Mailman" nickname is outdated... If deliveries were as consistent as this guy's, there'd be fewer complaints about the U.S. Postal Service... A league superstar... His numbers keep getting more impressive and, generally speaking, larger every season... Born July 24, 1963, at Summerfield, La....
Stock ebbed and flowed his junior year at Louisiana Tech, and when he went into the draft he dropped all the way to No. 13... Not an unlucky number in 1985 for Utah, ecstatic at chance to select him... Third in Rookie of Year voting, he's since been an automatic All-Star (and an All-Star Game MVP once)... Led the Jazz in minutes, shooting, rebounding, scoring again last season... Despite a 61-point game and a 31-point average, finished second in league scoring for second year in row to Michael Jordan... Positive influence on teammates, and almost always is affable to fans and cooperative with media.

Year	Team	G	FG	FG Pct.	FT	FT Pct.	Reb.	Ast.	TP	Avg.
1985-86	Utah	81	504	.496	195	.481	718	236	1203	14.9
1986-87	Utah	82	728	.512	323	.598	855	158	1779	21.7
1987-88	Utah	82	858	.520	552	.700	986	199	2268	27.7
1988-89	Utah	80	809	.519	703	.766	853	219	2326	29.1
1989-90	Utah	82	914	.562	696	.762	911	226	2540	31.0
	Totals	407	3813	.524	2469	.693	4323	1038	10116	24.9

JOHN STOCKTON 28 6-1 175   Guard

Feeds the hungry and not-so-hungry nightly... Old-timers yap that modern statisticians are too generous, but Stockton's assists are there to see and recount on tape... One of three different players to go over the 1,000-feed mark in a season... Stockton did it himself for the third straight time last season... Broke his own league mark (1,134, six more than in 1987-88) even though he missed four full games to injury... Born March

26, 1962, in Spokane, Wash. . . . Somewhat of a surprise and controversial pick at No. 16 out of Gonzaga in 1984 by Jazz . . . He's a career .500-plus FG and .800-plus FT shooter, and, along with keeping taller friends fed with passes for layups, he's elevated his double-figure scoring three years in a row.

Year	Team	G	FG	FG Pct.	FT	FT Pct.	Reb.	Ast.	TP	Avg.
1984-85	Utah	82	157	.471	142	.736	105	415	458	5.6
1985-86	Utah	82	228	.489	172	.839	179	610	630	7.7
1986-87	Utah	82	231	.499	179	.782	151	670	648	7.9
1987-88	Utah	82	454	.574	272	.840	237	1128	1204	14.7
1988-89	Utah	82	497	.538	390	.863	248	1118	1400	17.1
1989-90	Utah	78	472	.514	354	.819	206	1134	1345	17.2
	Totals	488	2039	.524	1509	.822	1126	5075	5685	11.6

THURL BAILEY 29 6-11 232   Forward

"The 6th Man Theme" is no longer the Jazz answer to "Name That Bailey Tune" . . . The game-plan scenario apparently has been re-written . . . The tall and elegantly striding Mr. T. got 33 starts last year and played more minutes than all teammates except Karl Malone and John Stockton . . . Dangerous open-court player, aggressive as shooter and rebounder from corners . . . Scoring average dropped off somewhat with changing role . . . Second on club in offensive rebounds and in blocks (rejecting twice as many as the fearsome Mailman) . . . Born April 7, 1961, in Washington, D.C. . . . Served as page in Congress during high-school years . . . Starred on the 1983 NCAA championship North Carolina State team . . . Jazz made him the No. 7 man taken in the 1983 draft . . . He's a musician (tuba, trombone and sax) and he's had several recordings played on Salt Lake City area stations.

Year	Team	G	FG	FG Pct.	FT	FT Pct.	Reb.	Ast.	TP	Avg.
1983-84	Utah	81	302	.512	88	.752	464	129	692	8.5
1984-85	Utah	80	507	.490	197	.842	525	138	1212	15.2
1985-86	Utah	82	483	.448	230	.830	493	153	1196	14.6
1986-87	Utah	81	463	.447	190	.805	432	102	1116	13.8
1987-88	Utah	82	633	.492	337	.826	531	158	1604	19.6
1988-89	Utah	82	615	.483	363	.825	447	138	1595	19.5
1989-90	Utah	82	470	.481	222	.779	410	137	1162	14.2
	Totals	570	3473	.478	1627	.815	3302	955	8577	15.0

MARK EATON 33 7-4 290   Center

Dropped to sixth in shots blocked (2.45 a game), but he's still the league's immovable object... Said journeyman forward Jay Vincent last year: "Shooting over Mark Eaton is like shooting over two helicopters, plus he's thick in the middle."... You can't teach height, his former coach, Frank Layden, always argued... But it took eight seasons (he did it last year) for Eaton to make more than half his shots, against his previous career .440 FG... Born Jan. 24, 1957, at Westminster, Cal.... Didn't go directly to college... Became bench-sitter at UCLA after transferring from Cypress, and then became an auto mechanic... Drafted twice, but only second one counted—by Utah as 72d pick in fourth round in 1982... Started each game in 1989-90 for third straight season but played fewest minutes since second year in pros.

Year	Team	G	FG	FG Pct.	FT	FT Pct.	Reb.	Ast.	TP	Avg.
1982-83	Utah	81	146	.414	59	.656	462	112	351	4.3
1983-84	Utah	82	194	.466	73	.593	595	113	461	5.6
1984-85	Utah	82	302	.449	190	.712	927	124	794	9.7
1985-86	Utah	80	277	.470	122	.604	675	101	676	8.5
1986-87	Utah	79	234	.400	140	.657	697	101	608	7.7
1987-88	Utah	82	226	.418	119	.623	717	55	571	7.0
1988-89	Utah	82	188	.462	132	.660	843	83	508	6.2
1989-90	Utah	82	158	.527	79	.669	601	39	395	4.8
	Totals	650	1725	.446	914	.651	5517	732	4364	6.7

JEFF MALONE 29 6-4 205   Guard

Hard as sponge, tough as crepe paper... That has always been the rap on a guy who can shoot with the best of them... Forever rumored in trade talks, was finally packaged just prior to 1990 draft to Utah in three-way deal involving Sacramento... Superb middle-distance shooter, also has rep for not hitting clutch shots... Was object of Bullets coach Wes Unseld's undisguised digs, but overall probably had his best season... Improved defensively... Michael Jordan scored 40 against every non-expansion team except Bullets, so that says something... Led team scoring for third straight year... Had 16 games of 30 or more points... Second all-time scorer in Bullet history...

First-round pick by Washington in 1983 out of Mississippi State
. . . Born June 28, 1961, in Mobile, Ala. . . . Earned $1.2 million.

Year	Team	G	FG	FG Pct.	FT	FT Pct.	Reb.	Ast.	TP	Avg.
1983-84	Washington	81	408	.444	142	.826	155	151	982	12.1
1984-85	Washington	76	605	.499	211	.844	206	184	1436	18.9
1985-86	Washington	80	735	.483	322	.868	288	191	1795	22.4
1986-87	Washington	80	689	.457	376	.885	218	298	1758	22.0
1987-88	Washington	80	648	.476	335	.882	206	237	1641	20.5
1988-89	Washington	76	677	.480	296	.871	179	219	1651	21.7
1989-90	Washington	75	781	.491	257	.877	206	243	1820	24.3
	Totals	548	4543	.477	1939	.869	1458	1523	11083	20.2

THEODORE (BLUE) EDWARDS 25 6-5 200   Guard

Had an admirable rookie year for a guy plucked
from virtual obscurity late in first round . . .
Born Oct. 31, 1965, in Washington, D.C. . . .
Former high-school high jumper . . . Performed
two of three years at East Carolina after a junior
college internship . . . Caught eye of Jazz with
.555 career shooting percentage and 26.7-point
scoring in senior year, the latter figure sixth-
best in nation . . . Picked 21st in 1989 by Utah . . . Earned 49 starts
and 23 minutes a game, appearing in all 82 . . . Not a bad rebounder
at the off-guard spot and probably is the man of the now-and-
future at that position for Jazz.

Year	Team	G	FG	FG Pct.	FT	FT Pct.	Reb.	Ast.	TP	Avg.
1989-90	Utah	82	286	.507	146	.719	251	145	727	8.9

DARRELL GRIFFITH 32 6-4 195   Guard

Has lost more than a step of quickness and
several inches from his once-great dunking
leap, but has not misplaced his shooting touch
. . . Made 80 of 215 attempts from beyond arc
for .372—best of his career for a twice NBA
three-point champion . . . Failed to average
double figures last season for first time in career
. . . But he actually shot better than at anytime
since losing the entire 1985-86 season with broken bone in foot
. . . Born June 16, 1958, in Louisville, Ky. . . . The 1980 College
Player of Year, he led Louisville to NCAA crown . . . Was known
as Dr. Dunkenstein . . . Picked No. 2 overall by Jazz (Joe Barry

Carroll was first) in 1980 draft and became 1981 Rookie of Year.

Year	Team	G	FG	FG Pct.	FT	FT Pct.	Reb.	Ast.	TP	Avg.
1980-81	Utah	81	716	.464	229	.716	288	194	1671	20.6
1981-82	Utah	80	689	.482	189	.697	305	187	1582	19.8
1982-83	Utah	77	752	.484	167	.679	304	270	1709	22.2
1983-84	Utah	82	697	.490	151	.696	338	283	1636	20.0
1984-85	Utah	78	728	.457	216	.725	344	243	1764	22.6
1985-86	Utah					Injured				
1986-87	Utah	76	463	.446	149	.703	227	129	1142	15.0
1987-88	Utah	52	251	.429	59	.641	127	91	589	11.3
1988-89	Utah	82	466	.446	142	.780	330	130	1135	13.8
1989-90	Utah	82	301	.464	51	.654	166	63	733	8.9
	Totals	690	5063	.466	1353	.706	2429	1590	11961	17.3

ERIC JOHNSON 24 6-2 205   Guard

Microwave's little brother . . . Free agent out of Nebraska who made team on hustle and grit . . . Got a chance to start twice when John Stockton was injured . . . Born Feb. 7, 1966, in Brooklyn, N.Y. . . . Played two seasons at Baylor and then transferred to Nebraska . . . Mostly a passer and ballhawk in college, although he twice scored more than 30 for Cornhuskers . . . Unselected in the two-round draft of 1989 and signed as a free-agent support player by personnel director Scott Layden . . . Averaged 5.7 minutes, 1.1 points and shot .238 FG in 48 first-year appearances.

Year	Team	G	FG	FG Pct.	FT	FT Pct.	Reb.	Ast.	TP	Avg.
1989-90	Utah	48	20	.238	13	.765	28	64	54	1.1

MIKE BROWN 27 6-9 260   Center-Forward

A bright young fellow and a mountain of persistence . . . Has become regular part of frontcourt rotation for Jerry Sloan, who doesn't believe in saving personal fouls for some other game . . . Born July 9, 1963, at Newark, N.J. . . . Played at George Washington University, where he mostly overpowered people with his bulk and from which he graduated in 3½ years . . . School's No. 2 career scorer and rebounder . . . His weight and a toe injury that messed up his senior year dropped his value as Chicago took him on the 69th spot in 1985 draft . . . Didn't like the money or roster prospects and played first pro season in Italy.

... Played two years for Bulls after that and then was exposed to expansion ... Claimed by Charlotte, he was packaged in the trade to Utah for Kelly Tripucka ... Made 82 appearances last year for first time and had career-high in minutes played, 17 a contest.

Year	Team	G	FG	FG Pct.	FT	FT Pct.	Reb.	Ast.	TP	Avg.
1986-87	Chicago	62	106	.527	46	.639	214	24	258	4.2
1987-88	Chicago	46	78	.448	41	.577	159	28	197	4.3
1988-89	Utah	66	104	.419	92	.708	258	41	300	4.5
1989-90	Utah	82	177	.515	157	.789	373	47	512	6.2
	Totals	256	465	.481	336	.712	1004	140	1267	4.9

DELANEY RUDD 28 6-2 195   Guard

Went three full seasons between being drafted and playing a minute in the league ... Born Nov. 8, 1962 ... Played high-school ball in Hollister, N.C., before attending Wake Forest ... Was passed over in the 1985 draft until fourth round ... Utah took a flyer on him with 83rd pick ... Cut by Jazz, he kicked around both the CBA and USBL ... Became a scoring star in Greece ... Milwaukee made him a late-camp cut before last season and he got second chance with Jazz ... Played 77 games and started twice for Utah and assists doubled his turnovers while averaging 3.5 points.

Year	Team	G	FG	FG Pct.	FT	FT Pct.	Reb.	Ast.	TP	Avg.
1989-90	Utah	77	111	.429	35	.660	55	177	273	3.5

RAYMOND BROWN 25 6-8 230   Forward

A rookie last year, he went unselected in draft ... Born July 5, 1965, in Atlanta ... Began his college career at Mississippi State, finished at Idaho ... Averaged 16.1 points as a junior, 15.5 as a senior and made All-Big Sky in final year ... After free-agent tryout with Jazz, was cut ... He played with Rapid City in the CBA before Utah re-signed him as bench insurance ... Scored a point a game in 56 minutes of 16 appearances.

Year	Team	G	FG	FG Pct.	FT	FT Pct.	Reb.	Ast.	TP	Avg.
1989-90	Utah	16	8	.286	0	.000	15	4	16	1.0

THE ROOKIE

WALTER PALMER 22 7-1 215   **Center**
Project center at No. 33 to replace traded Eric Leckner on bench
... First thing Jazz did when the slender youngster arrived in Salt
Lake City after draft was lead him to weight room ... Would like
to compete eventually at around 240 or 245 ... Lots of luck ...
Born Oct. 23, 1968, in Lexington, Va. ... Played four years at
Dartmouth ... Last season led the team in scoring (16.5), re-
bounding (6.5) and was 10th in nation (3.0) in shot-blocking
average ... Made All-Ivy team ... His dad and Rudy LaRusso
were Dartmouth teammates.

COACH JERRY SLOAN: The working-man's hero ...
Coaches the way he played: for 48 minutes,
intensely ... Took over 17 games into the
1988-89 season when Frank Layden abruptly
resigned ... Former Division II All-American
at Evansville, he went 40-25 with Jazz and took
Midwest Division title ... Last year, in his first
full season, Utah was an impressive 55-27, but
again bottomed up in playoffs—a disturbing
Jazz trend ... Born March 14, 1946, in Louis-
ville, Ky. ... Sloan had marvelous 11-year pro career (1965-76),
the statistics of which (14 ppg, for example) don't do him justice
... Four times was elected to NBA All-Defensive team ... Entered coaching at Chicago in 1979, but went 94-121 and was fired
in 1982, his third season ... Turned to scouting, joined Jazz as
an on-bench aide ... Could be in trouble if seasons keep ending
in May ... NBA coaching record is 181-173.

GREATEST REBOUNDER

Monument to self at 7-4, Mark Eaton stands amidst Utah's
defense. Eaton capitalized, by hard work and on the glandular

aberration, and has gained renown as a shot-blocker and collector of middle rebounds.

Many Eaton efforts, however, are brushed aside—not always softly—by Karl Malone. The Mailman stands 6-9, weighs 256 pounds, and doesn't limit himself to *collecting*.

Malone seeks, entices, harvests errors. Last season he averaged 11.1 boards per game, fourth in the league. Prior averages back to rookie year: 10.7, 12.0, 10.4, 8.9.

ALL-TIME JAZZ LEADERS

SEASON

Points: Karl Malone, 2,540, 1989-90
Assists: John Stockton, 1,134, 1989-90
Rebounds: Len Robinson, 1,288, 1977-78

GAME

Points: Pete Maravich, 68 vs. New York, 2/25/77
Assists: John Stockton, 26 vs. Portland, 4/14/88
Rebounds: Len Robinson, 27 vs. Los Angeles, 11/11/77

CAREER

Points: Adrian Dantley, 13,545, 1979-86
Assists: John Stockton, 5,075, 1984-90
Rebounds: Mark Eaton, 5,517, 1982-90

1990 NBA COLLEGE DRAFT

Sel. No.	Team	Name	College	Ht.
	FIRST ROUND			
1.	New Jersey	Derrick Coleman	Syracuse	6-10
2.	Seattle	Gary Payton	Oregon State	6-4
3.	Denver (from Miami)	Chris Jackson	LSU	6-1
4.	Orlando	Dennis Scott	Georgia Tech	6-8

Seattle made Oregon State's Gary Payton No. 2 in draft.

Sel. No.	Team	Name	College	Ht.
5.	Charlotte	Kendall Gill	Illinois	6-4
6.	Minnesota	Felton Spencer	Louisville	7-0
7.	Sacramento	Lionel Simmons	La Salle	6-8
8.	LA Clippers	Bo Kimble	Loyola Marymount	6-3
9.	Miami (from Washington via Dallas & Denver)	Willie Burton	Minnesota	6-6
10.	Atlanta (from Golden State)	Rumeal Robinson	Michigan	6-2
11.	Golden State (from Atlanta)	Tyrone Hill	Xavier	6-10
12.	a-Houston	Alec Kessler	Georgia	6-11
13.	LA Clippers (from Cleveland)	Loy Vaught	Michigan	6-9
14.	Sacramento (from Indiana via Dallas)	Travis Mays	Texas	6-2
15.	b-Miami (from Denver)	Dave Jamerson	Ohio	6-5
16.	c-Milwaukee	Terry Mills	Michigan	6-10

a-Rights traded to Miami
b-Rights traded to Houston
c-Traded to Denver

Orlando went for Georgia Tech's Dennis Scott as No. 4.

Sel. No.	Team	Name	College	Ht.
17.	New York	Jerrod Mustaf	Maryland	6-10
18.	Sacramento (from Dallas)	Duane Causwell	Temple	7-0
19.	Boston	Dee Brown	Jacksonville	6-1
20.	Minnesota (from Philadelphia)	Gerald Glass	Mississippi	6-6
21.	Phoenix	Jayson Williams	St. John's	6-8
22.	New Jersey (from Chicago)	Tate George	Connecticut	6-5
23.	Sacramento (from Utah)	Anthony Bonner	St. Louis	6-8
24.	San Antonio	Dwayne Schintzius	Florida	7-1
25.	Portland	Alaa Abdelnaby	Duke	6-10
26.	Detroit	Lance Blanks	Texas	6-4
27.	LA Lakers	Elden Campbell	Clemson	6-11

Louisville's Felton Spencer (No. 6) is a Timberwolf.

Sel. No.	Team	Name	College	Ht.
	SECOND ROUND			
28.	Golden State (from NJ via Atlanta)	Les Jepsen	Iowa	7-0
29.	Chicago (from Orlando)	Toni Kukoc	Jugoplastika Split	6-9
30.	b-Miami	Carl Herrera	Houston	6-9
31.	Phoenix (from Charlotte)	Negele Knight	Dayton	6-1
32.	Philadelphia (from Minnesota)	Brian Oliver	Georgia Tech	6-4
33.	Utah (from Sacramento)	Walter Palmer	Dartmouth	7-1
34.	Golden State (from LA Clippers)	Kevin Pritchard	Kansas	6-3
35.	Washington	Greg Foster	Texas-El Paso	7-0

b-Rights traded to Houston

Sacramento picked LaSalle's Lionel Simmons as No. 7.

Sel. No.	Team	Name	College	Ht.
36.	Atlanta (from Golden State)	Trevor Wilson	UCLA	6-7
37.	Washington (from Atlanta)	A.J. English	Virginia Union	6-5
38.	d-Seattle	Jud Buechler	Arizona	6-6
39.	Charlotte (from Houston)	Steve Scheffler	Purdue	6-9
40.	e-Sacramento (from Indiana)	Bimbo Coles	Virginia Tech	6-1
41.	Atlanta (from Cleveland via Miami & Golden State)	Steve Bardo	Illinois	6-5
42.	Denver	Marcus Liberty	Illinois	6-8
43.	San Antonio (from Milwaukee)	Tony Massenburg	Maryland	6-9
44.	Milwaukee (from New York via Seattle)	Steve Henson	Kansas State	6-1

d-Rights traded to New Jersey
e-Rights traded to Miami

Minnesota's Willie Burton (No. 9) will play for Miami.

Sel. No.	Team	Name	College	Ht.
45.	Indiana (from Dallas)	Antonio Davis	Texas El-Paso	6-9
46.	Indiana (from Boston)	Kenny Williams	Elizabeth City St.	6-9
47.	Philadelphia	Derek Strong	Xavier	6-7
48.	Phoenix	Cedric Ceballos	Cal-Fullerton	6-6
49.	Dallas (from Utah via Sacramento)	Phil Henderson	Duke	6-4
50.	f-Phoenix (from Chicago)	Milos Babic	Tenn. Tech	7-0
51.	LA Lakers (from San Antonio)	Tony Smith	Marquette	6-4
52.	g-Cleveland (from Detroit via Philadelphia)	Stefano Rusconi	Ranger Varese	6-9
53.	Seattle (from Portland)	Abdul Shamsid-Deen	Providence	6-10
54.	San Antonio (from LA Lakers)	Sean Higgins	Michigan	6-9

f-Rights traded to Cleveland
g-Rights traded to Phoenix

Michigan's Rumeal Robinson (No. 10) wound up a Hawk.

1989–90
NATIONAL BASKETBALL ASSOCIATION

FINAL STANDINGS

EASTERN CONFERENCE

Atlantic Division	Won	Lost	Pct.
Philadelphia	53	29	.646
Boston	52	30	.634
New York	45	37	.549
Washington	31	51	.378
Miami	18	64	.220
New Jersey	17	65	..207

Central Division	Won	Lost	Pct.
Detroit	59	23	.720
Chicago	55	27	.671
Milwaukee	44	38	.537
Cleveland	42	40	.512
Indiana	42	40	.512
Atlanta	41	41	.500
Orlando	18	64	.220

WESTERN CONFERENCE

Midwest Division	Won	Lost	Pct.
San Antonio	56	26	.683
Utah	55	27	.671
Dallas	47	35	.573
Denver	43	39	.524
Houston	41	41	.500
Minnesota	22	60	.268
Charlotte	19	63	.232

Pacific Division	Won	Lost	Pct.
L.A. Lakers	63	19	.768
Portland	59	23	.720
Phoenix	54	28	.659
Seattle	41	41	.500
Golden State	37	45	.451
L.A. Clippers	30	52	.366
Sacramento	23	59	.280

PLAYOFFS

EASTERN CONFERENCE	**WESTERN CONFERENCE**
First Round	**First Round**
New York defeated Boston (3-2)	L.A. Lakers defeated Houston (3-1)
Detroit defeated Indiana (3-0)	Phoenix defeated Utah (3-2)
Philadelphia defeated Cleveland (3-2)	San Antonio defeated Denver (3-0)
Chicago defeated Milwaukee (3-1)	Portland defeated Dallas (3-0)
Semifinals	**Semifinals**
Chicago defeated Philadelphia (4-1)	Portland defeated San Antonio (4-3)
Detroit defeated New York (4-1)	Phoenix defeated L.A. Lakers (4-1)
Finals	**Finals**
Detroit defeated Chicago (4-3)	Portland defeated Phoenix (4-2)

CHAMPIONSHIP
Detroit defeated Portland (4-1)

1989-90 INDIVIDUAL HIGHS

Most Minutes Played, Season: 3,238, McCray, Sacramento
Most Minutes Played, Game: 69, Ellis, Seattle vs. Milwaukee, 11/9 (5 OT)
Most Points, Game: 69, Jordan, Chicago, vs. Cleveland, 3/28 (OT)
　　　　　　　61, Malone, Utah, vs. Milwaukee, 1/27
Most Field Goals Made, Game: 23, Jordan, Chicago, vs. Cleveland, 3/28 (OT)
　　　　　　　22, Malone, Utah, vs. Charlotte, 12/22;
　　　　　　　Chambers, Phoenix, vs. Seattle, 3/24
Most Field Goal Attempts, Game: 43, Jordan, Chicago, vs. Orlando, 2/14 (OT)
　　　　　　　37, Jordan, Chicago, vs. Orlando, 12/20
Most 3-Pt. Field Goals Made, Game: 9, Ellis, Seattle, vs. L.A. Clippers, 4/20
Most 3-Pt. Field Goal Attempts, Game: 12, Jordan, Chicago, vs. Golden State, 1/18
Most Free Throws Made, Game: 23, K. Johnson, Phoenix, vs. Utah, 4/9 (OT)
　　　　　　　20, Malone, Utah, vs. Minnesota, 12/17
Most Free Throw Attempts, Game: 24, Malone, Utah, vs. Minnesota, 12/17;
　　　　　　　K. Johnson, Phoenix, vs. Utah, 4/9 (OT)
Most Rebounds, Game: 27, Donaldson, Dallas, vs. Portland, 12/29 (3 OT)
　　　　　　　26, Thorpe, Houston, vs. New York, 2/15
Most Offensive Rebounds, Game: 16, Cummings, San Antonio, vs. Golden State, 2/28 (OT)
　　　　　　　13, Ansley, Orlando, vs. Milwaukee, 2/1
Most Defensive Rebounds, Game: 22, Donaldson, Dallas, vs. Portland, 12/29 (3 OT); Olajuwon, Houston, vs. Detroit, 2/27 (OT)
Most Offensive Rebounds, Season: 364, Malone, Atlanta
Most Defensive Rebounds, Season: 850, Olajuwon, Houston
Most Assists, Game: 27, Stockton, Utah, vs. New York, 12/19
Most Blocked Shots, Game: 13, Bol, Golden State, vs. New Jersey, 2/2
Most Personal Fouls, Season: 328, Smits, Indiana
Most Games Disqualified, Season: 11, Long, Miami; Smits and Thompson, Indiana

INDIVIDUAL SCORING LEADERS
Minimum 70 games or 1,400 points

	G	FG	FT	Pts.	Avg.
Jordan, Chicago	82	1034	593	2753	33.6
Malone, Utah	82	914	696	2540	31.0
Ewing, New York	82	922	502	2347	28.6
Chambers, Phoenix	81	810	557	2201	27.2
Wilkins, Atlanta	80	810	459	2138	26.7
Barkley, Philadelphia	79	706	557	1989	25.2
Mullin, Garden State	78	682	505	1956	25.1
Miller, Indiana	82	661	544	2016	24.6
Olajuwon, Houston	82	806	382	1995	24.3
Robinson, San Antonio	82	690	613	1993	24.3
Bird, Boston	75	718	319	1820	24.3
Malone, Washington	75	781	257	1820	24.3
Drexler, Portland	73	670	333	1703	23.3
Campbell, Minnesota	82	723	448	1903	23.2
K. Johnson, Phoenix	74	578	501	1665	22.5
Cummings, San Antonio	81	728	343	1818	22.4
King, Washington	82	711	412	1837	22.4
Johnson, LA Lakers	79	546	567	1765	22.3
Tisdale, Sacramento	79	726	306	1758	22.3
Richmond, Golden State	78	640	406	1720	22.1

REBOUND LEADERS
Minimum 70 games or 800 rebounds

	G	Off.	Def.	Tot.	Avg.
Olajuwon, Houston	82	299	850	1149	14.0
Robinson, San Antonio	82	303	680	983	12.0
Barkley, Philadelphia	79	361	548	909	11.5
Malone, Utah	82	232	679	911	11.1
Ewing, New York	82	235	658	893	10.9
Seikaly, Miami	74	253	513	766	10.4
Parish, Boston	79	259	537	796	10.1
Malone, Atlanta	81	364	448	812	10.0
Cage, Seattle	82	306	515	821	10.0
Williams, Portland	82	250	550	800	9.8
Rodman, Detroit	82	336	456	792	9.7
Laimbeer, Detroit	81	166	614	780	9.6
Bird, Boston	75	90	622	712	9.5
Lever, Denver	79	230	504	734	9.3
Benjamin, LA Clippers	71	156	501	657	9.3
Thorpe, Houston	82	258	476	734	9.0
West, Phoenix	82	212	516	728	8.9
Walker, Washington	81	173	541	714	8.8
Green, LA Lakers	82	262	450	712	8.7
Donaldson, Dallas	73	155	475	630	8.6

Phoenix' Mark West was No. 1 in FG percentage.

FIELD-GOAL LEADERS
Minimum 300 FG Made

	FG	FGA	Pct.
West, Phoenix	331	530	.625
Barkley, Philadelphia	706	1177	.600
Parish, Boston	505	871	.580
Malone, Utah	914	1627	.562
Woolridge, LA Lakers	306	550	.556
Ewing, New York	922	1673	.551
McHale, Boston	648	1181	.549
Thorpe, Houston	547	998	.548
Worthy, LA Lakers	711	1298	.548
Williams, Portland	413	754	.548
Mullin, Garden State	682	1272	.536
Hornacek, Phoenix	483	901	.536
Manning, LA Clippers	440	826	.533
Smits, Indiana	515	967	.533

3-POINT FIELD-GOAL LEADERS
Minimum 25 Made

	FG	FGA	Pct.
Kerr, Cleveland	73	144	.507
Hodges, Chicago	87	181	.481
Petrovic, Portland	34	74	.459
Sundvold, Miami	44	100	.440
Scott, LA Lakers	93	220	.423
Hawkins, Philadelphia	84	200	.420
Ehlo, Cleveland	104	248	.419
Stockton, Utah	47	113	.416
Miller, Indiana	150	362	.414
Lever, Denver	36	87	.414
Hornacek, Phoenix	40	98	.408
Price, Cleveland	152	374	.406
Barros, Seattle	95	238	.399
Drew, LA Lakers	32	81	.395

FREE-THROW LEADERS
Minimum 125 FT Made

	FT	FTA	Pct.
Bird, Boston	319	343	.930
E. Johnson, Phoenix	188	205	.917
Davis, Denver	207	227	.912
Dumars, Detroit	297	330	.900
McHale, Boston	393	440	.893
Porter, Portland	421	472	.892
Johnson, LA Lakers	567	637	.890
Mullin, Golden State	505	568	.889
Hawkins, Philadelphia	387	436	.888
Price, Cleveland	300	338	.888
Sikma, Milwaukee	230	260	.885
Tripucka, Charlotte	310	351	.883

ASSISTS LEADERS
Minimum 70 Games or 400 assists

	G	A	Avg.
Stockton, Utah	78	1134	14.5
Johnson, LA Lakers	79	907	11.5
K. Johnson, Phoenix	74	846	11.4
Bogues, Charlotte	81	867	10.7
Grant, LA Clippers	44	442	10.0
Thomas, Detroit	81	765	9.4
Price, Cleveland	73	666	9.1
Porter, Portland	80	726	9.1
Hardaway, Golden State	79	689	8.7
Walker, Washington	81	652	8.0
Douglas, Miami	81	619	7.6
Bird, Boston	75	562	7.5

STEALS LEADERS
Minimum 70 games or 125 steals

	G	St.	Avg.
Jordan, Chicago	82	227	2.77
Stockton, Utah	78	207	2.65
Pippen, Chicago	82	211	2.57
Robertson, Milwaukee	81	207	2.56
Harper, Dallas	82	187	2.28
Corbin, Minnesota	82	175	2.13
Lever, Denver	79	168	2.13
Olajuwon, Houston	82	174	2.12
Conner, New Jersey	82	172	2.10
Hardaway, Golden State	79	165	2.09
Bogues, Charlotte	81	166	2.05
Drexler, Portland	73	145	1.99

BLOCKED-SHOTS LEADERS
Minimum 70 games or 100 blocked shots

	G	Blk.	Avg.
Olajuwon, Houston	82	376	4.59
Ewing, New York	82	327	3.99
Robinson, San Antonio	82	319	3.8
Bol, Golden State	75	238	3.17
Benjamin, LA Clippers	71	187	2.63
Eaton, Utah	82	201	2.45
Jones, Washington	81	197	2.43
West, Phoenix	82	184	2.24
Smits, Indiana	82	169	2.06
J. Williams, Cleveland	82	167	2.04
Nance, Cleveland	62	122	1.97
McHale, Boston	82	157	1.91

Cleveland's Steve Kerr led in 3-pt. FG percentage.

1989–90 ALL-NBA TEAM

FIRST

Pos.	Player, Team
G	Magic Johnson, Lakers
G	Michael Jordan, Bulls
C	Patrick Ewing, Knicks
F	Charles Barkley, 76ers
F	Karl Malone, Jazz

SECOND

Pos.	Player, Team
G	John Stockton, Jazz
G	Kevin Johnson, Suns
C	Akeem Olajuwon, Rockets
F	Tom Chambers, Suns
F	Larry Bird, Celtics

THIRD

Pos.	Player, Team
G	Clyde Drexler, Blazers
G	Joe Dumars, Pistons
C	David Robinson, Spurs
F	Chris Mullin, Warriors
F	James Worthy, Lakers

*1989–90 NBA ALL-ROOKIE TEAM

FIRST

David Robinson, Spurs
Tim Hardaway, Warriors
Vlade Divac, Lakers
Sherman Douglas, Heat
Pooh Richardson, Timberwolves

SECOND

J.R. Reid, Hornets
Sean Elliott, Spurs
Stacey King, Bulls
Blue Edwards, Jazz
Glen Rice, Heat

*Chosen without regard for position

1989–90 NBA ALL-DEFENSIVE TEAM

FIRST

Pos.	Player, Team
G	Joe Dumars, Pistons
G	Michael Jordan, Bulls
C	Akeem Olajuwon, Rockets
F	Dennis Rodman, Pistons
F	Buck Williams, Portland

SECOND

Pos.	Player, Team
G	Alvin Robertson, Bucks
G	Derek Harper, Mavericks
C	David Robinson, Spurs
F	Rick Mahorn, 76ers
F	Kevin McHale, Celtics

MOST VALUABLE PLAYER

1955-56	Bob Pettit, St. Louis	1973-74	Kareem Abdul-Jabbar, Milwaukee
1956-57	Bob Cousy, Boston	1974-75	Bob McAdoo, Buffalo
1957-58	Bill Russell, Boston	1975-76	Kareem Abdul-Jabbar, L.A.
1958-59	Bob Pettit, St. Louis	1976-77	Kareem Abdul-Jabbar, L.A.
1959-60	Wilt Chamberlain, Philadelphia	1977-78	Bill Walton, Portland
1960-61	Bill Russell, Boston	1978-79	Moses Malone, Houston
1961-62	Bill Russell, Boston	1979-80	Kareem Abdul-Jabbar, L.A.
1962-63	Bill Russell, Boston	1980-81	Julius Erving, Philadelphia
1963-64	Oscar Robertson, Cincinnati	1981-82	Moses Malone, Houston
1964-65	Bill Russell, Boston	1982-83	Moses Malone, Philadelphia
1965-66	Wilt Chamberlain, Philadelphia	1983-84	Larry Bird, Boston
1966-67	Wilt Chamberlain, Philadelphia	1984-85	Larry Bird, Boston
1967-68	Wilt Chamberlain, Philadelphia	1985-86	Larry Bird, Boston
1968-69	Wes Unseld, Baltimore	1986-87	Magic Johnson, L.A. Lakers
1969-70	Willis Reed, New York	1987-88	Michael Jordan, Chicago
1970-71	Lew Alcindor, Milwaukee	1988-89	Magic Johnson, L.A. Lakers
1971-72	Kareem Adbul-Jabbar, Milwaukee	1989-90	Magic Johnson, L.A. Lakers
1972-73	Dave Cowens, Boston		

FINALS MVP AWARD

1969	Jerry West, Los Angeles	1980	Magic Johnson, Los Angeles
1970	Willis Reed, New York	1981	Cedric Maxwell, Boston
1971	Kareem Abdul-Jabbar, Milwaukee	1982	Magic Johnson, Los Angeles
1972	Wilt Chamberlain, Los Angeles	1983	Moses Malone, Philadelphia
1973	Willis Reed, New York	1984	Larry Bird, Boston
1974	John Havlicek, Boston	1985	K. Abdul-Jabbar, L.A. Lakers
1975	Rick Barry, Golden State	1986	Larry Bird, Boston
1976	Jo Jo White, Boston	1987	Magic Johnson, L.A. Lakers
1977	Bill Walton, Portland	1988	James Worthy, L.A. Lakers
1978	Wes Unseld, Washington	1989	Joe Dumars, Detroit
1979	Dennis Johnson, Seattle	1990	Isiah Thomas, Detroit

ROOKIE OF THE YEAR

1952-53 Don Meineke, Fort Wayne	1971-72 Sidney Wicks, Portland
1953-54 Ray Felix, Baltimore	1972-73 Bob McAdoo, Buffalo
1954-55 Bob Pettit, Milwaukee	1973-74 Ernie DiGregorio, Buffalo
1955-56 Maurice Stokes, Rochester	1974-75 Keith Wilkes, Golden State
1956-57 Tom Heinsohn, Boston	1975-76 Alvan Adams, Phoenix
1957-58 Woody Sauldsberry, Philadelphia	1976-77 Adrian Dantley, Buffalo
1958-59 Elgin Baylor, Minneapolis	1977-78 Walter Davis, Phoenix
1959-60 Wilt Chamberlain, Philadelphia	1978-79 Phil Ford, Kansas City
1960-61 Oscar Robertson, Cincinnati	1979-80 Larry Bird, Boston
1961-62 Walt Bellamy, Chicago	1980-81 Darrell Griffith, Utah
1962-63 Terry Dischinger, Chicago	1981-82 Buck Williams, New Jersey
1963-64 Jerry Lucas, Cincinnati	1982-83 Terry Cummings, San Diego
1964-65 Willis Reed, New York	1983-84 Ralph Sampson, Houston
1965-66 Rick Barry, San Francisco	1984-85 Michael Jordan, Chicago
1966-67 Dave Bing, Detroit	1985-86 Patrick Ewing, New York
1967-68 Earl Monroe, Baltimore	1986-87 Chuck Person, Indiana
1968-69 Wes Unseld, Baltimore	1987-88 Mark Jackson, New York
1969-70 Lew Alcindor, Milwaukee	1988-89 Mitch Richmond, Golden State
1970-71 Dave Cowens, Boston	1989-90 David Robinson, San Antonio
Geoff Petrie, Portland	

COACH OF THE YEAR

1962-63 Harry Gallatin, St. Louis	1976-77 Tom Nissalke, Houston
1963-64 Alex Hannum, San Francisco	1977-78 Hubie Brown, Atlanta
1964-65 Red Auerbach, Boston	1978-79 Cotton Fitzsimmons, Kansas City
1965-66 Dolph Schayes, Philadelphia	1979-80 Bill Fitch, Boston
1966-67 Johnny Kerr, Chicago	1980-81 Jack McKinney, Indiana
1967-68 Richie Guerin, St. Louis	1981-82 Gene Shue, Washington
1968-69 Gene Shue, Baltimore	1982-83 Don Nelson, Milwaukee
1969-70 Red Holzman, New York	1983-84 Frank Layden, Utah
1970-71 Dick Motta, Chicago	1984-85 Don Nelson, Milwaukee
1971-72 Bill Sharman, Los Angeles	1985-86 Mike Fratello, Atlanta
1972-73 Tom Heinsohn, Boston	1986-87 Mike Schuler, Portland
1973-74 Ray Scott, Detroit	1987-88 Doug Moe, Denver
1974-75 Phil Johnson, Kansas City-Omaha	1988-89 Cotton Fitzsimmons, Phoenix
1975-76 Bill Fitch, Cleveland	1989-90 Pat Riley, L.A. Lakers

NBA SCORING CHAMPIONS

Season	Pts./Avg.	Top Scorer	Team
1946-47	1389	Joe Fulks	Philadelphia
1947-48	1007	Max Zaslofsky	Chicago
1948-49	1698	George Mikan	Minneapolis
1949-50	1865	George Mikan	Minneapolis
1950-51	1932	George Mikan	Minneapolis
1951-52	1674	Paul Arizin	Philadelphia
1952-53	1564	Neil Johnston	Philadelphia
1953-54	1759	Neil Johnston	Philadelphia
1954-55	1631	Neil Johnston	Philadelphia
1955-56	1849	Bob Pettit	St. Louis
1956-57	1817	Paul Arizin	Philadelphia
1957-58	2001	George Yardley	Detroit
1958-59	2105	Bob Pettit	St. Louis
1959-60	2707	Wilt Chamberlain	Philadelphia
1960-61	3033	Wilt Chamberlain	Philadelphia
1961-62	4029	Wilt Chamberlain	Philadelphia
1962-63	3586	Wilt Chamberlain	San Francisco
1963-64	2948	Wilt Chamberlain	San Francisco
1964-65	2534	Wilt Chamberlain	San Fran.-Phila.
1965-66	2649	Wilt Chamberlain	Philadelphia
1966-67	2775	Rick Barry	San Francisco
1967-68	2142	Dave Bing	Detroit
1968-69	2327	Elvin Hayes	San Diego
1969-70	31.2	Jerry West	Los Angeles
1970-71	31.7	Lew Alcindor	Milwaukee
1971-72	34.8	K. Abdul-Jabbar	Milwaukee
1972-73	34.0	Nate Archibald	K.C.-Omaha
1973-74	30.6	Bob McAdoo	Buffalo
1974-75	34.5	Bob McAdoo	Buffalo
1975-76	31.1	Bob McAdoo	Buffalo
1976-77	31.1	Pete Maravich	New Orleans
1977-78	27.2	George Gervin	San Antonio
1978-79	29.6	George Gervin	San Antonio
1979-80	33.1	George Gervin	San Antonio
1980-81	30.7	Adrian Dantley	Utah
1981-82	32.3	George Gervin	San Antonio
1982-83	28.4	Alex English	Denver
1983-84	30.6	Adrian Dantley	Utah
1984-85	32.9	Bernard King	New York
1985-86	30.3	Dominique Wilkins	Atlanta
1986-87	37.1	Michael Jordan	Chicago
1987-88	35.0	Michael Jordan	Chicago
1988-89	32.5	Michael Jordan	Chicago
1989-90	33.6	Michael Jordan	Chicago

NBA CHAMPIONS

Season	Champion	Eastern Division			Western Division		
		W.	L.		W.	L.	
1946-47	Philadelphia	49	11	Washington	39	22	Chicago
1947-48	Baltimore	27	21	Philadelphia	29	19	St. Louis
1948-49	Minneapolis	38	22	Washington	45	15	Rochester
1949-50	Minneapolis	51	13	Syracuse	39	25	Indianap.*
1950-51	Rochester	40	26	Philadelphia	44	24	Minneapolis
1951-52	Minneapolis	40	26	Syracuse	41	25	Rochester
1952-53	Minneapolis	47	23	New York	48	22	Minneapolis
1953-54	Minneapolis	44	28	New York	46	26	Minneapolis
1954-55	Syracuse	43	29	Syracuse	43	29	Ft. Wayne
1955-56	Philadelphia	45	27	Philadelphia	37	35	Ft. Wayne
1956-57	Boston	44	28	Boston	34	38	StL-Mpl-FtW
1957-58	St. Louis	49	23	Boston	41	31	St. Louis
1958-59	Boston	52	20	Boston	49	23	St. Louis
1959-60	Boston	59	16	Boston	46	29	St. Louis
1960-61	Boston	57	22	Boston	51	28	St. Louis
1961-62	Boston	60	20	Boston	54	26	Los Angeles
1962-63	Boston	58	22	Boston	53	27	Los Angeles
1963-64	Boston	59	21	Boston	48	32	San Fran.
1964-65	Boston	62	18	Boston	49	31	Los Angeles
1965-66	Boston	54	26	Boston	45	35	Los Angeles
1966-67	Philadelphia	68	13	Philadelphia	44	37	San Fran.
1967-68	Boston	54	28	Boston	52	30	Los Angeles
1968-69	Boston	48	34	Boston	55	27	Los Angeles
1969-70	New York	60	22	New York	46	36	Los Angeles
1970-71	Milwaukee	42	40	Baltimore	66	16	Milwaukee
1971-72	Los Angeles	48	34	New York	69	13	Los Angeles
1972-73	New York	57	25	New York	60	22	Los Angeles
1973-74	Boston	56	26	Boston	59	23	Milwaukee
1974-75	Golden State	60	22	Washington	48	34	Golden State
1975-76	Boston	54	28	Boston	42	40	Phoenix
1976-77	Portland	50	32	Philadelphia	49	33	Portland
1977-78	Washington	44	38	Washington	47	35	Seattle
1978-79	Seattle	54	28	Washington	52	30	Seattle
1979-80	Los Angeles	59	23	Philadelphia	60	22	Los Angeles
1980-81	Boston	62	20	Boston	40	42	Houston
1981-82	Los Angeles	58	24	Philadelphia	57	25	Los Angeles
1982-83	Philadelphia	65	17	Philadelphia	58	24	Los Angeles
1983-84	Boston	62	20	Boston	54	28	Los Angeles
1984-85	L.A. Lakers	63	19	Boston	62	20	L.A. Lakers

Season	Champion	Eastern Division			Western Division		
		W.	L.		W.	L.	
1985-86	Boston	67	15	Boston	51	31	Houston
1986-87	L.A. Lakers	59	23	Boston	65	17	L.A. Lakers
1987-88	L.A. Lakers	54	28	Detroit	62	20	L.A. Lakers
1988-89	Detroit	63	19	Detroit	57	25	L.A. Lakers
1989-90	Detroit	59	23	Detroit	59	23	Portland

*1949-50 Central Division Champion: Minneapolis and Rochester tied 51-17.

ALL-TIME NBA RECORDS

INDIVIDUAL
Single Game
Most Points: 100, Wilt Chamberlain, Philadelphia vs New York, at Hershey, Pa., Mar. 2, 1962

Most FG Attempted: 63, Wilt Chamberlain, Philadelphia vs New York, at Hershey, Pa., Mar. 2, 1962

Most FG Made: 36, Wilt Chamberlain, Philadelphia vs New York, at Hershey, Pa., Mar. 2, 1962

Most Consecutive FG Made: 18, Wilt Chamberlain, San Francisco vs New York, at Boston, Nov. 27, 1963; Wilt Chamberlain, Philadelphia vs Baltimore, at Pittsburgh, Feb. 24, 1967

Most FT Attempted: 34, Wilt Chamberlain, Philadelphia vs St. Louis, at Philadelphia, Feb. 22, 1962

Most FT Made: 28, Wilt Chamberlain, Philadelphia vs New York, at Hershey, Pa., Mar. 2, 1962; Adrian Dantley, Utah vs Houston at Las Vegas, Nev., Jan. 4, 1984

Most Consecutive FT Made: 19, Bob Pettit, St. Louis vs Boston, at Boston, Nov. 22, 1961; Bill Cartwright, New York vs Kansas City, at N.Y., Nov. 17, 1981; Adrian Dantley, Detroit vs Chicago, at Chicago, Dec. 15, 1987 (OT)

Most FT Missed: 22, Wilt Chamberlain, Philadelphia vs Seattle, at Boston, Dec. 1, 1967

Most Assists: 29, Kevin Porter, New Jersey vs Houston at N.J., Feb. 24, 1978

Most Personal Fouls: 8, Don Otten, Tri-Cities at Sheboygan, Nov. 24, 1949

Season
Most Points: 4,029, Wilt Chamberlain, Philadelphia, 1961-62
Highest Average: 50.4, Wilt Chamberlain, Philadelphia, 1961-62

Most FG Attempted: 3,159, Wilt Chamberlain, Philadelphia, 1961-62

Most FG Made: 1,597, Wilt Chamberlain, Philadelphia, 1961-62

Highest FG Percentage: .727, Wilt Chamberlain, Los Angeles, 1972-73

Most 3-Pt. FG Attempted: 466, Michael Adams, Denver, 1988-89

Most 3-Pt. FG Made: 166, Michael Adams, Denver, 1988-89

Highest 3-Pt. FG Percentage: .522, Jon Sundvold, Miami, 1988-89

Most FT Attempted: 1,363, Wilt Chamberlain, Philadelphia, 1961-62

Most FT Made: 840, Jerry West, Los Angeles, 1965-66

Highest FT Percentage: .958, Calvin Murphy, Houston, 1980-81

Most Rebounds: 2,149, Wilt Chamberlain, Philadelphia, 1960-61

Most Assists: 1,134, John Stockton, Utah, 1989-90

Most Personal Fouls: 386, Darryl Dawkins, New Jersey, 1983-84

Most Disqualifications: 26, Don Meineke, Fort Wayne, 1952-53

Career

Most Points Scored: 38,387, Kareem Abdul-Jabbar, Milwaukee and Los Angeles Lakers, 1970-89

Highest Scoring Average: 32.8, Michael Jordan, 1984-90

Most FG Attempted: 28,307, Kareem Abdul-Jabbar, Milwaukee and Los Angeles Lakers, 1970-89

Most FG Made: 15,837, Kareem Abdul-Jabbar, 1970-89

Highest FG Percentage: .599, Artis Gilmore, Chicago, San Antonio, Chicago, Boston, 1976-88

Most FT Attempted: 11,862, Wilt Chamberlain, 1960-73

Most FT Made: 7,694, Oscar Robertson, Cincinnati and Milwaukee, 1961-74

Highest FT Percentage: .900, Rick Barry, San Francisco/Golden State Warriors, Houston, 1965-67, 1972-80

Most Rebounds: 23,924, Wilt Chamberlain, 1960-73

Most Assists: 9,887, Oscar Robertson, 1961-74

Most Minutes: 57,446, Kareem Abdul-Jabbar, Milwaukee and Los Angeles Lakers, 1970-89

Most Games: 1,560, Kareem Abdul-Jabbar, Milwaukee and Los Angeles Lakers, 1970-89

Most Personal Fouls: 4,657, Kareem Abdul-Jabbar, Milwaukee and Los Angeles Lakers, 1970-89

Most Times Disqualified: 127, Vern Mikkelsen, Minneapolis, 1950-9

TEAM RECORDS

Single Game

Most Points, One Team: 173, Boston, vs Minneapolis at Boston, Feb. 27, 1959; 186, Detroit, vs Denver at Denver, Dec. 13, 1983 (3 overtimes)

Most Points, Two Teams: 318, Denver 163 vs San Antonio 155 at Denver, Jan. 11, 1984; 370, Detroit 186 vs Denver 184 at Denver, Dec. 13, 1983 (3 overtimes)

Most FG Attempted, One Team: 153, Philadelphia, vs Los Angeles at Philadelphia (3 overtimes), Dec. 8, 1961

Most FG Attempted, Two Teams: 291, Philadelphia 153 vs Los Angeles 138 at Philadelphia (3 overtimes), Dec. 8, 1961

Most FG Made, One Team: 72, Boston, vs Minneapolis at Boston, Feb. 27, 1959; 74, Denver, vs Detroit at Denver, Dec. 13, 1983 (3 overtimes)

Most FG Made, Two Teams: 142, Detroit 74 vs Denver 68 at Denver, Dec. 13, 1983 (3 overtimes)

Most FT Attempted, One Team: 86, Syracuse, vs Anderson at Syracuse (5 overtimes), Nov. 24, 1949

Most FT Attempted, Two Teams: 160, Syracuse 86 vs Anderson 74 at Syracuse (5 overtimes), Nov. 24, 1949

Most FT Made, One Team: 61, Phoenix, vs Utah, April 4, 1990 (1 overtime)

Most FT Made, Two Teams: 116, Syracuse 59 vs Anderson 57 at Syracuse (5 overtimes), Nov. 24, 1949

Most Rebounds, One Team: 109, Boston, vs Detroit at Boston, Dec. 24, 1960

Most Rebounds, Two Teams: 188, Philadelphia 98 vs Los Angeles 90 at Philadelphia, Dec. 8, 1961 (3 overtimes)

Most Assists, One Team: 53, Milwaukee, vs Detroit at Detroit, Dec. 26, 1978

Most Assists, Two Teams: 88, Phoenix 47 vs San Diego 41 at Tucson, Ariz., Mar. 15, 1969; San Antonio 50 vs Denver 38 at San Antonio, April 15, 1984

Most Assists, Two Teams, OT: 93, Detroit 47 vs Denver 46 at Denver, Dec. 13, 1983 (3 overtimes)

Most Personal Fouls, One Team: 66, Anderson, at Syracuse (5 overtimes), Nov. 24, 1949

Most Personal Fouls, Two Teams: 122, Anderson 66 vs Syracuse 56 at Syracuse (5 overtimes), Nov. 24, 1949

Most Disqualifications, One Team: 8, Syracuse, vs Baltimore at Syracuse (1 overtime), Nov. 15, 1952

Most Disqualifications, Two Teams: 13, Syracuse 8 vs Baltimore 5 at Syracuse (1 overtime), Nov. 15 1952

Most Points in a Losing Game: 184, Denver, vs Detroit at Denver Dec. 13, 1983 (3 overtimes)

Widest Point Spread: 63, Los Angeles 162 vs Golden State 99 at Los Angeles, Mar. 19, 1972

Most Consecutive Points in a Game: 24, Philadelphia, vs Baltimore at Baltimore, Mar. 20, 1966

Season

Most Games Won: 69, Los Angeles, 1971-72

Most Games Lost: 73, Philadelphia, 1972-73

Longest Winning Streak: 33, Los Angeles, Nov. 5, 1971 to Jan. 7, 1972

Longest Losing Streak: 20, Philadelphia, Jan. 9, 1973 to Feb. 11, 1973

Most Points Scored: 10,731, Denver, 1981-82

Most Points Allowed 10,328, Denver, 1981-82

Highest Scoring Average: 126.5, Denver, 1981-82

Highest Average, Points Allowed: 126.0, Denver, 1981-82

Most FG Attempted: 9,295, Boston, 1960-61

Most FG Made: 3,980, Denver, 1981-82

Highest FG Percentage: .545, Los Angeles, 1984-85

Most FT Attempted: 3,411, Philadelphia, 1966-67

Most FT Made: 2,313, Golden State, 1989-90

Highest FT Percentage: .832, Boston, 1989-90

Official 1990-91 NBA Schedule

*Afternoon Game
**Morning Game

Fri Nov 2
Cle at Bos
NY at Char
Wash at Mia
Orl at Atl
Mil at Det
NJ at Ind
Phil at Chi
Dal at Minn
GS at Den
**Phoe vs. Utah
at Tokyo
Sac at LAC
Hou at Port

Sat Nov 3
Bos at NY
NJ at Phil
Chi at Wash
Char at Orl
Ind at Atl
Cle at Det
Minn at Mil
Den at Dal
*LAL at SA
**Utah vs. Phoe
at Tokyo
Port at Sac
Hou at Sea

Sun Nov 4
GS at LAC

Tue Nov 6
Dal at NY
NJ at Char
Cle at Orl
Mil at Mia
Minn at Ind
Bos at Chi
Den at Hou
Port at LAL
LAC at GS
Atl at Sac
Det at Sea

Wed Nov 7
Dal at Phil
Char at Cle
Chi at Minn
Den at SA
GS at Phoe
Det at LAC

Thu Nov 8
Wash at NY
Mia at NJ
Phil at Mil
Orl at Hou
SA at Utah

Fri Nov 9
Chi at Bos
Mil at Wash
Cle at Ind
Char at Minn
Orl at Dal
Sea at Den
Sac at LAL
Atl at GS
Det at Port

Sat Nov 10
Bos at NJ
Ind at Mia
Phil at Cle
Char at Chi
Hou at SA
Den at Phoe
Atl at LAC
NY at Sac
GS vs. Sea
at Tacoma

Sun Nov 11
Orl at Minn
Utah at Hou
NY at LAL
LAC at Port

Mon Nov 12
Wash at NJ

Tue Nov 13
Wash at Char
Dal at Orl
Cle at Atl
Mia at Det
Phil at Ind
Bos at Mil
Minn at Hou
Chi at Utah
Phoe at LAL
*SA at GS
Den at Port
NY at Sea

Wed Nov 14
Char at Bos
Mil at NJ
Atl at Phil
Dal at Mia
Ind at Cle
Phoe at LAC

Thu Nov 15
Utah at Orl
LAL at Hou
Minn at Den
Chi at GS
SA at Sac
NY at Port

Fri Nov 16
Utah at Bos
Det at NJ
Wash at Phil
Char at Atl
Mil at Cle
Mia at Ind
LAL at Dal
LAC at Phoe

Sat Nov 17
Phil at NY
Bos at Wash
Cle at Char
Ind at Orl
Atl at Det

NJ at Mil
Mia at Hou
Phoe at SA
Port at Den
Sac at GS
Chi at Sea

Sun Nov 18
Utah at Minn
GS at LAL
Sea at LAC
Chi at Port

Mon Nov 19
Char at Phil
Utah at Mil
LAL at Den

Tue Nov 20
Hou at NY
Sac at Wash
Atl at Char
Det at Mia
Minn at Dal
Orl at GS
NJ at Sea

Wed Nov 21
Hou at Bos
Sac at Phil
Mia at Cle
Det at Ind
Atl at Mil
Minn at SA
Orl at Utah
Chi at Phoe
Den at LAL
NJ at LAC

Fri Nov 23
Sac at Bos
Cle at Phil
Mia at Char
Wash at Det
Hou at Ind
SA at Dal

Sea at Utah
NJ at Phoe
Chi at LAC
GS at Port

Sat Nov 24
*Mil at NY
Ind at Wash
Char at Mia
Phil at Atl
Bos at Cle
Utah at Dal
Chi at Den
Orl at LAL
NJ at GS

Sun Nov 25
Sac at Det
Hou at Minn
Orl at LAC
SA at Port

Mon Nov 26
Mia vs. Bos
at Hart

Tue Nov 27
Cle at NY
Phil at NJ
GS at Wash
Det at Atl
Ind at Mil
LAC at Hou
Orl at Den
Minn at Sac
Phoe at Port
SA at Sea

Wed Nov 28
Atl at Bos
Ind at Phil
Mil at Char
NJ at Mia
GS at Cle
NY at Det
Wash at Chi

LAC at Dal
Hou at Utah
SA at LAL

Thu Nov 29
Sac at Den
Sea at Phoe
Minn at Port

Fri Nov 30
Wash at Bos
GS at Orl
Cle at Atl
Phil at Det
Ind at Chi
NY at Mil
Minn at Utah

Sat Dec 1
Char at NY
Orl at NJ
Bos at Phil
Det at Wash
GS at Mia
Chi at Cle
Sac at Hou
Dal at SA
LAC at Den
LAL at Phoe
Port at Sea

Sun Dec 2
Mil at Ind
Minn at LAC
Utah at Port

Mon Dec 3
Sea at Bos
Wash at Utah

Tue Dec 4
Orl at NY
Sea at NJ
Mil at Phil
Port at Mia
Den at Cle
Phoe at Chi
Ind at Minn
Atl at Hou
Det at LAL
Dal at Sac

Wed Dec 5
Den at Bos
Port at Orl

Phoe at Ind
Cle at Mil
Atl at SA
Det at Utah
Dal at LAC
Wash at GS

Thu Dec 6
Sea at Mia
LAL at Minn
Char at Hou
Wash at Sac

Fri Dec 7
Phoe at NJ
Den at Phil
Sea at Orl
Mil at Atl
Port at Ind
NY at Chi
Bos at Dal
LAL at Utah
Det at GS

Sat Dec 8
Den at Char
Phoe at Orl
NY at Atl
Cle at Ind
Port at Chi
Hou at Dal
Bos at SA
Utah at LAC
Det at Sac

Sun Dec 9
Sea at Mil
Wash at LAL

Mon Dec 10
Bos at Hou

Tue Dec 11
Mia at NY
Char at NJ
Phil at Orl
SA at Det
Chi at Mil
LAC at Minn
Wash at Den
GS at Utah
Sac at Phoe
Ind at Port

Wed Dec 12
Mil at Bos

Hou at Phil
SA at Char
Atl at Mia
LAC at Cle
Dal at LAL
Ind at Sea

Thu Dec 13
NJ at Atl
NY at Minn
Den at Utah
Orl at Phoe
Sea at GS
Port at Sac

Fri Dec 14
Det at Bos
Mia at Phil
Hou at Wash
SA at Cle
LAC at Chi
Dal at Port

Sat Dec 15
NY at NJ
Hou at Char
Bos at Mia
Wash at Atl
Cle at Chi
LAC at Mil
SA at Minn
Phoe at Den
Ind at Utah
LAL at GS
Orl at Sac
Dal at Sea

Sun Dec 16
Ind at LAL
Orl at Port

Mon Dec 17
Utah at NJ
Atl at Cle

Tue Dec 18
LAL at NY
LAC at Phil
Utah at Char
Mia at Chi
Det at Mil
SA at Hou
Phoe at Dal
Minn at Sac
GS at Port
Orl at Sea

Wed Dec 19
Phil at Bos
LAC at NJ
NY at Mia
LAL at Cle
Chi at Det
Wash at Ind
Den at SA
Minn at Phoe

Thu Dec 20
Bos at Char
Utah at Atl
Orl at Hou
Port at GS
Sea at Sac

Fri Dec 21
Cle at NJ
NY at Wash
Phil at Mia
Atl at Det
Char at Ind
LAL at Chi
Mil at Dal
SA at Phoe
Port at LAC

Sat Dec 22
NJ at NY
Det at Phil
Utah at Orl
Wash at Cle
Ind at Chi
Phoe at Hou
Mil at SA
Dal at Den
Minn at GS
Sac at Sea

Sun Dec 23
Utah at Mia
Minn at LAL
Sac at LAC
Den at Port

Tue Dec 25
*Det at Chi

Wed Dec 26
Ind at Bos
Port at NY
Atl at NJ
Phil vs. Wash
at Balt

Hou at Orl
Sea at Cle
Char at Det
GS at Mil
Mia at SA
Dal at Phoe
LAL at LAC
Den at Sac

Thu Dec 27
Sea at Wash
Port at Char
GS at Chi
Mia at Den
Dal at Utah

Fri Dec 28
Hou at NJ
Bos at Atl
Det at Minn
Sac at SA
Phil at Phoe

Sat Dec 29
*Mil at NY
Den at Wash
Orl at Char
GS at Atl
Port at Cle
Hou at Det
NJ at Ind
Sea at Chi
Sac at Dal
*LAC at Utah
Mia at Phoe

Sun Dec 30
Den at Orl
Port at Mil
Sea at Minn
Phil at LAL
Mia at LAC

Wed Jan 2
NY at Bos
Mil at Char
LAC at Atl
Phoe at Cle
Den at Det
SA at Ind
Dal at Minn
Mia at Utah
Phil at Sea

Thu Jan 3
Den at NY

Warrior Tim Hardaway earned spot on All-Rookie Team.

Spurs' Sean Elliott was All-Rookie Second Team pick.

Char at Wash
LAC at Orl
Dal at Mil
Chi at Hou
GS at Sac
LAL at Port

Fri Jan 4
Phoe at Bos
SA at NJ
Ind at Atl
Det at Cle
Wash at Minn
Phil at Utah
LAL at GS
Mia at Sea

Sat Jan 5
LAC at Char
SA at Orl
Minn at Atl
NJ at Det
Cle at Chi
Phoe at Mil
Ind at Hou
Phil at Den
Utah at Sac
Mia at Port

Sun Jan 6
Dal at Bos
LAC at NY
GS at LAL
Sea at Port

Mon Jan 7
Dal at NJ
SA at Phil
Sac at Orl
Phoe at Minn

Tue Jan 8
Bos at NY
Det at Char
Sac at Mia
SA at Atl
LAC at Ind
NJ at Chi
Wash at Mil
Port at Hou
Cle at Utah
Den at GS
LAL at Sea

Wed Jan 9
Mil at Bos
Chi at Phil
Minn at Orl
Port at Dal
Cle at Phoe
Utah at LAL

Thu Jan 10
Ind at NY
LAC at Wash
Sac at Char
Orl at SA
Hou at Den
GS at Sea

Fri Jan 11
LAC at Bos
Minn at Mia
Port at Det
Atl at Chi
Phil at Mil
Utah at Dal
Hou at Phoe
Cle at LAL

Sat Jan 12
Atl at NY
NJ at Phil
Bos at Wash
Chi at Char
Mia at Det
Mil at Ind
Orl at Dal
Utah at SA
Cle at Den
Phoe at GS
Sea at Sac

Sun Jan 13
Port at NJ
Hou at LAL

Mon Jan 14
NY at Atl
Mil at Chi
Det at Dal
Hou at LAC

Tue Jan 15
GS at NJ
Orl at Mia
Atl at Ind
Port at Minn
SA at Utah

Wash at Phoe
Char at LAL
Den at Sea

Wed Jan 16
GS at Bos
Minn at NY
Chi at Orl
Mia at Cle
Ind at Mil
Dal at SA
Char at Den
Wash at LAC

Thu Jan 17
Det at Hou
LAL at Sac

Fri Jan 18
NJ at Bos
GS at Phil
NY at Mia
Chi at Atl
Utah at Cle
Orl at Mil
LAC at Dal
Char at SA
Det at Phoe
Sea at LAL
Wash at Port

Sat Jan 19
NY at Phil
NJ at Atl
Utah at Ind
GS at Minn
LAC at Hou
Char at Dal
SA at Den
Phoe at Sac
Wash at Sea

Sun Jan 20
Mil at Port

Mon Jan 21
*Phil at NY
*Orl at Wash
Chi at Mia
Bos at Det
LAL at Ind
*Minn at Den
Hou at Sac

Tues Jan 22
NJ at Char
LAL at Orl
Mia at Atl
LAC at SA
Hou at GS
Phoe at Port
Mil at Sea

Tue Jan 23
Det at Bos
Chi at NJ
Ind at Phil
Atl at Wash
Cle at Dal
NY at Utah
Mil at Sac

Thu Jan 24
LAL at Char
Minn at Hou
Cle at SA
NY at Den

Fri Jan 25
LAL at NJ
Bos at Phil
Ind vs. Wash
   at Balt
Dal at Det
Mia at Chi
Sac at Utah
Sea at Phoe
Mil at GS

Sat Jan 26
Dal at Wash
Phil at Char
Det at Orl
NJ at Mia
Cle at Hou
Minn at SA
Utah at Den
NY at Phoe
Mil at LAC
Sac at Port
Atl at Sea

Sun Jan 27
*LAL at Bos

Mon Jan 28
Wash at Det
Den at Chi
Bos at Minn

Sea at SA
NY at GS
NJ at Sac
Atl at Port

Tue Jan 29
Mia at Wash
Phoe at Orl
Char at Cle
Den at Mil
SA at Hou
Sea at Dal
Atl at Utah
NJ at LAL
NY at LAC

Wed Jan 30
Orl at Bos
Phoe at Mia
Cle at Det
Char at Ind
Sac at Minn

Thu Jan 31
Wash at NY
Sea at Hou
Chi at SA
NJ at Den
Port at Utah
Atl at LAL
LAC at GS

Fri Feb 1
Phoe at Phil
Det at Wash
Bos at Char
Ind at Mia
Sac at Mil
Chi at Dal
LAL at LAC
GS at Port

Sat Feb 2
Sac at NY
Mia at Orl
Minn at Cle
Sea at Ind
Hou at SA
Atl at Den
NJ at Utah

Sun Feb 3
*Wash at Bos
*Phoe at Det
*Char at Mil

*Phil at Minn
GS at Hou
*Chi at LAL

Mon Feb 4
Sea at Char
Mil at Cle
Chi at Sac
NJ at Port

Tue Feb 5
NY at Orl
Cle at Atl
Phil at Det
Utah at Minn
Ind at Dal
GS at SA
Den at Phoe
LAC at LAL

Wed Feb 6
Char at Bos
Mia at NJ
Wash at Phil
Hou at Mil
Phoe at Utah
Port at Sac
LAC at Sea

Thu Feb 7
Bos at NY
NJ at Wash
Minn at Orl
Char at Atl
Hou at Cle
Chi at Det
GS at Dal
Ind at SA

Sun Feb 10
*ALL-STAR
GAME at
CHARLOTTE

Tue Feb 12
Dal at Char
Den at Orl
Cle at Mia
NY at Ind
Atl at Chi
Wash at SA
Hou at Utah
LAL at Phoe
Minn at GS
LAC at Sac

Phil at Port
Bos at Sea

Wed Feb 13
Atl at NJ
Dal at Cle
Ind at Det
Minn at LAL

Thu Feb 14
Chi at NY
Sea at Orl
Den at Mia
Det at Mil
Wash at Hou
Phoe at SA
Bos at GS
Phil at Sac

Fri Feb 15
Den at NJ
Mil at Char
NY at Cle
Wash at Dal
Bos at LAL
Minn at LAC
Utah at Port

Sat Feb 16
Char at Mia
Sea at Atl
NJ at Chi
Phoe at Hou
SA at Dal
Minn at Utah
Phil at GS

Sun Feb 17
*Det at NY
*Cle vs. Wash
  at Balt
*Mil at Orl
*Sac at Ind
*Bos at Den
Port at LAL
Phil at LAC

Mon Feb 18
*Chi at Cle
Sea at Det
Den at Minn
*SA at Utah
Dal at GS

Tue Feb 19
Atl at NY
Sac at NJ
Sea at Phil
Ind at Char
Wash at Chi
Mia at Mil
LAL at Hou
Bos at Phoe
Dal at Port

Wed Feb 20
Sac at Cle
Atl at Det
Orl at Ind
GS at Minn
Phoe at LAC

Thu Feb 21
Sea at NY
Mia at Wash
Mil at Hou
LAL at Dal
Port at Den

Fri Feb 22
NJ vs. Bos
  at Hart
Det at Char
Phil at Mia
LAL at Atl
Ind at Cle
Sac at Chi
Orl at Minn
SA at LAC
Utah at GS
Phoe at Port

Sat Feb 23
Phil at NJ
NY at Wash
Dal at Atl
Char at Chi
Cle at Mil
GS at Den
Phoe at Sea

Sun Feb 24
Sac at Orl
NY at Mia
*LAL at Det
*Bos at Ind
*Hou at Minn
Den at LAC

SA at Port
Utah at Sea

Mon Feb 25
LAL at Phil
Sac at Atl
Char at Phoe

Tue Feb 26
Wash at NY
Ind at NJ
Mil at Mia
Det at Cle
Bos at Chi
Dal at Minn
Port at SA
Hou at Den
Orl at GS
LAC at Sea

Wed Feb 27
Minn at Bos
Atl at Phil
Dal at Ind
GS at Utah
Orl at Phoe
Char at Sac

Thu Feb 28
SA at NY
Mil at NJ
Det at Mia
Port at Atl
LAL at Den
Hou at LAC

Fri Mar 1
SA at Bos
Port at Phil
Utah at Det
Cle at Ind
Dal at Chi
Wash at Mil
Sac at Phoe
Orl at LAL
Char at Sea

Sat Mar 2
NY at NJ
Chi at Ind
LAC at Minn
Mia at Dal
Orl at Den
Char at GS
Sac at Sea

Sun Mar 3
*Port at Bos
*Utah at Phil
*SA at Wash
LAC at Det
*Atl at Mil
*Hou at LAL

Mon Mar 4
Ind vs. Bos
  at Hart
Phoe at Char
Utah at Orl
NJ at Dal
Sea at GS

Tue Mar 5
Phoe at NY
LAC at Mia
Den at Atl
Char at Ind
Mil at Chi
LAL at Minn
NJ at Hou
Phil at SA
GS at Sac
Cle at Sea

Wed Mar 6
Mia at Bos
Utah at Wash
LAC at Orl
NY at Det
Phil at Dal

Thu Mar 7
Phoe at Atl
Den at Ind
LAL at Mil
Sea at Minn
Dal at Hou
NJ at SA
Cle at GS

Fri Mar 8
Phoe at Wash
Den at Orl
Atl at Mia
Utah at Chi
Bos at LAC
Cle at Sac

Sat Mar 9
Utah at NY
LAL at Wash

Mavs' Derek Harper made All-Defensive Second Team.

Det at Ind
Char at Mil
Phil at Hou
Sea at SA

Sun Mar 10
LAL at Orl
*NJ at Mia
*Chi at Atl
*Phoe at Minn
*Dal at Den
Cle at LAC
*Sac at GS
Bos at Port

Mon Mar 11
NJ at NY
Mil at Det
Utah at SA
Cle at Port

Tue Mar 12
Wash at Char
LAL at Mia
Phil at Atl
Minn at Chi
Sea at Hou
LAC at Den
Ind at GS
Bos at Sac

Wed Mar 13
NY at Phil
Char at Det
Chi at Mil
Sea at Dal
Bos at Utah
Port at Phoe
SA at LAC

Thu Mar 14
Mia at NY
Det at NJ
Mil at Cle
Orl at Hou
Minn at Den
SA at GS
Ind at Sac

Fri Mar 15
Mia at Phil
Bos at Wash
Chi at Char
Atl at Dal
Port at Utah

Hou at Phoe
Den at LAL
Ind at LAC
Minn at Sea

Sat Mar 16
Wash at NJ
Chi at Cle
Orl at Det
GS at Dal
Atl at Phoe
SA at Sac
Utah at Sea

Sun Mar 17
*Phil at Bos
Char at NJ
*NY at Mil
*Mia at Minn
GS at Hou
*Ind at Den
SA at LAL
*LAC at Port

Mon Mar 18
Orl at Phil
Sac at Dal
Ind at Phoe

Tue Mar 19
NY at Char
Bos at Atl
Mia at Mil
Hou at Minn
Sac at SA
LAC at LAL
Port at GS

Wed Mar 20
Wash at Bos
Cle at NY
Minn at NJ
Det at Phil
Mia at Ind
Atl at Chi
Phoe at Dal
Utah at Den
Port at LAC
LAL at Sea

Thu Mar 21
SA at Orl
Sac at Hou
Char at Utah
Den at GS

Fri Mar 22
Chi at Phil
Atl vs. Wash
  at Balt
NJ at Det
Bos at Ind
Cle at Minn
NY at Dal
Sea at Phoe
Mil at LAL
Char at LAC

Sat Mar 23
Phil at Wash
Dal at Orl
Mia at Atl
NJ at Cle
Ind at Chi
NY at Hou
Mil at Den
Minn at Utah
LAC at GS
Phoe at Sac

Sun Mar 24
*Det at SA
Sea at LAL
*Char at Port

Mon Mar 25
NJ at Wash
GS at Orl
Hou at Chi
Det at Den
Mil at Utah
Phoe at LAC
LAL at Sac

Tue Mar 26
Phil at NJ
GS at Char
Cle at Mia
Atl at Ind
NY at SA
Minn at Phoe
Sea at Port

Wed Mar 27
Ind at Det
Orl at Dal
Utah at LAC
Port vs. Sea
  at Tacoma

Thu Mar 28
GS at NY
Chi at NJ
Phil at Char
Bos at Mia
Hou at Atl
Wash at Cle
Orl at SA
Mil at Phoe
Utah at Sac

Fri Mar 29
Cle at Bos
Char at Phil
Chi at Wash
GS at Det
Port at LAL
Dal at LAC
Minn at Sea

Sat Mar 30
NY at NJ
*Hou at Orl
Atl at Mil
Den at SA
Minn at Port
Dal at Sea

Sun Mar 31
*Chi at Bos
*Cle at Phil
*Char at Wash
Hou at Mia
*GS at Ind
Sac at LAL

Tue Apr 2
Bos at NJ
Mil at Phil
Cle at Wash
Det at Char
Orl at Chi
Port at Minn
Den at Dal
LAL at SA
Utah at Phoe
Mia at Sac

Wed Apr 3
NY at Cle
Phil at Ind
Dal at Hou
LAC at Utah
Mia at GS
Sac at Sea

Thu Apr 4
NJ at Bos
Chi at NY
Port at Wash
Atl at Char
SA at Mil
Den at Minn
LAL at Phoe

Fri Apr 5
Port at Orl
Char at Cle
Minn at Det
Wash at Ind
SA at Chi
Utah at Dal
Hou at Den
Mia at LAL
Sea at LAC
Phoe at GS

Sat Apr 6
Det at NY
Bos at Orl
Ind at Atl
NJ at Mil
Utah at Hou
GS at Sac

Sun Apr 7
*Cle at Char
*Phil at Chi
*SA at Minn
*Port at Dal
*Sea at Den
Phoe at LAL
Sac at LAC

Mon Apr 8
Wash at Atl
GS at SA
Orl at Utah
Den at Sea

Tue Apr 9
Ind at Char
Atl at Cle
NY at Det
Det at Mil
NJ at Minn
Port at Hou
GS at Phoe
Orl at LAC
Dal at Sac

Xavier's Tyrone Hill (11th pick) joins Warriors.

Wed Apr 10	Minn at Char	Mon Apr 15	Minn at Dal	Sac at Port
NY at Phil	Chi at Det	Mil at Chi	LAC at Phoe	Phoe at Sea
Wash at Mia	Dal at Phoe	Sac at Minn	LAL at GS	
Cle at Det	Den at LAC	Dal at LAL		**Sat Apr 20**
Chi at Ind	SA at Sea	Hou at Sea	**Thu Apr 18**	Char at NY
Port at SA			Bos at Phil	Mia at NJ
Dal at Utah	**Sat Apr 13**	**Tue Apr 16**	NJ at Wash	Ind at Mil
LAC vs. Sea	Mil at Atl	Phil at NY	SA at Hou	LAL at Utah
at Tacoma	NJ at Cle	Ind at NJ	Sea at Utah	
	Den at Utah	Mil at Wash	Den at Sac	**Sun Apr 21**
Thu Apr 11	Dal at GS	Mia at Char		*Atl at Bos
Bos at Mil	Hou at Sac	Atl at Orl	**Fri Apr 19**	*Minn at Wash
Atl at Minn	*LAL at Port	Bos at Det	Chi at Char	NJ at Orl
Utah at LAL	Orl at Sea	LAC at SA	Wash at Orl	*Phil at Cle
Hou at GS		Phoe at Den	Phil at Mia	*Det at Chi
Orl at Sac	**Sun Apr 14**	Sac at Utah	Det at Atl	Den at Hou
	*NY at Bos	Hou at Port	Bos at Cle	*Dal at SA
Fri Apr 12	*Minn at Phil		NY at Ind	*Port at Phoe
Mia at Bos	*Mia at Wash	**Wed Apr 17**	Mil at Minn	Sea at LAL
Ind at NY	*Det at Ind	Chi at Mia	Hou at Dal	*Utah at GS
Cle at NJ	*SA at Phoe	Char at Atl	SA at Den	*LAC at Sac
Wash at Phil	Orl at Port	Orl at Cle	GS at LAC	

Georgia's Alec Kessler (12th pick) wound up in Miami.

1990-91 NBA/NBC-TV Schedule

(starting times Eastern)

Day	Date	Game	Time
Sat	Nov 3	LAL at SA	3:30
Tue	Dec 25	Det at Chi	3:30
Sun	Jan 27	LAL at Bos	12:30
Sun	Feb 3	Phoe at Det	1:00
		Chi at LAL	3:30
Sun	Feb 10	41st ALL-STAR GAME	1:30
		(Charlotte Coliseum)	
Sun	Feb 17	Det at NY	1:30
Mon	Feb 18	Chi at Cle or	3:30
		SA at Utah	
Sun	Feb 24	Bos at Ind	1:00
		LAL at Det	3:30
Sun	Mar 3	Port at Bos or	1:00
		Utah at Phil	
		Hou at LAL	
Sun	Mar 10	Chi at Atl	12:00
Sun	Mar 17	Phil at Bos	12:00
Sun	Mar 24	Det at SA	1:00
Sun	Mar 31	Chi at Bos or	12:30
		Cle at Phil	
Sun	Apr 7	Phil at Chi or	3:30
		Port at Dal	
Sat	Apr 13	LAL at Port	3:30
Sun	Apr 14	NY at Bos	1:00
		SA at Phoe or	
		Det at Ind	
Sat	Apr 20	LAL at Utah	3:30
Sun	Apr 21	Det at Chi or	3:30
		Phil at Cle or	
		Dal at SA or	
		Utah at GS or	
		Port at Phoe	

Kings tabbed Texas' Travis Mays No. 14 in draft.

1990-91 NBA/TNT Schedule

(starting times Eastern)

Day	Date	Game	Time
Fri	Nov 2	Phil at Chi	8:00
		Phoe vs. Utah (at Tokyo)	11:00
Tue	Nov 6	Bos at Chi	8:00
		Atl at Sac	10:30
Fri	Nov 9	Cle at Ind	8:00
		Det at Port	10:30
Tue	Nov 13	SA at GS	8:00
Fri	Nov 16	LAL at Dal	8:00
Tue	Nov 20	Hou at NY	8:00
Fri	Nov 23	Chi at LAC	8:00
Tue	Nov 27	Phoe at Port	8:00
Fri	Nov 30	Phil at Det	8:00
Tue	Dec 4	Phoe at Chi	8:00
		Det at LAL	10:30
Fri	Dec 7	Bos at Dal	8:00
Tue	Dec 11	Chi at Mil	8:00
Fri	Dec 14	Det at Bos	8:00
Tue	Dec 18	LAL at NY	8:00
Fri	Dec 21	LAL at Chi	8:00
Wed	Jan 2	NY at Bos	8:00
Fri	Jan 4	SA at NJ	8:00
Tue	Jan 8	Det at Char	8:00
Fri	Jan 11	Port at Det	8:00
		Cle at LAL	10:30
Tue	Jan 15	Orl at Mia	8:00
Fri	Jan 18	Chi at Atl	8:00
Wed	Jan 23	Det at Bos	8:00
Fri	Jan 25	Sea at Phoe	10:00
Tue	Jan 29	SA at Hou	8:00
Fri	Feb 1	Det at Wash	8:00
Tue	Feb 5	Utah at Minn	8:00
Thu	Feb 7	Chi at Det	8:00
Tue	Feb 12	LAL at Phoe	8:00
Fri	Feb 15	NY at Cle	8:00
		Bos at LAL	10:30
Tue	Feb 19	Bos at Phoe	8:00
Fri	Feb 22	LAL at Atl	8:00
Tue	Feb 26	Hou at Den	8:00
Fri	Mar 1	SA at Bos	8:00
Tue	Mar 5	Phoe at NY	8:00
Wed	Mar 13	Bos at Utah	9:00
Wed	Mar 20	Det at Phil	8:00
Tue	Mar 26	NY at SA	8:00
Fri	Mar 29	Cle at Bos	8:00
		Port at LAL	10:30
Tue	Apr 2	LAL at SA	8:00
Fri	Apr 5	SA at Chi	8:00
Wed	Apr 10	NY at Phil	8:00
Mon	Apr 15	Mil at Chi	8:00
Fri	Apr 19	Wildcard Game	8:00

Revised and updated with over 75 all
new sports records and photographs!

THE ILLUSTRATED
SPORTS RECORD BOOK
Zander Hollander and David Schulz

Here, in a single book, are more than 350
all-time sports records with stories and
photos so vivid it's like "being there." All the
sports classics are here: Babe Ruth, Wilt
Chamberlain, Muhammad Ali ... plus the
stories of such active stars as Dwight Gooden
and Wayne Gretzky. This is the authoritative
book on what the great records are, and
who set them—an engrossing, fun-filled
reference guide filled with anecdotes of
hundreds of renowned athletes whose
remarkable records remain as fresh as when
they were set.
